JOURNAL · OF MORAL THEOLOGY

VOLUME 6, SPECIAL ISSUE 2
SEPTEMBER 2017

ENGAGING DISABILITY

Edited by Miguel J. Romero
and Mary Jo Iozzio

JOURNAL · OF
M · O · R · A · L
THEOLOGY

Journal of Moral Theology is published semiannually, with regular issues in January and June. Our mission is to publish scholarly articles in the field of Catholic moral theology, as well as theological treatments of related topics in philosophy, economics, political philosophy, and psychology.

Articles published in the *Journal of Moral Theology* undergo at least two double blind peer reviews. Authors are asked to submit articles electronically to jmt@msmary.edu. Submissions should be prepared for blind review. Microsoft Word format preferred. The editors assume that submissions are not being simultaneously considered for publication in another venue.

Journal of Moral Theology is indexed in the ATLA Catholic Periodical and Literature Index® (CPLI®), a product of the American Theological Library Association.

Email: atla@atla.com, www: http://www.atla.com.

ISSN 2166-2851 (print)
ISSN 2166-2118 (online)

Journal of Moral Theology is published by Mount St. Mary's University, 16300 Old Emmitsburg Road, Emmitsburg, MD 21727.

Copyright© 2017 individual authors and Mount St. Mary's University. All rights reserved.

Except for brief quotations in critical publications or reviews, no part of this book may be reproduced in any manner without prior written permission from the publisher. Write: Permissions. Wipf and Stock Publishers, 199 W. 8th Ave., Suite 3, Eugene, OR 97401.

Pickwick Publications, An Imprint of Wipf and Stock Publishers, 199 W. 8th Ave., Suite 3, Eugene, OR 97401. www.wipfandstock.com. ISBN 13: 978-1-5326-4031-5

JOURNAL OF MORAL THEOLOGY

EDITOR EMERITUS AND UNIVERSITY LIAISON
David M. McCarthy, *Mount St. Mary's University*

EDITOR
Jason King, *Saint Vincent College*

ASSOCIATE EDITOR
William J. Collinge, *Mount St. Mary's University*

MANAGING EDITOR
Kathy Criasia, *Mount St. Mary's University*

EDITORIAL BOARD
Melanie Barrett, *University of St. Mary of the Lake/Mundelein Seminary*
Jana M. Bennett, *University of Dayton*
Mara Brecht, *St. Norbert College*
Jim Caccamo, *St. Joseph's University*
Meghan Clark, *St. John's University*
David Cloutier, *The Catholic University of America*
Christopher Denny, *St. John's University*
John J. Fitzgerald, *St. John's University*
Mari Rapela Heidt, *Waukesha, Wisconsin*
Kelly Johnson, *University of Dayton*
Warren Kinghorn, *Duke University*
Kent Lasnoski, *Quincy University*
John Love, *Mount St. Mary's Seminary*
Ramon Luzarraga, *Benedictine University, Mesa*
M. Therese Lysaught, *Loyola University Chicago*
William C. Mattison III, *University of Notre Dame*
Christopher McMahon, *Saint Vincent College*
Joel Shuman, *Kings College*
Matthew Shadle, *Marymount University*
Msgr. Stuart Swetland, *Donnelly College*
Christopher P. Vogt, *St. John's University*
Brian Volck, *University of Cincinnati College of Medicine*
Paul Wadell, *St. Norbert College*
Greg Zuschlag, *Oblate School of Theology*

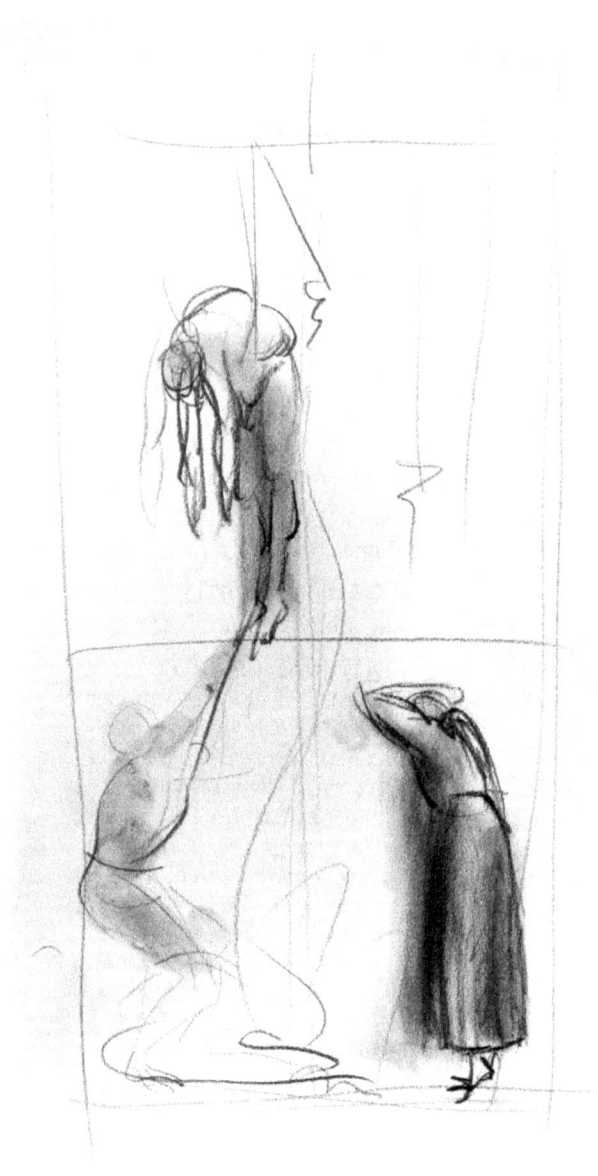

Giacomo Manzù, "Studio per Cristo in Croce,"
L'Archivio della Fondazione Giacomo Manzù;
© 2017 Artists Rights Society (ARS), New York / SIAE, Rome

JOURNAL OF MORAL THEOLOGY
VOLUME 6, SPECIAL ISSUE 2
SEPTEMBER 2017

CONTENTS

Preface: Engaging Disability
    Mary Jo Iozzio and Miguel J. Romero 1

God Bends Over Backwards to Accommodate Humankind ... While the Civil Rights Acts and the Americans with Disabilities Act Require [Only] the Minimum
    Mary Jo Iozzio 10

On "And Vulnerable": Catholic Social Thought and the Social Challenges of Cognitive Disability
    Matthew Gaudet 32

From Universal Precautions to Universal Design: Disclosure of Concealable Disability in the Case of HIV
    Mary M. Doyle Roche 54

Disability, the Healing of Infirmity, and the Theological Virtue of Hope: A Thomistic Approach
    Paul Gondreau 70

Seventeenth-Century Casuistry Regarding Persons with Disabilities: Antonino Diana's Tract "On the Mute, Deaf, and Blind"
    Julia A. Fleming 112

Blessed Silence: Explorations in Christian Contemplation and Hearing Loss
    Jana Bennett 138

Becoming Friends: Ethics in Friendship and in Doing Theology
    Lorraine Cuddeback 158

The Slow Journey Towards Beatitude: Disability in L'Arche, and Staying Human in High-Speed Society
    Jason Reimer Greig 180

The Goodness and Beauty of Our Fragile Flesh: Moral Theologians and Our Engagement With 'Disability'
    Miguel J. Romero 206

Contributors 254

Preface: Engaging Disability

Mary Jo Iozzio and Miguel J. Romero

THE COVER OF THIS ISSUE OF the *Journal of Moral Theology* presents a bronze panel depicting the death of Christ, from *La Porta della Morte*, which is found at the southernmost entryway into the nave of St. Peter's Basilica. Produced by the famed Italian artist Giacomo Manzú (1908-1991) and dedicated by Pope Paul VI in 1964, the ten panels of the bas-relief bronze door depict distinct episodes of human mortality and fragility. Manzú was concerned to illustrate the many ways that human beings encounter and experience mortality from the mundane to the glorious moments, exemplified in horrific violence (crucifixion, martyrdom, murder), in accident, and in the quiet peace of last breaths and rest for the weary. The door brings together distinct meditations on particular and particularizing instances of mortal fragility in human life. In so doing, Manzú presents a bronze-cast argument for both the unity and the hope of humanity: vulnerable beings, each implicated in the history of creations of beauty, of personal and social sin, and of the realities of evil, and yet each personally accommodated by and reconciled with God in Christ, and called to participate in the good news of God's loving care and merciful regard for all creation.

For Giacomo Manzú, artistic engagement with the particulars of mortality provides a vantage to illustrate aspects of the Gospel that are easy to overlook: the paradox of human vulnerability and the glory yet to be revealed. As paradox, *La Porta della Morte* is an apt metaphor for the editorial intuition animating the conception and development of this issue of the *Journal of Moral Theology*: Engaging Disability. Specifically, we are convinced that theo-ethical reflection on the complex realities and diverse experiences of disability provides a vantage to recognize aspects of contemporary life in Christ that are easy to overlook: the paradox of disability in a culture where errors of judgment and sinful practices concerning the normativity of the able body/able mind habituate into morally vicious forms of social and communal life. Oriented by the disciplinary perspectives and diverse methodologies of the Catholic moral tradition, we hope these articles will motivate, inspire, and provoke theologians working in Catholic theological ethics toward critical self-reflection on how their own interpretive and speculative work might engage disability regarding the human good, the common good, the practice of virtue, the call to happiness, discipleship, and service.

Before launching into the issue, we offer a brief introduction to the state of the academic specialization called "Disability Studies." An introductory bibliography follows this Preface. The specialized, scholarly study of disability is usually identified as beginning in the early 1990s, coincident with the passage of the Americans with Disabilities Act (1990). Over the last thirty years, the discourse of Disability Studies has continued to develop and its critical contributions have been recognized in many academic societies including the American Academy of Religion, Society of Biblical Literature, Modern Language Association, American Historical Association, American Educational Research Association, American Sociological Association, and others. Of the first wave of scholars specializing in disability, many had personal experience with a family member or someone close who lived with a disability, and it was through their formal academic training in theology, scripture, or history that they acquired the skills of critical reflection which empowered them to reflect on and interrogate that experience. (This is true also for most of the authors in this *Journal of Moral Theology* issue, even though they represent a second wave.) Over these years, among the principal developments in the field is the increasing presence of scholars with disabilities teaching, publishing, and encouraging their students and colleagues to recognize the interpretive advantage and speculative insights generated by the distinct hermeneutic of the disability critique emerging in academic, religious, social, political, and legal institutions. As with other critical studies that aim to retrieve the histories of people who were not members of the dominant communities and cultures in which they lived and were thereby marginalized and otherwise oppressed (e.g., women, children, ethnic and racial minorities), people with disabilities have a material history in culture and tradition that requires intentional focus and disciplined sensitivity to obscure, indirect, and implied references in the resources at our disposal. For the Catholic theological tradition, these sources include Scripture, the magisterial tradition, Church Councils, liturgy and the sacraments, theological reflection, and Canon Law.

Disability Studies encourages an interdisciplinary approach to critical and systematic investigation. It recognizes that the intersection of diverse experiences helps to expose distortions of truth, goodness, and beauty buried in un-interrogated notions of what is normal and natural and in simplistic binary categories of normal-abnormal/natural-unnatural. Our embodiment as creatures is a complex phenomenon that unfolds in time and includes both ability and disability. Importantly, scholars focused on disability have helped scholars in other disciplines recognize the incoherence of classifying the mere state of impairment or disability as a disqualifying defect, retributive punishment, threat, contagion, torment, or senseless fate. Much of the work in the field that debunks these associations refers to models of disability: religious/moral, tragedy/charity, medical, professional, rehabilitation, economic/customer, rights-based, and the social construction. The cultural and social practices described by these models are revealed in the ways that the roles of individuals and people with disabilities are determined by the dominant outlook of the cultures in which they live. As Nancy Eiesland, one of the first scholars to engage disability and religion, notes, "Disability is everywhere once you know how to look for it."[1]

With religious objects and texts—sacred sources, theological reflection, rituals, song, and material art—scholars specializing in disability have recognized as well a vital resource in the personal accounts and commentary on the lived experience of people with disabilities. Uncovering those histories requires the traditional courage and integrity to employ methods of detection that can include, for example, reading between the lines (à la Phyllis Trible[2]) of a text to identify who was there and who was missing. History is replete with allusions to the presence of persons at the margins of society, like women, people with disabilities, children, racial/linguistic/cultural minorities, slave or free persons, among others. Using a disability hermeneutic, scholars have begun to exhume the sources and resources of the Catholic tradition. Combined with knowledge and practical wisdom from the lived experiences of scholars with disabilities, theologians whose lives are shaped by the reality of disability and scholars who have recognized the importance of this disciplinary approach are well positioned to make important contributions to post-modern, post-colonial, and context-specific analyses of the way disability is understood today.

As "Engaging Disability" shows, the field of Disability Studies is developing along with its scholars and interested readers. Unfortunately, there is a notable dearth of contributions and interventions from Catholic theologians and Catholic theological ethicists. This absence is particularly striking given the ample sources and resources available for Catholic engagement in the field. Aside from work on making liturgies accessible, we believe that this collection is the first to bring Catholic theological ethicists together to

---

[1] Nancy Eiesland, "Integrating Disability in Religious Studies and Theological Education," Spotlight on Teaching, *Religious Studies News* (May 2005), rsnonline.org/indexe1f5.html?option=com_content&view=article&id=520&Itemid=604.

[2] See Phyllis Trible, *God and the Rhetoric of Sexuality* (Philadelphia, PA: Overtures to Biblical Theology, 1978).

explore some of the ways in which the tradition has engaged and can engage disability. May it not be the last.

The nine essays of the collection engage this work of excavation and are organized around three general themes. The issue opens with the contextual and content specific consideration of the traditions of Catholic social thought on matters of justice for people with disabilities. With a look to casuistry, prayer, and systematic thought, the issue turns next to the experiences of people with sensory and profound disabilities. Finally, the issue closes with theological reflections on friendship, beatitude, and vulnerability.

In "God Bends Over Backwards to Accommodate Humankind ... While the Civil Rights Acts and the Americans with Disabilities Act Require [Only] Minimum Effort," Mary Jo Iozzio articulates a call to solidarity and action by making connections between the U.S. Civil Rights Acts (1964 and 1965), the Americans with Disabilities Act (1990), Catholic social teaching, and the way God attends to humankind. Iozzio invokes the image of "bending over backwards" for its sense of limit-challenging regard in terms of the extra mile, the cloak given, or the offered cheek which Jesus asks of those who would follow him. She contends that, while the Civil Rights Acts granted protections from discrimination, the ADA law serves only as a directive, whereas a change of hearts (of the nondisabled toward people with disabilities) is the moral standard held by Christ and by those who would call themselves disciples. The imperatives of solidarity and the preferential option for the poor provide a robust dressing on the scaffolding of the law. Iozzio's essay provides a fitting introduction to this collection, emphasizing the radical nature of Christ's call to discipleship. Even as the call directs us toward forgotten persons at the margins of society, it is not "radical" because it is fringe or extraordinary. It is radical because it is fundamental to the ways human beings are related to one another. She argues this radical dependence with a theological anthropology based on Trinitarian relationality and Incarnational solidarity that inform and form human beings as the image of God.

In "On 'And Vulnerable': Catholic Social Thought and the Social Challenges of Cognitive Disability," Matthew Gaudet juxtaposes the opening lines of Vatican II's *Gaudium et Spes*—"The joys and the hopes, the griefs and the anxieties of the men of this age"—with the 1965 exposure of the scandalous state of conditions at New York's infamous Willowbrook State School. Gaudet sets the stage for the continuing struggles that people with intellectual and developmental disabilities still face with the promising trajectories of Catholic social thought for improvement. He contrasts the historical difference between the familial care provided for people with intellectual and developmental disabilities in agrarian communities with the dehumanizing institutional care provided in modern industrialized economies. The principles and ongoing development of human dignity, solidarity, and subsidiarity provide Gaudet with a framework to consider these challenges and to imagine a way forward.

In "From Universal Precautions to Universal Design: Disclosure of Concealable Disability in the Case of HIV," Mary M. Doyle Roche explores the challenges of disclosure that coincide with the inclusion of people with HIV-positive status among the class of persons covered by the protections from discrimination in the Americans with Disabilities Act. In particular, she considers the way the act of disclosure may exacerbate the stigma and exclusion experienced by persons with HIV-positive status and their caregivers within the Christian community. As a concealable condition, HIV-positive status prompts new theological thinking about the role of disclosure in building solidarity with persons who are living with HIV/AIDS. Transition from "universal precautions" to "universal design" prompts the Christian community itself to become a disclosure event and to initiate praxes of hospitality and liberation for persons living with HIV.

In "Disability, the Healing of Infirmity, and the Theological Virtue of Hope: A Thomistic Approach," Paul Gondreau considers two frescoes—one of the Final Judgment that includes a panel on the Resurrection where flesh is replaced on skeletons and bodies are changed from a former perishable to a new, immortal, and glorified nature, the other of St. Servulus, a man with severe cerebral palsy, lying on a cot, spending his days praising God and begging alms—to ask, "What does the Christian virtue of hope promise us in the final Resurrection, when our corruptible bodies attain to the *esse incorruptibile*?" Drawing upon the immersive experience of disability within his family, that of his brother and his son, Gondreau's principle concern is to understand the final destiny of our present infirmities. What shall not be wiped away, he argues, is the beauty of our sufferings and infirmities, inclusive of disability, in the measure that such beauty reflects the beauty of Christ's own suffering and infirmities. Gondreau cautions the parents, siblings, and healthcare providers of people with disabilities on the sins of despair and presumption in order to show the eschatological art of healing that hope sustains.

In "Seventeenth-Century Casuistry regarding Persons with Disabilities: Antonino Diana's Tract 'On the Mute, Deaf, and Blind,'" Julia A. Fleming presents Diana's case-study engagement with questions from his fellow casuists, confessors, missionaries, and pastors who encountered people with disabilities (or became disabled themselves). Diana, we learn, offers a range of opinions in answer to what degree of accommodation is necessary to ensure the participation of variously disabled persons in ecclesiastical and civil society.

Fleming highlights the Catholic casuist acknowledgement of both the moral aptitude and moral responsibilities of persons with impaired sensory and communication faculties. She concludes with an invitation to scholars working at the intersection of disability studies and theological ethics to consider Diana's text as a guide for considering the histories and circumstances of disability, reflecting on accommodation, and engaging with disability as the hermeneutic lens.

In "Blessed Silence: Explorations in Christian Contemplation and Hearing Loss," Jana Bennett uses a contemporary movement, Deaf Gain, which emphasizes the positive aspects of deafness (as opposed to "hearing loss"), to turn toward retrieving a critical appreciation for the practices of silent, contemplative prayer. Bennett locates her analysis in relation to the 2014 collection of essays entitled *Deaf Gain: Raising the Stakes for Human Diversity*, noting the absence of a theologian's voice in the collection and highlighting the intrigue of the *Deaf Gain* outlook for Christian theology (e.g., the presumed necessity to *hear* the Word, and the possibility that Jesus, the Incarnate Word of God, is a stumbling block for those who cannot hear). Bennett challenges the tendency to construct deafness as pathology under the medical model of disability; rather, she contends the silence that accompanies deafness can be a silence conducive to human flourishing and personal intimacy with the Spirit of God. She concludes with a discussion from the prophetic tradition in Scripture, proposing that while deafness is not an unmitigated good, from the Christian perspective, it can be a good in relation to our life in Christ.

In "Becoming Friends: Ethics in Friendship and in Doing Theology," Lorraine Cuddeback uses the methodological resources germane to ethnographic fieldwork to reflect on the experience of friendship among adult persons who have an intellectual disability and friendship between members of that community and adults who do not have intellectual disabilities. As researcher and theologian, Cuddeback is wary of both the tendency and the temptation to instrumentalize her research participants and the uncritical theological appeals to "friendship" as a solution to the problem of inclusion. As a way forward, Cuddeback argues that friendship requires both a love of and for the other as well as the justice capable of recognizing the real differences that mark every human relationship. She engages the remarks on friendship in Hans Reinders's theological anthropology and Tom Reynolds's remarks on difference and vulnerability as a way to unpack the narratives of her participants' claims to friendship, including their claim that she is, to them, a friend.

In "The Slow Journey towards Beatitude: Disability in L'Arche, and Staying Human in High-Speed Society," Jason Reimer Greig observes that contemporary conceptions of time create false anthropologies that thwart the journey toward becoming truly human and, as such, friends with God, with others, and with self. Reimer

Greig asks, "How can any follow Jesus at an accelerated world pace?" He argues for an alternate temporality as lived in L'Arche communities—a more human form of life and site of resistance to the western logic of speed. Like other authors in this issue, Reimer Greig mines the tradition's turn to the subject and social thought to ground a theological ethic of responsibility for the other, emphasizing human dignity, the inherently social nature of the person, and interdependence. Reimer Greig concludes with a reflection on the way Eucharist is celebrated in L'Arche communities as a practice that both forms and expresses the Christian concern to live according to "God's time."

Finally, in "The Goodness and Beauty of Our Fragile Flesh: Moral Theologians and Our Engagement with 'Disability,'" Miguel J. Romero raises the question and a concern about the way contemporary moral theologians think about the human body and, in particular, the goodness and beauty of our fragile flesh. Building upon the traditional Christian affirmations concerning the goodness of the human body and the fittingness of our corporeal vulnerability, Romero is concerned with the contemporary tendency in Christian moral discourse to treat impairment, illness, and injury as special topics, ancillary to standard theological reflection on the integral good proper to the human being. Drawing from Aquinas, Pope Saint John Paul II, Alasdair MacIntyre, and the critical theory approach to disability, Romero's aim is to show why the coherence and integrity of Catholic moral theology is undermined when theologians persistently avoid or consistently muddle the anthropological principles relevant to the human experience of impairment, illness, injury, and disability. Romero's essay provides a fitting summation for this issue of the *Journal of Moral Theology* of the ways contemporary theologians think about disability; their use of the concept to reflect upon impairment, illness, and injury; diverse understandings of embodied vulnerability; and a return to a theological anthropology of encounter, conversion, and transformation.

We co-editors are not of a single mind on the trajectories or the conclusions drawn in this issue of the *Journal of Moral Theology*. However, the claims made by each of the authors are substantiated with reliable evidence and reflect a line of thinking on disability that is accepted by one or another "school of thought." The experiences retold are verified as witness truths and the theo-ethical reflections sound. Thus, like us, some readers will recognize the merits of the social critique and others a critique of religious praxis. Some will cheer the politics of disablement and others the retrieval of historical developments. Some will favor a context-specific examination and others the systematic reflection on the experience of disability in the course of daily living. Some will prefer considerations on the practical responses to personal needs and others pious approaches of comfort. Still some will prefer "crip" empowerment and others attention to accompaniment. All approaches are welcome if we, as Catholic theologians and ethicists, are to engage disability—and, more importantly, ourselves and others living with disabilities—in constructive, hopeful, and life-affirming ways. We leave the implications to you, dear readers, and hope you will be encouraged to take, as an ever more deliberate cause, inclusion as a matter of what is right in all human affairs for all God's people: *misericordes sicut Pater*! M

Introductory Bibliography in Disability Studies

Avalos, Hector, Sarah J. Melcher, and Jeremy Schipper, eds. *This Abled Body: Rethinking Disabilities in Biblical Studies*. Atlanta, GA: Society of Biblical Literature, 2007.

Brock, Brian, and Jon Swinton, eds. *Disability in the Christian Tradition: A Reader*. Grand Rapids, MI: Wm. B. Eerdmans Publishing Company, 2012.

Carlson, Licia, *The Faces of Intellectual Disability: Philosophical Reflections*. Bloomington, IN: Indiana University Press, 2010.

Charlton, James I. *Nothing About Us Without Us*. Berkeley, CA: University of California Press, 1998.

Creamer, Deborah Beth. *Disability and Christian Theology: Embodied Limits and Constructive Possibilities*. Oxford, UK: Oxford University Press, 2009.

Davis, Lennard, ed. *The Disability Studies Reader*, 4th ed. New York, NY: Routledge, 2013.

Eiesland, Nancy L. *The Disabled God: Toward a Liberatory Theology of Disability*. Nashvillle, TN: Abingdon Press, 1994.

Finkelstein, Victor. *Attitudes and Disabled People*. New York, NY: World Rehabilitation Fund, Inc., 1980 [Monograph No. 5].

Garland-Thomson, Rosemarie. *Extraordinary Bodies: Figuring Physical Disability in American Culture and Literature*. New York, NY: Columbia University Press, 1997.

Goffman, Erving. *Stigma: Notes on the Management of Spoiled Identity*. New York, NY: Simon & Shuster, Inc., 1963.

Kittay, Eva Feder, and Licia Carlson, eds. *Cognitive Disability and its Challenge to Moral Philosophy*. Oxford, UK: Wiley-Blackwell, 2010.

Oliver, Michael and Colin Barnes. *The New Politics of Disablement*. Basingstoke, UK: Palgrave Macmillan, 2012 [See M. Oliver, *The Politics of Disablement*, 1990].

Reynolds, Thomas. *Vulnerable Communion: A Theology of Disability and Hospitality*. Grand Rapids, MI: Brazos Press, 2008.

Schumm, Darla and Michael Stoltzfus, eds. *Disability and World Religions: An Introduction*. Waco, TX: Baylor University Press, 2016.

Shakespeare, Tom. *Conceptualising Impairment and Disability in Sociological Perspective*. PhD diss., University of Cambridge, 1994.

Stiker, Henri-Jacques. *A History of Disability*. Ann Arbor, MI: University of Michigan Press, 2000 [Paris, FR: Éditions Aubier Montaigne, 1982; Paris, FR: Éditions Dunod, revised 1997, William Sayers, trans.].

Wolfensberger, Wolf. "Social Role Valorization: A Proposed New Term for the Principle of Normalization." *Mental Retardation* 21, no. 6 (1983): 234-239.

Yong, Amos. *Theology and Down Syndrome: Reimagining Disability in Late Modernity*. Waco, TX: Baylor University Press, 2017.

God Bends Over Backwards to Accommodate Humankind…While the Civil Rights Acts and the Americans with Disabilities Act Require [Only] Minimum Effort

Mary Jo Iozzio

THE CIVIL RIGHTS AND ADA LAWS IN the United States represent some of the results of the interrogations of privilege that attempt to ameliorate the disadvantages of servitude, marginalization, and the institutionalization of minoritized people with proactive measures for equality and access. However, these laws, like most laws, are limited in their ability to influence a change of heart among many. In this essay I consider some of the contours of these laws, I look at Catholic social teaching for insight on how to be with and for those who are poor and/or otherwise marginalized, and I reflect on what I think God wills we would do.

In 2015, the United States celebrated the fiftieth anniversary of the Voting Rights Act (1965) and the twenty-fifth anniversary of the Americans with Disabilities Act (1990). Some people in the United States and elsewhere celebrated these legislative measures that ensure legal protections against discrimination on the bases of race and/or disability; some did not. One of the concerns on the periphery of this essay is the apparent failure, if not outright hostility, that those not celebrating these legislative successes harbor against people belonging to one or both of these minorities in the United States and elsewhere. Another of my concerns is the failure to recognize that these and other laws require only a minimalist or anemic justice to avoid discriminatory behavior and other harms upon individuals and communities and/or the violation of citizens' exercise of their rights to common liberties and access to common goods. Mostly, while these laws are critically important for the real lives of those who are vulnerable, I am concerned about the theological implications of following or ignoring God's lead in accommodating humankind in all its diverse incarnations.

Why are these initiatives important? Because not one of us should have to wait for the Kingdom to know that we are loved, lovable, and capable of loving in return. Not one of us should have to witness another lynching, rape, institutionalization, sterilization, or insult to the humanity of another. Not one of us should ever think ourselves above or untouched by the fray in advantage or disadvantage. Moreover, we Christians may be especially indictable when we have failed to welcome strangers, clothe those naked, feed those hungry, shelter those without safe places to rest, visit those imprisoned—in jails, asylums, hospitals, detention centers, camps, and reservations—or announce the Good News.

From most accounts in Christian traditions and to the extent that it can be known, God's will for what God has wrought is that all creation flourish from the least to the greatest. God's lead goes far further than these laws in promoting the common goods they seek to distribute, and I find myself wanting to push law to its limits to accommodate people who have been left out of the goods that constitute the relationships with the One and the many. Insofar as God bends over backwards toward humankind and identifying especially with those who are vulnerable in the share of those goods, we Christians must go and do likewise.[1] I invoke the image of "bending over backwards" for its sense of no limit in terms of the extra mile, cloak or other cheek that Jesus asks of those who would follow him as well as for its sense of exposure by the one so bending/bent to vulnerability. To the extent that God's will can be known in God's becoming human, God has clearly gone the extra mile and experienced exposure even to an excruciating death. Since then, not one other person needs to so bend, except by her or his own choice and where or when injustice prevails.

In a time when suspicions about who count as legal members of our communities and who is protected by the laws of the land are raised by isolationist political camps, the image of God bending over backwards suggests another way to be with and to accommodate people in need of both justice and mercy. God's justice is not punitive; it is reconciliatory. God's mercy is scandalously generous; it is kenotic and favorably disposed to those who are marginalized on account of their deviance from assumed norms and privilege.

I engage this concern about God's designs for humankind from the perspective of disability studies at the intersections of theological ethics, race and anti-racism activism, and gender minority studies. I am committed to members of minoritized communities, particularly to those designated by hegemonic normativity—subsequent to an unrecognized or unacknowledged complacence by dominant

---

[1] Of course, other religious traditions have similar concerns for the weal of those in their midst who are vulnerable. Clearly, Judaism, the faith of Jesus of Nazareth, presents care for the widow, orphan, and sojourner as imperatives for the people, as important as the laws of the covenant. Islam too has among the pillars of faith support of those who are in need.

"majoritized" others—as undesirable on the basis of race and disability. These designations about some human beings offend justice at large and, in particular, their dignity as members of the one human community. That offense against the dignity of so many people disturbs the peace and ultimately offends the Creator in whose image each and every person is created and loved. I take the opportunity of these anniversaries to examine the nature of anti-discrimination laws and the protections they afford and to place those initiatives in dialogue with an ethics of virtue, the tools that the law has at its disposal to embrace as a teacher. I remain accountable to those about whom I write—people with disabilities and people of color—as well as to the guild of Catholic ethicists that turns to the implications of the Incarnation above all to find the means and the meanings of God's justice and mercy in a world distorted by sin.

The Civil Rights Acts (1964 and 1965) and the Americans with Disabilities Act (1990) offer protections against discrimination and, to a lesser extent, encourage opportunities for development and the participation of individuals and communities belonging to these protected classes in the local, state, national, and international communities of human commerce. These Acts represent landmark legislation and progress in fostering a sense of "liberty and justice for all" in pursuit of activities that bring people together in economic, educational, commercial, health, housing, legal, political, public, recreational, religious, and social venues. Unfortunately, both people identified with racial minorities and people with disabilities in the United States (and elsewhere) continue to experience limits to their liberty and justice. These limits are saturated by the long lasting residue of bias maintained by unexamined and unearned dominant white, male, hetero, Christian, and ableist privilege that remains preserved (covertly and well) in the systems from which human economies operate.[2] While charges are filed in the court systems and claims of multiple types of violation against these protected classes have been argued successfully in US courts,[3] the perpetuation of discrimination on the basis of race and disability reveals the limitations inherent to these laws. Those limitations point directly to an anemic conception of law where a more robust appreciation of the laws' pedagogical function better serves the common weal.

---

[2] Although there are parallels found in the discriminations against women, non-heterosexuals, and religious minorities in the United States, in what follows I confine my argument to the discriminations against and minimums afforded to people of color and people with disabilities.

[3] Since Fiscal Year 1997, more than 1.6 million charges have been filed with the EEOC. See "Charge Statistics, FY1997 Through FY 2015," *Enforcement and Litigation Statistics*, Equal Employment Opportunity Commission, eeoc.gov/eeoc/statistics/enforcement/charges.cfm.

Although the laws of a land serve as a guide in the development of individuals' and society's virtue, in forming upright and decent citizens and communities, laws today more often than not represent only a minimum (of decency let alone justice for the moment) owed between parties in human commerce. The notion of the law as a teacher is nearly lost.[4] As she builds upon the work of Aristotle and Aquinas, Cathleen Kaveny instructs that the key virtues about which law should teach are autonomy and solidarity.[5] Not coincidentally, these virtues are two of the most often referenced in calls for justice by advocacy groups. Yet for those who belong to and/or stand with communities of color and people with disabilities, recognition of their experiences exposes the laws' inadequacies and demonstrates that more than minimum is necessary, particularly when being black and/or having a disability is the reality questioned. When "being" is questioned, whose lives matter? It is simply "Not OK" to denigrate, discriminate, or disrespect any longer.[6]

It is all too clear that history has not been kind to people who differ from the dominant populations among which they are present and are presented by their families and/or friends to be acknowledged, recognized, and welcomed. While the United States experiment in democracy through the Constitution and more inclusively in subsequent Amendments purported (and still purports) equal opportunities and freedom for all, not everyone enjoys this equality among their neighbors, except on the papers that define the nation as sovereign and in the cultural imagination set in "The New Colossus" (a.k.a Lady Liberty) and "Manifest Destiny."[7] Sadly and scandalously, the nation's Original Sin of the theft of this land from and the near extinction of its Native Peoples, coupled with the slave trade and enshrined in its quintessential beliefs and myths about exceptionalism

---

[4] Among others, see Thomas Aquinas, "Treatise on Law," *Summa Theologiae*, I-II, q. 90-108; Cathleen Kaveny, *Law's Virtues: Fostering Autonomy and Solidarity in American* Society (Washington, DC: Georgetown University Press, 2012); and Robert P. George, "Law and Moral Purpose," *First Things*, January 2008, www.firstthings.com/article/2008/01/001-law-and-moral-purpose.
[5] See Kaveny, "Law as Moral Teacher," "Autonomy, Solidarity, and Law's Pedagogy," and "Law and Morality: Understanding the Relationship," *Law's Virtues*.
[6] With a single hand up in a sign language Stop Sign fashion, the Twitter feed #NotOK has "become a rallying cry of righteous indignation ... [against] the bland, generic violence of what we, as a patriarchal society, deem acceptable. ... the ironic challenge to our social complacency and normalized expectations of well-being in the face of injustice." See Laurence Scott, "Not OK: How a cunningly terse phrase elevates moral virtue over a bad status quo," *Boston Globe*, October 30, 2016, www.bostonglobe.com/ideas/2016/10/29/not/mBNeOrNivDfEWxRG072arK/story.html.
[7] For an interesting examination of the ambivalent relationship between this cultural imagination and the realities of nation-building, see Edward L. Widmer, *Ark of Liberties: America and the World* (New York: Farrar, Straus and Giroux, 2008), especially Chapter 6.

and democratic ideals,[8] is played out nearly daily in public and private spaces as news is told in the reports of promising and not-so-promising black lives lost to violence and/or complacence.[9] More than 50% of homicides committed in the United States are perpetrated against racialized minorities, with African Americans overwhelmingly among the dead. Similar violence against people with disabilities, though not as frequently reported on account of a cloak of invisibility and/or presumed rarity, plays on the vulnerability to the same losses from dominant narratives suspicious of danger to a mentality that assumes the victim is an easy target. Like crimes against Black men, a variety of hate crimes toward people with disabilities occur with impunity, and many are particularly vicious toward those with developmental and/or behavioral disabilities.[10] Moreover, women with disabilities are especially vulnerable to more kinds of, and more severe, sexual assaults, by more distinct perpetrators, and over a longer period of time than their non-disabled peers. The most recent report of the Federal Office of Justice Programs confirms the rate of violent crime against people with disabilities as two times greater than crimes against people without disabilities: at 14% of the total US population in 2013, people with disabilities numbered more than 21% of all violent crime victims.[11] This sinful history—from its original theft to its contemporary oppressive expressions—must not be ignored or glossed over, rather it must be exposed, reparations made, and its residue rejected. If our laws are to teach civility and virtue then the hope of equal regard as fully human and of equal access to human flourishing and to the nation's common goods—assuring the violence-free and hate-free exercise of personal autonomy as well as supporting solidarity in the work of community and national pride—will inform

---

[8] Among others, see Kelly Brown Douglas, *Stand Your Ground: Black Bodies and the Justice of God* (Maryknoll: Orbis Books, 2015).

[9] The FBI reports that more than 50% of homicide victims in 2015 are Black folk in a nation of 321 million where Blacks comprise a mere 13.3% of the population. That is, out of 13,455 murders 7,039 were Black folk. See Federal Bureau of Investigation, Uniform Crime Reporting, "Murder Victims by Race, Ethnicity, and Sex 2015,"ucr.fbi.gov/crime-in-the-u.s/2015/crime-in-the-u.s.2015/tables/expanded_homicide_data_table_1_murder_victims_by_race_ethnicity_and_sex_2015.xls. Data for 2016 are not yet available; however, the Black victim rate continues to rise. For one city's example, there were 798 homicides in Chicago in 2016. Of those 798, 624 are Black, 133 Hispanic, 41 White/Other. See Hey Jackass!, Illustrating Chicago Values, "Stats," heyjackass.com/category/2016-stats/.

[10] See Nora J. Baladerian, Thomas F. Coleman, and Jim Stream, *Abuse of People with Disabilities: Victims and Their Families Speak Out* (Los Angeles: Spectrum Institute, 2013), disability-abuse.com/survey/survey-report.pdf. Sadly, most of these crimes go unreported and, thereby, occur with ever-greater empowerment of the perpetrators (possibly with greater frequency) since they go unchallenged.

[11] See Erika Harrell, "Crime Against Persons with Disabilities, 2009-2013 –Statistical Tables," US Department of Justice, Office of Justice Programs, Bureau of Justice Statistics (May 2015), www.bjs.gov/content/pub/pdf/capd0913st.pdf.

the intents and the effects of the Civil Rights and Americans with Disabilities Acts.

A Primer on the Civil Rights and Americans with Disabilities Acts

The Civil Rights Act of 1964 outlaws discrimination against and segregation of people on the basis of race, color, religion, sex, and national origin.[12] The former ways of separate and unequal access to education, healthcare, transportation, dining, and other public facilities as well as employment discrimination would no longer suffice. The Voting Rights Act of 1965 outlaws racial discrimination in voting and (moderately) effectively enfranchised racial minorities. This legislation and subsequent amendments that clarify and/or extend provisions of the Act give local, state, and federal law enforcement agencies the capabilities that point back to the Civil Rights Act, to ensure thereby that the right of US citizens to vote is inviolable.[13] Overt and other more subtle disenfranchisement ploys, such as gerrymandering that manipulatively influence poll populations and precincts' results, and/or poll taxes were deemed illegal. The Americans with Disabilities Act of 1990 prohibits discrimination against persons with disabilities with protections similar to the Civil Rights Act, as well as requiring employers to provide reasonable accommodations to employees with disabilities and public venues to provide accessibility to patrons with disabilities.[14] The days of warehousing people with disabilities in asylums and the like or

---

[12] Civil Rights Act, Public Law 88-352, 88th Congress (July 2, 1964), media.nara.gov/rediscovery/02233.pdf: "An act to enforce the constitutional right to vote, to confer jurisdiction upon the district courts of the USA to provide injunctive relief against discrimination in public accommodations, to authorize the Attorney General to institute suits to protect constitutional rights in public facilities and public education, to extend the Commission on Civil Rights, to prevent discrimination in federally assisted programs, to establish a Commission on Equal Employment Opportunity [hereafter, EEOC], and for other purposes."

[13] Voting Rights Act, Public Law 89-110, 89th Congress (August 6, 1965), www.archives.gov/historical-docs/doc-content/images/voting-rights-act.pdf: "An act to enforce the Fifteenth Amendment [ratified February 3, 1870, prohibiting denial of a citizen's right to vote on account of "race, color, or previous condition of servitude"] to the Constitution of the United States, and for Other Purposes." Among the protections of the Voting Rights Act are the bans on literacy tests, English language comprehension (and provision of non-English ballots), and onerous (and superfluous) identification documents.

[14] Americans with Disabilities Act, Public Law 101-325, 101st Congress (July 26, 1990), www.ada.gov/pubs/adastatute08.htm: "An act to establish a clear and comprehensive prohibition of discrimination on the basis of disability." This legislation and subsequent amendments offer (moderately) comprehensive rights to employment, services of human commerce, and participation in the *polis*. Among the protections of the Americans with Disabilities Act are prohibitions of firing or refusing to hire, segregation, harassment, and denial of reasonable accommodation(s) or access on the basis of a disability(ies).

consigning them to substandard housing, inhumane and abusive treatment, and widespread exclusion in human work, other commerce, and play are no longer tolerated.

Each of these Acts reflects a major step in the direction of justice for many in the US. Those early steps followed the nation's widespread witness—through the increasingly available media outlets of newspapers, radio broadcasts, and both public and in-home television sets—of the struggles for freedom and fair play.[15] The discrimination against being black or other racial minority and/or having a disability, which these laws seek to jettison, exposes the intersections of common experience among individuals in the US belonging to non-dominant communities. In what follows I focus on ways to dismantle the edifice of dominant narratives and the power they wield through the strategic naming of injustice as these laws identify them.[16] I offer the terms of discriminating acts, I consider the elements of accountability the statutes employ, and I look at solidarity as the key to accommodate not only the minimum of rights but the fullness of life, work, and play that is God's way of reconciling perceived differences in the struggles for both racial and disability justice.

The Legal Terms Outlining Discrimination

While racialized skin color is often, though not always, apparent, disabilities may be and perhaps often are hidden and thereby render the categorizing of persons who would be protected by law both difficult and fungible. While, hopefully, the question of personhood is not asked, the question of "who" qualifies is asked, at times with impunity. These kinds of questions go to the heart of human dignity and raise suspicions about the presumptions that are based on philosophical and theological anthropologies in regard to who counts as human and who qualifies thereby for the protections offered in law.[17] Invisibilities or doubts that authorities may harbor about the

---

[15] In a nation where veterans of world wars and military conflicts worked alongside soldiers of different races, consider the visceral impact of media coverage on, for example, Brown vs. the Board of Education of Topeka (1954), the Montgomery Bus Boycott (1955-56), Freedom Riders (1961), the Birmingham Campaign (April-May 1963), and the March on Washington (August 1963). Consider too that through the efforts of Martin Luther King, Jr., the Southern Christian Leadership Conference, the Student Non-Violent Coordinating Committee, and their allies, the nation's hypocrisy was exposed and evidenced particularly in violent civilian, military, and police aggression against deliberately non-violent protesters.

[16] A good deal of my questioning and challenge to the dominant way of proceeding was inspired by anti-racism work with Pax Christi USA and critical theory à la Foucault. Among others, see Michel Foucault, *The Archaeology of Knowledge & The Discovery of Language* (New York: Pantheon Books, 1972).

[17] A good deal of discriminatory practices have been and continue to rely on dualist presumptions that place some people (those exemplifying a favored norm) over the

real (or in their view imagined) condition or experience of disability(ies) influence the determinations those authorities consider about the applicability of the law.

The Civil Rights Acts and the Americans with Disabilities Act serve to extend consciousness of widespread discrimination in human commerce and to enforce compliance that protects people from the injustices of humanity denied in terms of employment and access to other forms of human commerce. These acts use similar language to enfranchise and protect against discrimination. However, the legal terms point almost singularly to a denial of access based on presumptions of worth in comparison to those whose access is taken for granted. This is, discrimination will end only when access to vote, to schooling, healthcare, employment, religious/social/recreational activities, and movement about the commons will be equal to those whose access is at present unencumbered and free. The Equal Employment Opportunity Commission (EEOC) identifies eleven bases of employment discrimination:[18] race, sex, age, disability,[19] gender, pregnancy, national origin, religion, compensation, genetic information, and retaliation (termination, censure, demotion or failure to promote).

Unlike the Civil Rights Acts, which do not "qualify" what constitutes race or color, the Americans with Disabilities Act (hereafter ADA) does qualify what constitutes conditions that compel compliance. Title I Regulations of the ADA define the extent to which employers and public venues are to provide reasonable accommodations to people with disabilities (hereafter PWD). Title II of the ADA defines the conditions and/or impairments, with respect to an individual, that qualify or do not qualify for the protections against discrimination and recourse to the law as a champion of civil rights. Title II, Subpart A, "prohibits ... [and] protects qualified individuals with disabilities from discrimination on the basis of disabilities." Title III, Subpart A, offers that, "Disability means, with respect to an individual, a physical or mental impairment that substantially limits one or more of the major life activities of such individual; a record of such impairment; or being regarded as having such an impairment."[20] As a result, the ADA allows "qualifications" (as well as minimum requirements incumbent upon and minimum

---

mass of people who "fail" the norm. See Iozzio, "Norms Matter: A Hermeneutic of Disability/A Theological Anthropology of Radical Dependence," *ET-Studies* 4, no. 1 (2013): 89-106.

[18] See U.S. Equal Employment Opportunity Commission, "Prohibited Employment Policies/Practices" (2009), www.eeoc.gov/laws/practices/.

[19] The category disability was added in 1990 to the EEOC bases covered by the Civil Rights Act.

[20] See Code of Federal Regulations (ADA Title II) 28 CFR §35.104 Definitions and (ADA Title III) 28 CFR §36.104 Definitions.

compliance by employers, public and private institutions, and commercial venues) to make a way for and forward for PWD to enter into the determinations of discriminations against, equal opportunity for, or denied access to PWD. More often than not, these determined qualifications have undermined the intent to democratize employment of and social practices for PWD and have made recourse to the legal system all the more difficult for them and for their advocates and allies.[21]

The Elements of Accountability

Like the exacting force of definitions that determine the categories (e.g., race and/or gender) or classes of persons (e.g., children, elderly, PWD, patients,...), which the laws are designed to protect, coverage formulae outline the reach of the Federal Government to impose upon or relieve juridic persons from this or that requirement. Coverage formulae are most often used in the legal sphere on matters of voting rights and require a state and/or local municipality to seek permission of the courts before changing current practice regarding voting laws for protected classes of people. Coverage formulae are useful also in protecting the increase of access that PWD might experience across the spectrum of human commerce, including voting rights. Unfortunately, coverage formulae for the ADA are bound to factors of "qualified" entities as well as to their cost-to-revenue percentages (a mere 1% change in cost-to-revenue balances can be sufficient reason for disqualification on compliance and an opt-out to accommodate modifications for individuals and PWD) that grant a fairly widespread safe harbor exemption from being required to comply (i.e., to enjoy a status of non-compliance).[22] Similarly unfortunate, these formulae favor and protect the status quo of non-disabled/normate privilege.[23]

---

[21] On who qualifies, see Robert D. Dinerstein, "The Americans with Disabilities Act of 1990: Progeny of the Civil Rights Act of 1964," *Human Rights* 31, no. 3 (2004): www.americanbar.org/publications/human_rights_magazine_home/human_rights_vol31_2004/summer2004/irr_hr_summer04_disable.html. On reasonable accommodations, see Bonnie Poitras Tucker, "The ADA's Revolving Door: Inherent Flaws in the Civil Rights Paradigm," *Ohio State Law Journal* 62 (2001): 335-390.

[22] See U.S. Department of Justice, *Americans with Disabilities Act Title III Regulations: Nondiscrimination on the Basis of Disability by Public Accommodations and in Commercial Facilities*, "Supplementary Information" (Washington, DC: DOJ, 2010), www.ada.gov/regs2010/titleIII_2010/titleIII_2010_regulations.pdf.

[23] Rosemarie Garland Thomson has coined the term "normate." For her definition, see Garland Thomson, *Extraordinary Bodies: Figuring Physical Disability in American Culture and Literature* (New York: Columbia University Press, 1996), 8: "the veiled subject position of cultural self, the figure outlined by the array of deviant others whose marked bodies shore up the normate's boundaries. The term normate usefully designates the social figure through which people can represent themselves as definitive human beings. Normate, then, is the constructed identity of those who, by way of the bodily configurations and cultural capital they assume, can step into a position of authority and wield the power it grants them."

In community organizing, accountability has a meaning quite different from the legal definitions and assignments of responsibility for compliance used in federal, state, and local law. Social activists—to whom many of us are indebted in reference to the fifty-one (Voting Rights), fifty (Civil Rights), and twenty-five (ADA) year anniversaries of anti-discrimination acts celebrated in 2015—identify accountability as one of the measures used to ensure honesty and success in achieving the aims of liberty, access, and opportunity (that is, justice) for those whose capabilities to be agents of their own making have been systematically obstructed.[24] In the law, coverage formulae determine what entities must engage these and other laws and the extent to which anti-discrimination and reasonable accommodations laws are to reach; however, as the exemptions to compliance demonstrate, the law often betrays and even undermines its purpose to lead and teach as it remains a protectorate over a minimum measure of human dignity.

For example, in reference to the Voting Rights Act, following a series of legal challenges, coverage formulae were designed as a measure of accountability to prevent voter suppression through discriminatory testing, registration processes, language bias, identification cards, and precincts' boundaries through carefully crafted political gerrymandering.[25] In light of the ADA, PWD were added to the voting rolls and thereby covered by the Voting Rights Act as a specific class with previously limited enfranchisement. Regrettably, the U.S. Supreme Court decision in "Shelby County v. Holder" (2013) eliminated the requirement of states, counties, and municipalities to request and wait to receive Department of Justice (D.O.J.) approval before changing any local voting rules and practices.[26] D.O.J. oversight of safeguards against voter suppression

---

[24] In reference to these capabilities, I recognize that each of us/all of us develop them with the help of many others through the infrastructures provided in greater or lesser degrees by our local, national, and international villages.

[25] The coverage mandates have been challenged and, as recently as 2013, the US Supreme Court struck down as unconstitutional the requirement of certain jurisdictions, known for voter suppression, to preclear any voting changes with the federal government before implementing those changes. See Oluma Kas-Osoka, "A New Preclearance Coverage Formula: Renewing the Promise of the Voting Rights Act," *Washington University Journal of Law & Policy* 47, no. 1 (2015): 151-174.

[26] The vote leading up to the November 2016 presidential election was the first to test the effect of the 2013 Supreme Court ruling. Without the Department of Justice approval to change rules and practices, "people are turned away from the polls, or purged from the rolls, or refused ID," early voting is curtailed and something likened to a "hassle tax"—waiting in long lines to cast a ballot—imposed. See Emily Bazelon, "The Supreme Court Ruled That Voting Restrictions Were a Bygone Problem. Early Voting Results Suggest Otherwise," *The New York Times*, Nov. 7, 2016, www.nytimes.com/2016/11/07/magazine/the-supreme-court-ruled-that-voting-restrictions-were-a-bygone-problem-early-voting-results-suggest-otherwise.html?_r=0.

designed to protect minority voters is unraveling. Since Shelby County v. Holder and in time for the 2016 Presidential election, fourteen states instituted new voting restrictions, reducing both safeguards and D.O.J. oversight. For all intents and purposes, coverage formulae requirements have been annulled.[27]

In reference to the Civil Rights Acts inclusive of civil rights extended in the ADA, the coverage requirements of compliance against employment discrimination and access is limited. Accountability in the context of the ADA leans in favor of "entities" and away from PWD, exempting many entities from accommodations on account of an entity's employee base and on the determination of "reasonable" accommodations. Under the EEOC and authorized by the Civil Rights Acts and the ADA, businesses with fewer than fifteen employees are exempt from compliance in matters of both non-discrimination and reasonable accommodations, as are private "clubs" and religious organizations. Unfortunately, these formulary mechanisms of accountability demonstrate attention to only a minimum standard for recruitment and retention, a minimum that fails the tests of the nation's concern for those intangible yet inalienable rights to life, liberty, and the pursuit of happiness. Just as the challenges that conservative legislators have raised in as many as 20 states and as the Supreme Court ruled on June 25, 2013, to dismantle a key piece of the formula of Section 4(b) that identifies jurisdictions in need of a preclearance to make changes,[28] the ADA is similarly subject to revision and loss. Moreover, unlike civil rights laws, the ADA is perhaps more properly considered as a voluntary compliance law: employers are expected to comply even though they are not required to report on the raw data indicating the number of employees with disabilities and/or the requests they may have received and/or fulfilled for reasonable accommodations or their fulfillment of those requests. Nevertheless, and like the path to a restoration of voting rights denied through political machinations and district gerrymandering, resort after the fact to the courts may be the only recourse to result in remedies.[29]

---

[27] See Brennan Center for Justice, "New Voting Restrictions in Place for 2016 Presidential Election," *New York University School of Law*, www.brennancenter.org/voting-restrictions-first-time-2016.

[28] See The United States Department of Justice, "About Section 5 of the Voting Rights Act," *Shelby County Decision*, www.justice.gov/crt/about-section-5-voting-rights-act; and Dana Liebelson, "The Supreme Court Gutted the Voting Rights Act. What Happened in These 8 States Will Not Shock You," *Mother Jones*, April 8, 2014, www.motherjones.com/politics/2014/04/republican-voting-rights-supreme-court-id.

[29] See Julian Cardillo, "The Americans with Disabilities Act: 25 years later," *BrandeisNOW*, www.brandeis.edu/now/2015/july/parish-ada-qanda.html. Cardillo interviews Susan Parish, Professor and Dean, Heller School for Social Policy and Management, Brandeis University, who opines that injunctive relief yields small rewards to complainants to dis-incentivize legal recourse, and further even if

Solidarity in Reconciling Disability Justice and Racial Justice

Aside from the fact that these laws hold a minimum of expectations by which institutions—whether governmental, commercial, educational, recreational, or religious—are required to abide, the Civil Rights and Disability Rights movements call for more than protections from harms. Many people who belong to racial minorities and/or are PWD remain in need of programs and services that genuinely respond to opportunities for the development of their capabilities and talents that anti-discrimination laws and reasonable accommodations simply do not provide. Further, as made clear in the all-too-frequent harms inflicted upon and the murders of Black folk and the under-reported violence against PWD,[30] the minimum has failed in law's original intent to teach and guide in the ways of virtue and decency. Instead, witnesses learn something—first-hand and through media outlets—from violent crime and assault suffered by a person or group whom they resemble in terms of race, sex, gender, class, and/or religion to fear the "other." If the other resembles the witnesses in one way or another, they may internalize self-hate or hate the other, an experienced reinforced with graphic images instigating post-traumatic stress.[31]

Yet Aquinas, building on Aristotle about the law as teacher, argues, "every law is ordained to the common good" (ST I-II q. 90, a. 2c). Moreover, "it is evident that the proper effect of law is to lead its

---

defendant/employer loses the cost is low, and "Employers would be more likely to follow the law, and hire and promote people with disabilities, if the incentives were stronger."

[30] On the systemic vulnerability of Black lives in the US, particularly in vulnerability to law enforcement, see Richard Baudouin, ed, *Ku Klux Klan: A History of Racism and Violence* (Montgomery: The Southern Poverty Law Center, 2011); Tom McKay, "One Troubling Statistic Shows Just How Racist America's Police Brutality Problem Is," *News.Mic*, mic.com/articles/96452/one-troubling-statistic-shows-just-how-racist-america-s-police-brutality-problem-is - .bCo24uLiC; The Editorial Board, "The Truth of 'Black Lives Matter,'" *The New York Times*, September 3, 2015, www.nytimes.com/2015/09/04/opinion/the-truth-of-black-lives-matter.html?_r=0.

People with disabilities are at substantially greater risk for violence, 4 to 10 times more likely, than the general dominant population, see Karen Hughes, et al, "Prevalence and Risk of Violence Against Adults with Disabilities: A Systematic Review and Meta-analysis of Observational Studies," *The Lancet* 379 (2012): 1621-1629; Lisa Jones, et al., "Prevalence and Risk of Violence Against Children with Disabilities: A Systematic Review and Meta-analysis of Observational Studies," *The Lancet* 380 (2012): 899-907.

[31] See Kenya Downs, "When black death goes viral, it can trigger PTSD-like trauma," *PBS NewsHour*, www.pbs.org/newshour/rundown/black-pain-gone-viral-racism-graphic-videos-can-create-ptsd-like-trauma/. On exposure of systemic, institutionalized racism see Julian Zelizer, "Is America Repeating the Mistakes of 1968?," *The Atlantic*, July 8, 2016, www.theatlantic.com/politics/archive/2016/07/is-america-repeating-the-mistakes-of-1968/490568/.

subjects to their proper virtue; and since virtue is 'that which makes its subject good,' it follows that the proper effect of law is to make those to whom it is given, good, either simply or in some particular respect" (ST I-II q. 92, a. 1c). Further, "[Women and] men who are well disposed are led willingly to virtue by being admonished better than by coercion, but [women and] men who are evilly disposed are not led to virtue unless they are compelled" by the discipline of law (ST I-II q. 95, a .1, ad. 1).[32] Anti-discrimination laws protect, but, in theory, they could also inspire more noble qualities. That is (and I may be asking more than is reasonable), the law has failed to advance the cause of justice in policies that will reach into the consciousness and consciences of the polity to reject any denial of the humanity and the dignity with which all persons have been endowed. Many may argue that the law is not designed to advance these kinds of changes. However, as the tradition bears out, laws do encourage by means of external legislation the internal dispositions and the cultivation of the virtues toward right and just behavior between and among the people of the polis.

From ancient and pre-industrialized texts unearthed by archaeology—papyri, tablets, manuscripts, architecture, burial sites, battlefields, and other artifacts—to the contemporary and ubiquitous media, the norms of an imperial past that signal "best" and "most admired" and their opposites can be inferred. Influential agents of the past, who assigned norms and normative status to dominant group identifiers, relied on the force of physical power and prowess to silence the subaltern, the different, the "other."[33] Though fewer in number, other influential agents—the prophets of old, Jesus, and the early Christian communities among them—proffered norms of inclusivity and a welcome of diversity. As a result of a postcolonial consciousness, today these norms both proliferate and weaken as standards of superiority or best and most admired—on the basis of race, sex, gender, religion, and ability—are raised on a trajectory parallel to the disadvantages and implied inferiority to the very being and achievement of minority populations. The norms proliferate in overt and covert ways as more people become aware of a status that has been assigned as privileged or not, and paradoxically weaken as more people in both dominant and minority populations begin to interrogate why and how a dominant "better" and minority "worse" emerged.[34] In the meantime, the Civil Rights and ADA laws, among

---

[32] See also Kaveny, *Law's Virtues*, Part I: Law as Moral Teacher.
[33] Among others, see Gayatri Chakravorty Spivak, "Can the Subaltern Speak?" in *Marxism and the Interpretation of Culture*, ed. Cary Nelson and Lawrence Grossberg (Champaign: University of Illinois Press, 1988), 271-313; and Edward W. Said, *Orientalism* (New York: Random House, Inc/Vintage Books, 1979, 1978).
[34] On being an ally and in solidarity with individuals and communities who have been (and often remain) oppressed by the colonialism that protects systemic racism,

the results of those interrogations, attempt to ameliorate the disadvantages of past servitude, marginalization, and institutionalization (imprisonment/incarceration for Black and other racialized minorities, asylum and/or imprisonment for PWD[35]) with proactive measures for equality and access.

More is yet needed, particularly when people who are non-white, non-heterosexual, non-Christian, living with disabilities, and/or women are violated with scandalous impunity on account of their being in places and spaces where some members of the dominant culture prefer they not go. This "reluctance" on the part of some members of the dominant and normate culture to "let others be" suggests internalized prejudices against members of the non-dominant communities of a categorical kind that questions entrenched suppositions about who among them qualifies as fully human. It is this line of questioning and thinking that strikes at the heart of the Civil Rights Acts explored here. To whom, if not to everyone, do civil rights belong? Who counts as persons, and what remedies are to be applied to overcome and dismantle internalized apathy, unremarked hate speech, and/or lip service in the face of systemic structural obstacles against initiatives to thrive?

Sadly, racism continues to poison public and private spheres with exasperating frequency in the US and elsewhere, and, just as sadly, ableism too remains as entrenched. While derogatory name-calling may be on the decline, microaggressions against racial minorities and PWD occur far too often in and across a variety of contexts—at work, in school, in formal and informal settings—that make them especially covert, pernicious, and, thereby, ever more insidious. These aggressions "are everyday, seemingly minor verbal, nonverbal, or environmental slights or insults [providing] a glimpse of the communicator's conscious or unconscious assumptions and prejudices."[36]

At this juncture, a hermeneutic of solidarity and accountability, by means of the preferential option for those who are poor and otherwise marginalized, may serve this rights agenda as it reconciles work for justice against the prevailing hegemony of racism and ableism. Catholic social teaching is instructive on many levels for this purpose,

---

ableism, and heterosexism, see "Allyship & Solidarity Guidelines," *Unsettling America: Decolonization in Theory & Practice*, unsettlingamerica.wordpress.com/about/.

[35] See, for example, Michelle Alexander, *The New Jim Crow: Mass Incarceration in the Age of Colorblindness* (New York: The New Press, 2012); and Erving Goffman, *Asylums: Essays on the Social Situation of Mental Patients and Other Inmates* (New York: Anchor Books, 1961).

[36] See APA Presidential Task Force on Preventing Discrimination and Promoting Diversity, *Dual Pathways to a Better America* (Washington, DC: American Psychological Association, 2010), 19.

with solidarity and the preferential option for the poor as key. With the Second Vatican Council and the popes since, the Church has recognized solidarity as a fact of human life, as a norm of and for the relations on which each of us is interdependent, if not dependent, and as a virtue directed toward the common good.[37] A hermeneutic of solidarity invites dominant communities and their members to interrogate their privilege and share their space and use their power with, always with, those who have been marginalized. In addition, this hermeneutic invites minority communities and their members to interrogate their (self-imposed) silence and reject the stigmatizing otherness that the dominant have imposed. Then, speaking truth to power where the dominant and the minoritized people assemble and hear at once, a new dialogue of respect and care and love for one another can emerge. The ways and means of the preferential option for those who are marginalized requires that their voices and concerns are heard and are placed at the top of the list of what to achieve, where to start, and how to proceed. When solidarity is coupled with this preferential option: 1) an accounting of those who have been marginalized will be reconciled with the reality of human diversity writ large, 2) every individual will be honored as sister and brother of one human family, and 3) the goods of the earth and of human hands will be distributed according to need and the common good.[38]

While God Bends Over Backwards

The Civil Rights and Disability Rights movements have paved a way where the going was often steep and rocky and pockmarked and dangerous. Like the prophecy of Isaiah where a voice announces, "Every valley shall be lifted up, and every mountain and hill be made low; the uneven ground shall become level, and the rough places a plain" (Isaiah 40:4), these movements have sought to tread and, thereby, make a way for the people who have been exiled to assume or to return to their places in human commerce and relationship. However, many obstacles to inclusion and access to the places where the dominant go—work, school, shop, play, and worship—continue to hold sway instead of the fulfillment of Isaiah's prophecy and instead of anti-discrimination laws, equal access, and equal employment opportunities. In the face of God's justice and extraordinary concern for those who are disadvantaged by individuals, communities, and institutions of the dominant corps and the systems that are designed to

---

[37] Among others, see Vatican Council II, *Gaudium et Spes*; John Paul II, *Sollicitudo rei Socialis*; Benedict XVI, *Caritas in Veritate*; Francis, *Evangelii Gaudium*; see also Christine Firer Hinze, "The Drama of Social Sin and the (Im)Possibility of Solidarity: Reinhold Niebuhr and Modern Catholic Social Teaching," *Studies in Christian Ethics* 22, no. 4 (2009): 442-460.

[38] See Iozzio, "Solidarity: Restoring Communion with Those Who are Disabled," *Journal of Religion, Disability, & Health* 15, no. 2 (2011): 139-152.

oppress, the law is inadequate to the task.[39] While God bends over backwards to lighten the burdens of difference imposed on account of racism and/or ableism, complacence about the law and complicity in systemic injustice reveal persistent personal and social/structural sins—from exclusionary practices and microaggressions to outright hostility and violence—in dire need of redress.

In addition to the movements' ongoing efforts to support the advance of minorities, religionists are increasingly aware of the intersections of experience (overlapping discriminations and marginalizations) and concern (for liberation in the present and for the generations to come) among people who have been minoritized on account of race, sex, gender, religion, and/or disability.[40] Those working in theological or religious ethics give deliberate witness to a way of reconciling the dividing practices that have been institutionalized in the edifice of dominant narratives and the power they wield.[41] Moreover, for those of us who work to expose injustice for liberation purposes in the way that God wills it to be for all people, we have an obligation to witness and to do the work by weaving the multi-colored and variably malleable threads of warp and woof that reveal one and the same creative-created cloth, a tapestry of God's fecund imaginary and kaleidoscopic diversity.

Antithetical to one multi-colored/multi-dimensional tapestry and evident in artifacts from dominant communities in ancient and modern contexts, the stigma attached to minoritized people has traumatized them, literally (often abusively) and figuratively, and segregated them—in asylums to half-way houses to the streets—from the

---

[39] I often wonder if I am asking too much of the law or my expectations too high. Then again, many individuals–parents, teachers, clergy, communities of common faith and/or purpose, and institutions of an ecclesial, professional, governmental kind—could *and should* hold themselves to do more than the minimums that these laws require.

[40] The American Academy of Religion has been proactive in facilitating conversations on these intersections, particularly in the collaborative work and subsequent panel presentations and concurrent sessions sponsored by the AAR's four Standing Committees on the Status of 1) Women, 2) Racial and Ethnic Minorities, 3) Lesbian, Gay, Bisexual, Transgender, Intersex, & Queer Persons, and 4) People with Disabilities in the Profession (the order here follows the committees' inceptions from first to most recent). For disciplines noting intersectionality, see, for example, Jennifer C. James and Cynthia Wu, "Race, Ethnicity, Disability, and Literature: Intersections and Interventions," *MELUS* 31, no. 3 (2006): 3-13; and Beth Ferri, "A Dialogue We've Yet to Have: Race and Disability Studies," in *The Myth of the Normal Curve*, ed. Curt Dudley-Marling and Alex Gurn (New York: Peter Lang Publishing, Inc., 2010), 139-150.

[41] Among my colleagues in disability studies, those deliberately engaging ethics include Kecia Ali, Julia Watts Belser, Amy Laura Hall, Heike Peckruhn, Hans Reinders, Darla Schumm, and Jon Swinton.

communities in which they ought to number and contribute.[42] Historically, oppression occurred with the exercise of a tyrant and a cohort ruling party over the masses and laborers in their jurisdiction; empire- and religious-tradition building grew into colonizing initiatives recognized today as the disadvantaging injustice that the colonized suffer from the "well-intentioned" practices of paternalist lords and masters or their strong-arm demands. We (descendants of both the "in" and the "out" groups of those practices) have inherited a system maintained by unquestioned norms and structures that "are systematically reproduced in major economic, political, and cultural institutions."[43] Moreover, with the scientific/technological revolutions of the Enlightenment period, an ideology of hegemonic normativity has been insinuated across the globe. Such hegemony confounds the readily observable reality of the diversity of creation as much as it belies God's fecund creative imaginary. This ideological hegemony is evident in institutions of every sort, including our churches and the missions and ministries in which we are engaged.[44] Its hegemony has effectively divided and essentialized humankind into two groups, the normal and the defective, and distributed a power that privileges the one as it disables—by demonizing, marginalizing, and oppressing—the other.[45] Challenges to this normativity result in the assignment of stigma: "an attribute that is deeply discrediting" and ultimately dehumanizing.[46] Consider that 100,000 people with physical and developmental disabilities were the first victims of the Nazi program to eliminate inferior races. In capitalist economies, PWD are considered counter-productive, if not worthless, for profit. Few are employed. In day-to-day human commerce, PWD are regularly infantilized regardless of their age or physical or cognitive or developmental disability. This ideology of segregating exclusion has been inserted into nearly every social structure of human making, including the Church, and has corrupted the proclamation—by its "normative" interpretation—of the Good News in a way that defies the logic of the Incarnation. (Not coincidentally, the crucifixion

---

[42] The history is scandalous. Among others, see Henri Jacques Stiker, *A History of Disability* (Ann Arbor: University of Michigan Press, 2002); Bruce G. Link and Jo C. Phelan, "Conceptualizing Stigma," *Annual Review of Sociology* 27 (2001): 363-385; Erving Goffman, *Stigma: Notes on the Management of Spoiled Identity* (Upper Saddle River: Prentice Hall, 1963).

[43] Iris Marion Young, *Justice and the Politics of Difference*, "Five Faces of Oppression" (Princeton: Princeton University Press, 2011), 41.

[44] Among others, see Sharon V. Betcher, *Politics and the Spirit of Disablement* (Minneapolis: Augsburg Fortress Press, 2007).

[45] On normal, see Rosemary Garland Thomson, *Extraordinary Bodies: Figuring Physical Disability in American Culture and Literature* (New York: Columbia University Press, 1997); on power, see Michel Foucault, *Power*, ed. James D. Faubion, trans. Robert Hurley, et al (New York: The New Press, 2000).

[46] Goffman, *Stigma*, 3.

resulted in the "stigmata." While the Roman practice was certainly stigmatizing and scandalizing, devotion to the risen Christ eliminates the recoil open wounds would ordinarily evoke.) The results of that corruption, the residue of these sins—the ongoing exclusion and/or oppression of racial minorities and PWD as well as the internalized presumption of superiority (on the part of the dominant) or inferiority (on the part of minorities)—needs to be confessed and purged and vowed to never again dehumanize.

Here I call to mind the images that can be evoked by the idiom to bend over backwards. Consider the idiom as a metaphor for doing all that can be done to help someone, to go the extra mile, to be moved to relieve the hardship and the hardness of life among those who have been robbed of the means to thrive. Consider the idiom also as openness to vulnerability. Just think of the exposure of the human torso in such a position and the ease with which vital organs—from throat to pelvis—could be eviscerated. Clearly, this violence also suggests rape, and, considering the vulnerability of rape victims (vulnerable in the face of first violence and vulnerable to another, and another, and another attack), solidarity with and for these victims can be life-saving.

Now consider God so bending... for us.[47] In the *Spiritual Exercises* of St. Ignatius, retreatants are instructed to contemplate the Trinity as the Divine Persons look upon Earth and its human inhabitants to see the mess into which we had gotten ourselves. Pity the people: vicious in word and deed, blasphemous against one another and against the *imago Dei* to be hallowed in each. But no, the Divine Persons proclaim, "Let us work the redemption of the human race."[48] In the Incarnation, in the Divine self-emptying *kenosis*, God bends over backwards—so in love with and merciful toward humankind is God for us—so as to become human. No minimum of effort or formulary limit can be found in that *kenosis*. In fact, even to death does Jesus bend—nearly eviscerated, possibly raped/impaled,[49] and rather completely, shamefully, and demonstratively stigmatized—in command and loving all the way to crucifixion and resurrected life. *Kenosis*, folly to the Greeks and blasphemy to the Jews, is shameful and illustrative of the lengths to which God bends for us. God is simply not capable of anything but the most and the best and more, including the self-emptying into human matter and spirit, that God can, would,

---

[47] See especially Catherine Mowry LaCugna, *God for Us: The Trinity and Christian Life* (New York: HarperCollins Publishers, 1991).

[48] Louis J. Puhl, SJ, *The Spiritual Exercises of St. Ignatius: Based on Studies in the Language of the Autograph* (Chicago: Loyola University Press, 1951), 50.

[49] Although not immediately related to the point, the tradition of Ancient Near East and Roman crucifixion included, frequently enough, impalement. See David Tombs, "Crucifixion, State Terror, and Sexual Abuse," *Union Seminary Quarterly Review* 53, no. 1-2 (1999): 89-109.

and does do. Admittedly, we human beings fail to so bend time and again. We begrudge equal employment opportunities, equal access to education and healthcare, equal welcome to our places of gathering and worship, and we fail thereby solidarity and the preferential option: we fail to do what God wills. Nevertheless, we each are called to persevere in aligning our wills to God's will as well to God's will for others who we do not yet know. We human beings also succeed in bending, I venture, more often than not in spite of the scandalizing horror in war-torn locales, in refugee flight, in mass incarceration, in urban neighborhoods, in environmental degradation.[50]

It is all too clear that the Civil Rights Acts of anti-discrimination and enfranchisement have not lived up to their purposes, as many people had hoped. The unfortunate minimum applications of the law have been structured and institutionalized in deliberately anemic fashion, evident especially in the coverage formulae and, for the benefit of the privileged, without a program to teach and guide the populace how to pursue happiness and the common good with liberty and justice for all. Law's pedagogical value remains underutilized while God's example is often forgotten, even when just a little give-and-take in place of fully backwards may be sufficient bending to accommodate an expressed need.

What practical take-away can be used to increase accountability to and solidarity with people so as to live a preferential option for those who are marginalized, to do what is right and just and best? As a start, interrogate the past with a view to interrogate the present.

> 1) Retrieve the dangerous memories and scandals of the past. Listen to the voices of wisdom with those who have been marginalized on the basis of her, his, and their "deviance" from the dominant norms and follow their lead for change. PWD in particular experience violent crime—rape, sexual assault, robbery, aggravated assault and simple assault—at twice the rate of non-disabled people

---

[50] Among others, on war, see Theresa S. Betancourt, Jessica Agnew-Blais, Stephen E. Gilmar, David R. Williams, and B. Heidi Ellis, "Past Horrors, Present Struggles: The Role of Stigma in the Association Between War Experiences and Psychosocial Adjustment Among Former Child Soldiers in Sierra Leone," *Social Science & Medicine* 70, no. 1 (2010): 17-26; on refugees, see Pavan Joseph and Nasir Warfa, "Suicide and Self-Harm Among Refugees and Asylum Seekers," in *Suicidal Behavior of Immigrants and Ethnic Minorities in Europe*, ed. Diana D. van Bergen, Amanda Heredia Montesinos, and Meryam Schouler-Ocak (Boston: Hogrefe Publishing, 2015); on incarceration, see Alexander Mikulich, Laurie Cassidy, and Margie Pfeil, *The Scandal of White Complicity in US Hyper-incarceration: A Nonviolent Spirituality of White Resistance* (New York: Palgrave Macmillan, 2013); on urban violence, see Javier Auyero, Philippe Bourgois, and Nancy Scheper-Hughes, eds., *Violence at the Urban Margins* (New York: Oxford University Press, 2015); on the environment, see Alexandre Berthe and Luc Elie, "Mechanisms Explaining the Impact of Economic Inequality on Environmental Deterioration," *Ecological Economics* 116 (2015): 191-200.

in the US (and young teens with disabilities at three times the rate). More personally, perhaps less violently but marginalizing and oppressive nonetheless, members of minoritized communities have been excluded for far too long. The systemic institutionalized segregations of minority populations from the dominant power is no longer tolerable. Not unlike truth and justice commissions for restorative justice, PWD and other minoritized people must be heeded.

2) Dismantle what those who have been marginalized identify as oppressive and repressive structures and attitudes, inclusive of veiled microaggressions, that lead to internalized inferiority and self-hate among minoritized people while, at the same time, empower and embolden the dominant to dominate again. Regardless of race, sex, gender, class, and/or disability-ability each of us unconsciously learns from our respective places—as if it is in the air we breathe—the stereotypes about groups of people and individuals belonging to that group. Bullying, mocking, dismissing others reinforces assumptions of superiority in dominant folks while it sadistically reinforces self-doubt and assumptions of inferiority in minoritized people. Dismantling institutionalized and structural oppressions requires a thorough examination of conscious and unconscious speech and behaviors by oppressor and oppressed alike. Success will require moderated conversations to expose the failures to recognize and honor the *imago Dei* present in everyone.

3) Internalize a hermeneutic of solidarity with and a preferential option for those who are marginalized. In the language of social justice movements, become an ally. Regardless of which side of the spectrum you stand on: know yourself, learn about others different from you in formal and informal ways, take chances on friendship, develop empowering communication skills, take action and advocate with and for those who are marginalized.

4) Then, look in and around common spaces—churches, schools, commercial and recreational venues, and government, in every gathering of the people—to note who is there and who absent. Perform a regular check on inclusion. Where the gatherings are monochrome and/or mono-abled, there exclusionary practices of physical and/or attitudinal obstacles persist.

5) Repeat: listen and speak again with equal regard, then together assess results of initiatives to dismantle oppression, brainstorm next steps with additional expertise, and follow the lead of wisdom for solidarity and the preferential option to make change.

Concluding Thoughts

Envisioning justice as God wills it, while weaving in by warp and woof the threads of diversity, reveals the potentials of solidarity and the preferential option for the poor that require instruction on more than the status quo minimum interpretation of civil rights law. Consider too the standard that Jesus presents on fulfillment of the law versus the demands of the Commandments and the Beatitudes.[51] To so weave is to seek justice and mercy, the "two dimensions of a single reality that unfolds progressively until it culminates in the fullness of love" (*Misericordiae Vultus*, no. 20). Surely, God's justice wills the halt of the pervasive recurrence of discriminations, access denied, and violence experienced daily by too many members of minoritized peoples. Just as surely, God, who is Creator, has a plan of flourishing for all creation. That plan, God's will, is that all the parts are welcome, to have a place and role in a future blessedness sustained in and by the "laws" of justice and mercy as found in the parables of, for example, the Lost Coin (Luke 15:8-10), the Prodigal Son (Luke 15:11-32), and, par excellence, the Good Samaritan (Luke 10:25-37).[52] Finally and comprehensively, God's way of reconciling justice and mercy is definitive in the plain words and action of the Paschal Mystery: the whole story begun with the Incarnation through the stigma-scandalizing death and culminating in life restored and forgiveness won.

This kind of justice reflects the right relations between the parts: between persons (one to another), between persons and communities (along with their institutions, systems, and social structures), and between persons/communities and the goods of creation and those made by human hands to be shared not so as to simply survive but to thrive. Understood in Aristotelian terms (and followed by medieval scholars), those relations are determinable according to the being or properties distinguishing the nature(s) of persons and things (ST II-II, q. 57-61). Once those relations are determined, given the fundamental equality with which God creates all that is, moving forward in solidarity requires that we human beings, like God, bend over backwards in our efforts to dismantle the systems that assign diminished "property" status and oppress individuals and communities thereby.

Misericordes sicut Pater! As Pope Francis and the tradition teach:

Mercy: the word reveals the very mystery of the Most Holy Trinity.
Mercy: the ultimate and supreme act by which God comes to meet us.
Mercy: the fundamental law that dwells in the heart of every person who looks sincerely into the eyes of ... brothers and sisters on the path

---

[51] See Yiu Sing Lúcás Chan, *The Ten Commandments and the Beatitudes: Biblical Studies and Ethics for Real Life* (Lanham: Rowman & Littlefield Publishers, 2012).
[52] So conclude Venerable Bede, William Spohn, James Keenan, and Pope Francis, among others.

to life. Mercy: the bridge that connects God and [human beings], opening our hearts to the hope of being loved forever despite our sinfulness. (*Misericordiae Vultus*, no. 2)

Mercy, which appears to defy the logic of justice, is its obverse. Mercy calls us to do more always and especially for those who have been downtrodden by the imposition of norms that do not reflect the encounter God wills. Mercy reflects "our willingness to enter into the chaos of another,"[53] including the chaos that is the scandal of stigma, of those who are voiceless, forgotten by indifference, and deliberately not counted, wounded, shot, lynched, bullied, ridiculed, institutionalized, raped, abused and denied their humanity. "During this Jubilee, the Church will be called even more to heal these wounds, to assuage them with the oil of consolation, to bind them with mercy and cure them with solidarity and vigilant care" (*Misericordiae Vultus*, no. 15). God bends human ineptitude toward justice and mercy, calls humankind to accountability for unearned and unexamined privilege, and accommodates each and every one who has been bowed low so as to take their places and participate in every manner of human commerce. It is scandalous to do anything less. M

---

[53] James F. Keenan, SJ, *The Works of Mercy: The Heart of Catholicism* (Lanham: Rowman & Littlefield Publishers Inc., 2008), 4. See also Keenan, "The Scandal of Mercy Excludes No One," *Thinking Faith, Jesuit Media Initiatives*, December 2, 2015, www.thinkingfaith.org/articles/scandal-mercy-excludes-no-one.

On "And Vulnerable": Catholic Social Thought and the Social Challenges of Cognitive Disability

Matthew Gaudet

IN SEPTEMBER 1965, THE BISHOPS OF THE Second Vatican Council were deep into the drafting process of *Gaudium et Spes*. That document began with the now famous words: "The joys and the hopes, the griefs and the anxieties of the men of this age, especially those who are poor or in any way afflicted, these are the joys and hopes, the griefs and anxieties of the followers of Christ" (*Gaudium et Spes*, no. 1). That same month, Senator Robert F. Kennedy paid a surprise visit to the Willowbrook State School, a state-supported institution for children and young adults with intellectual and developmental disabilities (IDD) in Staten Island, NY.[1] Kennedy was astounded and disgusted by what he saw. At the time, Willowbrook was housing 6000 individuals in a space designed for 4000. The facilities were understaffed and in disrepair, disease was rampant, and education was non-existent. Kennedy described the situation as one that "borders on a snake pit...[where] the children live in filth...[and] many of our fellow citizens are suffering tremendously because of a lack of attention, lack of imagination, lack of adequate manpower."[2]

I raise the chronological nearness of these two events in order to highlight just how important the words "in any way afflicted" are to

---

[1] It is important, at the outset, to note a distinction between the terms "impairment" and "disability." These terms have been used in various ways throughout the growing field of disability studies, but, for my purposes here, I will distinguish between the biological conditions which impair one's cognitive abilities (i.e. cognitive impairment) and cultural meaning and identity ascribed to those with such a condition (i.e. intellectual and developmental disability). I address this distinction in greater detail later in this essay.

[2] "Senator Robert Kennedy Visiting Institutions in New York," *Parallels in Time: A History of Developmental Disabilities*, mn.gov/mnddc/parallels/five/5b/bobby-kennedy-snakepits.html. In the video, Kennedy's use of the term "snake pit" is likely a reference to the 1949 movie "The Snake Pit," a semi-autobiographical story about one women's experience in a mental institution. The movie's authentic telling of conditions in a mental institution is credited with inspiring a series of reforms in mental institutions in the 1950s; see "The Snake Pit," *Turner Classic Movies*, www.tcm.com/this-month/article/2768380/The-Snake-Pit.html.

the bold and beautiful claim that opens *Gaudium et Spes*. The suffering experienced by the residents of Willowbrook and other 'schools' like it ranks among the greatest atrocities committed in this country. While it would be a stretch to believe that the authors of *Gaudium et Spes* were thinking of Willowbrook when they claimed the griefs and anxieties of those "in any way afflicted" as a central concern of the Church, there should be little doubt that the suffering of those with IDD fits well under it, both in the institution system of the mid-twentieth century and at the hands of modern constructs today.

Thankfully, today, the inhuman conditions of institutions like Willowbrook have been exposed and the institutionalization model for persons with IDD has been largely dismantled. Moreover, with the establishment of the Americans with Disabilities Act (ADA) in 1990, protections have been set to ensure that such a situation will not be repeated. However, neither of these advancements have fully alleviated the particular griefs and anxieties experienced by persons with IDD in the modern world. The ADA certainty aspired to such a task when it set the lofty but worthwhile goals of "assur[ing] equality of opportunity, full participation, independent living, and economic self-sufficiency" for people with disabilities.[3] However, now more than twenty-five years on, much work remains to be done. While the challenges differ in degree, when compared to the institution era, intentional and unintentional segregation of those with disabilities remains a serious roadblock to "full participation" and a causal factor in the perpetuation of stigma. In turn, social stigma and inadequate advocacy severely limits the achievement of "equality of opportunity" as a norm. Likewise, community-based housing and employment programs—while well-envisioned for developing the conditions for "independent living" and "economic self-sufficiency"—suffer from inadequate funding, shortages of qualified care providers, and an overall lack of political will to respond to inadequacies in the system.

In light of the ongoing social challenges or issues facing individuals with IDD in our time, I want to highlight some underappreciated aspects of Catholic social teaching that we would do well to recall. The discussion proceeds in four parts. First, I identify several key contemporary social challenges that continue to face individuals with IDD. Second, I trace the root of those particular challenges to the social forces of industrialization, urbanization, and social Darwinism in the second half of the nineteenth century. Third, on the basis of that historical framework, I argue that the contemporary Catholic response to the various social challenges of disabled persons has much to gain from serious consideration of Catholic social

---

[3] Americans with Disabilities Act of 1990, Public Law 101-336. 108th Congress, 2nd session (July 26, 1990), www.ada.gov/pubs/adastatute08mark.htm.

thought's beginnings in *Rerum Novarum*—the Church's response to the suffering of the working class, as they bore the burden of the nineteenth century social forces just mentioned. So conceived, developments in Catholic social teaching since *Rerum Novarum* offer clues as to how the tradition can be applied to the particular social challenges facing cognitively impaired persons. Finally, I conclude with a proposal on how this interpretation of the tradition might further be developed and promoted.

THE CURRENT STATE OF COGNITIVE DISABILITY IN AMERICAN SOCIETY

I focus on four overlapping social challenges or issues facing individuals with IDD today: segregation and stigma; inadequate, unfulfilling, and unlivable wage-earning employment opportunities; lack of adequate housing and care; and poor education and training. These are by no means the only issues at stake, but they are some of the larger blocks to achieving the ADA goals of "equality of opportunity, full participation, independent living, and economic self-sufficiency."

According to the Shriver Report, a survey conducted by the Harris Institute in 2015, only 56% of Americans personally know someone with a cognitive disability and a mere 13% say they have a friend with a cognitive disability. In contrast, a whopping 42% of Americans have had no personal contact with someone with a cognitive disability. Similarly, while 93% of Americans believe that adults with cognitive disabilities should be encouraged to work, and 80% said that they would be willing to hire someone with a cognitive disability, a paltry 5% have actually worked with someone with a cognitive disability.[4]

One of the primary reasons that only 5% of the national population reports having worked with someone with a cognitive disability is that only 6% of adults with a cognitive disability actually work in the community. According to a survey of family members of adults with cognitive disabilities, collected by the disability advocacy group, The Arc, 9% of those surveyed indicate that their family member was working in a "sheltered workshop or enclave setting" while a massive 85% of families report that their family members were unemployed. This despite the fact that "the majority of people with [cognitive] disabilities want to have a job in the community."[5]

Making matters worse, even among those working, nearly half work for less than minimum wage. Subminimum wages, which can be

---

[4] "Insight into Intellectual Disabilities in the 21st Century," *Disabled World*, www.disabled-world.com/disability/types/cognitive/21st-century.php.

[5] "Still in the Shadows with Their Future Uncertain: A Report on Family and Individual Needs for Disability Supports (FINDS)." *The Arc*, www.thearc.org/document.doc?id=3672.

as low as $0.25 per hour, are legal loopholes built into the Fair Labor Standards Act of 1938 with the intention of encouraging the hiring of people with disabilities.[6] Among those unemployed, or severely underemployed, approximately 4.9 million Americans with a cognitive disability—those with extremely low wages or unemployed, and lacking other resources—rely on Supplemental Security Income (SSI) for their basic survival. However, in 2014, the average annual income of a single individual receiving SSI payments was $8,995, 23% below the federal poverty level. Twenty-one states do supplement federal SSI payments, but these are also meager, ranging from a high of $362 in Alaska to a low of $5 in Nebraska. Moreover, these supplements have declined by 7% since 1998.[7]

One consequence of these paltry rations is that those who do not live with family are effectively priced out of a decent living arrangement. The 2014 national average annual rent for a modest one-bedroom unit was $9,360 or 104% of SSI income, and the national average rent for a studio was $8088 or 90% of an average SSI payment.[8] The U.S. Department of Housing and Urban Development (HUD) Section 811 Supportive Housing program was established to help solve this cost by producing affordable, accessible housing units that are specifically designed for people with disabilities, but the program has historically been unable to keep up with identified demand.[9]

Housing is just one of many government-funded services with extremely long waiting lists, including personal assistance, therapy, employment supports, and transportation. One third of those interviewed for The Arc's study reported that they are on a waiting list for government-funded services of some kind. "A conservative estimate is that there are more than 1 million people with [cognitive disabilities] waiting for services that may never come."[10] At the same time, threats of a further shortage loom as nearly 900,000 individuals currently live with a caregiver (typically a family member) who is over

---

[6] "Still in the Shadows"; Cheryl Corley, "Subminimum Wages For The Disabled: Godsend Or Exploitation?" *National Public Radio*, www.npr.org/2014/04/23/305854409/subminimum-wages-for-the-disabled-godsend-or-exploitation.

[7] Emily Cooper et al., "Priced Out in 2014: The Housing Crisis for People with Disabilities," *Technical Assistance Collaborative*, www.tacinc.org/knowledge-resources/priced-out-findings/.

[8] Cooper et al., "Priced Out in 2014."

[9] The Frank Melville Supportive Housing Investment Act of 2010 was aimed at modernizing the Section 811 program to more efficiently meet demand as they have not before. Significant waiting lists remain, however.

[10] "Still in the Shadows." See also "In California, Aid Withers For People With Developmental Disabilities," *National Public Radio*, www.npr.org/sections/health-shots/2015/12/04/458458916/in-california-aid-withers-for-people-with-developmental-disabilities.

60 years old and thus will soon not be able to continue to care for the individual with a disability.[11]

Finally, there is an argument to be made that part of the reason the low employment rate for adults with cognitive disabilities is because they are not receiving proper education when they are young. In The Arc study, 52% of families reported that their family member left school without receiving a high school diploma—a necessary prerequisite for employment in many cases. At the same time, fewer than one third of students with cognitive disabilities are fully integrated into mainstream classes, while more than one third of students are completely segregated from the mainstream students.[12] Thus, our special educational system, beneficial as it is in many cases, is for most people the first encounter with the normativity of segregation that remains in our society and consequently serves to reinforce a norm of segregation throughout the lives of people with IDD. As it is normative in schools, it should be no wonder that 42% of American adults have had no personal contact with someone with a cognitive disability.

THE MODERN SOCIAL CONSTRUCTION OF COGNITIVE DISABILITY

As with many social issues, alleviating the suffering of individuals with IDD will require more than the establishment of rights or a mere material response (i.e. proper funding of housing, education, and employment programs). Addressing the challenges just laid out will require a shift in the social understanding of disability. Thus, it is important to recall the distinction between disability and impairment:

> Disability is not a physical or mental defect but a cultural and minority identity. To call disability an identity is to recognize that it is not a biological or natural property but an elastic social category both subject to social control and capable of effecting social change.[13]

This distinction is important because, while cognitive impairments are a natural part of the human experience and have been throughout history, the social boundaries that emerge in response to those impairments operate uniquely in each given society and are, in fact, a product of that society and its history. Historians of disability have frequently observed that our understanding—who is considered disabled, how disability is defined, what cultural meanings are

---

[11] Cooper et al., "Priced Out in 2014."
[12] "Still in the Shadows."
[13] Tobin Siebers, *Disability Theory* (Ann Arbor: University of Michigan Press, 2008), 4, hdl.handle.net/2027/mdp.39015082696892.

ascribed to a particular disability—is shaped largely by the social context of and the historical moment in which disability occurs.[14]

Moreover, not only are conceptions of disability historically located, but they are in fact the product of human effort. "Social problems like mental retardation are in fact social constructions...built from a variety of materials: the desire to help and the need to control, infatuation with science and technique and professional status, responses to social change and instability."[15] With this in mind, I argue that our contemporary understanding of IDD has emerged in large part from the changes in the social status of those with cognitive impairments during the second half of the nineteenth century.[16] I contend that three factors—in particular, urbanization, industrialization, and the rise of social Darwinism—converged to lay the foundations of much of our contemporary understanding of IDD.

---

[14] Katherine Castles, "'Nice Average Americans,'" in *Mental Retardation in America*, ed. Steven Noll and James W. Trent Jr., (New York: New York University Press, 2004), 352.

[15] James W. Trent, Jr., *Inventing the Feeble Mind: A History of Mental Retardation in the United States* (Berkeley: University of California Press, 1994), 6.

[16] Space constraints limit my attempt to only a broad stroke summary in these pages. For a more detailed examination of the social construction of cognitive disability, see Trent, Jr., *Inventing the Feeble Mind*; Michael Wehmeyer, ed., *The Story of Intellectual Disability: An Evolution of Meaning, Understanding, and Public Perception*, 1st ed. (Baltimore: Brookes Publishing, 2013); David Wright, *Downs: The History of a Disability* (Oxford: Oxford University Press, 2011), chap. 1; and C. F. Goodey, *A History of Intelligence and "Intellectual Disability": The Shaping of Psychology in Early Modern Europe*, Kindle Edition (Burlington: Ashgate Publishing, 2013). Additionally, Henri-Jacques Stiker's *A History of Disability*, trans. William Sayers (Ann Arbor: University of Michigan Press, 1999), focuses primarily on physical and sensory disability with occasional reference to cognitive disability but offers an important examination of the social construction of disability, widely construed, going back to antiquity. Similarly, Michel Foucault's landmark text, *History of Madness*, ed. Jean Khalfa (New York: Routledge, 2006), while primarily an inquiry into mental illness and not cognitive disability, nevertheless offers important insight into the social construction of normalcy and abnormality with regard to human reason. See Shelley Lynn Tremain, ed., *Foucault and the Government of Disability* (Ann Arbor: University of Michigan Press, 2010), 11: "An argument about disability that takes Foucault's approach would be concerned to show that there is indeed a causal relation between impairment and disability, and it is precisely this: the category of impairment emerged and, in many respects, persists in order to legitimize the governmental practices that generated it in the first place." Foucault occupies an important enough place in the field to be noted here, but a full Foucaultian critique leads away from the present topic. For more, therefore, Foucault's ideas find application to disability in two important works edited by Shelley Tremain: the collection of essays *Foucault and the Government of Disability* as well as the June 2015 issue of the journal *Foucault Studies* offered on the 10th anniversary of the book (*Foucault Studies*, no 9).

COGNITIVE DISABILITY IN THE PRE-INDUSTRIAL WORLD

In 1835, Thomas Cameron was a young postmaster in rural North Carolina; ten-year-old Lloyd Fuller was studying alongside his older brothers in their middle class New England home. Thomas and Lloyd would today be considered developmentally disabled; in the 1830s, that difference alone did not disqualify them from work, education, social invitations, or travel.[17]

Literature and historical accounts as far back as the sixteenth century give us images of the "village idiot" who was left to wander about in public, but, as historian David Wright notes, there is little historical evidence to sustain this stereotype as normative.[18] More typically, in the centuries leading up to the industrial revolution, individuals with cognitive impairments were integrated members of society and, more fundamentally, their families. The centrality of the family in this regard is evident in legal statutes going back at least to the thirteenth century English court document *Prerogativa Regis* (Kings Prerogative), which gave the King the right to seize the property of *fatui naturales* (natural fools) who were deemed unable to rule the estate themselves and place it in the care of a more capable family member, "who would commit themselves to administering the property (and maintaining the idiot and his family) in a responsible manner."[19] When the "fool" passed away, his lands and title would be returned to his heirs. Similarly, at the other end of the economic spectrum, under the Poor Laws established under Elizabeth I, local parishes in England and Wales were deemed responsible for providing relief to the impoverished in their locality, including those with cognitive impairments. However, aid for those who could not care for themselves fell again to kin. Even when family was not available, aid took the form of "boarding out," a form of early foster care (thus again following a familial model, artificial as it was).

That this familial care norm would continue well into the nineteenth century should not be surprising. During that time, the family was the fundamental social and economic unit of society. On the economic side, family farms and family businesses dominated the economy, and in America's pre-industrial agrarian economy there was no lack of unskilled labor to be done. For the vast majority of society, education was largely provided at home. As such, families made a

---

[17] Penny Richards, "Beside Her Sat Her Idiot Child: Families and Developmental Disability in Mid-Nineteenth-Century America," in *Mental Retardation in America: A Historical Reader*, ed. Steven Noll and James Trent (New York: New York University Press, 2004), 65.
[18] Wright, *Downs*, 24.
[19] Wright, *Downs*, 21.

place for all members of the clan, regardless of their abilities or disabilities. Social hierarchies in all classes remained very tied to familial lines. Hereditary rights remained a large part of the organization of society. Even as families served as the primary social unit, local communities also operated as an extension of the family as evidenced by the responsibility of the local parish in the Elizabethan Poor Laws and boarding out.

Early twentieth century sociologist Emil Durkheim identified these traditional, familial and community based networks as constructed on what he termed "mechanical solidarity."[20] In mechanical solidarity, relationships are held together by commonality. Local communities in the pre-industrial West shared the same rituals, worshiped at the same churches, attended the same schools, and partook of the same festivals. They also shared the same immediate history: when a drought hit a localized agrarian community or when a harvest was plentiful, all in the community were affected. According to Durkheim, these shared experiences were what held society together.

CARE FOR DISABILITY IN AN URBANIZED WORLD

The nineteenth century was a period of exponential growth, massive change, and important tests for America. The nation expanded its borders, its population, its economy and its power. It was a century of turmoil and new beginnings. Near the eve of the century, America mourned the death of its first president and by mid-century survived its bloodiest and only civil war. And yet, over the course of the century, technology advanced like never before:

> By the end of the 1880s, workers in urban settings rode elevators up to their offices in the amazing 10-story skyscrapers that were popping up seemingly everywhere. Once at their desks, they turned on the lights in their electrically lit offices, made calls on one of Bell's amazing telephones, and typed letters on their new Remington typewriters.[21]

The advance of technology had a tremendous effect on society at large. New farm machinery meant that less manual labor was needed on the farms. At the same time, the rise of technology created an insatiable appetite for factory work. These two factors catalyzed a mass migration from rural areas to urban cities in America.

---

[20] Emile Durkheim, *The Division of Labor in Society* (New York: Simon and Schuster, 2014), 57ff.

[21] Phillip M. Ferguson, "The Development of Systems of Supports: Intellectual Disabilities in Middle Modern Times (1800 CE to 1899 CE)," in *The Story of Intellectual Disability: An Evolution of Meaning, Understanding, and Public Perception*, ed. Michael Wehmeyer (Baltimore: Brookes Publishing, 2013), 81.

The urbanization of America had a weakening effect on family bonds. With less work needed on the farms, many young adults left their family for work in the city. Distanced from traditional familial structures, urbanized workers sought new social structures in their new environment. The factory, rather than family, became the economic hub of society, while class replaced family as the fundamental unit of culture. Moreover, in the cities, factory work and especially the assembly line were made efficient by a specialization of labor.

The urban living environment encouraged specialization in other areas as well. No longer did each family own its own cow and churn its own butter. Rather, these former domestic tasks became centralized and sold as commodities. These shifting conditions created a functional difference in the forces that previously held society together. Under mechanical solidarity, similarity drew neighbors into community, but, in the new urbanized, centralized, and individualized world, society was held together by an individualized need of the other, or what Durkheim termed "organic solidarity." When each individual has a highly specialized task in society, both the survival of the individual and the functioning of society as a whole rely on the specialization of countless others.[22]

Amidst these vast changes in society, it was likely inevitable that our societal response to cognitive impairment would also change.

> Although people with intellectual disability seldom drove the engines of change, they were carried along with dramatic shifts in both definition and response to what was perceived to be a growing population of unproductive and dependent people, draining energy from the marketplace and distracting families from their proper role as sources of labor and respite for a hard-working population.[23]

While individuals with cognitive impairments found a natural place in the family and local community under the bonds of mechanical solidarity, in the urbanized, industrialized, and individualized economy, where an individual was measured by what they could bring to the table, what they could offer to the collective machine, those who were "unproductive" and "dependent" had no natural place.

WORK AND DISABILITY IN AN INDUSTRIALIZED WORLD

In the midst of the great industrialization and urbanization of the nineteenth century, two economic downturns (1837-1843 and 1857-1861) prompted a need for an economic safety net in the new urbanized landscape. As noted above, in traditional economies, entire

---

[22] Durkheim, *The Division of Labor in Society*, 88ff.
[23] Ferguson, "The Development of Systems of Supports," 81.

communities would bear their fates together, sharing the burdens of economic hardships around the community. In the new industrialized economy, social structures built around individualism meant that some would remain afloat while others sank. For those in the latter category, a wide array of "institutional solutions for all types of devalued, or simply nonproductive, groups of people" arose.[24]

The first of these "institutional solutions" was the explosion of government-run almshouses in the late eighteenth and early nineteenth centuries.[25] These almshouses were intended to serve as a temporary respite for unemployed individuals as they got back on their feet. While these almshouses did serve a social good, they were also viewed with disdain—a last resort solution that marked the lowest point for a prideful worker. During this same time, work was also becoming more technical as the operation of machinery replaced many simple manual tasks, while mass urbanization prompted tremendous competition amongst workers for available jobs. Thus, even when a task was relatively low skill, competition favored those who could do low skill tasks faster and more efficiently. Soon a class of individuals emerged that had a very difficult time of ever securing and holding a job in this new economy and so remained dependent on the almshouses. In this environment, a distinction arose between the temporary poor and those with disabilities or mental illness. Those with disabilities had come to be understood as the "legitimate" poor, free from public disdain: "*True or justifiable* poverty entailed disability."[26] When the economy recovered in the 1860s, public almshouses fell out of favor, but the view that those with disabilities should "legitimately" be supported by the state remained, demanding a new solution for the organized care of "idiots."

EDUCATION AND DISABILITY IN A MODERN WORLD

It was around this same time, psychology began to emerge as a distinct academic discipline and the specialized study of "idiocy" (as opposed to "insanity") grew as its own sub-discipline. In 1840, a French doctor named Edward Séguin had begun a school in Paris dedicated to the education of individuals with cognitive disabilities. Public education for mainstream children was only just becoming a public priority, so the idea of specialized education for those with disabilities was especially novel. Seguin's model was rooted in an

---

[24] Phillip M. Ferguson, "The Legacy of the Almshouse," *Mental Retardation in America: A Historical Reader*, eds. Steven Noll and James Trent (New York: New York University Press, 2004), 48.
[25] Between 1824 and 1850, Massachusetts went from 83 almshouses to 204. In the same years, New York went from 30 local almshouses in the metropolitan areas of the state to a county almshouse system in which 56 of 60 counties had centralized almshouses by 1857. See Ferguson, "The Legacy of the Almshouse," 48.
[26] Ferguson, "The Legacy of the Almshouse," 51; original emphasis.

assumption that education could only be effective if the students were segregated from family and community. The belief was that, with the proper education, individuals with cognitive disabilities could be "freed from inactivity and no longer a burden to their families" and would return to their families and communities upon completion of the program.[27]

Within a decade, schools using Seguin's model emerged in the United States. The Massachusetts Asylum for Idiotic and Feebleminded Youth (est. 1847) and the New York Asylum for Idiots (est. 1851) were two of the first. When Séguin, himself, emigrated to America in 1850, his stature in the world medical community added legitimacy to the cause, and, by 1870, the state school had replaced the almshouse as a "solution" for disability in America.[28]

Initially, this education movement met some successes in training and graduating "productive idiots." However, for every successful case, there were other residents whose "limitations were great and whose eventual release was doubtful."[29] For those that did "graduate," expectations of a smooth transition into the community never materialized. The turbulent economic landscape meant that many could not find work in their home communities. With no place to go in the community, many graduates were forced back to the asylums. By the 1880s, the focus of the state schools began shifting from education and graduation to care and custody.

SEGREGATION AND DISABILITY IN AN EVOLVING WORLD

In the 1860s, John Langdon Down (for whom Down syndrome is named) was the medical superintendent at the Earlswood Asylum for Idiots in England. Down had made a name for himself as a proponent of separating idiot asylums from lunatic asylums. (Cognitive disability and mental illness had previously been treated as similar conditions.) The Earlswood Asylum was the first asylum dedicated specifically to individuals with cognitive impairments in England.

Down was also a strong proponent of specialized education and separate treatment for individuals with cognitive impairments. Down, however, came up a generation after Seguin, Howe, and Wilbur and thus was influenced to a much greater degree by Darwinism and the biological experiments and hereditary studies of Gregor Mendel, O.S.A. Down began to speculate whether cognitive disability represented a regression of species to an earlier form. Drawing on popular notions that non-Caucasian races represented less developed species, Down claimed that each of these conditions represented a

---

[27] Trent, Jr., *Inventing the Feeble Mind*, 26; Ferguson, "The Development of Systems of Supports," 87.
[28] Trent, Jr., *Inventing the Feeble Mind*, 17–18.
[29] Trent, Jr., *Inventing the Feeble Mind*, 28.

regression to an earlier form of humanity and began to classify different types of idiots according to the races they most resembled. The most well-known of these was the "Mongolian idiot" (the condition now called Down syndrome), but other classifications included "Malay," "Ethiopian," "Aztec," and "Caucasian."[30] Down claimed that this "great Mongolian family" represented "the reversion of Caucasian children to an earlier 'less developed' race."[31] While the racially discriminatory undertones of this analysis cannot be ignored, Down's ethnic classification was never fully adopted by medical science, and, in the 1930s, Lionel Penrose conducted blood type studies that debunked Down's devolutionary theory. Socially, however, the lasting effects of Down's work and the notion that those with disabilities were somehow less human were immeasurable.

Down was not the only person who saw implications for disability in Darwinism. In the 1870s, the eugenics movement emerged in Europe and America. This movement proposed that, if Darwin's theory of evolution is correct, then it places upon society a moral burden to actively advance our species in future generations.[32] The simplest way to accomplish this was by eliminating from our reproducing population traits that could be viewed as negative and unproductive.[33] In the United States, this meant segregation (and later sterilization) of those with "undesirable traits," such as cognitive disabilities. During this time, the view of those with disabilities as "legitimate poor" gave way to a view of disability as a menace to society. In 1870, the U.S. census, which had counted "idiots" as a separate category since 1840, began placing this category in the same column as criminals and convicts. And in 1882, Congress passed the "Undesirables Act," which excluded convicts, paupers, the insane, and idiots from immigrating to the United States.[34] In 1878, Josephine Shaw Lowell opened the Custodial Asylum for Feeble Minded

---

[30] Down noted that Mongolian idiocy was the most prevalent at Earlswood. This observation has proven indicative of the greater population as Down syndrome remains the most common condition of cognitive disability.

[31] David Wright, "Mongols in our Midst," in *Mental Retardation in America: A Historical Reader*, ed. Steven Noll and James Trent (New York: New York University Press, 2004), 102. Historians today are quick to note that while these classifications seem offensive today, they were actually considered liberal in Victorian England. While the common theory of the time was that other races represented completely different species of lesser value, Down's theories understood that all humans evolved from the same species. See Wright, "Mongols in our Midst," 103-104.

[32] It should be noted that the 19th century not only marked the rise of evolutionary theory in biology, but also utilitarian theory in philosophy. Eugenics represented the merger of the absolutist forms of both of these theories.

[33] Of course, the industrial revolution had simultaneously helped to solidify the commonly-held view that "success" was defined in terms of productivity, and productivity was a function of intelligence.

[34] Trent, Jr., *Inventing the Feeble Mind*, 86.

Women in Newark, N.Y., marking the first American institution established specifically for the custodial care (as opposed to the education) for individuals with IDD.

> Shall the State of New York suffer a moral leprosy to spread and taint her future generations, because she lacks the courage to set apart those who have inherited the deadly poison and who will hand it down to their children, even to third and fourth generations?[35]

The Custodial Asylum represented a new model of care in which segregation was permanent and the end in and of itself. In the state schools, education was the goal, and the "boarding" nature of the school was a means to that end. Moreover, while the original state schools were set up close to state capitals, as custodial care became the primary focus, institutions were designed as farm colonies in remote rural environments. During this time, families were discouraged from visiting individuals in the asylums and instead encouraged to forget that the family member even existed. Finally, in contrast to the state schools, there was little hope in the institutions that anyone would be able to "graduate" and return to mainstream society. Under this model, custodial care was permanent, non-educational, and as far removed from mainstream society as possible.

In summary, in the span of three generations in the second half of the nineteenth century, the typical life of an American with a cognitive disability went from being an integrated part of the education, work, and social life of one's family and local community to a menial and segregated existence of custodial care, removed from family and community as a menace to mainstream social life. Today, while the most glaringly undignified aspects of this era have been dismantled, several social constructs regarding disability remain. First and foremost, even as society moves, in theory, toward greater integration of those with cognitive impairments into mainstream society, the legacy of cognitive disability understood as a menace, mystery, and drain on society still looms large in our current context and creates a reality in which nearly half of American adults have never had any serious contact with an individual with a cognitive impairment.[36] Second, the shift away from a traditional family structure and toward

---

[35] Josephine Shaw Lowell, "One Means for Preventing Pauperism," in *Proceedings of the National Conference of Charities and Correction* (1879): 189-200, as quoted in Nicole Rafter, "The Criminalization of Mental Retardation," in *Mental Retardation in America*, ed. Steven Noll and James W. Trent Jr. (New York: New York University Press, 2004), 239.

[36] Couple this history with a nearly a century of institutionalization in which the typical American neighborhood, school, and church did not include cognitive disability, and a certain mystery and trepidation about how to relate to those with cognitive impairments compounds the issue all the more.

government provided care, education, housing, and employment for those with disabilities remains at least partially normative today. Even those who continue to live with their families into adulthood still often participate in public special education and other training, draw SSI and other government funds, and partake of other public services for those with disabilities, making the current role of the family as much advocacy as caregiving. Third, the post-industrial capitalist economy that is built on organic solidarity and values individuals based on their skill, ability, and contribution remains our standard today as it was at the height of the industrial revolution. Such a society can only locate individuals with cognitive disabilities at the economic bottom and dependent on either a social safety net or the charity of others (an economic state that is underscored by a historical legacy in which disability was synonymous with a condition of legitimate poverty.)

CATHOLIC SOCIAL THOUGHT: A RESPONSE TO SOCIAL UPHEAVAL

It is no coincidence that modern Catholic social thought emerged around the same time that institutionalization was becoming the new standard of care for individuals with IDD, for when he wrote *Rerum Novarum,* Pope Leo XIII was aiming to address many of the same social forces that gave rise to such treatment of individuals with IDD. In his opening soliloquy that set the stage for the entirety of the tradition, Leo wrote,

> The elements of the conflict now raging are unmistakable, in the vast expansion of industrial pursuits and the marvelous discoveries of science; in the changed relations between masters and workmen; in the enormous fortunes of some few individuals, and the utter poverty of the masses; the increased self-reliance and closer mutual combination of the working classes; as also, finally, in the prevailing moral degeneracy. The momentous gravity of the state of things now obtaining fills every mind with painful apprehension; wise men are discussing it; practical men are proposing schemes; popular meetings, legislatures, and rulers of nations are all busied with it - actually there is no question which has taken deeper hold on the public mind.
>
> Therefore, venerable brethren, as on former occasions when it seemed opportune to refute false teaching…, We thought it expedient now to speak on the condition of the working classes. (*Rerum Novarum,* no. 1)

Leo XIII leaves no doubt that the ultimate object of his work is the plight of working people of that age. While Leo XIII's words are not directly addressed to individuals with IDD, in identifying the social shifts of the urbanized, industrialized, modern world as the cause of the plight of the working classes, *Rerum Novarum* and the Catholic social tradition it spurred offer a theologically grounded critique of modernism that is useful for the task at hand.

LAYING THE GROUNDWORK: THE THEOLOGICAL IMPORTANCE OF HUMAN DIGNITY

The cornerstone of Catholic social teaching is the fundamental dignity of the human person. "God has imprinted his own image and likeness on man (see Gen 1:26), conferring upon him an incomparable dignity.... In effect, beyond the rights which man acquires by his own work, there exist rights which do not correspond to any work he performs, but which flow from his essential dignity as a person" (*Centesimus Annus*, no 11). This dignity is unique to humans—as the only part of creation made in the image of God—but universal to all humans, regardless of age, race, gender, creed, or (dis)ability. A simplistic application of this theme would argue that those with disabilities are made in the image of God and thus share in the unique dignity of humanity. Equally human, the Church and her members have a duty to protect the dignity of those with disabilities against the forces in this world that would seek to take that dignity away. As the US Catholic Bishops note, human dignity defines the fundamental and basic orientation each must take towards another: "Human personhood must be respected with a reverence that is religious. When we deal with each other, we should do so with the sense of awe that arises in the presence of something holy and sacred. For that is what human beings are: we are created in the image of God."[37]

From John Langdon Down's devolutionary theory of disability to capitalism's emphasis on material production as the means of valuation for individuals, significant forces in the modern world have contributed to the view that individuals with disabilities are of less value than those who are not disabled. In response, Catholic social teaching appeals to the dignity of humanity as the theological justification for the establishment of basic rights (*Gaudium et Spes*, no. 26ff), such as those laid out in the ADA. This is all good, so far as it goes, but, as I have noted, the establishment of rights alone is insufficient for addressing the depth and the breadth of the social constructions that are embedded into our very understanding of disability. Fortunately, while Catholic social thought provides a framework for rights, it does not end with the bare assertion of rights.

---

[37] National Conference of Catholic Bishops, *Economic Justice for All: Pastoral Letter on Catholic Social Teaching and the U.S. Economy*, 10th Anniversary edition, www.usccb.org/upload/economic_justice_for_all.pdf, no. 28.

RELIEVING THE TENSION BETWEEN FREEDOM AND COMMUNITY IN THE MODERN WORLD

For Catholic social teaching, human dignity, rooted in the *Imago Dei*, also provides the theological grounding for both human freedom and human community.

> For Sacred Scripture teaches that man was created "to the image of God," is capable of knowing and loving his Creator, and was appointed by Him as master of all earthly creatures that he might subdue them and use them to God's glory. "What is man that you should care for him? You have made him little less than the angels, and crowned him with glory and honor. You have given him rule over the works of your hands, putting all things under his feet" (Ps. 8:5-7). But God did not create man as a solitary, for from the beginning "male and female he created them" (Gen. 1:27). Their companionship produces the primary form of interpersonal communion. For by his innermost nature man is a social being, and unless he relates himself to others he can neither live nor develop his potential. (*Gaudium et Spes*, no. 12)

Human freedom, present in each individual from the moment of creation, is our freedom to make choices and act independently from the Divine will of God. However, even as humans are free to abuse this freedom, we are called to perfect our freedom by directing our choices toward God (*Catechism*, no. 1731). Community emerges from freedom as one of the primary commands of the Divine will:

> God, Who has fatherly concern for everyone, has willed that all men should constitute one family and treat one another in a spirit of brotherhood. For having been created in the image of God, Who "from one man has created the whole human race and made them live all over the face of the earth" (Acts 17:26), all men are called to one and the same goal, namely God Himself.
>
> For this reason, love for God and neighbor is the first and greatest commandment. Sacred Scripture, however, teaches us that the love of God cannot be separated from love of neighbor: "If there is any other commandment, it is summed up in this saying: Thou shalt love thy neighbor as thyself .... Love therefore is the fulfillment of the Law" (Rom. 13:9-10; see 1 John 4:20). To men growing daily more dependent on one another, and to a world becoming more unified every day, this truth proves to be of paramount importance. (*Gaudium et Spes*, no. 24)

Thus, while freedom is fundamental to our humanity, the proper use of that freedom is to serve God and serve each other.

The concepts of freedom and community are important as the devastating forces that emerged in the wake of the industrial revolution were, in many ways, a perversion and overindulgence of human freedom and the undermining of human community. The status quo in 1891 was a condition in which freedom went unchecked by Church, state, or other communal organization:

> [S]ome opportune remedy must be found quickly for the misery and wretchedness pressing so unjustly on the majority of the working class: for the ancient workingmen's guilds were abolished in the last century, and no other protective organization took their place. Public institutions and the laws set aside the ancient religion. Hence, by degrees it has come to pass that working men have been surrendered, isolated and helpless, to the hardheartedness of employers and the greed of unchecked competition. (*Rerum Novarum*, no. 9)

Leo's solution was to recognize the moral burden borne by the owner to each worker in accordance with natural law and the dignity of each human person: "The following duties bind the wealthy owner and the employer: not to look upon their work people as their bondsmen, but to respect in every man his dignity as a person ennobled by Christian character" (*Rerum Novarum,* no 20). That is, the owner ought to use his freedom in the service of God and community.

At the same time, Leo cautioned about inverting the paradigm, and placing the community as the sole value to the exclusion of the exercise of individual human freedom, as the communists proposed. Leo defended private property and sought limits on the power of the communal government:

> The contention, then, that the civil government should at its option intrude into and exercise intimate control over the family and the household is a great and pernicious error. True, if a family finds itself in exceeding distress, utterly deprived of the counsel of friends, and without any prospect of extricating itself, it is right that extreme necessity be met by public aid, since each family is a part of the commonwealth. In like manner, if within the precincts of the household there occur grave disturbance of mutual rights, public authority should intervene to force each party to yield to the other its proper due; for this is not to deprive citizens of their rights, but justly and properly to safeguard and strengthen them. (*Rerum Novarum*, no. 16)

Here again, however, he does not reject the notion of communal authority and the need for public aid on the part of the commonwealth. Rather, he takes what modern society has placed at odds—individual freedom and the common good—and instead draws them together in service of the same ends: service of God and neighbor.

There is a lesson in this for cognitive disability. Of the various social structures put in place to respond to cognitive disability, those systems that allow too much individual freedom and favor the capitalist market will inevitably leave individuals with IDD in a position of scarcity and suffering. We saw this in the early industrial age, prior to the state schools. On the other hand, efforts to restrict freedom and create tightly controlled environments, such as in the institutional era, find philosophical parallels in the centralizing functions of communism. History has shown that overreaching by central authorities in the name of the common good leads to poor results for those with disabilities.

It is in this impasse that society finds itself today. In recent decades, American society has stepped away from the atrocity of the institution system with the creation of successful community-based programs that seek explicitly to allow the greatest degree of freedom possible. At the same time, certain legacy factors keep society from being able to achieve such a state. On the one hand, society is still built on individualism and organic solidarity, so if the system allows too much individualized freedom—as is the case, for example, with employment today—then individuals with IDD will inevitably be left out. On the other hand, the legacy of centralized control means that funding and authority for any of these programs still runs through the centralized state, and, since individuals with IDD rank fairly low when it comes to governmental priorities, funding shortages and waitlists are common.

In *Rerum Novarum,* Leo argued that "no practical solution for this [impoverishment] will ever be found apart from the intervention of religion and the Church" (no. 16). This is as true for disability as it was (and is) for poverty, for solving either of these issues requires a teleological anthropology that orients our freedom toward the love of God and neighbor. Secular documents of rights, while necessary to avoid a regression into atrocity, merely set a floor for societal treatment of those with disabilities. The recognition of the *Imago Dei* serves as a reminder that, by the grace of God, all are free and equal in dignity. Recognition of the *Imago Dei* in others, reminds us that in that freedom and in dignity, God calls us to community.

A 'THIRD WAY' OF SOLIDARITY

Being called to community requires the Church, both the institution and its membership, to be intentional about the basis of communal life. Earlier in this essay, I noted that, in his examination of the shift from traditional to modern economies, sociologist Emil Durkheim identified two types of solidarity. Durkheim's "organic" solidarity was rooted in interdependence. I interact with you because I need something from you. This is the way of the modern world, built on a robust individualism, market capitalism, the division of labor, and exchange of goods. It is also one of the most fundamental stumbling blocks to the advancement of people or individuals or persons with disabilities, since they often have less (materially) to offer than the nondisabled in the exchange and, consequently, are often excluded from active participation in society.

Durkheim's "mechanical" solidarity, on the other hand, arose not out of need for what the other can offer but out of commonality with the other. I interact with you because I share something in common with you. For Durkheim, mechanical solidarity typified the traditional way of life in small towns, where experiences, good and bad, were shared by all. Today, society cannot return to its pre-industrial norms, nor should it. The local bonds of mechanical solidarity, while perhaps a better state of affairs for people with disabilities, also gave rise to tremendous violence. Such bonds, rooted in cultural and material similarity, are at the very root of war, slavery, ethnic cleansing, racism, and genocide.

Catholic social teaching calls individuals to solidarity but not in either of the senses that Durkheim uses the term. Catholic solidarity, by contrast, is a prescriptive command derived from our shared creation and existence.

> Interdependence must be transformed into *solidarity*, based upon the principle that the goods of creation are meant for all. That which human industry produces through the processing of raw materials, with the contribution of work, must serve equally for the good of all. (*Sollicitudo Rei Socialis*, no. 39)

Or, as interpreted by the US Bishops:

> We have to move from our devotion to independence, through an understanding of interdependence, to a commitment to human solidarity. That challenge must find its realization in the kind of community we build among us. Love implies concern for all - especially the poor - and a continued search for those social and economic structures that permit everyone to share in a community that is a part of a redeemed creation. (*Economic Justice for All*, no. 365)

By calling individuals each to embrace a solidarity that is rooted in a shared humanity rather than material interdependence (organic solidarity), Catholic social teaching includes people with disabilities as a fundamental part of society, rather than a dependent burden on society.

SUBSIDIARITY, THE PRIMACY OF THE FAMILY, AND LOCAL ASSOCIATIONS

For the Church, the primary model of solidarity is the nuclear family. The family is "the most intimate sphere in which people cooperate..., [It is] the 'first cell of society.'"[38] As such, it is notable that families do not operate out of any type of functional interdependence. At birth, a child is fully dependent on her or his parents, and, the power of a smile or a giggle aside, an infant offers nothing of material value in exchange for his or her care. Rather, families are the most intimate and fundamental example of the bonds inherent in our nature as social beings.

I have already noted the important advocacy role that family members play on behalf of individuals with disabilities today. Despite the efforts of the Church, the industrialized world continues to reward individuals on the basis of material merit and, thus, reject those who seem to have little of material value to offer. By exalting the bonds of family, however, Catholic social teaching acknowledges the family as the fundamental social unit to which individuals belong regardless of material merits. As such, it also gives warrant to the family's role as advocate for individuals with IDD.

The Church does not expect families to carry the load themselves, however. The bonds of the family, strong as they are, also offer the model of solidarity for the rest of the world to emulate.

> The roots of the contradiction between the solemn affirmation of human rights and their tragic denial in practice lies in a notion of freedom which exalts the isolated individual in an absolute way, and gives no place to solidarity, to openness to others and service of them ... [E]very [person] is his "brother's keeper," because God entrusts us to one another. (*Evangelium Vitae,* no. 19)

While the call to solidarity is universal, the Church also recognizes the importance of it being fulfilled locally.

> Government should not replace or destroy smaller communities and individual initiative. Rather it should help them contribute more effectively to social well-being and supplement their activity when the demands of justice exceed their capacities. This does not mean, however, that the government that governs least, governs best. Rather it defines good government intervention as that which truly "helps" other social groups contribute to the common good by directing, urging, restraining, and regulating economic activity as "the occasion requires and necessity demands." (*Economic Justice for All,* no. 124)

This principle of "subsidiarity" offers valuable caution against the centralized and institutionalized responses to social problems that have, time and time again, failed to adequately respect the human dignity of individuals with disabilities.

---

[38] Thomas Massaro, *Living Justice: Catholic Social Teaching in Action* (Lanham: Rowan & Littlefield Publisher, 2000), 124–125.

IN DEFENSE OF "AND VULNERABLE"

If the principle of human dignity provides the cornerstone of Catholic social thought, then the principle of a Preferential Option for the Poor and Vulnerable is its capstone, that which completes the arch and holds it all together. For the past few decades the Preferential Option for the Poor has served as a summative claim, bringing together the whole of Catholic social thought into the singular idea. This principle places special burdens on those who are blessed with great fortune—be it material riches or physical or cognitive abilities—and special rights on those who do not.

> Whoever has received from the divine bounty a large share of temporal blessings, whether they be external and material, or *gifts of the mind*, has received them for the purpose of using them for the perfecting of his own nature, and, at the same time, that he may employ them, as the steward of God's providence, for the benefit of others. "He that hath a talent," said St. Gregory the Great, "let him see that he hide it not; he that hath abundance, let him quicken himself to mercy and generosity; he that hath art and skill, let him do his best to share the use and the utility hereof with his neighbor." (*Rerum Novarum*, no. 23)[39]

In this way, the preferential option inverts the typical paradigm in which those with fortune and power may wield those resources to gain more fortune and power, while those who lack these riches remain powerless and often, thereby, victimized. Without the principle of the preferential option, a follower of Catholic social thought might well be satisfied with equal treatment of the powerful and the powerless. A preferential option for the poor and vulnerable calls those who possess power and privilege to aim beyond equal treatment and, instead, seek a special place for those who are poor, lowly, and vulnerable.

Often, however, the "and vulnerable" clause of the principle is omitted, thus reducing Catholic social concerns only to the materially poor. This is a mistake. A preferential option *for those with disabilities* suggests that it is not enough to simply tear down the institutions and asylums and return individuals with disabilities to mainstream society. Rather, the Church must give special attention to the needs of people with disabilities in a modern world that otherwise leaves no place for them. Special education, specialized group homes, and dedicated work programs that help to promote the livelihood of those with disabilities are necessary, but, as a society, we must also be mindful that an overemphasis on "special" programs encourages segregation rather that integration.

---

[39] Leo XIII cites Gregory the Great, *Hom. in Evang.*, 9, n. 7 (PL 76, 1109B). Emphasis added.

As a capstone, the Preferential Option for the Poor and Vulnerable not only stands on its own, but it also draws our attention to all of the other principles of Catholic social thought. As such, while the promotion of the dignity and freedom of the human person are noteworthy goals, a preferential option for people with disabilities, ensures that efforts are aimed at the promotion of human dignity and the protection of the freedom *of individuals with disabilities specifically*. Similarly, while the advancement of community is vital for sustaining human life, consideration to the principles of subsidiarity and solidarity and special attention to the role of the family will ensure that we are doing our best to serve the vulnerable in community first. It is only when all of these points are taken in sum that we can truly be making a preferential option for people with disabilities. M

From Universal Precautions to Universal Design: Disclosure of Concealable Disability in the Case of HIV

Mary M. Doyle Roche

HIV IS INCLUDED AMONG THE DISABLING conditions covered by the Americans with Disabilities Act, which has provided important protections for persons who are HIV-positive. Viewing HIV through a theology of disability lens highlights the need to overcome the stigma that leaves persons and their caregivers excluded from Christian community and other aspects of social life. However, the nature of HIV as an infectious disease and the "fight against AIDS" present challenges to some of the assumptions in disability studies. As a concealable condition, HIV-positive status prompts new theological thinking about the role of disclosure in building solidarity with persons who are living with HIV and AIDS and their caregivers. Making the transition from universal precautions to universal design suggests that the Christian community itself can be a disclosure event that can initiate praxes of hospitality and liberation for persons living with HIV.

HIV, AIDS, AND THE ADA

The Americans with Disabilities Act (ADA) celebrated its twenty-fifth anniversary in 2015. The ADA protects persons with disabilities from discrimination in employment, public accommodations, and government services. According to the ADA, "An individual is considered to have a 'disability' if he or she has a physical or mental impairment that substantially limits one or more major life activities, has a record of such impairment, or is regarded as having such impairment." Following a 1998 Supreme Court case, *Bragdon v. Abbott*, in which a dentist turned away a patient who was HIV-positive (the court ruled in favor of the patient), and the ADA Amendments Act of 2008, HIV and AIDS were listed among the disabling conditions covered by the ADA: "Persons with HIV disease, either symptomatic or asymptomatic, have physical impairments that substantially limit one or more major life activities and thus are protected by the ADA. Persons who are discriminated against because they are regarded as being HIV-positive are also protected. For example, the ADA would protect a person who is denied an occupational license or admission to a school on the basis of a rumor or assumption that he has HIV or AIDS, even if he does not."[1]

The ADA website notes the "physical impairments" experienced by people who are HIV-positive or who have AIDS (due primarily to a severely compromised immune system). It is also true to say that stigma lies at the heart of discrimination against persons who are HIV-positive or who have AIDS. As the fictional attorney Andy Beckett says as he researches an employment discrimination suit in the 1993 film *Philadelphia*, "prejudice surrounding AIDS exacts a *social death* which precedes the actual, physical death." Discrimination is based not on an employee's merits, or even on physical limitations, but on the employee's "membership in a group with shared characteristics."[2] At the time, these "shared characteristics" included not only HIV status or a diagnosis of AIDS, but membership in one of the four *H*'s: homosexual men, heroin users, Haitians, and/or hemophiliacs. With the exception of hemophilia, these were already stigmatized groups in the US, and HIV and AIDS exacerbated the discrimination and isolation faced by these persons. In the absence of effective treatment, HIV progressed more rapidly to AIDS, and AIDS was in many ways a visible condition (due to the onset of skin lesions associated with Kaposi sarcoma or wasting).

With the advent of effective anti-retroviral therapies (ARV's) in the 1990's, persons who are HIV-positive live longer, healthier lives, and HIV is now frequently described as a chronic illness in places like the United States where people have ready (and affordable) access to medications. An ARV regimen is not an easy course, and persons who are HIV-positive may still experience physical limitations brought on by fatigue, nausea, headache, dizziness and other side effects of treatment.[3] Since persons who are HIV-positive and have access to treatment can now live longer without symptoms, HIV status has become in many ways an invisible disability. HIV is a concealable, stigmatized identity. The hiddenness of HIV has a number of ethical implications that are not limited to concerns about transmission but include moral practices of disclosure and the potential obstacles to building communities of solidarity. It also presents challenges to theologies of disability in so far as they have focused primarily on visible and apparent conditions.

---

[1] See www.ada.gov/aids/ and www.ada.gov/aids/ada_aids_discrimination.htm.
[2] *Philadelphia*, directed by Jonathan Demme (TriStar Pictures, 1993).
[3] Centers for Disease Control and Prevention, "Act Against AIDS: HIV Treatment," www.cdc.gov/actagainstaids/campaigns/hivtreatmentworks/stayincare/treatment.html.

HIV, AIDS, AND THEOLOGIES OF DISABILITY

The ADA has been an important tool in addressing discrimination against people who are HIV-positive or who have AIDS. Fear and misunderstanding around HIV remain alive and well, and people continue to be refused medical treatment and access to educational opportunities based on their HIV status. Nevertheless, the inclusion of HIV in the ADA and its Amendments is not without ambiguity. The fields of disability studies, disabilities rights movements, and theologies of disability have emphasized inclusion and accepting persons with disabling conditions as they are. Disabilities are not necessarily conditions to be fixed or changed. Mary Jo Iozzio, noting the broad spectrum of disabling conditions and, depending on the operative definition of disability, the significant percentages of people in whom such conditions are present, claims, "Rather than anomalies, I am suggesting that this rate of incidence indicates the wondrous diversity of humankind."[4] Persons with disabling conditions are members of God's "kaleidoscopic" creation.[5]

Sociologist Linda Blum echoes this thinking in her work with mothers of children who have relatively invisible learning and intellectual disabilities that she describes as representing "neurodiversity." She notes, "The disability rights' frame of the neurodiverse repudiates the search for a cure. In this sense it bears a stronger resemblance to deaf community activists and scholars arguing for the autonomous culture of American Sign Language speakers."[6] She calls for an appreciation of neurodiversity. Persons with invisible cognitive differences resist the rhetoric of cure, and Blum notes that the "more sincere protests… have emerged from young adults reclaiming their stigmatized identities through identity-based movement discourse."[7]

According to Blum, advocates for persons who have concealable conditions face particular challenges, "If those with clearly visible stigma faced a lack of privacy and 'displeasure in being exposed' in public, they might also more readily find 'sympathetic others' than those faced with continuous, anxious decisions about the 'management of undisclosed discrediting information' and 'invisible failings.'" She continues, "many of the mothers I came to know … drew pained comparisons to the disregard which they and their children received and to their responsibilities for concealing,

---

[4] See Mary Jo Iozzio, "Thinking about Disabilities with Justice, Liberation, and Mercy," *Horizons* 36, no. 1 (Spring 2009): 34. Iozzio notes the plurality of disabling conditions and categories, and among these she includes medical disabilities.

[5] Iozzio, "Thinking about Disabilities," 36.

[6] Linda M. Blum, *Raising Generation Rx: Mothering Kids with Invisible Disabilities in an Age of Inequality* (New York: New York University Press, 2015), 17.

[7] Blum, *Raising Generation Rx*, 17.

revealing, or managing discrediting information."[8] Disability rights advocates have done much to educate people about how stares, however unintentional they might be, are perceived by people with physical disabilities whose conditions are immediately apparent to others. Yet, for the mothers interviewed by Blum, *not* being noticed or seen by others also has negative implications. Finding "sympathetic others" requires the risk of disclosure and prudentially negotiating often competing desires for both community and privacy. This balancing act consumes significant amounts of precious time and energy.

Even though people may take many different kinds of precautions to prevent the occurrence of disabling conditions (through prenatal care and nutrition, wearing seatbelts or helmets to prevent injury, etc.), the emphasis within theologies of disability is on liberation from oppression perpetuated by individuals and social structures, as well as on a failure of hospitality toward persons with disabilities. Such hospitality may take the form of the removal of physical barriers and the addition of other elements to an environment that would facilitate ease of use. The principles of universal design press even further: re-imagining spaces "from the ground up" rather than relying solely on a practice of "accommodation" for particular individuals that leaves the architecture of exclusion intact. Moreover, some practices of accommodation require that persons disclose a disability to an appropriate agent (though best practices make every attempt to insure confidentiality). Examples of the accommodations approach include responses to students with invisible learning disabilities who may require extended time for testing, a reduced distraction environment, or a scribe for note-taking.

This perspective challenges the medical model of disability, with important distinctions drawn between disabling conditions and illness. Jennie Weiss Block notes, "This [medical] model has become pervasive and widespread, focusing on diagnosis, treatment, and cure. While some people become disabled as a result of an illness, most people with disabilities are not sick; and illness is a separate and not necessarily related experience."[9] Disabilities are not "contagious" and not necessarily in want of a cure. Disabilities arise from biological conditions but are also socially constructed, and the experiences of exclusion and oppression are often rooted in social constructions that impact how persons with disabling conditions interact with other people and their environment.

For Christians, the distinction between illness and disability challenges unexamined interpretations of the healing narratives within

---

[8] Blum, *Raising Generation Rx*, 18.
[9] Jennie Weiss Block, *Copious Hosting: A Theology of Access for People with Disabilities* (New York: Continuum, 2002), 50.

the Gospels. Jesus's encounters with persons with disabilities (which Weiss Block distinguishes from his encounters with persons experiencing illness) may be less about cure and more about restoring persons who had been stigmatized due to their condition and marginalized from membership in the community. It is important to note that even though Jesus performs "miracle cures," cure is not a precondition for relationship with Jesus. Again, Iozzio is instructive,

> Further, we must recall Jesus' concern for the outcast oppressed. Jesus is explicitly attentive to those who are sick, disabled, and marginalized; they are the first in the Kingdom of God. He expresses affection for them as a result of their closeness to God because God suffers with and has a preferential option for the poor.[10]

Jesus's encounters with persons with leprosy have become paradigmatic for Christian responses to persons with HIV and AIDS. There are important resonances here for Christian communities who are striving to overcome stigma. Like lepers in the ancient world (and down to today), persons with HIV and AIDS are "untouchable," marginalized from their communities. They have been denied access to important social and spiritual supports. Jesus moves beyond the social and religious boundaries of his age, drawing near to those who are suffering both because of their illness and because of their isolation. In her essay, "Kissing the Leprous: A Theological Praxis for AIDS," Maria Clara Lucchetti Bingemer highlights Jesus's physical nearness to those who have been rejected and his willingness to touch them while others let fear of contagion guide them.[11] She writes, "Jesus's ministry forms the basis for a Christian praxis of proximity, of affection, friendship and mercy even if it means enduring rejection as one who associates with outcasts."[12]

So, biblical passages that narrate Jesus's interaction with lepers provide an opening for a "liberating" approach to HIV and AIDS. However, the analogy is not without problems. The use of leprosy may perpetuate misunderstanding about the nature of HIV and its transmission. Though "leprosy" in the Bible is likely to have included a range of illnesses and conditions, its association with contagion remains strong. Calling persons who are HIV-positive or who have AIDS "the lepers of our time," continues to signal their "untouchableness" and can fuel associations with sinfulness, viewing HIV and AIDS as punishments for infractions of the dominant moral code.

---

[10] Iozzio, "Thinking about Disabilities," 47.
[11] Maria Clara Lucchetti Bingemer, "Kissing the Leprous: A Theological Praxis for AIDS" in *Calling for Justice Throughout the World: Catholic Women Theologians on the HIV/AIDS Pandemic,* eds. Mary Jo Iozzio, Mary M. Doyle Roche, and Elsie Miranda (New York: Continuum, 2008): 206.
[12] Bingemer, "Kissing the Leprous," 210-211.

If the use of leprosy as an analogy is problematic and the aim is to frame praxes of hospitality and liberation, how then ought we to speak about HIV and AIDS? HIV and AIDS are cases in which the disabling condition is related to illness and to the social constructions of illness in general and infectious diseases in particular. HIV is infectious. That is to say, it is caused by a "microorganism and therefore potentially infinitely transferable to new individuals." Infectious illnesses may or may not be communicable. A communicable illness is infectious and "can be transmitted from one source to another by infectious bacteria or viral organisms." Infectious and communicable diseases may also be contagious in the sense that they are "capable of spreading rapidly from one person to another by contact or close proximity."[13] Technically, HIV fits all of these categories, though use of the term "contagious" often leads to misinformation and misunderstanding about risk of exposure (AIDS, properly speaking, is defined by low CD4 counts or by the appearance of a constellation of opportunistic infections and is not in itself communicable or contagious). It may be more helpful to describe HIV as infectious and refrain from using contagious, which in the popular imagination brings to mind illnesses that are transmitted easily through the air or by touching infected surfaces.[14] While the risks are very real and complicated by a number of other factors, HIV is, for example, harder to "catch" than measles.

Understanding HIV transmission and speaking about it accurately from a medical perspective is crucial in order to overcome stigma and to speak well about it theologically. That HIV is infectious and communicable presents a challenge to languages of disability theologies that distinguish disability from illness. In order to protect persons who are HIV-positive from stigma and discrimination, health care providers and others who may be in proximity to bodily fluids through their work adopt universal precautions. That is to say, rather than making a determination about HIV risk based on the identity of a person in their care (because they are assumed to be homosexual, an intravenous drug user, engaged in sex work, etc.), all bodily fluids, from all people, are treated as if they were "contaminated" with infectious and communicable disease. Taking universal precautions is basically a defensive posture aimed at protecting caregivers from HIV transmission (though in one sense, those in close proximity to persons with HIV pose more of a threat to the HIV-positive person whose immune system is compromised, leaving those who are HIV-positive at increased vulnerability to infection transmitted by others). These precautions take a step toward reducing stigma since no person is singled out and the hope is that these precautions will insure that

---

[13] See Centers for Disease Control, emergency.cdc.gov/preparedness/quarantine/.
[14] Thank you to my colleague and immunologist Ann Sheehy for discussing the finer points of language used to describe HIV and AIDS.

patients in particular will not be turned away or avoided based on an HIV or AIDS diagnosis (or the presumption that a person is HIV-positive or has AIDS).

In the context of HIV and AIDS, the priority on inclusion and overcoming stigma is crucial and has yet to be entirely realized. At the same time, the rhetorical language used in the context of HIV and AIDS can be in tension with these goals. The rhetoric espouses militaristic metaphors: a battle is being waged against HIV and AIDS. It is not a battle against persons who are HIV-positive, who have AIDS, or those whose lives have been impacted by the pandemic, but it is a battle nonetheless. The ultimate goal within the scientific, medical, and public health communities is a world without HIV and AIDS. Reaching this goal requires important resources to be marshaled in the fight against AIDS.[15] The goal in light of theologies of disability is not necessarily a world without disabling conditions though surely a world without disabling access and attitudes. Striving to eliminate disabling conditions can slip all too easily into eliminating persons with disabling conditions or preventing their existence in the first place. It fails to acknowledge the broad spectrum of conditions and can obscure the "kaleidoscopic" diversity that gives God glory. In the case of HIV and AIDS, particularly in the early days of the epidemic in the U.S., some in the "moral majority" made claims that AIDS was punishment from God, that AIDS was (is) God's way of eliminating those who had violated Christian moral codes (primarily, heteronormative sexual codes).

Preventing transmission is a key strategy in the fight against AIDS and the practices that could dramatically reduce transmission rates are well established even though education about transmission and access and ability to use prophylaxis remains a challenge. For example, mother-to-child transmission has all but been eliminated in regions with adequate prenatal care and access to ARV's for mother and child. A world in which no child is born HIV-positive is desirable. That the case of HIV and AIDS does not rest easily in the context of theologies of disability and challenges some working assumptions, does not imply however that thinking and speaking theologically about HIV and AIDS cannot benefit from a disability studies lens.

Theologies of disability done in liberationist perspective draw attention to the social construction of disability and to the forms of

---

[15] For a critique of metaphors of illness, and military metaphors in particular, see Susan Sontag, *Illness as Metaphor and AIDS and Its Metaphors* (New York: Picador, 2001). While militaristic language might alert communities to the urgency of the matter at hand and unite people against a common "enemy," this posture is liable to take on utilitarian approaches that tend toward an "ends justify means" rationality that undermines the dignity of persons and communities. Moreover, the rhetoric too easily slips from eradicating the virus to eradicating those persons carrying the virus and living with AIDS.

institutionalized violence that persons with disabling conditions experience. As Iozzio notes, liberationist practices move from first, doing no harm to those with disabling conditions, to second, restoring those who have been marginalized to the community, to third, making a way open to "the many."[16] In the context of HIV, this demands movement through universal precautions and universal design that accounts for and strives to eliminate the many concrete challenges that persons with HIV face but that also welcomes persons as gifts to the community and signs of God's grace and mercy.

INVISIBLE DISABILITIES AND CONCEALABLE STIGMATIZED IDENTITIES

Before effective treatments were available, HIV progressed rapidly to AIDS and patients exhibited dramatic weight loss or wasting, skin lesions caused by Kaposi sarcoma, fever and cough. AIDS was visible. Now that HIV is a chronic illness in places where there is ready access to ARV treatments, progression to AIDS may take decades and persons can live an "average" life span. AIDS has become less prevalent (though not in regions of the world without access to treatment), and HIV status is an invisible and concealable reality. HIV-positive status joins other invisible disabling conditions like learning disabilities, including ADHD and autism spectrum disorders in their mild to moderate forms.

We have every reason to rejoice that effective treatments have been developed and strive mightily to insure that they are available to all people who require them. However, this situation has not done much to reduce stigma around HIV, and the danger that HIV-positive persons become invisible members of our communities is real. Religious communities may perpetuate the assumption that HIV is "out there" as opposed to being "in here." The practice of "othering" may continue in subtle ways, and the suffering, struggle, and resilience of HIV-positive persons may be ignored. Iozzio notes the ease with which persons with disabling conditions are ignored and how their absence from community goes unnoticed, "Scandalously, this invisibility is a result of the stigmatizing social constructions and internalized assumptions that have hidden many in their homes, in institutional residential facilities, or in culpably ignorant oblivion on the part of the non-disabled majority."[17]

Iozzio is highlighting the reality that excluding practices and architecture (itself a practice) have forced the absence of persons with disabling conditions, resulting in an impoverished communal life. In the case of invisible and concealable disabling conditions, persons with these conditions may in fact be present, even though the

---

[16] Iozzio, "Thinking about Disabilities," 33.
[17] Iozzio, "Thinking about Disabilities," 45.

community is unaware of their presence as the result of either unconscious bias or deliberate self-deception. The reality of HIV is ignored or spoken about in ways that marginalize HIV-positive persons. So, HIV and AIDS are problems in Africa or among groups of people who are assumed to be absent from the community's midst (but, if anyone here is living with HIV, keep quiet about it!). The environment, though it appears with a veneer of hospitality, becomes hostile. Disclosing HIV-status becomes less likely, fraught as it is with the risk of isolation and abandonment.

ETHICS OF DISCLOSURE AND THE ROAD TO SOLIDARITY

College student Paige Rawl opens her memoir, *Positive*, "Today, when I tell people that I took medicine every single day for almost a decade without ever once wondering why, they sometimes look at me like I have three heads." She continues,

> There I am as a very young child, scrambling up onto the kitchen counter, folding my legs crisscross-applesauce, and waiting patiently. And there is my mother, twisting the child safety lid off a white plastic jar, scooping a heap of powder, and stirring it, still lumpy, into a plastic sippy cup filled with milk... I make a face and begin to drink... I drink it all. I would have every time, even if my mother hadn't been watching me closely, her eyes focused on this ritual as my life depended on it. It did of course, although I didn't know it yet.[18]

Paige's medical regimen is for her, simply a fact of life, nothing extraordinary. She enjoys the regular visits to her physician, whom she admires and aspires to emulate someday. She does not know, as her mother clearly does, what is at stake in her adherence to this routine. That Paige's HIV status was concealed from her seems reasonable and developmentally appropriate, especially since the virus was being effectively managed with medication and her prognosis was good.

As she grew and the powdered drinks were replaced by pills, Paige "began to pay more attention" to the words she saw written in medical charts and on the information materials posted on the walls of her doctor's office. In fourth grade, she put the question to her mother directly, "Am I HIV positive or negative?" In the conversation that followed, her mother told Paige about her HIV-positive status, that she had been HIV-positive since birth, that her mother too was HIV-positive, and that her father (whom she had not known but met once in the hospital near the end of his life) had died of AIDS.[19] Paige seemed to take all of this in stride. It was confusing information to be sure, but, at this point, Paige was able to understand more about the

---

[18] Paige Rawl with Ali Benjamin, *Positive: A Memoir* (New York: HarperCollins, 2014), 3.
[19] Rawl, *Positive*, 55-56.

virus, how it is and is not transmitted, and that, with proper medication, she could continue to live well and engage in the activities she enjoyed. It is not clear in her narrative if they discussed whether or not this information should be kept private and why.

One day, as a close friend shared with Paige her personal story of a family member's illness and how unsettling it was for her, Paige thought, "I understood she was telling me something important. I wanted her to feel better, to feel less alone." Moved by compassion, Paige discloses her HIV status,

> Everybody's got something, I told her… And then I told her that I had something too. I told her I had HIV. If her face changed at all when I told her, I didn't notice it. If she looked at me differently, I didn't see it. … I really meant what I said to Yasmine: everybody had something. HIV just happened to be my thing.[20]

Paige was happy to have shared this part of herself with someone as an expression of friendship and solidarity so that her friend would not feel alone in her suffering. Paige did not comprehend the implications of this disclosure beyond the trusting friendship she was trying to build. Word of her HIV status, shared in a personal encounter with one friend, spread rapidly throughout the school and, by the end of the day, the name-calling had begun. Paige would face relentless bullying by other students, parents, and school officials who, as in many instances of bullying, placed the burden of blame on Paige. It is not a stretch to claim that school officials conspired to shield the school from any accountability for what was happening to her.

Paige's story demonstrates how critical the experience of disclosure can be. Her first disclosure experience, having her own and her mother's status disclosed, was positive overall. Her first attempt to disclose on her own was initially positive, but the ensuing consequences created an intolerable situation for Paige. In their review of the psychological literature, Chaudoir, Fisher and Simoni note, "Disclosure of HIV status is one of the most complex psychosocial challenges facing individuals who live with HIV/AIDS; it has important implications for both individual and public health outcomes."[21] Disclosure can be a first step in gaining HIV-specific social support, helping to prevent sero-conversion of HIV-negative individuals, and facilitating adherence to ARV medication regimens.[22] Even though disclosure can result in access to support, they also note

---

[20] Rawl, *Positive*, 61.
[21] Stephenie R. Chaudoir, Jeffrey D. Fisher, and Jane M. Simoni, "Understanding HIV Disclosure: A Review and Application of the Disclosure Process Model," *Social Science and Medicine* 72, no. 10 (2011): 1618.
[22] Chaudoir, Fisher, and Simoni, "Understanding HIV Disclosure," 1618.

that there are risks that include stigmatizing reactions, physical harm and discrimination.

Chaudoir, Fisher, and Simoni ask "When and why is disclosure beneficial?" and propose the Disclosure Process Model (DPM), which attends to the outcomes of disclosure, both advantageous and detrimental, rather than focusing on disclosure as an "endpoint."[23] They note "the DPM posits that disclosure is regulated by two distinct goal, or motivational, systems that represent approach and avoidance motivations.... Approach goals are focused on pursuing a rewarding or desired end state, while avoidance goals are focused on avoiding a punishing or undesired end state."[24] Approach goals might include "strengthening an important relationship," in much the way that Paige Rawl disclosed her status to a friend in a time of need. Her thoughts about disclosure after the first event were shaped by her very realistic desire to avoid ridicule and stigma.

It was not until she attended a camp for children and young people impacted by HIV and AIDS (both for those who are HIV positive themselves and for those who have loved ones who are HIV positive) that Paige's disclosure motivations and goals would shift again. Disclosure would help her build solidarity with others and feel supported by a trusted community. Attending the camp and participating in AIDS walks and other awareness events, according to Chaudoir and colleagues, can "introduce new information about HIV status 'in the open' where this information can shape perceptions and behavior in both the immediate and broader social context."[25] Disclosure creates a "feedback loop in which [persons living with HIV or AIDS] who have positive disclosure events will become increasingly open about their HIV status whereas individuals who have negative disclosure events will become increasingly concealed."[26] The quality of the disclosure event is critical, and there is some evidence that positive disclosure events can impact psychological and physical well-being.[27] Among children, HIV disclosure can have a negative impact especially if the child is asked to keep the information a secret.[28]

The Office of the Medical Director of the New York State Department of AIDS Institute in collaboration with Johns Hopkins University Division of Infectious Diseases has developed a resource of best practices regarding disclosure to children and young people. They note, "HIV disclosure to infected children and adolescents

---

[23] Chaudoir, Fisher, and Simoni, "Understanding HIV Disclosure," 1619.
[24] Chaudoir, Fisher, and Simoni, "Understanding HIV Disclosure," 1619.
[25] Chaudoir, Fisher, and Simoni, "Understanding HIV Disclosure," 1620.
[26] Chaudoir, Fisher, and Simoni, "Understanding HIV Disclosure," 1620.
[27] Chaudoir, Fisher, and Simoni, "Understanding HIV Disclosure," 1622-1624.
[28] Chaudoir, Fisher, and Simoni, "Understanding HIV Disclosure," 1625.

should take place in a supportive environment with collaboration and cooperation among caregivers and providers. Disclosure is contingent on the caregiver's acknowledgment of the illness, the readiness to disclose, and the child's cognitive skills and emotional maturity." There are several cornerstones to their approach that include: collaboration among providers and caregivers, developmentally appropriate and truthful explanations of the illness, validation of the child's concerns and clarifications of misconceptions, and ongoing support. They note, disclosure of HIV status is not a one-time event but rather a process, involving ongoing discussions about the disease as the child matures cognitively, emotionally, and sexually.[29]

A number of factors might keep caregivers from disclosing HIV status to children. These include concern that a child might inappropriately disclose their status, fear of stigma and loss of social support, and a desire to protect the child from anxiety and depression.[30] Practical guidelines for disclosure include: carefully chosen date of disclosure, clear and developmentally appropriate language, opportunity to share feelings with an accompanying acceptance of silence, opportunity to ask questions, availability of resource materials, and the inclusion of the healthcare team and caregivers in the process.[31]

In his discussion of the ethics of disclosure, James Keenan turns to virtue ethics to highlight the balance that must be struck by two values, confidentiality and the common good. The virtue of fidelity "grounds the priority of all confidences" and justice "protects the common good."[32] With respect to HIV, the issue for Keenan is whether and to whom physicians may disclose the HIV status of a patient. In the context of HIV and AIDS, the argument has usually revolved around the need to prevent the transmission of HIV. So, could confidentiality be breached in order to protect a patient's sexual partners (in this case HIV status is not a threat to public health writ large but potential threats facing particular others)?[33] Ideally, the patient would consent to this type of notification. Since the moral agent in Keenan's case is the physician and not necessarily the patient, Keenan does not explore

---

[29] The Office of the Medical Director of the New York State Department of AIDS Institute in collaboration with Johns Hopkins University Division of Infectious Diseases, "HIV Clinical Resource: Disclosure of HIV to Perinatally Infected Children and Adolescents," www.hivguidelines.org/clinicalguidelines/adolescents/disclosure-of-hiv-to-perinatally-infected-children-and-adolescents-2/.
[30] "HIV Clinical Resource."
[31] "HIV Clinical Resource."
[32] James Keenan, "Confidentiality, Disclosure, and Fiduciary Responsibility," *Theological Studies* 54, no. 1 (1993): 143. Disclosure was particularly problematic for adults at the time of Keenan's writing, before medications to thwart onset of AIDS and the determination of HIV as a chronic condition.
[33] Keenan, "Confidentiality,"158.

the role of his other cardinal virtue of self-care and how self-care might guide personal disclosure to others (to both particular others, such as sexual partner(s), family and friends, and general others in the process of raising awareness about HIV and AIDS). Self-care might involve keeping one's status confidential in the interest of protecting the self from stigma, though it may also lead to a "silencing of the self" in ways that are destructive of voice and moral agency. Self-care might also lead one to disclose in order to gain support and reduce the stress that keeping secrets can induce.

Keeping justice, fidelity and self-care, each guided by prudence, in the frame opens a way to consider the common good in another way, more broadly than the public health issue of transmission. Protecting the common good surely involves reducing rates of transmission and protecting those who are particularly vulnerable to infection. Promoting the common good might also include the desire that a community grow in its ability to be in solidarity with persons who are HIV-positive or whose lives and relationships are impacted by HIV and AIDS. Is it good for a community to know that there are HIV-positive persons in its midst? If it is good then how might justice, fidelity, and self-care provide a safe space for disclosure that leads to solidarity?

I teach a course on HIV, AIDS, and ethics encouraging students to be aware of how we speak about HIV remains a challenge. HIV-positive persons and those impacted by the pandemic are "out there." It is difficult to shake "us/them" language. Students are rarely cognizant of the possibility that someone else "in the room" is touched by HIV in deeply personal ways. All members of the class participate, anonymously, in an exercise in which personal connections are disclosed. When asked to write down people with HIV on slips of paper, responses have included Magic Johnson (far and away the most frequent person named) and also "my high school teacher," "my aunt," and several given names. Representatives from a local agency that supports persons with HIV and offers educational and advocacy programs in the community visit our class. Even after a semester of critical study, the students are thrown off guard when our visitors disclose their HIV-positive status. Their comments tend to be something like, "I knew they worked for the agency, but I didn't know they were also HIV-positive themselves." In spite of what they might know intellectually about HIV, about transmission and treatment, they are surprised when the person doesn't "look" like they have HIV. They "look" just like "anyone else."

This experience is among the most powerful in the course and marks a transition point for students in terms of confronting unacknowledged biases and expectations. The representatives speak about their personal journeys including the process of disclosure, which includes accepting their status (a kind of disclosure to self), recognizing that they have dignity and are worthy of respect and love, and finding relationships of trust. They hope that their disclosure at these events raises awareness and is a step on the road to greater justice and compassion for persons impacted by HIV and AIDS. These representatives exhibit the virtues of prudence and self-care, solidarity, and justice in the form of the common good.

Paige Rawl experienced a space of acceptance when she attended a camp for children who are impacted by HIV. Writing her memoir, making a very public disclosure, is a way in which Paige serves others and contributes to the common good by helping to break down stigma and reach people who often feel like they cannot meaningfully participate in common life, either because they are HIV-positive, because they are being bullied, or simply because they are young. Serving the common good benefited Paige as well. The common good does not overwhelm the needs or rights of individuals, and all goods that are the fruit of participation in common life redound to individuals.

Paige's memoir advanced her dignity and well-being. Her disclosure in this way certainly came with risk, but the disclosure did not sacrifice her personal dignity so that others could become better educated about an urgent moral issue. In some ways, Paige's participation in the camp made her memoir possible, one disclosure leading to another in ways that enhanced her voice and her freedom. Recognizing the role of the camp in the process also highlights a critical element: the camp's prior disclosure of itself as a community of solidarity that would be faithful to the confidences of its participants is crucial to solidarity especially for those with concealable stigmatized identities. Solidarity shifts the moral responsibility of disclosure on to the community and away from the person with HIV even though the burden, and potentially the gift, of this responsibility will continue to shift back and forth from community to individual.

THE CHRISTIAN COMMUNITY AND UNIVERSAL DESIGN: A DISCLOSURE EVENT

Disclosure of HIV status, as well as disclosure of other invisible disabling conditions, illnesses and concealable stigmatized identities, can be a crucial element of personal well-being and may advance social support and solidarity. Communities and individuals benefit when there is a safe space in which to disclose HIV-status. The perspective of universal precautions is a step along the way, but it remains a defensive and accommodating stance with respect to persons with disabilities. Communities must speak and act on the assumption that persons impacted with HIV are in their midst. Donald Messer notes that theologically, the Church, the Body of Christ, is

HIV-positive. The Body of Christ has AIDS.[34] The risen Christ bears the wounds of the passion. This revelation cannot be merely a matter of adjusting language so as not to offend, exclude, isolate, or silence "unseen" and "unheard" persons.

If universal precautions are an important step, universal design is the next crucial element. As Iozzio notes, this "opens the way for many." Universal design must not only shape our architecture but also our speech and other practices. Universal design principles assume the "kaleidoscopic" beauty of creation and the unique contributions of persons with disabling conditions whether they are the result of injury, illness, or genetic make-up. This posture of welcome and hospitality recognizes the giftedness of persons of all abilities, acknowledges the reality that many, if not most, persons will experience a disabling condition at some point in their lives and that, as we live longer, many more of us may spend a significant time in our lives with chronic illnesses and physical or cognitive disabilities.

Universal design takes "a long loving look at the real" as Walter Burghardt, S.J., once described the practice of prayer. It pays close attention to the diversity of God's creation and "walks a mile in someone else's shoes" in order to capture potential obstacles that may otherwise go unnoticed. It also captures the many assets that persons with disabling conditions can bring to a community that is ready to accept them. Universal design facilitates this loving acceptance. Persons with disabling conditions do not present a problem to be addressed but are rather gifts, as all people are to one another, from a passionately loving God. Some of the limits imposed on persons with disabling conditions are a consequence of the conditions themselves. Other limits are socially constructed. The former can be "accommodated" and the latter can be deconstructed in a community willing to reflect deeply on its practices of welcome.

The focus of universal design is not on the accommodation of individuals, a practice that continues to maintain a narrow vision of what is "normal" in human functioning. The emphasis is on the dependence and interdependence that we experience as an element of human finitude and on broadening our moral imaginations to include "the many." The practice of accommodation places the burden of disclosure on persons with disabling conditions in order to gain access to communal life in all of its richness. Universal design, considered from a theological perspective, implies that it is the community that bears the responsibility of disclosure. If Christian communities are unreflective about disability in general and about invisible disabilities and concealable stigmatized identities in particular, they will disclose,

---

[34] Donald Messer, *Breaking the Conspiracy of Silence: Christian Churches and the Global AIDS Crisis* (Minneapolis: Fortress Press, 2004).

intentionally or not, communities of obstacles at best and hostility at worst.

The Church community is itself a disclosure event. Gathered to hear the good news, to offer a sign of peace, to share the Eucharistic meal, the Church discloses God's kingdom. Brought together for sacrament, service and social justice, the community offers a glimpse of new life in the Resurrection. It bears witness to Jesus Christ who offered cure and healing to the vulnerable and outcast, restoring them to community. It bears witness to the ministry of Jesus who was himself, on several occasions, surprised by those who made claims on him. This disclosure on the part of the Christian community is the prerequisite for the safe and meaningful disclosure of HIV status, which can in turn lead to greater solidarity and social support.

Disclosure may take the form of homilies and prayers of the faithful that speak about HIV and AIDS (and not only on World AIDS Day); ministries to persons with HIV that include pastoral ministers who are impacted by the virus; education and awareness programs that are developmentally appropriate, speak plainly, frankly, and accurately about HIV prevention, transmission, and treatment; prophetic speech and action on behalf of those who face compounded stigma due to sexual orientation, gender, race, or drug addiction. These praxes of hospitality and liberation become part of the positive feedback loop that may help sustain persons in other hostile environments and during negative disclosure experiences. As Paul instructs those at Corinth to "glorify God in your body" (1 Corinthians 6:20) and as solidarity demands resources directed at preventing, treating, and curing HIV and AIDS, the revealed HIV-positive disabled body of Christ gives God glory in God's universal design of mercy and compassion. ■

Disability, the Healing of Infirmity, and the Theological Virtue of Hope: A Thomistic Approach

Paul Gondreau

WHEN ONE STEPS INTO THE FOURTEENTH-century cathedral of Orvieto, Italy, and ventures into the side chapel near the right of the sanctuary, one beholds a masterpiece of the early High Renaissance: frescoes dedicated to the Final Judgment, painted by Luca Signorelli between 1500 and 1503. Having received instruction from unnamed theologians (the contract for these frescoes, still on record in the archives of the cathedral, stipulates that Signorelli should consult the "Masters of the Sacred Page" before commencing his painting), Signorelli succeeded in infusing his frescoes with evident theological depth and insight. Divided into several panels corresponding to the various events that, according to traditional Christian belief, will occur at the *eschaton*, Signorelli's Final Judgment chapel offers one panel in particular that, to my mind, holds special relevance for a theological account of disability, as, indeed, of the corruptibility of the human body in general: that of the *Resurrection of the Flesh*. Here Signorelli's mastery of the human form, realized in the dynamic action of various nude bodies whose flesh is being placed back on their bones, comes to the fore.

More to the point of this essay, Signorelli's *Resurrection of the Flesh* panel places before its onlooker one of the "secondary goods" that are integral to the proper object of the theological virtue of hope (the *visio Dei*): the glorified reunion of body and soul in virtue of the body's resurrection. To put it in the words of the Nicene-Constantinopolitan Creed, Christians "look forward to the resurrection of the dead and the life of the world to come." Recall, in this connection, the biblical foundation of this credal profession. The Old Testament promises that the "dead shall live, their bodies shall rise" (Isaiah 26:19), and offers a vision of "dry bones" having "sinews," "flesh" and "skin" placed back on them, followed by "breath" put in them, "and [they] shall live" (Ezekiel 37:1-14). For the New Testament, the words of St. Paul are especially sonorous: "We shall all be changed, in a moment, in the twinkling of an eye, at the last trumpet. For the trumpet will sound and the dead will be raised imperishable, and we shall be changed. For this perishable nature must put on the imperishable, and this mortal nature must put on immortality" (1 Corinthians 15:51-53; see also 1 Thessalonians 4:14-18). As if elaborating on this change attested to by St. Paul, the Book of Revelation sees in the eschatological "new heavens and new earth" a time when God "will wipe away every tear from their eyes," and where "death shall be no more, neither shall there be mourning nor crying nor pain any more, for the former things [will] have passed away" (Revelation 21:1-4).

The precise nature of this "passing away" of former things and "change" from a perishable, mortal nature to an imperishable and immortal one, that is, to a glorified nature, for all persons with corruptible bodies, but especially for those with disabilities, marks the chief consideration of this essay. The relevance that this change bears in regard to hope hinges strictly upon our gaining a proper understanding of what it involves.

For his part, Signorelli attempts to depict this change by placing in his fresco only the fully mature human form—neither elderly or middle-aged bodies on the "back" (degenerating) side of the attainment of full physical maturity nor prepubescent or adolescent bodies on the "front" (developing) side—devoid of any and all impairments or infirmities. He paints only bodies in the prime of life and in full vigor and which are quite visibly sound, youthful, integral, whole, robust, perfectly proportional.

At the same time, the artistic and theological magnificence of Signorelli's *Resurrection of the Flesh* panel notwithstanding, we might ask whether his fresco omits for our consideration another aspect of the resurrected body. For an indication of this other aspect, we can turn to an additional fresco, this one in the city of Rome itself. In the Basilica of San Clemente, within eyeshot of the Coliseum, there exists a little-known fresco on the right-hand clerestory just after one enters the main doors of the church building. The fresco shows a certain St. Servulus lying on a cot while listening to the Scriptures being read to him. A sixth-century saint who had a severe case of cerebral palsy, by which he was unable to stand, sit upright, put his hand to his mouth, or turn from one side to the other, Servulus was cared for by his mother and brothers and would spend his days praising God while begging for alms in the portico of this same church, San Clemente. (His body is buried beneath the fresco.) In a homily, Pope St. Gregory the Great, who speaks as if he knew Servulus personally, holds up this man with a severe disability as an example of heroic forbearance and gratitude and as a rebuke to the able bodied who complain about the slightest hardship they have to endure. "His bed of pain was a pulpit of preaching, from which he converted souls," exclaims Gregory of Servulus in a marvelous phrase.[1]

So, yes, in the final resurrection, the human body will enjoy a perfection, a vigor, a beauty, and thus—especially pertinent for people with disabilities—a healing that, commensurate with the imperishable and immortal condition of that state, cannot be attained in this life. Yet, considering the role of physical disability in the life not just of St. Servulus but of countless other saints as well and how inextricably linked their disability is to their holiness, what exactly shall become of physical disability in the healing that accompanies the glorified condition of the resurrected body?[2] Shall the wiping away of every tear and the passing away of former things attested to in Revelation 21:4 include the wiping away of every form of disability, or shall the marks of disability in some way remain, much like how the marks of Christ's crucifixion remain? Is there, in other words, a fuller way of conceiving the perfection and beauty of the resurrected body than what we find depicted in Signorelli's *Resurrection of the Flesh* panel, one that is inclusive of disability and which the "beauty" revealed in Christ's Cross demands?

---

[1] Gregory the Great, *Homilia* 15 *(Homiliae xl in Evangelia)*, on Lk 8:4-15 (PL 76.1491 [cols. 1133-4]). Gregory says much the same thing of Servulus in his *Dialogues*, Bk 4.14.

[2] The May 2015 issue of *Magnificat* showcased on each day of the month a particular saint who suffered from a physical disability: St. Rafqa Pietra Choboq Ar-Rayès (†1914), a Lebanese saint who suffered from a paralysis that confined her to her bed; St. Miguel Febres Cordero (†1910), a Spanish saint who was born with club feet and who could neither walk nor stand on his own; St. Joan of France (†1505), a French saint who was hunchbacked and pockmarked; St. Sabinus of Canosa (†566), an Italian saint known to us also through Pope St. Gregory the Great's *Dialogues* and who suffered total blindness in his old age; St. Gilbert of Sempringham (†1189), an English saint who suffered some sort of physical deformity; St. Gerald of Sauve-Majeure (†1095), a French saint who suffered from severe shingles; the well-known Italian St. Charles Borromeo (†1584), who suffered from a speech defect (probably a chronic stammer); St. Mellitus (†624), a Roman saint and missionary to England who became crippled with gout; St. John of Dukla (†1484), a Polish saint who became blind in his later years; St. Pacificus of San Severino (†1721), an Italian saint who suffered from ulcers on his legs that made walking difficult and who also lost his eyesight and hearing; St. Joseph Cafasso (†1860), an Italian saint who was born with a twisted spine; St. Bernard Tolomei (†1348), an Italian saint who suffered from blindness; St. Odilia (†*c.* 720), a Frankish saint who was born blind and rejected by her father; St. Jaime Hilario (†1937), a Spanish saint who suffered from deafness; St. Rafael Arnáiz Barón (†1938), a Spanish saint who was troubled with fever and pleurisy and who suffered from diabetes mellitus; St. Fina (†1254), an Italian saint who was struck by a severe disease that made her become disfigured and paralyzed; St. Mary Joseph Rossello (†1880), an Italian saint who suffered from heart trouble and who lost the use of her legs; St. Hervé († 6th century), a French saint who was born blind; St. Aleydis (†1250), a Belgian saint who suffered from leprosy and who lost her eyesight near the end of her life; St. Gemma Galgani (†1903), an Italian saint who suffered from tuberculosis of the spine, which twisted her body and caused excruciating headaches.

In this connection, Cardinal Joseph Ratzinger (the future Pope Benedict XVI), in a little-known address, observes how beauty itself is transformed and given "new depth and new realism" in the scandal of Christ's Cross.[3] He draws this conclusion from the paradoxical fact that, while there was "no beauty, no majesty to draw our eyes, no grace to make us delight in him" (Isaiah 53:2) when he hung upon the Cross, Christ remained all the same and in that very moment on the Cross "the fairest of the children of men" (Psalm 45:2). Does the example of St. Servulus and of all those saints with disabilities, given their intimate sharing in Christ's suffering, not allow us to see in disability a reflection of the same beauty of Christ on the Cross? Can we not say, in other words, that disability participates in the "new depth and new realism" of beauty that is revealed in the Cross of Christ? If so, by extension we may include people with disabilities among "the fairest of the children of men," and the beauty of their disability, like the beauty of Christ's crucifixion wounds, should be reflected somehow in the beauty of the resurrected body.[4]

In what follows, I consider what the theological virtue of hope offers all of us, though with particular emphasis on people with disabilities, as regards the glorification of our humanity, when the soul is reunited with the risen body. At all points in this essay, I draw chiefly from the thought of St. Thomas Aquinas, as I believe his insights on hope, imbedded within a larger theological and philosophical anthropology and a comprehensive system of thought, have much to offer contemporary disability studies.[5] In a first move, I argue that, commensurate with the imperishable condition of the resurrected state, people with disabilities, indeed, all people (able bodied and all), shall attain to complete bodily healing in the final resurrection. God shall bring our corruptible bodies, our disabled bodies, to full healing, in the very measure that he shall "wipe away

---

[3] Joseph Ratzinger, "The Feelings of Things, the Contemplation of Beauty: Message of His Eminence Card. Joseph Ratzinger to the Communion and Liberation (CL) Meeting at Rimini (24-30 August 2002)," vatican.va/roman_curia/congrega-tions/cfaith/documents/rc_con_cfaith_doc_20020824_ratzinger-cl-rimini_en.html.

[4] Ratzinger also observes in this same address: "I have often affirmed my conviction that the true apology of Christian faith, the most convincing demonstration of its truth against every denial, are the saints, and the beauty that the faith has generated. Today, for faith to grow, we must lead ourselves and the persons we meet to encounter the saints and to enter into contact with the Beautiful."

[5] Particular acknowledgement goes to Miguel J. Romero for his efforts at inserting the voice of Aquinas into disability studies. See his "The Happiness of 'Those Who Lack the Use of Reason,'" *Thomist* 80, no. 1 (2016): 49-96; and "Aquinas on the *corporis infirmitas*: Broken Flesh and the Grammar of Grace," in *Disability in the Christian Tradition: A Reader*, ed. Brian Brock and John Swinton (Michigan: Eerdmans, 2012), 101-151. See also John Berkman, "Are Persons with Profound Intellectual Disabilities Sacramental Icons of Heavenly Life? Aquinas on Impairment," *Studies in Christian Ethics* 26, no. 1 (2013): 83-96.

every tear from our eyes." At the same time, because of their participation in the beauty of the glorified wounds of Christ, the marks of disability, I argue, shall remain in the glorified risen body. Hope assures us of nothing less.

In a second move, I consider the two sins opposed to hope—despair (the extreme of defect) and presumption (the extreme of excess)—and how they bear on this promised healing and glorification. Practical suggestions on overcoming these vices are offered, with special emphasis on the role that healthcare practitioners play in the effort at living by hope amidst a condition of corruptibility and disability. There is a much grander project of healing at work than what simply takes place in the here and now, and therapists and other healthcare practitioners play an indispensable part in this grander project. I attempt to show that "the art of healing," to use Pope St. John Paul II's phrase from his apostolic letter on the Christian Meaning of Human Suffering, *Salvifici Doloris* (no. 5), is ultimately eschatological in meaning and significance. Particular emphasis is given as well to the way the sin of presumption can sometimes impede a proper administration of the sacraments to people with disabilities.

In the interests of full disclosure, I should acknowledge at the outset of this essay that I have personally lived with the reality of disability for many years. My older brother has been a quadriplegic since the age of seventeen (he severed his spinal cord in a diving accident, when I was just entering high school), and my own son, now twelve, has a severe and complex form of cerebral palsy (he has, in fact, two forms of cerebral palsy superimposed on each other). Some readers may recall seeing images of my son with Pope Francis from a few years back. On Easter Sunday, 2013, just two weeks after his election as pope, Francis embraced my son (whose name is Dominic) while touring St. Peter's Square. Images of this embrace went viral and quickly became an iconic emblem of Pope Francis's special devotion to the poor and marginalized that would in short order become a hallmark feature of his pontificate. Issuing from the pen of both a theologian and a parent of a child with a severe disability, this essay owes to my own lived experience with disability, particularly with that of my son, and of my theological reflection on this experience. Closely resembling St. Servulus both in physical disability and in holiness (everyone in my family thinks this), my son has taught me a great deal. In many respects, this essay marks my justification of his very existence in a culture whose outlook could easily call it into question. While I attempt to integrate Dominic's voice at various points of this essay, I am mindful that, for obvious reasons, the perspective of this essay comes predominantly from me, his parent. I apologize in advance if this gives a somewhat one-sided view of disability (of his disability especially), though, again, I attempt to counterbalance it with occasional insertions of Dominic's voice. I dedicate this essay to him.

A NOTE ON TERMINOLOGY

Disability studies has its own established lexicon of sorts and recognizes various models or common approaches to theorizing "disability" (e.g., medical model, social model, rights model, cultural model, etc.).[6] In some respects, however, this lexicon and these models stand at variance with a Thomistic method and approach (the method and approach of this study), and thus at variance—though not necessarily at odds—with distinctive Thomistic language. For this reason, I put forward the following definition of key terms in hopes of avoiding potential misunderstanding, confusion, or disagreement. At all points, the goal is not so much to promote a parallel use of language as to put forward a critically complementary voice in disability studies. I believe the Thomistic method and approach, informed by a nuanced interpretive tradition, can offer a valuable contribution to contemporary disability studies.

As for disability itself, Thomistic usage would define this term against the backdrop of a robust metaphysics of human nature and thus of a proper understanding of objective goods to which our nature is ordered by its design. Seen in this light, disability would signify an impairment (whether of a physical or intellectual sort) and thus an "evil" or wound of nature. It is a privation of a good that should be present, a failure of human nature to attain, particularly in terms of operation or function, what God the Author of our nature has designed it to attain.[7] Thomists routinely distinguish between physical evil (something like cancer or blindness) and moral evil (sin or vice).[8] Disability, whether it be physical (such as cerebral palsy or multiple sclerosis) or intellectual (such as Down syndrome or autism), would clearly belong in the former category. For the purposes of this essay, disability is used throughout to signify an evil of a functional (or physical) sort rather than of an ontological (let alone moral) sort.

---

[6] For a useful guide, albeit with particular reference to intellectual disability, see Licia Carlson, *The Faces of Intellectual Disability: Philosophical Reflections* (Bloomington: Indiana University Press, 2010).

[7] Because, so far as I can tell, no express metaphysical regard for the human person stands behind her understanding of disability, Candida R. Moss, in "Heavenly Healing: Eschatological Cleansing and the Resurrection of the Dead in the Early Church," *Journal of the American Academy of Religion* 79, no. 4 (2011): 1-27, refuses to consider disability as an evil or an impairment, even in a purely physical sense.

[8] See, for instance, Charles Journet, *Le mal. Essai théologique* (Saint-Maurice, Switzerland: Édition Saint-Augustin, 1988, 3rd ed.); and Jacques Maritain, *St. Thomas and the Problem of Evil*, "The Aquinas Lecture, 1942" (Milwaukee: Marquette University Press, 1942).

Disability means a debilitating, privative limitation, and thus a functional infirmity or impairment.

While such an understanding identifies disability as an evil or wound of nature, it does not preclude our valuing disability positively—as we shall see below when considering disability as a source of holiness in and through Christ. Moreover, because disability constitutes a functional rather than an ontological evil, the dignity of persons with disabilities (their human ontology) remains whole and intact, along with all the human rights accruing to their dignity as persons. No matter the strong language—indeed, in virtue of a right understanding of its language—a Thomistic approach leaves no room for a utopian or eugenic social regard for disability, whereby unjust exclusion or abuse of people with disabilities, let alone nefarious social engineering programs for people with disabilities, are tolerated or justified.

Because disability, on a Thomistic account, marks a functional impairment or infirmity, a debilitating wound of nature, it necessarily involves a condition of suffering. Here we need to be clear, since many will object to the view that would seem to conflate disability with suffering.[9] Certainly, limitation or weakness in themselves need not equate with suffering. An infant does not "suffer" simply because she is limited, weak, or dependent on others. Further, not all people with disabilities "suffer" in the sense of "feel pain" or feel, subjectively speaking, an awareness of their disagreeable state or condition of infirmity. Objectively speaking, however, disability (whether physical disability or intellectual disability) involves a debilitating condition, whereby human nature is impaired from acting or functioning in the way it is designed to act and otherwise should be acting: "[The human being] particularly suffers when he ought—in the normal order of things—to have a share in this good [of his nature] and does not have it," writes John Paul II (*Salvifici Doloris*, no. 7).[10] Such is not the case, say, for the infant who remains in a developmental stage and thus in potency of the type of operation to which her nature is ordered to performing at a later, more fully developed stage of life. Missing out on a kind of action (like motor functioning in the case of my son's cerebral palsy) that, all things being equal, one should not be missing out on is quite different from not yet being able to perform that action.

---

[9] For an engaging reflection on the relationship between suffering and disability (especially of a developmental sort), see Stanley Hauerwas, "Suffering the Retarded: Should We Prevent Retardation?" in *Suffering Presence: Theological Reflections on Medicine, the Mentally Handicapped, and the Church* (South Bend: University of Notre Dame Press, 1986), 159-182 (reprinted in John Swinton, *Critical Reflections of Stanley Hauerwas' Theology of Disability: Disabling Society, Enabling Theology* [London: Routledge, 2004], 87-112).

[10] For the difference between the subjective and objective dimensions of suffering, see no. 5.

Suffering—or, better, passibility or disagreeable passibility—in its strict scholastic sense means the soul or the body's being altered from a natural state to a contrary one. For Aquinas, as for the entire patristic and scholastic tradition that he inherits (though contrary to some scholars writing on disability today), we suffer now and are subject to disagreeable passibility (whether of an affective or bodily sort) because of the introduction of sin into the world by our first parents.[11] "[S]uffering cannot be divorced from the sin of the beginnings," *Salvifici Doloris* (no. 15) observes, even if, at the same time, we ought never affirm the "direct dependence" of suffering on an individual's concrete sins. The introduction of sin into the world by our first parents explains why we find ourselves susceptible to disability or infirmity. Passibility or suffering (whether affective or bodily) did not belong to the prelapsarian state of our first parents as it issued from the creative hand of God. For this reason, Aquinas assigns passibility (suffering) to the *reatus poenae*, that is, to the state of punishment due to sin (as distinguished from the *macula culpae*, the stain of guilt).[12] At the same time, and this is important (particularly as regards the relationship between suffering and disability), passibility/suffering is from a certain point of view "natural" *(naturalis)* to us as owing to our bodily makeup or to our having a body "composed of contraries" and thus given to corruption. All the same, passibility/suffering remains a "defect" *(defectus)* and "penal" *(poenalis)* on account of the loss of the grace of original justice, whereby God made our first parents immune to all disagreeable passibility, as to all suffering.[13] In this

---

[11] Thus, Candida Moss ("Heavenly Healing," 20-21), who is severely critical of the writings of the early Church Fathers on disability for having, as she says, "utilize[d] traditions in which disability is associated with sin, and healing is equated with divine forgiveness or salvation."

[12] For more on passibility or affective suffering as a consequence of sin, see my *The Passions of Christ's Soul in the Theology of St. Thomas Aquinas* (Münster, Germany: Aschendorff, 2002; reprinted, Scranton: University of Scranton Press, 2009), 227-233. For key texts in Aquinas, see ST I q. 97, aa. 1-2; I-II, q. 85, a. 6; *De malo* q. 5, a. 5; and *II Sent* d. 19, q. 1, a. 4. This view was commonplace among the thirteenth-century Masters, as in: Bonaventure, *Breviloquium* pt. 2, ch. 10 (ed. Quaracchi, 228); Alexander of Hales, *III Sent* d. 15, n. 22 (ed. Quaracchi, 158); Albert the Great, *III Sent* d. 15, aa. 2-8. For Aquinas on passibility belonging to the *reatus poenae*, see ST I-II q. 87, a. 6; III q. 14, a. 1 and q. 22, a. 3; see as well ST I-II q. 85, a. 5: "The removal of original justice has the character of punishment, as does the withdrawal of grace. Therefore, death and all consequent bodily defects are punishments of original sin." This distinction between the punishment of sin and the guilt of sin can be found in Peter Lombard, *III Sent* d. 15, ch. 1; and d. 16, ch. 2 (ed. Coll. Bonav., 93 and 105). Translations of Aquinas's *Summa Theologiae* are, with the exception of occasional modifications per my discretion, taken from the Fathers of the English Dominican Province 1947 Benziger Bros. edition.

[13] What Aquinas says about death, then, being both "natural" and "penal" could equally be said of passibility: "Death is both natural on account of [our] condition pertaining to matter [or to our body], and penal on account of the loss of the divine

respect, suffering is practically "inseparable from [the human] earthly existence" and is "deeply rooted in humanity itself," to quote again *Salvifici Doloris* (nos. 3 and 5).

So that there be no misunderstanding when speaking of passibility or suffering (and, by extension, disability) as a "defect" *(defectus)*, it should be observed that the technical scholastic understanding of *defectus* has nothing whatsoever to do with the eugenic and utopian senses of "human defect." According to this latter, the practice of labeling people with disabilities as medically "defective" means that they may be disqualified from humanity or excluded from the social order.[14] This stands quite opposed to the Thomistic sense of defect in relation to disability. The same goes for the term *infirmitas*, infirmity, which Aquinas sometimes uses interchangeably with *defectus*, usually in reference to the body.[15]

Finally, because a Thomistic regard associates disability with suffering, that is, with a condition of functional privation, disability stands at all points in need of healing. Hence, this essay's focused attention on healing that the theological virtue of hope promises. Note that the healing hoped for will be of a functional rather than an ontological sort: namely, the body's (or the soul's) attaining to the ability to operate in the way intended by nature (the attaining to proper motor control, proper cognitive functioning, etc.). This is the kind of healing that marks the object of my daily prayer for my son Dominic. While I do not presume to know how my son will be healed in this life, the virtue of hope assures me that my prayers will indeed be answered in "the life of the world to come." On the Last Day, my son will be fully healed (as shall we all).

THE THEOLOGICAL VIRTUE OF HOPE
Longing, expectation, waiting ... in hopes of a future good

In his treatise on the theological virtue of hope in the *Summa Theologiae* II-II, qq. 17-22, St. Thomas Aquinas highlights how hope concerns God as the First Good, as the uncreated infinite Good, though

---

favor preserving man from death." ST II-II q. 164, a. 1 ad. 1. For the natural corruptibility and passibility of human life, see ST III q. 14, a. 2; and q. 15, a. 5 ad. 1 and ad. 2. Aquinas here echoes Albert the Great (*III Sent* d. 15, a. 11) and Bonaventure (*III Sent* d. 16, a. 1, q. 3 [ed. Quar.], 351). For an approach to disability that is amenable (somewhat) to looking upon disability as a defect (she prefers a "limits model"), see Deborah Beth Creamer, *Disability and Christian Theology: Embodied Limits and Constructive Possibilities* (New York: Oxford University Press, 2009).

[14] For more on the history of this, see Steven Noll and James Trent, eds., *Mental Retardation in America: A Historical Reader* (New York: New York University Press, 2004).

[15] For an interchangeable use of *defectus* and *infirmitas* in Aquinas, see his treatment of the "defects of body" co-assumed by Christ in ST III q. 14, aa. 1-4.

as not-yet attained and therefore as desirable (*bonum delectabile*).[16] This virtue, in other words, heals and perfects (as all grace heals and perfects) human desire, since hope is nothing other than a type of desire—namely, a struggled desire. In this regard, Aquinas relates this virtue to the passion of hope (whence the identical name), in that both target a future good that is difficult yet possible to obtain: a bodily good (*arduum sensibile*) in the case of the passion of hope, and which our lower animal-like sense appetitive power desires; and, in the case of the theological virtue of hope, the divine or "supra-intelligible" good *(arduum intelligibile vel potius supra intellectum existens)*— namely, the good of "eternal life, which consists in the enjoyment of God himself"—and which our higher rational appetite, the will, desires.[17]

Longing, expectation, waiting, all in view of future divine promises—this is a theme that stretches from beginning to end in the biblical witness. As the French moral theologian Michel Labourdette, O.P., reminds us, "Abraham is no less an example of hope as of faith," and hope resonates particularly in many of the psalms and in the prophets, as in Jeremiah 29:11: "For I know the plans I have for you, says the Lord, plans for welfare and not for evil, to give you a future and a hope."[18] Inaugurating a series of Wednesday-audience catecheses on Christian hope in early December 2016, Pope Francis announced in the first address: "The Scriptures show us how Christ's birth was prepared for by men and women—like Mary, Joseph, Zechariah, and Elizabeth—who never lost their trust in God's promises. May we imitate their hope, and await the coming of the Saviour, who turns the desert of our lives into a garden of delight."[19] With Christ's coming, of course, the proper and ultimate end point of God's promises—eternal life with God himself—comes into clear and direct focus.

---

[16] Aquinas also treats the theological virtue of hope in *III Sent* d. 26, in *Summa Contra Gentiles* (hereafter SCG) 3.153, and especially in *Quaestiones disputatae de Virtutibus* q. 4 (*De Spe*).

[17] Aquinas, ST II-II q. 17, a. 2; and q. 18, a. 1 ad. 1: "The object of the irascible [passion of hope] is an arduous sensible (*arduum sensibile*), whereas the object of the virtue of hope is an arduous intelligible (*arduum intelligibile*), or rather supra intelligible [namely, the divine good]." See also ST II-II q. 17, a. 1, *corpus* and ad. 1, where Aquinas maintains that the virtue of hope "is not a passion but a spiritual habit (*habitus mentis*)." For the object of the passion of hope, see ST I-II q. 40, a. 1.

[18] Michel Labourdette, *Cours de théologie morale, 9: L'espérance* (Secunda-Secundae, q. 17-22) (unpublished course notes, Toulouse, academic year 1959-1960), 10; all translations of this text are my own. These course notes have recently been published as *"Grand cours" de théologie morale: Tome 9, L'espérance*, "Bibliothèque de la *Revue thomiste*" (Les Plans sur Bex, Switzerland: Parole et Silence, 2012).

[19] Pope Francis, General audience, December 7, 2016, press.vatican.va/content/salas tampa/it/bollettino/pubblico/2016/12/07/0883/01952.html.

To be Christian, then, is to be a people of hope. It is to walk by hope. Liturgically, the season of Advent showcases in a privileged way the virtue of hope, as it occasions (for Catholics, at least) the opportunity to relive each year the longing for the coming of the Messiah, both in his first coming and in his glorious return on the Last Day. For this reason, Labourdette observes that hope concerns the imperfect state "*in via,*" our present imperfect life here below (or in Purgatory).[20] "Human hope is founded on an ontology of *not-yet-being*, [that is, on] the existential uncertainty of the human being," writes Bernard Schumacher in reference to the thought of the Thomist philosopher Josef Pieper.[21]

Hope, then, perfects human struggled desire, particularly as this desire reaches ultimately unto God himself, the infinite Good. Hope regulates our desires as we keep our sights set on eternal life. "Whatever else hope expects to obtain," Aquinas writes, "it hopes for it in reference to God as the last end, or as the first efficient cause" (ST II-II q. 17, a. 5 ad. 1). As Labourdette puts it, "The great supernatural desire of hope carries us unto the beatitude that otherwise, naturally speaking, remains out of our reach."[22] Since beatitude, that is, eternal life and the enjoyment of God, marks an end to which we are not proportioned and thus incapable of attaining on our own ("naturally speaking, out of our reach," to use Labourdette's phrase), the object of hope includes the divine assistance required for procuring this end of eternal life.[23]

Aquinas's phrase, "whatever else hope expects to obtain" (*quaecumque alia spes adipisci expectat*), casts a wide net. Labourdette puts it, "Hope also has secondary objects, in the order of the created: all those goods that are ordered to the beatifying God and which are integral to our supreme end (*finis quo*), yet which exceed our power."[24] At the top of the list would sit "the resurrection of the dead and the life of the world to come," to cite the Nicene-Constantinopolitan Creed. Put in other terms, Christian faith looks forward to the glorification of our humanity, inclusive of the body and soul's complete healing and, more particularly for the purposes of this essay, the "wiping away" of every form of suffering associated with disability (whether physical or intellectual), even if (as we shall soon

---

[20] Michel Labourdette, *L'espérance*, 17 and 45 (commentary on ST II-II q. 17, a. 1; and q. 18, a. 3).

[21] Bernard Schumacher, *A Philosophy of Hope: Josef Pieper and the Contemporary Debate on Hope*, trans. D. C. Schindler (New York: Fordham University Press, 2003), 39 and 46. Schumacher goes on to relate Pieper's ontology of *not-yet-being*, which situates the human being between the metaphysical categories of *minimal-being* and *full-being*, to the thought of Martin Heidegger and Ernst Bloch (40-46).

[22] Labourdette, *L'espérance*, 9.

[23] See ST II-II q. 17, a. 6.

[24] Labourdette, *L'espérance*, 19 (commentary on ST II-II q. 17, a. 2).

see) certain marks of disability remain. This stands at the heart of the struggled desires of those who find themselves faced with a disability, severe or otherwise, as they live with the disability and keep their sights set on eternal life. Longing, expectation, waiting, all in hopes of a future good—not only eschatological healing and glorification, but also more proximate goods, such as social inclusion and welcoming—these are known only too well by people with disabilities.

The esse incorruptibile *of the glorified body*

On Aquinas's account, eternal union with God, the *visio Dei*, is first and foremost of a spiritual nature, as God has no body. Yet, because of our hylemorphic design, whereby the human person is constituted of a body and a soul, that is, is a composite of matter joined to form (an organic body of an animal sort joined to a rational soul), the experience of complete human beatitude requires the integral presence of the body—the identical body we all possess in life. This is the fundamental metaphysical reason for belief in the general resurrection on the Last Day, when the soul will be reunited with the risen flesh after the manner of Jesus's own resurrection (and the Virgin Mary's assumption). It is a tenet of the faith: the body will share in the soul's glorification.[25]

Since, however, the *visio Dei* is primarily intellectual in nature, the body's glorification will be consequent upon the soul's glorification and, indeed, in virtue of the soul's glorification. With the soul rejoined to the body as form to matter, the glory of the beatified soul will redound or overflow into the resurrected body: "glory overflowing (*redundantem*) from a beatified soul" (ST III q. 54, a. 2 ad. 2) is how St. Thomas puts it in his description of Christ's glorified resurrected body (which shall be the cause of own bodily resurrection, as per 1 Corinthians 15:43).[26] In the treatise on hope, Aquinas writes:

> Since hope is a theological virtue having God for its object, its principal object is the glory of the soul, which consists in the enjoyment of God, and not the glory of the body. Moreover…the glory of the body is a very small thing as compared with the glory of the soul, and one who has the glory of the soul has *already the*

---

[25] For more on how our beatitude, on Aquinas's account, will only be fully realized, at least in terms of the *subject* of human beatitude rather than the *object* (God), when the soul is reunited with the risen flesh, see Bryan Kromholtz, O.P., "La perfection de la nature: la doctrine de saint Thomas d'Aquin sur la Résurrection du corps, sa réception et son développement," *Revue thomiste* 116 (2016): 57-70.

[26] For a deeper reflection upon this, particularly from a Thomistic angle, see Philippe-Marie Margelidon, O.P., *Les fins dernières, De la résurrection du Christ à la résurrection des morts* (Paris: Éditions Lethielleux, 2016, 2nd ed.). See also Jean-Pierre Torrell, O.P., *Résurrection de Jésus et résurrection des morts: Foi, histoire et théologie* (Paris: Cerf, 2012).

sufficient cause of the glory of the body. (ST II-II q. 18, a. 2 ad. 4; emphasis mine)

Explaining further what it means to say the glory of the soul "causes" the glory of the body, Aquinas writes the following:

> The incorruptible form [namely, the spiritual soul] bestows an incorruptible being on the body in spite of its composition from contraries, because in respect to corruption the matter of the human body will be entirely subject to the human soul. But the glory and power of the soul elevated to the divine vision will add something more ample to the body united to itself. For this body will be entirely subject to the soul—the divine power will achieve this—not only in regard to its being, but also in regard to action, passion, movements, and bodily qualities. (SCG 4.86)

Following a long tradition, St. Thomas, elaborating on the body's receiving an "incorruptible being" (*esse incorruptibile*) at the final resurrection extending unto its very "actions, passions, movements, and qualities," enumerates four characteristic attributes of the glorified body *qua* glorified body (or what he also calls the "spiritual" or "heavenly" body): impassibility (*impassibilitas*), agility (*agilitas*), luminosity or clarity (*claritas*), and subtlety (*subtilitas*).[27] In short, the spiritualized glorified body, which shall be numerically identical to the body we possess in this life (despite what may revert after death to nothingness through decomposition, cremation, or the like), will: *first*, suffer no injury, harm, defect (*defectus*), infirmity, debilitation, or corruption (impassibility);[28] *second*, it will enact the soul's every command and enjoy complete freedom of movement without any difficulty, hardship or hindrance (agility), as when the risen Christ

---

[27] I owe a debt of gratitude to Christopher M. Brown, "St. Thomas on the Subtlety, Spirituality, and Sexuality of the Glorified Body," Presented at the 51st International Congress on Medieval Studies, Kalamazoo, Michigan, May 13, 2016. His paper alerted me to the texts in Aquinas that treat the condition of the glorified body.

[28] "[The soul's] desire [will] be filled by the removal of every evil, for with the highest good no evil has a place. Therefore, the body perfected by the soul will be, proportionally to the soul, immune from every evil, both in regard to act and in regard to potency. This will be actually so, indeed, because there will not be in them any corruption, any deformity, any defect. It will be potentially so, however, because they will not be able to suffer anything which is harmful to them. For this reason they will be incapable of suffering (*impassibilia*)." Aquinas, SCG 4.86; see also ST Suppl q. 82, aa. 1-4; *Compendium theologiae* (hereafter *CT*) ch. 168. For the numerical identity of the risen body, see SCG 4.80-81; ST Suppl q. 79, a. 1; *CT* ch. 153; for patristic foundation of the numerical identity of the risen body, see Irenaeus of Lyon, *Adversus Haereses (Against the Heresies)*, 5.13.1; found in Anti-Nicene Fathers, vol. 1 (Grand Rapids: Eerdmans, 1950), 539.

passed through the locked doors of the upper room;[29] *third*, it will radiate brightness and beauty, as the soul's splendor will overflow into the body (luminosity/clarity, or radiance *[raggio]*, to use Dante's term from the *Divine Comedy*);[30] and, *fourth*, it will be perfectly subject to the soul (subtlety), in that the body will not hinder but share fully in the soul's spiritual enjoyment of God—which means it will not engage in the bodily activities of eating, drinking, and sexual union, as these "serve the corruptible life."[31] St. Thomas concludes,

> Just as the soul of man will be elevated to the glory of heavenly spirits to see God in His essence so also will his body be raised up to the properties of heavenly bodies: it will be luminous (*clarum*), incapable of suffering (*impassibile*), without difficulty and labor in movement, and most perfectly perfected (*perfectissime perfectum*) by its form. For this reason, the Apostle [Paul] speaks [in 1 Cor 15:40] of the bodies of the risen as heavenly, referring not to their nature, but to their glory. (SCG 4.86)

As we saw at the outset of this essay in the reference to Signorelli's *Resurrection of the Flesh* panel, one voice in the Christian tradition (a strong voice) understands the body's being "most perfectly perfected by its form [the soul]" (to use Aquinas's terms) to mean that the resurrected, imperishable body shall rise in the prime of life, that is, it shall be: fully mature, youthful, sound, whole, integral (any organs or limbs that were missing or lost through malformation or through some type of accident or violent action will be restored), and perfectly

---

[29] "[T]he soul which will enjoy the divine vision, united to its ultimate end, will in all matters experience the fulfillment of desire. And since it is out of the soul's desire that the body is moved, the consequence will be the body's utter obedience to the spirit's slightest wish. Hence, the bodies of the blessed when they rise are going to have agility (*agilia*)." Aquinas, SCG 4.86; see also ST Suppl q. 84, aa. 1-3; *CT* ch. 168.

[30] "[J]ust as the soul which enjoys the divine vision will be filled with a kind of spiritual luminosity *(spirituali claritate)*, so by a certain overflow *(quandam redundantiam)* from the soul to the body, the body will in its own way put on the luminosity of glory *(claritatis gloriae)*." Aquinas, SCG 4.86; see also ST Suppl q. 85, aa. 1-3; *CT* ch. 168. In *Paradiso*, Canto XIV, Dante affirms how our humanity will be "lovelier for being whole" when our souls are "robed about" once again in the "radiance of the flesh" (that is, in the glorified risen body) (see trans. Anthony Esolen [New York: Modern Library, 2004], 147).

[31] "[T]he soul which is enjoying God will cleave to Him most perfectly, and will in its own fashion share in His goodness to the highest degree; and thus will the body be perfectly within the soul's dominion, and will share in what is the soul's very own properties so far as possible, in the perspicuity of sense knowledge, in the ordering of bodily appetite, and in the all-round perfection of nature; for as a thing is the more perfect in nature, the more its matter is dominated by its form…. The body of the risen will be spiritual, indeed, but not because it is a spirit—as some have badly understood the point—whether in the sense of a spiritual substance, or in the sense of air or wind; it will be spiritual because it will be entirely subject to the spirit." Aquinas, SCG 4.86; see also ch. 83; ST Suppl q. 83, aa. 1-6; *CT* ch. 168.

proportional (no overweight or underweight bodies, nor disproportionately structured bodies). Influential in this regard is the following passage from St. Augustine's *De Civitate Dei*, a text that would prove seminal in western thought:

> [T]here shall be no deformity resulting from want of proportion in that state in which all that is wrong is corrected.... [A]ll that is excessive [shall be] removed without destroying the integrity of the substance.... [I]n the resurrection of the flesh the body shall be of that size which it either had attained or should have attained in the flower of its youth, and shall enjoy the beauty that arises from preserving symmetry and proportion in all its members.[32] (Augustine, *City of God*, 22.19-20)

As we already suggested, however, we have good reason to question whether Signorelli presents a somewhat one-sided, or at least incomplete, view of what the "perfectly perfected" body will be like. To be sure, as we shall see below, the same Augustine offers another passage in the *De Civitate Dei* that will serve to relativize and temper these very words of his on the perfect proportionality and symmetry of the risen body. This other passage will have significant bearing on the question of the role of disability in the risen state.

For his part, Aquinas remains a bit more circumspect in his language, preferring to lay stress on what is essential to our humanity from a metaphysical point of view. For instance, he makes clear that, given the numerical identity of the resurrected body and the essential role that sexuality plays in our nature, the biological sex that we possess in this life (inclusive of our sexual organs) will be retained in the glorified state.[33] As for the age of the resurrected body, St. Thomas gives a Christological resonance to Augustine's "flower of youth" statement:

> [A]ll must rise in the age of Christ, which is that of youth, by reason of the perfection of nature which is found in that age alone [namely, about the age of thirty]. For the age of boyhood has not yet achieved

---

[32] I believe Candida Moss ("Heavenly Healing," 18) fails to grasp the metaphysical and theological thrust of Augustine's argument when she labels his position "an intensely materialistic and physical understanding of the [general] resurrection."

[33] See SCG 4.88; and ST Suppl q. 81, a. 3, where Thomas writes: "(Humans) shall rise again of different sex. And though there be difference of sex, there will be no shame in seeing one another, since there will be no lust to invite them to shameful deeds which are the cause of shame." For an extended discussion of the metaphysics of human sexuality in the thought of Aquinas, see my *The Passions of Christ's Soul*, 147-149; see as well my "The 'Inseparable Connection' between Procreation and Unitive Love (*Humanae Vitae*, §12) and Thomistic Hylemorphic Anthropology," *Nova et Vetera* 6, no. 1 (2008): 731-764.

the perfection of nature through increase; and by decrease old age has already withdrawn from that perfection. (SCG 4.88)[34]

That our bodies should "rise in the age of Christ" is fitting (*conveniens*), and not only because Christ died in the prime of life (the age of the "perfection of nature"), but because the entire Christian life is Christo-conforming.[35] This holds especially for what shall be bestowed upon us on the Last Day. After all, as Labourdette reminds us, "In Christ's death and resurrection, the end of salvation history has been reached. Salvation is accomplished. The Parousia will be nothing other than the *manifestation* of this salvation in its ultimate consequences [inclusive of the glorification of our humanity] and in the final triumph over death."[36] Or as Pope Francis puts it in his inaugural address on Christian hope:

> Today [December 7, 2016] we begin a new series of catecheses dealing with Christian hope. In these times, when evil often seems to have the upper hand, hope comforts us with the assurance of Christ's lordship, his victory over sin, and his constant presence in our midst.[37]

Agilitas for the physically disabled

What the four aforementioned attributes of the glorified body—*impassibilitas, agilitas, claritas, subtilitas*—spell in terms of hope is awe-inspiring not only for those of us who have a physical or cognitive impairment (not to mention a mental illness, since, as Aquinas again observes, the glory of the soul will far exceed that of the body) but especially for those whose impairment (disability) is severe. Speaking as an individual who lives among and cares for a person with severe cerebral palsy, I find myself quite often meditating upon the condition of the glorified risen body. My son Dominic, for his part, expresses great excitement and joy (his eyes brighten and he breaks out into a beautiful smile) when I ask him if he looks forward to the glorification of his body, and in particular to his sharing in the attribute of *agilitas*—the attribute that is particularly relevant to his severe motor functioning impairment.

This son of mine, who moves his body with such tremendous difficulty and labor due to his cerebral palsy, often taking several

---

[34] See also ST Suppl q. 81, a. 1.
[35] For more on the how notion of *conveniens* (fittingness, suitability) floods Aquinas's Christology, see my *The Passions of Christ's Soul*, 181-188; and Gilbert Narcisse, *Les raisons de Dieu. Argument de convenance et esthétique théologique selon saint Thomas d'Aquin et Hans Urs von Balthasar* (Fribourg, Switzerland: Editions Universitaires, 1997).
[36] Labourdette, *L'espérance*, 12; emphasis his.
[37] Pope Francis, General audience, December 7, 2016, press.vatican.va/content/salastampa/it/bollettino/pubblico/2016/12/07/0883/01952.html.

minutes to accomplish the simplest of intentional bodily movements, shall one day, on the Last Day, be endowed with the attribute of *agilitas* as owing to his body's newfound *esse incorruptibile*. On that Day, he shall move his body "without difficulty and labor" (*absque difficultate et labore*), to quote Aquinas's description of *agilitas*. Of course, we shall all attain to this *agilitas* as well. And if we consider how our peak physical condition and agility in the life, wounded as it is by sin, is but a dim and clumsy trace of the *agilitas* to come, we can appreciate how especially pronounced will be the *agilitas* in those who experience here below a severe physical impairment.

For those who care for him, it is difficult to imagine Dominic moving his body "without difficulty and labor." Yet the virtue of hope promises exactly this. When we profess in the Creed that we "look forward to the resurrection of the dead," we know that this is what those who, like Dominic, live with a physical disability have to "look forward to." As indicated in the opening section of this essay, I often tell people that I pray every day for Dominic's healing. While I do not presume to know what that healing will entail on this side of the veil of death, I have the certitude of knowing that on the Last Day my prayers will be fully answered. (Labourdette reminds us that the certitude of Christian hope, while "conditional," cannot be reduced simply to subjective "wishful thinking," as the certitude of hope rests upon the objective indefectibility of the faith, that is, upon God himself, "and this cannot mislead" [see Romans 5:5]).[38] For, on that Day, my son's body will be healed, whole, and strong. Indeed, it will be glorified, and, endowed with the attribute of *agilitas* as owing to his body's newfound *esse incorruptibile*, he shall enjoy perfect motor functioning "without difficulty and labor."

The weakness of God that "shames" the strong

At the same time, as the scandal of the Cross paradoxically signifies humankind's greatest blessing, the "curse" of a disability can act as a great blessing, as almost anyone who cares for a person with a disability will attest. There is, on Joseph Ratzinger's account, a "new depth and new realism" to beauty that is revealed in Christ's suffering, given that it was incarnate Beauty itself that hung upon the Cross.[39] We find in the Cross of Christ, in other words, a reversal of an all-too limited notion of beauty, perfection, wisdom, power that otherwise

---

[38] Labourdette, *L'espérance*, 17 and 48 (commentary on ST II-II q. 17, a. 1; and q. 18, a. 4): "considered in itself, theological hope cannot err, as its foundation is indefectible.... It is not upon oneself that one counts to obtain beatitude, but solely upon God, and this cannot mislead." For a deeper Thomistic analysis of the (conditional) certitude of hope, see L.-B. Gillon, O.P., "Certitude de notre espérance," *Revue thomiste* 47, no. 2 (1939): 232-248.

[39] Again, this came in Ratzinger's "The Feelings of Things, the Contemplation of Beauty."

dominates human discourse. Because it has the power to conform one so intimately to the suffering Christ on the Cross, disability, I would argue, gives one the opportunity, through cooperation, to participate in a privileged manner in this "new depth and new realism" of beauty rooted in Christ. "[*I*]*n suffering*," John Paul II writes, "*there is concealed a particular power that draws a person interiorly close to Christ*, a special grace" (*Salvifici Doloris*, no. 26; emphasis his).

To be sure, there is a beauty of soul, apparent to nearly anyone who has eyes to see, that is commonly experienced among people with disabilities. "He was one of the most beautiful souls I have ever met in my life," Cardinal Ersilio Tonino, Archbishop of Macerata and Ravenna, once said of Venerable Luigi Rocchi (1932-1979). Stricken with muscular dystrophy that confined him to a wheelchair by the age of twenty and that made him completely immobile by twenty-eight, Rocchi exuded great joy and good cheer and would encourage others to find happiness in their impairment. "I have never seen anyone as happy as he," Cardinal Tonino said.[40] As for my son Dominic, I could easily list his many exemplary virtues and attractive qualities, beginning with his humility and heroic forbearance, his patience, his honesty and purity, his joyful and playful spirit, his boyish sense of humor and infectious smile, his bright eyes and countenance, his extraordinary tolerance and acceptance of his limitations, his eagerness to learn and to please others with his cooperation, his inspiring work ethic (physical therapists often note how they enjoy the guaranteed full effort they get from Dominic), his evident compassion and earnest empathy (he often expresses the desire to give a "hug" to a family member who is experiencing a difficult moment). Indeed, in families with a person with special needs, that person is quite often a magnet and a "light" of love and affection for everyone in the family. This has been a recurring theme in the countless conversations I have had with parents of children with disabilities. With good reason did Pope Francis, in an address at the Convention for the Disabled in June of 2016, challenge the Church to look upon people with disabilities as "hidden treasures able to renew our Christian communities."[41]

Disability united with Christ, in other words, is taken up into that grand theme of the theo-drama of salvation history where God, who "sees not as man sees," since he "looks at the heart" rather than "the outward appearance" (see 1 Samuel 16:7), accomplishes the extraordinary through the ordinary, the great through the small, the strong through the weak: "The stone rejected by the builders has

---

[40] For the story of Luigi Rocchi, see Heather King, "Credible Witnesses: Venerable Luigi Rocchi," *Magnificat*, January 2017, 91-92.
[41] "May Christian communities be 'homes' where all suffering encounters 'compassion': The Pope at the Convention for the Disabled," June 11, 2016, press.vatican.va/content/salastampa/en/bollettino/pubblico/2016/06/11/160611a.html.

become the cornerstone" (Psalm 118:22; Mark 12:10; Acts 4:11). This is the theme of the "folly of God" and the "weakness of God" that "shame the wise [and] the strong" that St. Paul, holding principally in mind the Cross of Christ, famously proclaims in 1 Corinthians 1:17-28.

When we see people with disabilities, we, who "look at the outward appearance," see limitations, weakness, and, speaking as a parent of a child with special needs (and who tends to see my relationship with my son in a one-sided manner), we see a burden and demands of time and energy. Yet, as with the Cross, these very limitations and weaknesses, these disabilities may "shame" (in the Pauline sense) those among us who are able bodied and without an identified disability, particularly when we attend to the beauty of the soul that is often found in persons with disability. In this connection, a physical-therapist friend of mine once recounted to me how his brother, diagnosed with schizophrenia, would often go out for a walk when the two of them lived together in a shady part of a southern New England city years ago. Only later did this therapist friend discover that his brother was doing this in order to help a blind woman cross busy streets so that she could get to certain stores that she needed to get to. "I felt shamed," this therapist friend told me, "since doing such a deed would never have occurred to me, nor would I have done the deed even if it had. My schizophrenic brother opened my eyes to what is most important in life and he taught me how to treat others in need." In a privileged participatory way, persons with disability can help make the reality and beauty of the Cross of Christ concretely present to those who live with and/or care for them.

"Marks of honor"

With this in mind, we should ask: will the condition of disability not somehow remain in our glorified state, no matter our longing for the Last Day when all disease and all infirmity shall be wiped away "in a moment, in a twinkling of any eye, at the last trumpet" (1 Corinthians 15:51)? On this question, it seems to me that the example of the risen Christ, who appeared with the marks of his wounds, is determinative: "'See my hands and my feet, that it is I myself; handle me, and see; for a spirit has not flesh and bones as you see that I have.' And when he had said this, he showed them his hands and his feet" (Luke 24:39-40; see also John 20:26-27). Should we not say the same of those whose disability allows them to participate in a privileged way in the sacred wounds of Christ?[42] Here is where the other passage

---

[42] For her part, Candida Moss ("Heavenly Healing," 12-13) sees opposition between the risen body of Jesus, which still bears his crucified wounds, and the "transformed" risen bodies of all at the general resurrection: "Despite the fact that the resurrection of Jesus is the prototype of the general resurrection of the dead, Jesus's own pierced

from St. Augustine's *De Civitate Dei*, which speculates on the fate of the wounds of the martyrs in the risen flesh, may prove useful.

> [T]he marks of the wounds which the blessed martyrs received for the name of Christ we shall possibly see [in their risen bodies]. For these will not be a deformity (*deformitas*), but a mark of honor, and will add luster to their appearance, as well as a spiritual, if not a bodily beauty.... [And if] some marks of these wounds [suffered by the martyrs, to the point of their losing bodily members] will still be visible in that [resurrected] immortal flesh, the places where they have been wounded or mutilated shall retain the scars without any of the members being lost. While, therefore, it is quite true that no blemishes which the body has sustained shall appear in the resurrection, yet we are not to reckon or name these marks of virtue blemishes. (Augustine, *City of God*, 22.19)

The key idea here is that since the wounds of the martyrs, on Augustine's account (as well as Aquinas's who follows Augustine here), should be considered "marks of honor (*dignitas*) [and] virtue (*virtutis indicia*)" rather than as "deformities" (*deformitas*) or "blemishes" (*vitia*), it would only be fitting that they somehow remain in the glorified resurrected state (without of course causing the least bit of suffering or discomfort), as in the case of the wounds of the risen Christ.[43] We see a faint (very faint) foreshadowing of this here below in the case of the stigmatist saints, where the crucifixion wounds granted to them possess properties that are not natural to the body. This includes the blood smelling of perfume or flowers, or the wounds never becoming infected, both of which occurred in Padre Pio's case.

Extending this line of reasoning to the various conditions of disability, we can, with good reason, affirm the real likelihood of disabilities remaining in the glorified risen state as "marks of honor" rather than as veritable disabilities (in the Augustinian sense of "deformity," *deformitas*, or "blemishes," *vitia*). After all, since disabilities grant persons who have them the opportunity to share more intimately in the suffering Christ on the Cross, these persons, when they cooperate with this "grace of the Crucified Redeemer" (as *Salvifici Doloris*, no. 26, calls it), share more profoundly in Christ's redemptive power.

In my own family's case, it seems clear to us that our son's cerebral palsy acts as the proximate instrumental cause not only of his own

---

body is not prototypical for the form of resurrected bodies." In my mind, this assertion wrongly presumes an incompatibility between the marks of wounds and a "transformed" glorified body, especially when we consider all those who experience a profound participation in Christ's suffering, whether through disability or some other form of suffering.

[43] For Aquinas's agreement, see ST Suppl q. 82, a. 1 ad. 5.

sanctification but especially of the sanctification of those around him. I recounted one time to a priest friend how a certified nursing assistant who had once cared for Dominic and who had spent a considerable amount of time with our family had gone through a conversion experience as a result of the experience. This priest immediately observed, "And it was all on account of Dominic." And this is to say nothing of the widespread impact that Dominic had on various persons around the world through his embrace with Pope Francis. This includes the mother of a child with cerebral palsy who returned to the Church after seeing the video of this embrace, as attested by Greg Burke, the current Director of the Holy See Press Office, in an interview with *Relevant Radio* on July 25, 2013. Indeed, a woman who was in St. Peter's Square at the moment of the embrace shouted to my wife immediately afterward, "Your son is here to show people how to love." *To show people how to love*—could there be a nobler vocation, a nobler path of helping to sanctify others? To be sure, our family commonly looks upon Dominic as the "saint" of our family. This does not preclude his struggles with his own spiritual shortcomings—what saint does not know such struggles? Yet his holiness, in our view, exhibits itself nearly every day we interact with him. He is, as it were and as indicated at the outset of this essay, our own St. Servulus.

It would only seem fitting, then, that our son's condition of disability (not to mention that of St. Servulus) somehow remain as a "mark of honor"(*dignitatis indicia*) in his risen body—without in any way mitigating his glorified body's *agilitas* or *subtilitas*, let alone its *impassibilitas*. Adapting somewhat St. Augustine's phrasing, we might put it as follows: "The marks of disability from which some suffered after the manner of Christ we shall possibly see in the risen body. For these will not be disabling, but will be marks of honor, and will add luster to their appearance, as well as a spiritual, if not a bodily beauty." As the scars and wounds of the martyrs shall remain present in the risen body, albeit no longer as blemishes (*vitia*) but as "beauty marks" (or "crowns" in the case of limbs lost in the act of martyrdom but restored in the risen body, as the martyred brother of 2 Maccabees 7:10-11 hopes for in regards to his tongue and hands), so too shall my son's cerebral palsy remain in his risen body. It shall remain not as a debilitating condition (*deformitas*) but as a transformed "capacitating" or "actuating" condition which he shall wear as a "crown."

Dominic's impairment will become its opposite, though still bearing a resemblance to the condition of his body as we know it now, just as the martyr's "beauty mark" will bear a resemblance to the wound inflicted on account of the faith. It will attract us for its comeliness. The *dis*ability will become something akin to a *super* ability. Like the poor man Lazarus—who was considered low in human estimation for having "received evil things" in his lifetime, such as a body "full of sores" that dogs "came and licked" as he lay at the gate of the rich man's house, but who found himself "carried by the angels to the bosom of Abraham" upon his death and who was "comforted [t]here" (see Luke 16:19-25)—so shall those beset with the "evil" of disability find themselves "comforted" with a particular glorification and radiance fitted to them in their disability-turned "mark of honor."

An eschatological pledge of full and lasting healing

We know by faith that God wants our complete healing and desires that we be free of all impairments and suffering and that he *will* heal us completely and make us whole. "God founded human nature without defect, and just so will he restore it without defect," is how Aquinas expresses this truth (ST Suppl q. 81, a. 1). Because God desires our full healing, we remain here below, I would argue, bound to work towards this healing (to the best of our abilities and respecting the bounds of reason). *God Does Not Want Us to Suffer* is how the French Orthodox theologian Jean-Claude Larchet, highlighting a central theme in Greek patristic theology, alluringly titles his manuscript on the role of affective suffering (or of human passibility as a consequence of sin) in the divine plan.[44] This theme is also found in Augustine and Boethius, as well as Aquinas, who follows closely the Greek Fathers on this point.[45] Larchet gives his work this title in order to stress that what God willed for the human family at the dawn of our existence he continues to will; namely, that God, still today, does not desire us to suffer.

As noted at the outset of this essay, we suffer now and are subject to disagreeable passibility because of the introduction of sin into the world by our first parents. Again, passibility or suffering, and by extension disability, is from a certain point of view natural to us as owing to our having corruptible bodies. All the same, it belongs to the *reatus poenae*, the state of punishment or defect due to sin and the loss of the grace of original justice. To promote healing here and now then is to participate in the final and complete healing that shall arrive on the Last Day, when corruptibility, infirmity, sin, death, indeed, when "[a]ll things are put in subjection under Christ" (1 Corinthians 15:27). God wants us to be healed, and this places upon us the duty of participating here and now in the art of healing. God wills that the art

---

[44] Jean-Claude Larchet, *Dieu ne veut pas la souffrance des hommes* (Paris: Éditions du Cerf, 2008, 2nd ed.).

[45] One key Greek Father, especially considering his impact on Aquinas, who stresses this is John Damascene; see his *De fide orthodoxa* 2.11, ed. E. M. Buytaert (New York: Franciscan Institute, 1955), 108. See also John Chrysostom, *In Matt. homil.* 74-5 (PG 58.681-5). For key passages in Augustine, see *De Genesi ad litteram* 6.25 (CSEL 28,1, 197); *Enarr. in Ps* 87.3 (CSEL 39, 1209); for Boethius, see *Liber contra Eutychen et Nestorium*, ch. 8, ed. Stewart (Loeb Classical Library, Cambridge, Mass.: Harvard University Press, 1973), 123.

of healing not belong to him alone. Granted, we do not wish to conflate health or wellness in this life, wounded as it is by sin, with the *esse incorruptibile* of the resurrected body. But it would be equally mistaken to place a hard and firm barrier between the corruptible condition of the body in this life and the body's glorified *esse incorruptibile* of the next.

Here the crucial role that healthcare practitioners—not only surgeons, but especially therapists—play in the art of healing deserves special mention. There exist, for instance, certain methods of physical therapy that seek to assist the body in its inherent structural ability to heal itself (the immediate coagulation of blood in response to the body's detection of an open cut provides a simple example of how God has structurally designed the human body to heal itself, albeit in a limited capacity). These methods take a combined "structural" and "functional," rather than exclusively functional, approach to physical therapy, one more akin to naturopathy. To be sure, the latest research from what one leading medical doctor terms "the frontiers of neuroplasticity" (that is, research on the malleability of the brain) confirms the ability of the brain to rewire itself and to create new pathways that promote healing from neurological trauma and injury.[46] My own son Dominic has for years benefited from such a structural-functional approach to physical therapy (at a place called Crossroads Physical Therapy in Columbia, Connecticut), which expressly targets neuroplastic change via its therapeutic practice. One time during treatment, for instance, a therapist placed my son's body in a position that helped to disengage the cerebellum (the part of the brain that triggers instinctive motor movements, such as occurs when one's hand touches a hot stove, and which is dominant in my son's case) and engage the frontal lobe (the part of the brain that regulates intentional motor control). This allowed my son, who otherwise exercises almost no control over the movement of his hand, to place his head in midline, hold a pen in his hand, and legibly write the first three letters of his name!

Certainly, the *agilitas* hoped for in the resurrection, commensurate with the *esse incorruptibile* of glorified state, differs in kind and not only in degree from whatever measure of health and physical well-being we can enjoy in the corruptible life here below. Still, by setting us on a trajectory that has as its proper endpoint the attainment of the *agilitas* of our glorified state, the healing that these methods of physical therapy accomplish (as, indeed, with any healing

---

[46] See, for instance, the *New York Times* Bestseller by Norman Doidge, M.D., *The Brain's Way of Healing: Remarkable Discoveries and Recoveries from the Frontiers of Neuroplasticity* (New York: Penguin Books, 2016); see as well Dr. Doidge's earlier *New York Times* Bestseller, *The Brain that Changes Itself: Stories of Personal Triumph from the Frontiers of Brain Science* (New York: Penguin Books, 2007).

accomplished by whatever method) anticipates our complete healing at the *eschaton*. While remaining transitory and unable to stave off death (the *terminus ad quem* of bodily corruptibility), such healing at the same time participates, however faintly, in the full healing that awaits, and announces the eschatological imminence of its attainment.

It is imperative for physical therapists, as for all healthcare practitioners, particularly those of Christian faith, to realize that the healing work they do is not confined to the here and now. Rather, it is caught up in a much larger project, a much grander work of healing, where God is the primary healer and they act as his secondary healers ("secondary supports, instruments of the divine Power," to quote Labourdette). For the sake of our ennoblement, God intends us to enjoy the dignity of being healers. Healthcare practitioners exercise their professional expertise in the art of healing to assist God in the healing that he will bring to completion on the Last Day.[47] Without, again, denying the limited and transitory quality of health and wellness in this life, or of the incommensurability between this life and the next, the healing that healthcare practitioners accomplish, however small in human estimation, extends by way of participation unto the *esse incorruptibile* of eternal life.

Such healing is somewhat akin, then, to the healing miracles Jesus performed during his earthly ministry. None of these miracles conferred full or lasting healing, since all who benefited from them eventually succumbed to death (including those who, like Lazarus, were raised from the dead). By prefiguring and participating in the full and lasting healing that Jesus will grant when "he come[s] again in glory," however, these miracles act as an eschatological pledge of this full and everlasting healing that awaits.[48] Addressing whether the suffering associated with physical disability or infirmity will remain in the resurrected body, the early Christian work *De Resurrectione (On the Resurrection)*, once attributed to Justin Martyr but penned instead possibly by Hippolytus of Rome or Athenagoras of Athens, seems to make this very argument.

> [I]n the resurrection the flesh shall rise entire. For if on earth He [the Savior] healed the sickness of the flesh, and made the body whole, much more will He do this in the resurrection, so that the flesh shall

---

[47] Labourdette, *L'espérance*, 28 (commentary on ST II-II q. 17, a. 4).

[48] For more on a Thomistic account of the resurrection that will occur at the time of Christ's coming in glory, with particular emphasis on the connection between Christ, the rest of creation, and the human community, see Bryan Kromholtz, O.P., *On the Last Day: The Time of the Resurrection of the Dead according to Thomas Aquinas*, "Studia Friburgensia" 110 (Fribourg, Switzerland: Academic Press Fribourg, 2010); for a shorter study of the same, see Bryan Kromholtz, "La résurrection au dernier jour selon saint Thomas d'Aquin," *Revue thomiste* 109, no. 1 (2009): 55-78.

rise perfect and entire. In this manner, then, shall those dreaded difficulties of theirs be healed.[49]

THE SINS OPPOSED TO HOPE: THE STRUGGLE WITH DESPAIR AND PRESUMPTION

As hope steers therapists and healthcare practitioners (to say nothing of family members and all those who care for people with disabilities) to work towards the full and lasting healing that awaits the *eschaton*, the two sins opposed to hope—despair and presumption—threaten to derail our struggled desires, particularly as they bear on this healing.[50] When it comes to the effort at healing the impairment associated with disability, it is easy "either to presume above one's capability, or to despair of things of which one is capable," to quote St. Thomas, who does note that hope, as a theological virtue with God as its proper object, has no *true* mean or extremes, "since it is impossible to trust too much in the Divine assistance" (ST II-II q. 17, a. 5 ad. 2). Many, of course, know the struggle with the sins of despair (the extreme of defect) and presumption (the extreme of excess), but it can be especially acute among persons with disabilities and their caregivers (I have often seen this struggle, especially with despair, when talking to parents of children with special needs). Of the two, despair, Labourdette tells us, is more grave, and "is more directly opposed to hope," while presumption marks a kind of superficial "counterfeit" of hope. Both, in any case, are characterized "by a slackening of spiritual vigor, by a reliance upon oneself or upon goods within our scope, and, correlatively, by a lack of confidence in God's help."[51]

Disability and the Sin of Despair

Aquinas observes that despair always comes in response to the concrete or the particular, so that one may continue to hope "in the

---

[49] *On the Resurrection*, found in Anti-Nicene Fathers, vol. 1 (Grand Rapids: Eerdmans, 1950), 344 (cited in Candida Moss, "Heavenly Healing," 15; Moss correctly observes that the *De Resurrectione*'s read on salvation history is one of "a history of healing"). For the case that Hippolytus of Rome is to be considered the author of the *De Resurrectione*, see A. Whealey, "Pseudo-Justin's *De Resurrectione:* Athenagoras or Hippolytus?" *Vigiliae Christianae* 60, no. 4 (2006): 420-430. For the case that Athenagoras of Athens should be considered the author, see Martin Heimgartner, *Pseudo-Justin: Über die Auferstehung,* Patristische Texte und Studien 54 (Berlin: Walter de Gruyter, 2001); this work offers the best critical edition of the text on 102-131 (otherwise the text can be found in PG 6.1572D-1592A). We should add here, no matter if the author fails to mention it or have it in mind, that this healing of the 'dreaded difficulties' does not, as argued above, preclude marks of disability from remaining as marks of honor in a 'perfect and entire' resurrected body.

[50] For more on despair and presumption, the extreme opposites of hope, in the thought of Josef Pieper, see Bernard Schumacher, *A Philosophy of Hope*, 135-147.

[51] Labourdette, *L'espérance*, 77 (commentary on ST II-II q. 20).

universal" but despair "in a particular matter."⁵² Thus, one might believe that full and everlasting healing shall be bestowed upon all in the Final Age but, as I heard one parent of a child with severe cerebral palsy once say, "Healing might be in store for others, but my son's disability is too debilitating to hope for any meaningful improvement in his condition." Following Labourdette, we should understand despair to signify "not simply the absence of hope, but a real and positive appetitive movement, though in an inverse sense: despondency and retreat, withdrawing from a good."⁵³ In the case of a physical disability, especially where the impairment is severe, this withdrawal from a good could cause one to despair of the goodness of the body.

Aquinas further remarks that since despair results from our being "excessively downcast" (*nimia deiectione*) with respect to the particular case at hand, despair issues from a deeper vicious disposition: that of acedia or sloth (*acedia*), that is, from "an oppressive sorrow" (*tristitia aggravans*) that makes us give up on the end as too great, too difficult, too troublesome, and as practically impossible (or so we deem).⁵⁴ Many of those living with disability, at least from what I have seen from my experience, know what it is like to struggle, almost on a daily basis, with the temptation to forsake healing and amelioration, in whatever small or large degree, as too

---

⁵² ST II-II q. 20, a. 2: "It may happen that a man, while having [in his intellect] a right opinion in the universal [since the intellect is about universals], is not rightly disposed as to his appetitive movement [which always moves the soul towards the particular], his estimate being corrupted in a particular matter, because, in order to pass from the universal opinion to the appetite for a particular thing, it is necessary to have a particular estimate.... Hence the fornicator, by choosing fornication as a good for himself at this particular moment, has a corrupt estimate in a particular matter, although he retains the true universal estimate according to faith, viz. that fornication is a mortal sin. In the same way, a man while retaining in the universal the true estimate of faith, viz. that there is in the Church the power of forgiving sins, may suffer a movement of despair, namely, that for him, being in such a state, there is no hope of forgiveness, his estimate being corrupted in a particular matter." As Labourdette (*L'espérance*, 78; commentary on this article) observes: "In despair, as in any sin, there is always an inconsistency, an error. But it is not at the level of universal knowledge where this error occurs..., it is in the estimation of a particular case."

⁵³ Labourdette, *L'espérance*, 16 (commentary on ST II-II q. 17, a. 1).

⁵⁴ ST II-II q. 20, a. 4: "[T]he fact that a man deems an arduous good impossible to obtain, either by himself or by another, is due to his being excessively downcast, because when this state of mind dominates his affections, it seems to him that he will never be able to rise to any good. And since acedia or sloth *(acedia)* is a sadness that casts down the spirit, in this way despair is born of acedia or sloth *(ex acedia generatur)*." Drawing upon John Damascene (*De fide orth.* 2.14), Aquinas defines acedia or sloth (in *ST* II-II q. 35, a. 1) as "an oppressive sorrow *(tristitia aggravans)* that so weighs upon a man's mind that he wants to do nothing." In q. 35, a. 2, he adds: "Sloth shuns spiritual good as toilsome *(laboriosum)*, or troublesome to the body *(molestum corpori)*, or as a hindrance to the body's pleasure."

toilsome, if not as impossible. Labourdette's observation that "[t]he slackening that is characteristic of despair arises especially from our excessive attachment to immediate bodily pleasures"[55] certainly bears out in my son's case. Daily care for my son requires constant strenuous physical effort (and he is yet only twelve years old!), so that the pleasure of bodily repose ever beckons and allures (for myself, at least) in the face of Dominic's needs. Dominic, for his part, sometimes experiences the same. Despite his body's proclivity to a sometimes-interminable hypertonia that overwhelms him and which causes him much discomfort, Dominic can, with much intentional effort, override his hypertonia and calm his motor functioning. Sometimes, though, he admits that he thinks this is too strenuous for him and that it is useless to attempt to overcome his hypertonia. In a word, he despairs.

A physical-therapist acquaintance of mine who excels at the "structural-functional" method described above once told me that, in his mind, healthcare practitioners and therapists too often limit themselves by focusing on what people with disabilities are unable to do and on the body's "corruption" (his word, which we can take in its strict philosophical sense of the body's being composed of contraries, and thus given to breaking down). This is especially so in my son Dominic's case, as he again suffers from a rather complex form of cerebral palsy, where two types of cerebral palsy are superimposed on each other. Too often, this physical therapist continued, we focus on the weakness, on the "dark," on the *dis*ability, and so aim at the lowest common denominator. This spills into a conviction of what the person "won't" do either because we despair in what can be attained or because we presume to know what the person will be able to do.

Countering despair by keeping our sights set on healing

To live by hope means, then, that we, like the God who "sees not as man sees" and who "writes straight with crooked lines" (to quote the popular Portuguese proverb), take our cue from Christ's Cross, where ultimate weakness and folly turn into ultimate strength and wisdom. Faced with disability (cerebral palsy, paralysis, multiple sclerosis, Down syndrome, autism, bipolar, etc.), hope steers us to focus on the positive, not the dark. It drives us to lay stress on strength and *a*-bility, rather than weakness, limitation or *dis*-ability. Hope impels us to aim high (as God always does), not low. "Maybe Dominic will walk someday," the theological virtue of hope leads me to say, rather than, "Dominic will never be able to walk, or hold himself up straight without assistance, or sit in midline, or...." *Fully Alive* is what Timothy Shriver, Chairman of Special Olympics and co-founder of the Collaborative for Academic, Social, and Emotional Learning

---

[55] Labourdette, *L'espérance*, 80 (commentary on ST II-II q. 20, a. 4).

(CASEL), appropriately titles his memoir on overcoming the challenges that disability in all its forms presents.[56]

To live by hope means that we (both those with disabilities and their caregivers, though the former are usually more limited in view of their impairments) embrace the moral duty to work towards the healing that God desires to accomplish through us—and which he promises to bring to completion in the Final Age. To focus for a moment on the role of caregivers in fulfilling this moral charge, my wife and I, as parents of a child with severe cerebral palsy, navigate the gambit of special services (physical therapy and otherwise) in the interests of attaining a certain degree of healing (greater mobility) for our son, in as much as the limits of finances, time, and distance allow. To do anything less would be to adopt a "quietist"-like approach to disability, where "inaction" is the defining trait, or where we renounce our secondary causal role and leave the art of healing exclusively to God. No matter the transitory and limited nature of their craft, secondary healers (whether healthcare practitioners, therapists, or any type of caregiver) remain true healers, even if dependent upon God the First Healer. At no point does secondary instrumental healing fail to participate in the larger project of healing directed by God the Principal Healer.

Hope also requires my wife and me to make prudential judgments when faced not only with the limits of finances, time, and distance, but also with attitudes of despair and presumption, not to mention prejudices, particularly among healthcare practitioners. This has required us at times, and will continue to require us, to seek out alternative sources of information, other professional opinions, and to conduct our own research and explore naturopathic alternatives. It also requires us to learn from Dominic himself, so as to gain a better grasp of his personal struggles *and* strengths, as well as the way his cerebral palsy impairs him uniquely. The goal at all points is to arrive at a critically informed judgment and to work towards the healing that God desires through our best efforts and to the best of our abilities.

With God as its proper object, the theological virtue of hope demands on our part self-abandonment to divine providence. The well-being of persons with disability rests, as does the well-being of all persons, in God's providential hands. God knows what lies in store for healing and amelioration for each of us in this life whereas we do not. He knows what awaits the development and growth of persons with disability while we do not. The lesson of Job, as *Salvifici Doloris* (nos. 10-11) points out, here remains perennial, "The Lord answered Job out of the whirlwind: 'Where were you when I laid the foundation of the earth? Tell me, if you have understanding.'" (Job 38:1-4). We

---

[56] Timothy Shriver, *Fully Alive: Discovering What Matters Most* (New York: Sarah Crichton Books, 2014).

might put it this way: Where were we when God founded human nature without defect and where were we when God raised Jesus from the dead to prove to us that he shall restore human nature without defect? Let us speak only if we have perfect understanding.

To live by hope means we take each day as it comes. I am always tempted to despair when I think too far down the road. Will Dominic ever know what it is like to play on a playground? Will he get a "normal" education and go to college? Will he get married? How will he function in today's world, and who will care for him when my wife and I are unable to? What shall we do when he is too heavy to carry? My wife and I do what is best for our son today to the best of our abilities, and we leave the rest to God, particularly with regard to the future, all with a proper attitude of spiritual detachment.

To this end, Dominic is himself an example to both of us. Let me say it again: he exhibits a remarkable tolerance and acceptance of the severe limits of his motor functioning. While he loves to be around his siblings when they are playing, he almost never expresses frustration that he is unable to play alongside them. He is rather content simply to be present with them—though his siblings involve him in their play marvelously in whatever way they can and no matter the effort this requires. In short, Dominic feels loved, and I am sure that this largely accounts for his contentment simply to be present with his siblings alongside their activity. If he experiences the temptation to despair via the type of questions that tempt my wife and me, he does not show it.

Disability and the Sin of Presumption

We move to presumption, or what we might call, with Aquinas, "inordinate hope" (*spes inordinata*),[57] or again, with Labourdette, "counterfeit hope" (whereas despair would qualify as deficient or inadequate hope). Following Aquinas, we can distinguish two rather different types of presumption. The first arises from pride or vanity (*inanis gloria*), that is, from an excessive reliance upon oneself or upon an inflated and false estimation of one's abilities, and which counters especially the moral virtue of magnanimity. Magnanimity regulates the passion of hope according to the good of reason by directing human action toward noble works and purposes, though with due regard for one's abilities. The second type of presumption, which is of a more properly theological sort, also arises from pride. This type of presumption consists in an "inordinate trust in the Divine mercy or power," as it leads one to hope to obtain "glory without merits, or forgiveness without repentance."[58] For Labourdette, this type of

---

[57] ST II-II q. 21, a. 2.

[58] ST II-II q. 21, a. 4: "Presumption is twofold; one whereby a man relies on his own power, when he attempts something beyond his power, as though it were possible to him. Such like presumption clearly arises from vainglory; for it is owing to a great

presumption induces one to think that when standing before the judgment seat of God, "all obstacles shall collapse, like the walls of Jericho, and that God can only but hold the person in high esteem."[59]

Of the two types of presumption, the first one, I think, more directly concerns people with disabilities and their caregivers. If it is easy to succumb to despair when faced with a disability, it is no less easy for those living with a disability to presume that little or nothing is expected from them because of their impairment or to presume a right to special consideration or to a lower moral standard, almost as if they are exempt from the fallen condition of the human family. As for caregivers, it is no less easy to trust too much in one's estimation of what the person with a disability needs or doesn't need, to trust too much in modern medicine or in the opinion of medical doctors, to trust too much in the human ability to overcome disability and to obtain complete (or near complete) healing. If human agents can act as secondary causes of healing, they remain all the same *secondary* healers and act as such only in the measure by which they are moved by the First Cause of healing. This is to say that outside the Principal Healer, they cause no healing. Labourdette once again sounds the key notion here when he explains that whatever help the divine Assistance uses as instruments in the obtaining of our end, God, to whom "all other assistance adds nothing," remains "the only proper and specifying reason for our hope…. The All-Powerful helper is immediately proportioned, as efficient Cause, to the end to which hope tends."[60]

This holds especially for attaining full and everlasting healing, as owing to the *esse incorruptibile* that shall be bestowed upon the body. The divine Power alone can accomplish this, given that attaining to an *esse incorruptibile* exceeds the body's natural principles. The sin of presumption would consist, for example, in healthcare practitioners acting as if healing depended primarily (rather than secondarily or instrumentally) upon them and their expertise.[61]

---

desire for glory, that a man attempts things beyond his power, and especially novelties which call for greater admiration…. The other presumption is an inordinate trust in the Divine mercy or power, consisting in the hope of obtaining glory without merits, or forgiveness without repentance. Such like presumption seems to arise directly from pride, as though man thought so much of himself as to esteem that God would not punish him or exclude him from glory, however much he might be a sinner."

[59] Labourdette, *L'espérance*, 83 (commentary on ST II-II q. 21, a. 1). As for the gravity of the two sins relative to each other, if despair is worse, it is because, as Labourdette observes, presumption "attains to God less directly than despair: the judgment that it complies with is less false, as it is more proper to God to forgive than to punish, for forgiving and fulfilling are proper to God on account of himself (the infinite Good), whereas punishing is proper to God only on account of our sins."

[60] Labourdette, *L'espérance*, 28-29 (commentary on ST II-II q. 17, aa. 4-5).

[61] For Labourdette (*L'espérance*, 85; commentary on ST II-II q. 21, a. 4), if pride incites "the flowering of presumption, it is not simply because it exalts the idea one

Presumption of the first type: an inflated estimation of one's expertise

While my wife and I have benefitted over the years from the services of some rather exceptional medical doctors and healthcare practitioners in the treatment of our son, we have also seen pride and vanity spilling into presumption emerge all too commonly among healthcare practitioners (especially surgeons and medical doctors). (Pride, on Labourdette's account, signifies "the disordered desire for one's own excellence, the desire not simply to appear superior, but to be superior, to hold oneself above the limits of one's created condition," whereas vanity denotes "the disordered desire both to appear and to be honored and praised.")[62] Too often, for instance, medical doctors hold the views either of the parents of children with disabilities or of the adults with disabilities in little esteem, despite the fact that no one has a better handle on these persons than the parents (in the case of disabled children) or the persons themselves (particularly in the case of adults). Harboring an inflated estimation of their expertise, these doctors can assert this expertise in a somewhat dismissive and authoritarian manner, as if expecting to be blindly obeyed. Not infrequently, they can show little interest in the input and informed feedback of the parents or of the disabled adults, and they display little tolerance for their judgments being questioned or outright called into question by the parents or by these adults.

Medical doctors can also presume, based upon an excessively specialized (and thus narrow) perspective from their field, that a certain course of action marks the optimal (if not only) course of action for a respective attempt at improving, to whatever degree, the impaired condition. Once a highly respected orthopedic surgeon prescribed a certain surgical procedure for our son's hip condition that horrified many of his physical therapists, given the grave trauma and potential long-lasting functional setbacks it would likely cause. Another time, several professional nutritionists insisted that the exclusive use of a gastrointestinal tube was strictly required to overcome a quite severe digestive issue our son had developed. Yet, as my wife and I soon discovered afterward through our own research, it was possible to heal our son's gastrointestinal tract, and by that means resolve his digestive issues, through following a regimen based solely on whole foods (a kind of food therapy, as it were). While rather slow in showing its beneficial effects and quite labor intensive in preparation (one nutritionist even counseled us to put our son on a feeding tube not because it was better for him, but because it made our lives easier),

---

has of one's proper strengths, but because it diminishes the feeling of one's need for God and of the necessity of his help."
[62] Labourdette, *L'espérance*, 85.

this whole-foods-based regimen did in fact, at the length of three years, restore our son to perfect digestive health. A certain well-respected pediatrician, seeing our son only one time, which was at the low point of his decline from his digestive disorder, and without knowing anything of his history or seeking any detailed information of his condition from my wife and me, wrote a formal letter after the visit with a veiled threat of contacting Child Protective Services for neglect, given our son's dangerously low weight! Many times subsequent to the restoration of our son's digestive health, my wife and I have remarked on how tragic it would have been had we taken away the pleasure of eating from our son by putting him on a feeding tube. If we often mention this, it is not only because persons on feeding tubes clearly do not thrive, let alone enjoy vim, vigor and vitality, but because our son, who is deprived of countless bodily pleasures on account of his cerebral palsy and who has a fierce appetite as a result of the burning of calories through hypertonia, takes great delight in the pleasures of eating "real" (especially savory) food! This is not to deny that a gastrointestinal tube may offer the appropriate course of action in certain instances, but, too often, such a course of action is too hastily prescribed and sometimes for insufficiently valid health reasons (such as to ease the burdens of one's family life).

In short, and without again taking anything away from those truly exceptional medical practitioners, it is not uncommon for medical professionals, harboring an inflated estimation of their knowledge and expertise, to presume to know what persons, especially children, with disabilities need or do not need, what these children will or will never do, what they will or will not be like, whether five years from now or fifty. The same can hold for parents who presume to know the needs of their children. This is purely and simply to play God, since it usurps the knowledge and "expertise" that are proper to God. "God is the real healer," a physical therapist, truly exceptional in his field, once said to me, "and so who are we to say what a child with a disability will or will never do? Since we cannot know how God will heal a person, I believe it is incumbent upon me as a physical therapist never to utter the word 'never' in reference to a child's accomplishing such or such a task."

Presumption of the second type: downplaying the gravity of human shortcoming

We can encounter presumption in the face of disability among the Church's ministers as well. I once was speaking to a priest who was the chaplain of a diocesan office that provides catechesis and sacramental ministry to persons with intellectual and developmental disabilities. Speaking of the sacrament of reconciliation, he told me he thought it was sufficient to offer general absolution to persons with intellectual and developmental disabilities, since it was unclear if such persons were truly guilty of committing actual sins, thereby voiding (in his mind) their need for individual confession. This position, it seems clear to me, commits the sin of presumption of the second type, that of placing an inordinate trust in God's mercy by downplaying the gravity of human sin.

Sparing no criticism, the moral theologian Stanley Hauerwas does not hesitate to castigate this view for the "sentimental" way by which it both "rob[s]" persons with disabilities of their moral agency, and thus of their "right" to sin (even mortally), and "forget[s] that there is no more disparaging way to treat another than to assume that they [particularly those with disabilities] can do nothing wrong."[63] Like all human persons, people with disabilities remain children of Adam who have inherited original sin and who thus stand in need of Christ's healing grace. No member of the human race gets a pass on the moral and spiritual struggles that are part and parcel of our fallen condition.[64] To be sure, persons with disabilities are like everyone else potentially aware of their moral failings, particularly if they have been instructed well, even if such failings are merely occasional and venial. Our son Dominic, for instance, makes it clear to us that he would very much like to go to confession when we offer the opportunity to him, and we know from his priest confessors (without their breaking the seal of confession) that Dominic possesses an acute sense of his moral shortcomings. The need for and right to individual one-on-one confession should, then, not be denied to persons with disabilities.[65]

Presumption of the first type and the model of exclusion or segregation

In the field of disability, there emerges another approach that I believe falls prey to that first type of presumption bred of

---

[63] Stanley Hauerwas, "Having and Learning to Care for Retarded Children," in *Truthfulness and Tragedy: Further Investigations into Christian Ethics* (South Bend: University of Notre Dame Press, 1977), 147-156; reprinted in John Swinton, *Critical Reflections on Stanley Hauerwas' Theology of Disability*, 149-159 (from which the current citation is taken on p. 157). The larger citation goes as follows: "[H]eroic stories can lead us to forms of sentimental care and protection that rob these children of the demands to grow as they are able.... [T]o care for these children as if they are somehow specially innocent...is to rob them of the right to be the same kind of selfish, grasping, manipulative children that other children have the right to be.... We forget that there is no more disparaging way to treat another than to assume that they can do nothing wrong." The reader should note that while this essay of Hauerwas, originally published in 1977, uses terminology (like "retarded") that has since become infelicitous, it would be inappropriate to use today's lexical standard to hold this against Hauerwas.

[64] For support, see Romero, "The Happiness of 'Those Who Lack the Use of Reason,'" 49-96.

[65] For a Thomistic argument in support of this, Romero, "Aquinas on the *corporis infirmitas*," 101-151.

overestimation of human knowledge and ability, where we presume to know what is best for persons with disabilities, especially children. We might call it the practice of exclusion or segregation, and we see it exhibited in sacramental administration, in the educational arena, as, indeed, in general quotidian living. It consists in placing persons with disabilities into their own separate groups, such as in a school, in the presumed view of what best meets the educational and social needs of those with disabilities. All the students with moderate to severe disabilities are placed together in a classroom set apart from the other children, with little or no interaction with the rest of the student population and where they receive exclusive "special" education.

On its face, though, this practice signals the message that persons with disabilities inhabit their own isolated sphere of activity, disconnected from the larger human population (that of the able bodied or able minded), without the need for integration with this larger population. It fosters an attitude of "us versus them" and it reinforces negative stereotypes. Despite our foregoing praise of its chairman Timothy Shriver, the Special Olympics provides a high-profile example of a segregated program (without denying its creating an opportunity for competition that otherwise would not exist). As one such published criticism noted in its opening salvo, "Despite decades of research, advocacy, and program development, most adults with severe disabilities live lives of segregation."[66] Not surprisingly, we have learned that this model works not in the best interests either of those with disabilities or of the larger human population. And why should it, since too often it leads the able bodied (or the non-disabled) to ignore, neglect, shut out, and refuse to be confronted by those who live with a disability?

When the able bodied *are* confronted or brought into direct contact with disability, they can find themselves "disturbed" and shaken out of their moral "comfort zone." They find themselves confronted by the existential reality of human weakness and limitation, to which none are immune. It is not unlike how the image of a crucifix, characterized by its disturbing gruesomeness, confronts us with the dreadful reality of human sin. Yet, if the crucifix confronts us with terrible suffering and death, at the same time it confronts us with the highest expression of virtue, holiness, and love. To quote again Cardinal Ratzinger: "The One who is Beauty itself let himself be slapped in the face, spat upon, crowned with thorns.... However, in his Face that is so disfigured, there appears the genuine, extreme

---

[66] Keith Storey, "The More Things Change, the More They Are the Same: Continuing Concerns with the Special Olympics," *Research & Practice for Persons with Severe Disabilities* 33, no. 3 (2008): 134-142.

beauty: the beauty of love that goes *'to the very end'*."[67] Similarly, and as already observed in connection with Pope St. Gregory the Great's preaching on St. Servulus, the virtues and the beauty of soul of persons with disability often convict those around them in their vices and ugliness of soul, in their moral turpitude.

Practicing the model of inclusion or integration

We gain much, then, when we observe the model not of exclusion or segregation, but of inclusion or integration.[68] More to the point of this essay, the theological virtue of hope, I would submit, places upon us the moral duty of practicing this model, as it counters the presumption that can so often engender the practice of exclusion or segregation.[69] Most families shaped by the experience of disability live the model of inclusion or integration naturally and so know firsthand its virtues. When I see how my other children interact with my son Dominic, how they treat him as one of the family, how they joke with him, how they include him in so many of their activities and prove that disability can be experienced as a "normal" feature of life, how they respond to him when he is in need, sometimes by intuition or even anticipation, and especially how they exhibit special love and affection for him, I consider how fortunate and blessed they are to have a brother with a severe disability and how fortunate and blessed he is to have such siblings. I see, in other words, how crucial a role he has played in the development of their character and their sense of humanity *and* how crucial a role they have played in the development of his character by meeting his physical, affective, intellectual, developmental, social, and spiritual needs. This extends beyond the home. Whenever my children find themselves in a public setting with other individuals with disabilities, they hardly seem to notice the disability and interact naturally and comfortably with these persons as if they were able-bodied.

For the purposes of this essay, I would propose that we observe, in the interests of living according to hope, sacramental inclusion, educational inclusion, and quotidian inclusion.[70]

---

[67] Joseph Ratzinger, "The Feelings of Things, the Contemplation of Beauty"; emphasis his.

[68] Much literature on this model abounds, but M. Will, *Supported Employment for Adults with Severe Disabilities: An OSERS Program Initiative* (Washington, D.C.: Office of Special Education and Rehabilitative Services, 1984) defines it as implying "regular access [for people with disabilities] to interactions with individuals without identified handicaps and regular use of normal community resources."

[69] Labourdette (*L'espérance*, 83 [commentary on ST II-II q. 21, a. 1]) observes that the presumption that arises from an inflated estimation of one's knowledge and abilities is typically of a properly natural and moral, rather than theological sort.

[70] For references to official Church documents and resources, see Miguel J. Romero, "Profound Cognitive Impairment, Moral Virtue, and Our Life in Christ," *Church Life* 3, no. 4 (2015): 80-94.

Sacramental inclusion

As for the first, no less an authority than Pope Francis has offered his public support for this approach to disability. In his address to the Convention for the Disabled in June of 2016, Pope Francis challenged Catholics "to help the vulnerable be fully part of our community" through their practice of "true inclusion and full participation that becomes ordinary and normal," noting in particular that "the decisive place for the inclusion of the disabled is [in] their admission to the Sacraments": "the Christian community," he insisted, "is called to work to allow every baptized person to experience Christ in the Sacraments."[71] Calling "for broader integration of persons with disabilities into the full life of the Church," the United States Conference of Catholic Bishops, for its part, has offered guidelines on the administration of the sacraments to people with disabilities, as well as a statement on "access and inclusion" of persons with disabilities.[72]

Sacramental inclusion works best, I would submit, when we treat persons with disability in sacramental practice and administration as we treat persons without disabilities. If, following Pope Francis, this means that we admit them to the sacraments, this should be done with due diligence and at the standard ages, particularly in regards to the sacraments of initiation.[73] I know parents of a girl with Down syndrome who did not know what to do about their daughter's First Communion. And so, with their parish priest offering no express encouragement to see her through instruction and reception, they let it tarry some years beyond what is standard. I also know a forty-year-old Catholic man with severe cerebral palsy who has yet to receive the sacrament of confirmation for the same reason. Failure to admit persons with disabilities with due diligence to the sacraments risks committing that type of presumption which places an inordinate trust in God's mercy by downplaying the human need to experience Christ in the Sacraments. Such failure downplays the human need for the grace of justification and the deifying power of the sacraments.[74]

---

[71] Pope Francis, "May Christian communities be 'homes,'" November 6, 2016, press.vatican.va/content/salastampa/en/bollettino/pubblico/2016/06/11/160611a.html.

[72] USCCB, "Guidelines for the Celebration of the Sacraments with Persons with Disabilities," 1995, www.usccb.org/beliefs-and-teachings/how-we-teach/catechesis/upload/guidelines-for-sacraments-disabilities.pdf; and USCCB, "Welcome and Justice for Persons with Disabilities: A Framework of Access and Inclusion," 1998, www.usccb.org/upload/justice-persons-disabilities-bulletin-insert.pdf.

[73] On the administration of the sacrament of confirmation, Canon 890 of the 1983 Code of Canon Law stipulates: "The faithful are bound to receive this sacraments at the proper time."

[74] In Aquinas's sacramental theology, the grace of the sacraments, the *res tantum*, acts as both healing medicine and divinizing power, that is, it acts as "a remedy against sin" and as "strength to do and wish supernatural good." See ST III q. 63, a. 1: "[T]he

Integrating persons with disability into the sacramental life of the Church also means observing the liturgical and sacramental norm whenever possible, and not to depart from this norm needlessly. Some persons with disability may need special assistance, which may require creative adaptations where necessary, all the while respecting the bounds of sacramental and liturgical propriety. At all points though, we should strive to have these persons participate *with* and *alongside* the faithful gathered in liturgical worship. We should, in as much as is practicable, avoid setting people with disabilities apart or treating them differently from the non-disabled. This latter can occur, say, when they are removed from the rest of the congregation during the Liturgy of the Word at Mass in order to experience their own "special-needs" Liturgy of the Word. I know one diocese that organizes this as an integral part of their ministry to the disabled. In my own son's case, I will, for instance, have him sit with me in the pew (one for the physically disabled) at Mass rather than leave him in his chair. I stand him when it is time to stand, sit him alongside me when is time to sit. While this may demand exertion on my part (some Sundays more than others), not to mention constant handling, it better "includes" and integrates Dominic in the communal celebration of the Mass. He tells me he much prefers this to remaining in his chair during the entire Mass.

As for the sacrament of reconciliation, what my family does with Dominic provides a good example, I think, of what I mean by "creative adaptations, where necessary." To repeat, Dominic bears no cognitive impairment, and, while his ability to communicate verbally is quite limited, he can respond with a clear yes or no (such as when we ask him if he wants to go to confession, which always elicits an enthusiastic affirmative). We have Dominic receive the sacrament of reconciliation by having a priest friend of the family come to our house and go into a room with him (Dominic remains in his seat positioning chair). The first time this happened, the priest had been to our home many times, had interacted with Dominic a fair bit, and could thus

---

sacraments of the New Law are ordained, first, as a remedy against sin and, second, for the perfecting of the soul in things pertaining to the divine worship." This is even clearer in I-II q. 109, aa. 2 and 5: "[I]n the state of corrupt nature, [man needs a gratuitous strength added to natural strength, i.e., he needs sanctifying grace] in order to be healed, and in order to do and wish supernatural good [and thus] to carry out works of supernatural virtue.... [Indeed, since] everlasting life is an end exceeding the proportion of human nature... a higher force is needed, namely, the force of grace." See also ST I-II, q. 112, a. 1. For more on deification in the thought of Thomas Aquinas, see Daria Spezzano, *The Glory of God's Grace: Deification according to St. Thomas Aquinas* (Washington, D.C.: Catholic University of America Press, 2015); Jean-Pierre Torrell, O.P., *Saint Thomas Aquinas,* Vol. 2: *Spiritual Master,* trans. Robert Royal (Washington, D.C.: Catholic University of America Press, 2003), 126-128; and Luc-Thomas Somme, O.P., *Thomas d'Aquin, La divinisation dans le Christ* (Geneva: Ad Solem, 1998).

devise certain questions to ask him (with my wife and me, knowing our son's struggles, providing ideas of possible questions). Following a practice that priests often perform with penitents who struggle in knowing what to confess, this priest also went through an examination of conscience with Dominic as befitting a boy his age. Without providing us with specifics (which the seal excludes, of course), this priest was able to tell us that his experience with Dominic in this sacrament was a powerful and rather edifying moment in his (young) priesthood, as "for the first time" he felt like he was truly communicating directly with Dominic. He assured us that Dominic clearly understood what he, the priest, was asking and that Dominic had a distinct idea of what he wanted to confess. After reviewing with him what he understood Dominic to be saying, the priest received confirmation from Dominic that his understanding was accurate. Dominic corrected him at least once. The priest proceeded to ask if he was missing anything, and, after Dominic replied in the affirmative, the priest asked a series of questions until Dominic made it clear everything had been covered. When Dominic emerged from the room with the priest, he was quite noticeably proud of his accomplishment and of having been able to partake in the same sacrament that everyone else in the family (including his younger twin sisters) had partaken in. Our son has the need for the sacrament of confession, he wants to go to confession, and he wants to experience it like anyone else to the degree that he can. We are happy to accommodate these needs.

All the same, the priest in this anecdote and the recommendations of Pope Francis notwithstanding, there remains a noticeable need for many of the Church's pastors, particularly at the parochial and diocesan levels, to take more of a leadership role in offering creative and responsive ways of meeting the sacramental needs of persons with disability. Naturally, this type of pastoral concern sits more at the forefront of the minds of the family members who care for persons with disability. Still, a conscientious pastor who knows his flock well should always make sure that his parish members with disabilities never "slip through the cracks," particularly in the administration of the sacraments of initiation, or be otherwise neglected and marginalized. Here special mention must be made of the way the National Catholic Partnership on Disability, which works in close tandem with the United States Conference of Catholic Bishops, has helped make advancements on all these fronts at the national level of the Church in the United States.[75]

---

[75] See the website of the National Catholic Partnership on Disability (www.ncpd.org) for all its resources and accomplishments.

Educational inclusion

As for the model of educational inclusion or integration, in which informed choice and self-determination play a crucial role, we have learned that children with intellectual and developmental disabilities learn best not when segregated into isolated groups, into "special-education" classrooms, with little or no interaction with the general student population, but when included in the "regular" classroom setting—though with the requisite special, one-on-one services that meet their needs being provided to them. To repeat, this serves to the benefit of the general student population as well, since it leads students without an identified disability to encounter those with disabilities as genuine persons and not simply as "the kid in the chair." It fosters the experience of a "common humanity."

A film called *Including Samuel* captures this beautifully.[76] In it, Keith, a man in his forties with cerebral palsy, who looks back at the inadequacies of the special-education services he received in the 1970s for how they segregated him and consistently lowballed his educational abilities. As he expresses it, he got tired of gluing popsicle sticks and, instead, found himself wanting to shout out, "Hey, how about some math over here! I'd like to learn some math!" For my part, I have noticed a similar pattern with my son. Because of the severity of my son's physical impairment, many will assume he suffers from a corresponding cognitive impairment (which he does not). So instead of reading books befitting his age to him, care providers will sometimes read young children's books to him. It goes without saying that as a twelve-year-old boy with no cognitive impairment, Dominic likes to hear stories that interest a typical twelve-year old boy, not a six-year old boy or girl.

No less an authority than the U.S. Department of Education, reviewing the legal provisions of a Free and Appropriate Public Education (FAPE) for students with disabilities as stipulated by the Individuals with Disability Education Act (IDEA) and the Rehabilitation Act of 1973, mandates the model of inclusion (albeit without calling it that), as it asserts on its website: "Students with disabilities and students without disabilities must be placed in the same setting, to the maximum extent appropriate to the education needs of the students with disabilities."[77] The Learning Disabilities

---

[76] This film can be found at www.includingsamuel.com/film.

[77] U.S. Department of Education, Office for Civil Rights, "Free and Appropriate Public Education for Students with Disabilities: Requirements Under Section 504 of the Rehabilitation Act of 1973," www2.ed.gov/about/offices/list/ocr/docs/edlite-FAPE504.html: "The Section 504 regulation requires a school district to provide a 'free appropriate public education' (FAPE) to each qualified person with a disability who is in the school district's jurisdiction, regardless of the nature or severity of the person's disability.... An appropriate education may comprise education in regular classes, education in regular classes with the use of related aids and services, or special

Association of America, for its part, puts the notion of educational inclusion or integration this way: "'Full inclusion', 'full integration', 'unified system', 'inclusive education' are terms used to describe a popular policy/practice in which all students with disabilities, regardless of the nature or the severity of the disability and need for related services, receive their total education within the regular education classroom in their home school."[78]

Quotidian inclusion

Inclusion or integration extends to all areas of life, to quotidian life. I have been sensitive to this since my high-school days, as my older quadriplegic brother always wanted to be treated and included like everyone else. As for my son Dominic, I observed above how my other children naturally include him in all areas of our domestic life. To them, Dominic is simply a member of the family (albeit with severe limitations), not so much a boy with cerebral palsy.

A formative experience for a physical-therapist acquaintance of mine helps to illustrate this model of inclusion in everyday life. When this physical-therapist acquaintance was yet in high school, a good friend and classmate of his suffered a stroke. Paralyzed in one entire half of his body, the friend was told by his doctors that he would never use that side of his body again. Practicing the model of recreational inclusion by intuition, this physical therapist and his other classmates, when they would gather to play basketball, would situate their classmate who had suffered the stroke alongside the court in a chair and place a ball under his paralyzed arm. The motivation of wanting to join his classmates on the court was enough for this person to begin

---

education and related services in separate classrooms for all or portions of the school day. Special education may include specially designed instruction in classrooms, at home, or in private or public institutions, and may be accompanied by related services such as speech therapy, occupational and physical therapy, psychological counseling, and medical diagnostic services necessary to the child's education.... To be appropriate, education programs for students with disabilities must be designed to meet their individual needs to the same extent that the needs of nondisabled students are met. An appropriate education may include regular or special education and related aids and services to accommodate the unique needs of individuals with disabilities.... Students with disabilities and students without disabilities must be placed in the same setting, to the maximum extent appropriate to the education needs of the students with disabilities.... As necessary, specific related aids and services must be provided for students with disabilities to ensure an appropriate education setting. Supplementary aids may include interpreters for students who are deaf, readers for students who are blind, and door-to-door transportation for students with mobility impairments.... The requirements for FAPE under *IDEA* are more detailed than those under Section 504."

[78] Learning Disabilities Association of America (2012), "Full Inclusion of All Students with Learning Disabilities in the Regular Education Classroom," www.ldaamerica.org/advocacy/lda-position-papers/full-inclusion-of-all-students-with-learning-disabilities-in-the-regular-education-classroom/.

moving his arm again. "If you saw him today," this physical-therapist acquaintance finished by telling me, "you would never know he was paralyzed, let alone that his doctors had told him that he would never overcome his paralysis." Time and again, the model of inclusion or integration has shown that the developmental and functional challenges that persons with disabilities face can be heroically overcome through commonplace interaction with peers and the larger community.

Conclusion

I close this essay by returning to the image of Pope Francis embracing my son. By providentially orchestrating an embrace between the Holy Father and my son Dominic on Easter Sunday, God, I believe, made an eschatological promise to him and to all those with disabilities—indeed, to all of us. Easter Sunday marks, as it were, the feast of the glorification of the body, of how Christ's bodily resurrection points toward and anticipates the Final Age when our own corruptible bodies will be healed and made whole in full vigor and glory as owing to the *esse incorruptibile* that will be bestowed upon them. On the Last Day, Dominic—along with my quadriplegic brother, as well as you and me with our own infirmities, whether of a physical, emotional, or intellectual sort—will be healed. His body, our bodies, and our souls will be "made new" (Revelation 21:5). They will be made whole and healthy. Our bodies will be glorified. They will be radiant.

Those who profess the Christian faith live in hope of this. To that end, let us take to heart the words of St. Paul, who writes the following as if addressing the quandary of a loving God permitting innocent ones, like children with disabilities or anyone with a particularly onerous disability, to suffer: "I consider that the sufferings of this present time are as nothing compared with the glory that is to be revealed to us" (Romans 8:18). May these words ever echo in my ears whenever I look upon my son Dominic and ponder how the myriad of ways he in his cerebral palsy suffers impairment here below anticipates the glory that shall be his in "the life of the world to come." When we behold him in that glory, he will be radiant not in spite of or in absence of his disability, but *in and through* his disability. The marks of his disability shall remain, as they will testify to his having shared intimately in the Cross of Christ. Like the risen Christ with his glorified wounds, my risen son will shine with the glorified signs of his disability, albeit his disability-turned mark of honor.

It is imperative that we hold on to hope and not live with disability out of fear, sorrow, despair, or presumption. At all points, we need to recall that our stories, particularly the stories of those with disabilities, are not fully written yet. The ending shall be written on the Last Day, when all disease, all infirmity, all chronic conditions will be wiped

Disability, the Healing of Infirmity, the Virtue of Hope 111

away "in a moment, in a twinkling of any eye, at the last trumpet." Yet what shall not be wiped away is the beauty of these selfsame sufferings, in the measure that such beauty reflects the beauty of Christ's own suffering. While we yet labor under the consequences of sin and suffer our fallen condition, we must never fail to recall that whatever healing we experience now is partial and is but a foretaste of the healing yet to come. Faith in the glorified risen body professes faith in a God who, never intending us to suffer, yet permits our suffering, if only because in the Final Age we shall be glorified through our suffering.

St. Servulus, pray for us! 🅼

Seventeenth-Century Casuistry Regarding Persons with Disabilities: Antonino Diana's Tract 'On the Mute, Deaf, and Blind'

Julia A. Fleming

IN 1639, THE FAMOUS THEATINE casuist Antonino Diana published the fifth part of his *Resolutiones morales*, a volume that included a tract regarding the mute, deaf, and blind.[1] Structured as a series of cases (i.e., questions and answers), its form resembles tracts in Diana's other volumes concerning members of particular groups, such as vowed religious, slaves, and executors of wills.[2] While the arrangement of cases within the tract is not systematic, they tend to fall into two broad categories, the first regarding the status of persons with specified disabilities in the Church and the second in civil society. Diana draws the cases from a wide variety of sources, from Thomas Aquinas and Gratian to later experts in theology, pastoral practice, canon law, and civil law. The tract is thus a reference collection rather than a monograph, although Diana occasionally proposes a new question for his colleagues' consideration.

"On the Mute, Deaf, and Blind" addresses thirty-seven different cases, some focused upon persons with a single disability, and others, on persons with combination of these three disabilities. Specific cases hinge upon further distinctions. Is the individual in question completely or partially blind, totally deaf or hard of hearing, mute or beset with a speech impediment? Was the condition present from birth

---

[1] Antonino Diana, *Resolutionum moralium pars quinta* (hereafter *RM* 5) (Lyon, France: Sumpt. Laurent. Durand, 1639), 161-172 (tract 6). All citations to the works of Diana in this article rely upon volumes digitized by Google. For background on Diana's theology, see Santo Burgio, *Teologia barocca: Il probabilismo in Sicilia nell'epoca di Filippo IV* (Catania, Italy: Società di Storia Patria per la Sicilia Orientale, 1998); Pierre Hurtubise, *La casuistique dans tous ses états: de Martin Azpilcueta à Alphonse de Liguori* (Ottawa, Canada: Novalis, 2005), 35-37,125-137.

[2] On slaves, see Antonino Diana, *Resolutionum moralium pars septima* ... (hereafter *RM* 7), Editio Secunda Veneta (Venice: Apud Franciscum Baba, 1650), 141-165, (tract 7); on religious, see Antonino Diana, *Resolutionum moralium pars tertia...* (*herafter RM* 3) (Lyon, France: Sumptibus Jacobi Prost, 1633), 21-69 (tract 2); on executors of wills, see Antonino Diana, *Resolutionum moralium pars octava...* (hereafter *RM* 8) (Lyon, France: Haered. Petri Prost, Philippi Borde, & Laurentii Arnaud, 1647), 366-407 (tract 5).

or did it develop later, as the result of illness or injury? Do the subject's intellect, education, or communicative skills offset his or her sensory deficiencies? When taken as a whole, Diana's collection of cases provides a fascinating window into Early Modern Roman Catholic assessments of the capacities and responsibilities of this group of disabled persons.

Why should Diana's tract interest Catholic ethicists focused on "engaging disability" today? First, the collection illustrates at least some of the practical questions that arose during the seventeenth century when pastors, missionaries, religious superiors, and magistrates interacted with the disabled, or, in some cases, became disabled themselves.[3] It also indicates the range of expert opinions on the appropriate resolution of these practical issues. Considering Diana's tract thus enhances our appreciation of the history of Roman Catholic ethical engagement with disability.

Moreover, the tract provides evidence for several significant conclusions regarding Roman Catholic casuistry's approaches to the disabled during the early seventeenth century. First, Early Modern Roman Catholic casuistry recognized and acknowledged the capacities of the disabled, in both the religious and the civil spheres, even though persons' disabilities excluded them from some positions of authority. Second, seventeenth century casuists assumed that mute, deaf, and blind Catholics had responsibilities within the Church, as lay Christians, vowed religious, or members of the clergy. Third, this collection of casuistry demonstrates that Early Modern pastoral practice and civil law provided some accommodations for the disabled, both to enable them to fulfill their ordinary responsibilities and to avoid the imposition of unfair burdens upon them. In fact, one may reasonably argue that the implicit concern behind Diana's treatise—as evidenced by the cases he proposes and the resolutions he supports—is to safeguard the participation of the disabled within the Church and civil society in light of their capacities for moral agency.

To provide a context for my interpretation of Diana's tract, this paper begins with a brief introduction to the meaning and historical situation of Roman Catholic casuistry in the seventeenth century, before turning to Diana's life and his literary project, the *Resolutiones morales*, and the place of "On the Mute, Deaf, and Blind" within that work. This background grounds the paper's central claims that the tract reflects seventeenth century Roman Catholic casuistry's acknowledgment of the capacities and responsibilities of the hearing, seeing, or vocally impaired, and its consideration (albeit to a much

---

[3] I deliberately use the word *some* because Diana was not systematic in his approach. He makes no claim to have compiled all the relevant cases regarding this sub-group of the disabled.

lesser degree) of the accommodations necessary to allow them to fulfill their responsibilities.

The paper concludes with a brief and admittedly provisional introduction of three topics for further investigation, i.e., questions that experts in disability ethics might wish to develop, in dialogue with Diana's text. These questions concern the significance of personal histories and circumstances for the analysis of disability; the application within disability ethics of the distinction between an alternative means and an unduly burdensome means of fulfilling one's responsibilities; and finally, the value of the situation of the disabled as a lens for theological analysis. Ultimately, however, any inspiration that this tract can offer for contemporary theologies of disability arises from its central presumption that the mute, deaf, and blind are members of communities and, thus, that questions about their modes of participation in those communities presuppose a web of existing relationships with their fellow human beings, fellow believers, and fellow citizens.

CASUISTRY AND CASUISTS IN THE FIRST HALF OF THE SEVENTEENTH CENTURY

Early Modern Roman Catholic casuistry was the art of resolving cases of conscience, questions regarding the identification of appropriate and inappropriate Christian practices.[4] Such questions were often ethical problems in the modern sense. For example, is it legitimate to use deadly force in self-defense? However, they could also concern devotional practices, such as Jubilee indulgences or the maintenance of private oratories.[5] Finally, Roman Catholic casuistry often addressed problems of sacramental administration and pastoral jurisdiction.[6] By their nature, many cases of conscience involved the application of canon law.

Casuists were experts in the principles and precedents necessary to resolve these practical dilemmas of the Christian life. They evaluated extant cases, drawn from earlier theologians or from their own contemporaries. New problems, such as the significance of chocolate consumption or tobacco use for the Eucharistic fast, also drew their

---

[4] For a general introduction to the concept of casuistry, see Albert R. Jonsen and Stephen Toulmin, *The Abuse of Casuistry: A History of Moral Reasoning* (Berkeley: University of California Press, 1988); and Hurtubise, *La casuistique dans tous ses états*, 13-23.

[5] Diana discusses indulgences and Jubilee in *RM* 5, 317-340 (tract. 12). A tract on private oratories appears in *Resolutionum moralium pars nona...* (hereafter *RM* 9) (Venice, Italy: Apud Iuntas & Baba, 1650), 1-32 (tract. 1).

[6] On the broad meaning of the term *mores*, especially at the Council of Trent, see John Mahoney, *The Making of Moral Theology: A Study of the Roman Catholic Tradition* (Oxford: Clarendon Press, 1989), 120-135.

comments.[7] Well-known casuists such as Diana might add cases that came to their attention when someone asked for their opinion, either in person or by letter. Casuists thus served as ethical consultants for political leaders as well as private individuals. The Spanish crown created councils of theologians, "customarily assembled to pronounce where questions of conscience impinged on matters of state."[8] Casuists even debated whether accepting money for giving their opinions constituted simony (the selling of holy things).[9]

In discussing cases, the casuist's principle role was to identify, outline, and evaluate the various solutions proposed for a particular practical question. His greatest responsibility was to distinguish options that were acceptable in practice from those that were not (e.g., because they had been rejected by central Church authorities or because of weaknesses in the arguments and expert endorsements that supported them). Naturally, professional opinions sometimes differed, especially in their assessment of the comparative strength of the various alternatives. By the end of Diana's career, such disagreements had blossomed into a full-fledged methodological dispute regarding the sufficiency of probable opinion as a warrant for action.[10] While a casuist might, and often did, assert the superiority of one option over the others, he educated those involved in the formation of consciences by outlining positions other than his own, particularly those he regarded as safe in practice.

As Pierre Hurtubise points out, the production of works of casuistry was very much a growth industry in the Early Modern period, especially in the seventeenth century, which saw the publication of more than 750 volumes on the subject.[11] Significantly, the market for works of casuistry extended beyond the clerical elites, as evidenced by the popularity of condensed versions of texts like Diana's *Resolutiones morales*.[12] The ecclesiological impetus for this extensive interest in casuistry was the Council of Trent's teaching on

---

[7] See Diana, *RM* 5, 142, 341-343 (resol. 11; resol. 1). Because a single page often includes more than one case, I will include the number of the specific case resolution in parenthesis after the page numbers in my citations, unless the reference is to a tract in its entirety.

[8] J.H. Elliott, *The Count-Duke of Olivares: The Statesman in an Age of Decline* (New Haven: Yale University Press, 1986), 227.

[9] See Diana, *RM* 5, 388 (resol. 4).

[10] On this history, see Jean Delumeau, *L'aveu et le pardon: Les difficultés de la confession XIIIe-XVIIIe siècle* (Paris: Fayard, 1990), 123-149; Jean-Louis Quantin, *Le rigorisme chrétien* (Paris: Les Éditions du Cerf, 2001), 71-106; Julia Fleming, *Defending Probabilism: The Moral Theology of Juan Caramuel* (Washington, D.C.: Georgetown, 2006), 4-7, 14-19; Jonsen and Toulmin, *The Abuse of Casuistry*, 164-175; Mahoney, *The Making of Moral Theology*, 135-43; and Burgio, *Teologia barocca*, 136-180.

[11] Hurtubise, *La casuistique dans tous ses états*, 25-31.

[12] See Hurtubise, *La casuistique dans tous ses états*, 36-37.

private confession, especially its insistence that penitents confess their sins according to number and species (i.e., according to frequency and type of sin committed).[13] This last requirement necessitated the education of confessors skilled in classifying sins, given the complicated taxonomy of wrong actions operative within Roman Catholic moral theology. The emphasis upon confession as an instrument for the formation and discipline of the laity during this period also heightened the importance of casuistry, as an educational tool for Church reform.[14]

An added challenge for the conscientious bishop, religious superior, or confessor arose from the post-Tridentine expansion in central Church regulations, particularly surrounding the administration of penance, a development that one can trace in Giovanni Pittoni's *Constitutiones pontificiae et romanarum Congregationum decisiones ad confessarios utriusque cleri spectantes*, published in Venice in 1715.[15] While Pittoni identifies only 221 rulings regarding penance between 1023 and 1563 (the year in which the Council of Trent ended), he cites over 500 papal or congregational decisions on the subject issued between 1564 and September of 1628, when Diana received permission to publish the first two installments of the *Resolutiones morales*.[16] There would be another 200 such rulings by the end of Diana's literary career.[17] Helping to keep confessors abreast of these developments became another service that casuists such as Diana could provide.

Not all casuistry, of course, was intended for the same audience or served the same authorial purpose. For example, some casuistry appears within textbooks for the author's students, as in the works of Juan Azor, S.J.[18] Naturally, works aimed at students include a great

---

[13] See Council of Trent, Session 14, 25 November 1551, canons 7-9, and ch. 5, *de confessione* in Norman P. Tanner, S.J., ed., *Decrees of the Ecumenical Councils, Vol. II, Trent to Vatican II*, ed. (London: Sheed and Ward, 1990), 712, 705-707. See also the comments of Mahoney, *The Making of Moral Theology*, 22-26.

[14] See Adriano Prosperi, *Tribunali della coscienza: Inquisitori, confessori, missionary,* nuove ed. (Torino, Italy: Piccola Biblioteca Einaudi, 2009).

[15] Giovanni Pittoni, *Constitutiones pontificiae et romanarum Congregationum decisiones ad confessarios utriusque cleri spectantes* (Venice, Italy: Leonardus Pittonus Collectoris Pater, 1715).

[16] Pittoni, *Constitutiones pontificiae*, 1-76, 76-218. One can determine the dates on which Diana received permission to publish by consulting the unnumbered preliminary pages of each volume. Volume 1 of the 1636 Venice edition (hereafter, *RM* 1), *Resolutiones morales in quatuor partes distributae* ... (Apud Franciscum Baba), reprints the 1628 permissions on a such a page under the heading "*Approbationes.*"

[17] By September of 1655, Diana's Superior General gave permission for the publication of Volume 12. See Antonino Diana, *Resolutionum moralium pars duodecima* ... (hereafter *RM* 12) (Venice: Apud Franciscum Baba, 1657), untitled preliminary page (no heading); and Pittone, *Constitutiones pontificiae*, 218-275.

[18] On Azor, see Hurtubise, *La casuistique dans tous ses états*, 106-112.

deal of what one might describe as stock casuistry or standard casuistry, i.e., settled cases discussed simply to educate the reader. By contrast, one can also find volumes of casuistry that are really illustrations of ethical theory, as when Juan Caramuel developed his *Theologiae Praeterintentionalis* around cases largely drawn from Diana's *Resolutiones morales*.[19] As we shall see, Diana was neither an academic nor a theorist. His goal was to provide a reference collection for knowledgeable colleagues.[20] Virtually his entire literary corpus concerns the resolution of cases of conscience.[21]

Antonino Diana, the Theatines, and the Resolutiones morales

Unfortunately, there is no biography, either Early Modern or recent, to flesh out the basic outline of Diana's personal history. Born in Palermo in 1585, Antonino Diana was the child of a noble Sicilian family with a history of involvement in city governance, and in service to the Spanish Inquisition.[22] His educational background is presently a matter of conjecture, but five vernacular poems, created in his adolescence, but published near the end of his life in another author's anthology of Sicilian verse, suggest that he received humanistic training.[23]

Apparently, Diana was already a priest when he entered the Congregation of Regular Clerics (commonly known as the Theatines) in 1614 or 1615.[24] This was a new religious community, founded in

---

[19] Juan Caramuel, *Theologia Praeterintentionalis* ... (Lyon: Sumptibus Philippi Borde, Laurentii Arnaud, Petri Borde, & Guillemi Barbier, 1664).

[20] See Hurtubise, *La casuistique dans tous ses états*, 128, 135.

[21] Diana, *RM* 9, 389-419, contains a text of Diana's that had originally been a separate work: *De primatu solius D. Petri, ac differentia inter ipsum et D. Paulum, disceptationes apologeticae*. On its publication history, see Antonio Francesco Vezzosi, *I scrittori de' Cherici Regolari detti teatini, parte prima* (Rome: Sacra Congregazione di Propaganda Fide, 1780), 313.

[22] For brief accounts of his career, see Gaetano M. Cottone, C.R., *De scriptoribus venerabilis domûs divi Josephi Clericorum Regularium urbis Panormi...* (Palermo: ex Typographia Angeli Felicella, 1733), 12-38; and Antonino Mongitore, *Bibliotheca sicula, sive de scriptoribus siculis...* (Palermo: ex Typographia Didaci Bua, 1707), 45-47. Both digitized by Google. See also Paolo Portone, "Diana, Antonino," *Dizionario biografico degli italiani Treccani* (Rome: Instituto della Enciclopedia Italiana Treccani, 1991), 39:645-647. On the family, see Filadelfo Mugnos, *Teatro genologico delle famiglie nobili, titolate, feudatarie ed antiche nobili del fidelissimo regno di Sicilie viventi ed estinte* (Palermo: Pietro Coppola, 1647), 329-330. For references to two members of the Diana family, including Antonio Guiscardo de Diana, a doctor of both civil and canon law, as familiars of the Inquisition in Palermo in 1561, see Francesco Giunta, *Dossier inquisizione in Sicilia: l'organigramma del Sant'Uffizio a metà del Cinquecento* (Palermo: Sellerio, 1991), 46, 47.

[23] Pier Giuseppe Sanclemente, *Le muse siciliane, overo, Scelta di tutte le canzoni della Sicilia* (Palermo: Giuseppe Bisagni, 1662), Part 2, Vol. 1, 84-87. Digitized by Google. See also Cottone, *De scriptoribus venerabilis*, 12.

[24] On the sources for the two different dates, see Vezzosi, *I scrittori de' Cherici Regolari detti teatini*, 301, n. 3.

1524 by four members of the Roman branch of the Oratory of Divine Love who had concluded that they could best serve the confraternity's goal of fostering lay piety, sacramental devotion, and participation in the corporal works of mercy by creating a new religious order that would model these practices for ordinary Christians.[25] Drawing inspiration from the monastic model that Augustine had created for his clergy at Hippo, the new group's members lived in community and recited (rather than sang) the liturgy of the hours. Their pastoral ministries included care of the sick, preaching, and hearing confessions. New members of the community typically were clerics seeking a stricter way of life and a reformed model of living out their pastoral vocation.[26]

Created as a community subject to the pope and to their own elected superior, the Theatines collaborated with the Vatican on a number of important projects following the Council of Trent. Members of the order, for example, were involved in the revision of the Vulgate, the Roman breviary, and the missal.[27] By the time that the community reached its centenary, it had produced forty-five bishops.[28] Much of this influence was the legacy of the most famous of the group's original founders, Gian Pietro Carafa, who promoted the order after his election to the papacy in 1555. (The name *Theatine*, in fact, reflects Carafa's one-time position as bishop of Chieti, one of the two episcopal offices that he resigned when the order received formal Vatican recognition).[29] As the community's first Superior and, later, as Pope Paul IV, Carafa exercised significant influence over the Theatines' development, especially since the group did not create a constitution until early in the seventeenth century.[30] Moreover, the agenda of Paul IV, the promulgator of the Roman Index, the creator of the Roman ghetto, and the hardline opponent of any concessions to Protestantism, inevitably affected the image and self-understanding of the religious community that he had helped to create.[31]

Until the seventeenth century, the Theatines did not expand beyond Italy. Despite their influence within the Italian ecclesiastical orbit, their numbers remained small. The first Theatine house in Palermo,

---

[25] For background on the Theatines, see Kenneth J. Jorgensen, S.J., "The Theatines," in *Religious Orders of the Catholic Reformation: In Honor of John C. Olin on His Seventy-Fifth Birthday*, ed. Richard L. DeMolen (New York: Fordham University Press, 1994), 1-29; and William V. Hudon, *Theatine Spirituality: Selected Writings* (New York: Paulist Press, 1996), 1-29.

[26] See Jorgensen, "The Theatines," 10-11, 13, 14, 18-19; Hudon, *Theatine Spirituality* 17, 21, 22-23.

[27] Hudon, *Theatine Spirituality*, 27.

[28] Jorgensen, "The Theatines," 18.

[29] Hudon, *Theatine Spirituality*, 20-22, 27, 29.

[30] Jorgensen, "The Theatines," 3, 5, 8-9: Hudon, *Theatine Spirituality*, 23-26.

[31] Jorgensen, "The Theatines," 5-7, 16-18.

Diana's birthplace, was established in 1602, and S. Giuseppe, the house in which he would later be admitted to the community, was founded a year later.[32]

In light of the present investigation, it is interesting that Diana required special accommodations from his order's General Chapter in 1630 before he could become a full voting member of the Theatines, since ill health precluded him from participating in some of the ordinary responsibilities of the community.[33] Evidently, he had provided alternative service by concentrating upon his studies in standards for Christian practice. In the preface to the first volume of the *Resolutiones morales*, he tells that reader that he has served as a consultant regarding moral problems in Palermo for many years.[34] Various volumes of his text refer to consultations with political authorities in his native city.[35] The work's title page also identifies Diana as a consultor for the Spanish Inquisition, operative in Sicily, then a possession of the Spanish Hapsburgs, as part of the tribunal of Aragon.[36] The responsibilities of this (unpaid) appointment would have included giving advice about whether there was sufficient evidence or legal grounds to justify an arrest or torture of someone suspected of heresy and providing similar advice about the punishment of those convicted.[37] Diana eventually addressed a number of cases regarding the Inquisition within the fourth volume of the *Resolutiones morales*.[38]

In 1628, Diana, by then in his late forties, received permission to publish the first installment of what would become his life's literary project. In his preliminary message to the reader, Diana provides important clues for interpreting the work, in reference to both its intended audience and its purpose. Diana begins with the conceit that his reader has already expended great energy in the study of moral questions and has wandered, overworked, through a variety of prolix

---

[32] Marcella Campanelli, *I Teatini*. L'Inchiesta di Innocenzo X sui regolari in Italia, ed. Giuseppe Galasso (Rome: Edizioni di Storia e Letteratura, 1987), 68; Vezzosi, *I scrittori de' Cherici Regolari detti teatini*, 301.

[33] Vezzosi, *I scrittori de' Cherici Regolari detti teatini*, 301-302; Hurtubise, *La casuistique dans tous ses états*, 126.

[34] Diana, *RM* 1, unnumbered preliminary page, "Auctor ad Lectorem."

[35] See, for example, Diana, *RM* 5, 343 (resol. 2); Antonino Diana, *Resolutiones moralium pars secunda...* (hereafter *RM* 2) (Lyon, France: Sumpt. Iacobi Prost, 1633) 76 (resol. 67). See the last paragraph of this resolution.

[36] On the tribunal in Sicily, see William Monter, *Frontiers of Heresy: The Spanish Inquisition from the Basque Lands to Sicily* (Cambridge: Cambridge University Press, 1990), 164-185; and Henry Charles Lea, *The Inquisition in the Spanish Dependencies: Sicily—Naples—Sardinia—Milan—The Canaries—Mexico—Peru—New Granada* (New York: Macmillan, 1922), 1-44.

[37] Antonino Diana, *Resolutionum moralium pars quarta ...* (hereafter *RM 4*) (Venice: Apud Franciscum Baba, 1636), 229, 190, 202- 204 (res. 11; res. 25; res. 7, res. 8).

[38] See Diana, *RM* 4, 163-258 (tracts 5-8).

tomes.[39] This compliment to the reader, in fact, reflects an important characteristic of the text: Diana is writing for those who already have a background in the discipline rather than for students or neophytes. He presumes that the reader will understand the background for the cases he discusses so that there is no need for a preliminary excursus into foundational issues in theology, sacramental practices, or canon law. This presumption also allows Diana to move straight into the controversial cases without a systematic review of the settled cases relevant to their resolution. In reading Diana, it is important to remember that his targeted audience member is the expert rather than the novice.

What, then, does Diana offer to such a knowledgeable reader? In essence, the *Resolutiones morales* is a reference book, the distillation of his vast research into complex questions of moral theology, sacramental administration, and canon law. It is also a précis of alternative moral assessments of these questions, predominantly drawn from recent or contemporary sources.[40] While the cumulative scope of the *Resolutiones morales* is vast, Diana's treatment of individual cases is often very short, so that a single page might well present several cases. In an interesting acknowledgment of his own ongoing disability, Diana tells the reader that both ill health and his other responsibilities would have precluded him from composing an extensive analysis of particular moral questions, even if he were inclined to pursue such a project. What he hopes to provide instead is a guidebook to resolutions for complex problems of Christian practice, the strongest arguments surrounding them, and their most important advocates.[41]

In writing for his fellow casuists, Diana takes care to expose the range of possible options for the conundrums under consideration. In some cases, he asserts, truth and natural law mandate a single course of action from which any deviation would be wicked. In other cases, however, God allows greater scope for human freedom, so that the prudent have more than one responsible choice. Diana is particularly concerned to identify the "more benign [*benigniores*]" alternatives for his readers, to aid them in receiving confessions or resolving others' perplexities. They must not, he warns, attack God's supreme impartiality and the "sweet yoke [*suaveque...iugum*]" of divine law.[42]

Whatever Diana's original hopes or intentions for his work, the publishing records of the *Resolutiones morales* testify to its influence

---

[39] See Diana, *RM* 1, "Auctor ad lectorem."
[40] See Hurtubise's comments regarding Diana's sources, *La casuistique dans tous ses états*, 133-36. However, I would note that this tract includes several references to Aquinas and to Gratian. See Diana, *RM* 5, 162, 167, 172 (resols. 2, 3, 18, 20, 35).
[41] Diana, *RM* 1, "Auctor ad lectorem."
[42] Diana, *RM* 1, "Auctor ad lectorem."

and success. Printers in Lyon, Rome, Venice, Madrid, Antwerp, Munich, and Paris (among others) released versions of Diana's volumes.[43] Within five years, Diana's work had also given rise to condensed versions, which continued to be published—sometimes with Diana's approval and sometimes to his dismay—both during and beyond their author's lifetime.[44]

For the next twenty-eight years, Diana continued to publish installments of the *Resolutiones morales*.[45] Later volumes followed the same basic format as the first, with very brief presentations of individual cases combined into tracts. Diana often returned to cases that he had considered in earlier volumes, updating the analysis and describing new discussions of the case or other writers' responses to his positions.[46] Over time, this meant that multiple volumes could contain treatments of the same question. Diana never systematically revised the entire work. Others would undertake this effort after the last volume of the *Resolutiones morales* appeared, and it was more than another decade before this mammoth collection was published, several years after Diana's death.[47]

Diana's move to Rome in 1637 encouraged his scholarly work, even though he undertook other responsibilities for his order and for the Vatican, where he served as an examiner of bishops under Urban VIII, Innocent X, and Alexander VII.[48] From Pope Innocent, to whom Diana dedicated the seventh volume of the *Resolutiones morales*, the Theatine purportedly received both personal approbation and financial support for his research.[49] In his account of Diana's work, the Theatine Gaetano Maria Cottone includes a long catalogue of laudatory references to the author of the *Resolutiones morales* taken from their own writings or preserved in the records of the Theatine community

---

[43] See Vezzosi, *I scrittori de' Cherici Regolari detti teatini*, 307.

[44] Compare the statement of approbation from Diana that appears within the *Summa Diana* of Antonio Cottoni (published with the compiler's name listed under the anagram *Ausonio Noctinot*) with Diana's warning against the early abridged version of Jean de Val. For the first, see the last page of the unnumbered preliminary address "lectori benevolo" in *Summa Diana ... pars prior* (Lyon: Sumptib. Haered. Prost, Borde, & Arnaud, 1644). For the second, see *RM* 1, where Diana's warning appears on the unnumbered page "*Auctor ad lectorem*," under the heading: "*Iterum auctor lectori benevolo.*"

[45] See Vezzosi, *I scrittori de' Cherici Regolari detti teatini*, 304-307.

[46] For an example of this regarding a case discussed in "On the Mute, Deaf, and Blind," see note 96.

[47] See Vezzosi, *I scrittori de' Cherici Regolari detti teatini*, 307-309.

[48] See Hurtubise, *La casuistique dans tous ses états*, 127; Vezzosi, *I scrittori de' Cherici Regolari detti teatini*, 303-304.

[49] See Vezzosi, *I scrittori de' Cherici Regolari detti teatini*, 306; Mongitore, *Bibliotheca sicula*, 1:45-46.

in Palermo.[50] By any standard, Diana enjoyed great success for most of his career.

Ironically, Diana is probably best known today as one of Pascal's targets in the *Provincial Letters* and, more broadly, as one of the writers associated with the controversies over probabilism and laxism that dominated the history of Roman Catholic moral theology in the second half of the seventeenth century.[51] However, it is important to note that many of these events post-date Diana's publishing career, since the last volume of the *Resolutiones morales* appeared in the same year that Pascal began to release his satirical epistles.[52] While Diana certainly lived to see the beginnings of these controversies, he never responded to them in print. Indeed, the dedicatory epistle to Alexander VII at the beginning of volume 12 makes many references to Diana's age and his failing health.[53] The deterioration of his eyesight made him incapable of the intensive reading demanded for the production of the *Resolutiones morales*.[54] Diana died in Rome in 1663, less than a decade after his last volume's publication.[55]

The Tract "On the Mute, Deaf, and Blind"

Diana's tract "On the Mute, Deaf, and Blind," appears within *Resolutiones morales* 5, the first volume published after its author's move from Palermo to Rome. Neither the tract itself nor the volume's introductory message to the reader provides any clues about what inspired Diana to take up these questions. While one can sometimes connect the production of a tract in the *Resolutiones morales* to a particular book that had drawn Diana's interest (or his ire), the cases in "On the Mute, Deaf, and Blind" seem to have come from a wide variety of sources.[56] Even the tract's placement in the volume provides

---

[50] See Cottone, *De scriptoribus venerabilis*, 16-38.

[51] See Quantin, *Le rigorisme chrétien*, 54-70; and Jonsen and Toulmin, *The Abuse of Casuistry*, 156-57, 248; Jean-Pascal Gay, *Morales en conflit: Théologie et polémique au Grand Siècle (1640-1700)* (Paris: Les Éditions du Cerf, 2011), 37, 183-184, 194, 566-567, 789, 803.

[52] On Pascal's impact, see Gay, *Morales en conflit*, 171-202; Burgio, *Teologia barocca*, 154-159; Quantin, *Le rigorisme chrétien*, 71-106; and Jonsen and Toulmin, *The Abuse of Casuistry*, 231-249.

[53] See Diana, *RM* 12, unnumbered page with the heading, "*Alexandro VII P.O.M.*"

[54] See Hurtubise, *La casuistique dans tous ses états*, 134, n. 17; Juan Caramuel, *Apologema pro antiquissima et universalissima doctrina, de probabilitate...* (Lyon: Sumptibus Laurentii Anisson, 1663) 10, 92.

[55] See Mongitore, *Bibliotheca sicula*, 1:46; Vezzosi, *I scrittori de' Cherici Regolari detti teatini*, 304.

[56] See the first tract in Diana, *RM* 5, which is clearly directed against Mario Cutelli's *Codicis legum Sicularum libri iv ...* (see page 1, resol. 1).

no assistance, since "On the Mute, Deaf, and Blind" follows the tract on parvity of matter and precedes the tract on scandal.[57]

But if Diana's motivations remain a mystery, the cases themselves give us grounds to speculate about another important issue: who would have benefited from having answers to the questions that Diana poses in this tract? The most obvious audience for such information is the pastor seeking to respond to the needs of a disabled parishioner, especially in reference to sacramental administration. Perhaps the tract's cases regarding wills and donations would also have been of special interest to pastors, who often witnessed or recorded deathbed testaments during this period.[58] But one can also imagine many of these cases arising in the context of a dialogue—a dialogue, for example, between a pastor and the parents of a disabled child regarding the child's status in the Church and civil society and the vocational options available to him or her. Moreover, in at least two cases, a disabled person clearly initiated the exchange that became the basis for Diana's reflections. Thus, disabled persons, their caretakers, and their pastors appear as potential beneficiaries of the options that the tract outlines.

Yet, there is another group that might also have been particularly interested in Diana's analysis: those in the process of going deaf or blind. At least a quarter of the tract's cases ask whether those who have become disabled are still obligated to perform their former duties and whether they remain eligible to fulfill particular roles (e.g., reciting the breviary, celebrating mass, serving as judges, voting in elections for religious superiors).[59] In an age without cataract surgery or hearing aids, debilitating loss of vision and hearing were no doubt familiar specters of the aging process. Diana lost his sight in the last years of his life; so, later, did his friend Juan Caramuel, the bishop of Vigevano, who managed to conceal his blindness in one eye from his clergy until he lost sight in the other.[60] In the seventeenth century, as in the twenty-first, progressive disability must have been a painful adjustment, both for the disabled and for their caregivers. For religious superiors, consideration of an aging community member's rights and responsibilities might well have been a common preoccupation. Thus, in addition to addressing the needs of the currently disabled, Diana's

---

[57] Diana, *RM 5*, 137-160, 173-194 (tracts 5 and 7). This is by no means unusual for Diana, who follows no evident system in the arrangement of his tracts.

[58] On the role of Catholic priests regarding wills in seventeenth century France, see S. Amana Eurich, "Between the Living and the Dead: Preserving Confessional Identity in Early Modern France," in *Defining Community in Early Modern Europe*, ed. Michael J. Halvorson and Karen E. Spierling (Aldershot: Ashgate Publishing, 2008), 43-61 at 45-46.

[59] Diana, *RM 5*, 166-167, 172 (resols. 13-22, 36).

[60] See Julián Velarde Lombraña, *Juan Caramuel: vida y obra* (Oviedo, Spain: Pentalfa, 1989), 374.

tract addressed future problems that persons could anticipate, in the face of either their own progressive disabilities or the decline of those for whom they were responsible. In contrast to some of his other tracts, which addressed a comparatively narrow band of human experience, "On the Mute, Deaf, and Blind" considers problems that extend across the life cycle.

INTERPRETATION OF THE TRACT

Any effort to interpret Antonino Diana's tract "On the Mute, Deaf, and Blind," as evidence for seventeenth century casuistry's engagement with issues surrounding these disabilities must begin with three important clarifications regarding the project. First, although Diana is the compiler of the tract, he is not the formulator of the cases, except perhaps in one instance.[61] Thus, the tract is a record less of Diana's own speculations about disability than of what he found, and judged to be of interest, in the writings of others. Obviously, Diana chose the cases, responded to the arguments proposed, and combined them into a unit of his broader literary work, but one must not treat the text as if it articulated the reflections of a single author. In a sense, this makes the work more interesting, since it reveals the arguments and disagreements among a broad group of experts over questions of disability.

Second, Diana was not systematic in choosing his cases and targeted his work toward knowledgeable professionals rather than neophytes. As we have noted, this allowed him to move directly into analyzing the cases that posed the greatest challenge, without reviewing related cases.[62] But it also means that many practical questions regarding interactions with the disabled may be missing from this tract, precisely because Diana assumed that his intended audience already knew the answers. Diana's work is thus a better guide to complex cases regarding the disabled than to the resolution of obvious ones.

Third, unlike many other Christian casuists, Diana never composed works of spiritual or systematic theology that would provide a framework for interpreting his case resolutions or, indeed, his interpretation of disabilities. The *Resolutiones morales* includes no explicit presentation on theological anthropology.[63] Thus, the interpreter cannot hope to offer an analysis of Diana's thought relevant to a theology of disability comparable to Miguel J. Romero's

---

[61] See Diana, *RM* 5, 163-164 (resol. 7).
[62] Notice, for example, that the first case in the tract concerns a deaf-mute adult from the New World who requests baptism (Diana, *RM* 5, 161). Diana never asks whether the case would be different for a deaf-mute adult raised in a majority Christian culture (e.g., a Jew raised in the Roman ghetto).
[63] See Hurtubise, *La casuistique dans tous ses états*, 131.

interpretation of Aquinas.[64] Indeed, the most theoretical speculation regarding disability in Diana's tract comes from medicine rather than theology, as he discusses physicians' hypotheses about whether those born deaf are necessarily incapable of speech.[65] Diana's theological presumptions about disability remain implicit. The sources figuring most prominently in this tract are precedent and practical experience, as Diana (and the writers upon whom he relies) invoke the guidance that they have received from the Tradition and their observations of interactions with the disabled.[66] What emerges, by necessity, is a casuistry of encounters with the mute, deaf, and blind, rather than a casuistry of disability *per se*.

Nonetheless, despite these limitations, Diana's tract does support the claim that seventeenth century casuistry recognized the capacities and emphasized the ecclesiastical responsibilities of the mute, deaf, and blind, while at the same time acknowledging (at least to some degree) their need for special accommodations in this regard. Accordingly, it approached them primarily as members of the human, ecclesiastical, and civil communities whose circumstances required special consideration. Because defense of this claim requires illustrations from the tract itself, the interpretation of Diana's text that follows addresses first its treatment of the capacities, second, of the ecclesiastical responsibilities, and third, of the accommodations necessary to insure the participation of the mute, deaf, and blind in the various communities to which they belonged.

Capacities of Persons with Particular Disabilities

From its outset, Diana's tract on the mute, deaf, and blind analyzes the capacities of persons with disabilities and, accordingly, evaluates their potential to participate in rites of the Church or to perform specific roles within the Christian community or civil society. The tract begins with a case from the New World regarding baptism. Among a group of indigenous persons requesting the sacrament was a mute adult who had been born deaf. Diana's source for the case, the Dominican Luis Lopez, reports that his missionary confreres feared to administer baptism under such circumstances because adult baptism requires both explicit faith and repentance for sin. Christ's command to the disciples to baptize all nations is preceded by the command to teach them, a process that engenders both faith and awareness of one's need for conversion. Since the deaf could not hear the preaching of the missionaries, the friars concluded that they could not be prepared for

---

[64] Miguel J. Romero, "Aquinas on the *corporis infirmitas*: Broken Flesh and the Grammar of Grace," in *Disability in the Christian Tradition: A Reader*, ed. Brian Brock and John Swinton (Grand Rapids: Eerdmans, 2012), 101-151.
[65] See Diana, *RM* 5, 168 (resol. 24).
[66] See, for example, Diana, *RM* 5, 162, 163, 164, 170 (resols. 3, 6, 7, 9, 29).

adult baptism, either intellectually or morally. Under these circumstances, their disability undermined their capacity for reception into the Christian community.[67]

Diana reports extensively upon Lopez's rejection of these arguments. To deny baptism closes the way to salvation for persons seeking it. Instead, one should presume that God has somehow enlightened such persons with supernatural faith, if they express their contrition with gestures. Out of concern for the persuasiveness of the arguments against baptism however, Lopez argues that the missionary should defer the case to the local bishop, who must then determine whether a particular deaf-mute candidate has gained sufficient knowledge of the faith through sharpness of mind, divine inspiration, or exposure to Christian practices. Diana seems impressed by the arguments in favor of baptism, but he is less convinced of the need for episcopal intervention. Instead Diana cites the concession of a Spanish bishop that no such consultation is necessary if distance renders it impractical.[68] Yet whenever and wherever the examination of the deaf-mute occurs, Lopez, Diana, and the bishop agree that the expression of the candidate's capacity for baptism can come through gestures rather than words.

This case illustrates a recurrent question of great practical significance within the tract: do persons with particular disabilities, especially deaf-mutes, have the capacity to communicate their intentions and understanding to others? Two resolutions regarding whether the deaf can make wills distinguish those who are deaf and mute from those who are deaf but not mute. Deaf persons who can speak—whether they are literate or illiterate—can make wills.[69] However, *Resolutio* 23 reflects considerable disagreement among the authorities about whether and under what circumstances a deaf-mute can be permitted to do so. For example, does it matter whether the disabilities were present from birth, whether the deaf-mute is literate, whether he is a soldier or the recipient of some other privilege granted by a prince, or whether the will concerns bequests to pious causes?[70] By contrast, the long discussion of the wills of the blind focuses upon procedures for preventing malfeasance in transmission of the testament, since there is no doubt regarding these testators' capacity to express their wishes verbally.[71]

These arguments might initially suggest that the casuists regarded only conventional speech as an adequate form of self-expression. However, the tract also refers to alternative forms of communication

---

[67] Diana, *RM* 5, 161 (resol. 1).
[68] Diana, *RM* 5, 161 (resol. 1).
[69] Diana, *RM* 5, 168 (resol. 24).
[70] Diana, *RM* 5, 167-168 (resol. 23).
[71] Diana, *RM* 5, 169-170 (resol. 26).

among those without conventional speech or hearing, including nods and gestures, signs that can be interpreted by friends or family members, lip reading, and, of course, writing.[72] Thus, according to a number of Diana's experts, deaf-mutes are capable of marrying, making religious vows, engaging in commerce, guaranteeing others' debts, and giving testimony (under some circumstances).[73]

Perhaps because the blind can speak for themselves in conventional ways, the tract does not pose any question about their capacity for marriage or religious profession, except when blind persons are also deaf-mutes.[74] Similarly, there is no case about whether the blind can serve as witnesses, although the tract does explicitly defend their capacity to guarantee others' debts.[75] While noting that the deaf, the mute, and the blind are precluded from serving as others' legal counsel, Diana cites Sanchez's argument that it is no sin for a mute with the necessary legal expertise to proffer a written opinion.[76]

The tract also gives explicit attention to the capacities of the disabled to fulfill other functions within the civil order. Because the role involves speaking publicly for another, for example, a mute person cannot act as a guardian. Yet, it is conceivable that the mute, deaf, and blind might act as advocates on their own behalf.[77] A blind person can serve as a judge.[78] If capable of performing the specified service to their lords, mute, deaf, or blind persons can even inherit feudal rights.[79] In the secular sphere, just as in the ecclesiastical sphere, the tract's cases reflect great concern for the specific circumstances surrounding the capacities of the disabled and their possibilities for communicating their intentions and serving the common good.

Since canon law treated deafness, muteness, and blindness as impediments to ordination, Diana presumes that persons with these conditions are barred from receiving Holy Orders.[80] Diana's single case on the subject carefully distinguishes the completely disabled

---

[72] Diana, *RM* 5, 162-165, 168, 170-171 (resols. 3, 4, 7, 9, 12, 23, 29, 31, 33, 34).

[73] Diana, *RM* 5, 164-165, 171-172, 165, 170, 171 (resols. 9, 34, 12, 29, 32).

[74] Diana, *RM* 5, 165, 171-172 (resols. 10, 34). Notice that Diana mentions sources who do not reject marriage in all cases for those who are both blind and deaf-mute, although he does not accept these conclusions.

[75] Diana, *RM* 5, 170 (resol. 29).

[76] Diana, *RM* 5, 170 (resol. 27).

[77] Diana, *RM* 5, 172, 170 (resols. 35, 27).

[78] Diana, *RM* 5, 172 (resol. 36).

[79] Diana, *RM* 5, 167 (resol. 21).

[80] These prohibitions are not part of 1983 Code of Canon Law, but they were applied in reference to canon 984, no. 2, of the 1917 Code. For a commentary on this point in the older code, see Charles Augustine (Bachfen), O.S.B., *A Commentary on the New Code of Canon Law*, Book III, Vol. 4 (St. Louis: B. Herder Book Company, 1920), 4:481. Digitized by LLMC Digital.

from the partially disabled, emphasizing that the hearing and speech-impaired (unlike the deaf and mute) are not automatically excluded from ordained ministry.[81] However, the tract also poses a number of cases in which the cleric's disability developed after ordination. Can a blind priest celebrate the Eucharist? Can a mute priest, in emergency circumstances, administer the Eucharist to others? Can a deaf priest serve as a confessor, if no one else is available? The answer to all these questions is "yes."[82] Furthermore, while disabled clerics cannot become prelates, they do not lose their rights to vote in elections of prelates (e.g., religious superiors).[83] Clerical identity remains, even when disability restricts the ordinary exercise of ministerial or administrative roles.

When considered as a whole therefore, Diana's collection of cases reflects a broad recognition within seventeenth century Roman Catholic casuistry of the capacities of the mute, deaf, and blind to participate in the life of both the ecclesiastical and civil communities. Implicit in this analysis is an assumption that all persons share the responsibility to contribute to the common good. As a result, while particular disabilities may influence the form of a person's participation in the common good, they do not supersede this basic human vocation.

The Ecclesiastical Responsibilities of the Mute, Deaf, and/or Blind

If Diana's tract provides evidence that seventeenth century casuistry recognized the capacities of the mute, deaf, and blind, it also demonstrates that such casuistry emphasized the ecclesiastical responsibilities of the disabled. One striking case asks whether the duty to "hear" mass on festival days applies to deaf-mutes who are

---

[81] Diana, *RM* 5, 167 (resol. 22). According to Diana, the case of the blind is more complex, since both the completely blind man and the man who has lost one eye (e.g., to injury) are deemed irregular, although the man who has lost his sight in one eye is not. The loss of an eye (as opposed to the loss of vision in an eye) prevented candidates from meeting the standards for acceptable physical appearance required of potential clergy. Regarding these regulations, see the commentary mentioned in the previous footnote and R.M. Helmholz, *The Spirit of Classical Canon Law* (Athens: University of Georgia Press, 1996), 64-65. See also the discussion from Aquinas's commentary on Lombard's Fourth Book of Sentences that appears in St. Thomas Aquinas, *Summa Theologica, Supplement*, q. 39, art. 6.

[82] Diana, *RM* 5, 166-167 (resols. 17-19). Diana returns to the case of the visually impaired priest and the Eucharistic celebration in *RM* 9, 344 (resol. 30). Here, he mentions his advice to a priest experiencing double vision.

[83] Diana, *RM 5,* 166 (resol. 13). Diana also discusses the debated case of religious appointed as visitor (i.e., as a travelling inspector of his community's houses and ministries) who loses his eyesight while these responsibilities are ongoing (Diana, *RM* 5, 167 [resol. 20]). In a later volume, he addresses a related case regarding the rights of a blind religious to intervene in a general chapter. See Antonino Diana, *Resolutionium moralium pars decima...* (Venice: Apud Franciscum Baba, 1652), 430-431 (resol. 45). Hereafter, *RM* 10.

also blind. While the reader might expect a negative answer, given the tract's denial of the capacity of such persons for marriage, Diana does not cite a single author who argues that they are not obliged to attend mass.[84] The precept does not require one to "hear" mass in the literal sense, he explains. There are circumstances in which mass-goers without any hearing impairment will be unable to perceive the spoken words, as for example, if they are present during a priest's private mass or during a large, crowded celebration.[85] Those who are mute, deaf, and blind simply share the obligation to attend mass incumbent upon other Christians.

Diana and his sources also agree that those who are mute (including the deaf) have an obligation to confess through nods and gestures, assuming that they are capable of doing so.[86] A more controversial question is whether mute persons who are able to write are obliged to put pen to paper so that they can make an integral confession. Here the experts are divided. On the one hand, when such an important precept of the Church is at stake, writing down sins that one already remembers is not a particularly arduous task. (In fact, presenting a written list to one's confessor is likely to arouse less shame than reciting the same list out loud.) On the other hand, writing sins down risks their accidental public exposure. There is always a chance that the penitent might lose the paper through accident or theft. The Jesuit Jacobus Granadus, whom Diana cites at length for the affirmative position, suggests that penitents protect themselves by writing their sins on one sheet of paper, and the corresponding numbers of these sins on another, apparently, so that content of the confession does not become apparent until the two pages are aligned. After the confession is finished, the confessor is to destroy the pages immediately![87]

Yet it is precisely the risk of inadvertent revelation that leads other thinkers to conclude that literate mutes have no obligation to confess in writing. The precept of the Church does not require annual *public* confession. Writing is a medium susceptible to publicity, should the text fall into the wrong hands. Ergo, written confession is not obligatory for mute persons capable of employing this means. Diana calls both positions probable (i.e., defensible), although he seems inclined to the negative view.[88]

These arguments suggest an intriguing calculus about the obligations of the disabled. In respect to the basic duty to confess

---

[84] Diana, *RM* 5, 164 (resol. 8). On marriage, compare resols. 9 and 10. Note, however, the range of opinions in *resolutio* 10.

[85] Diana, *RM* 5, 164 (resol. 8).

[86] Diana, *RM* 5, 162 (resol. 3).

[87] Diana, *RM* 5, 162-163 (resol. 4).

[88] Diana, *RM* 5, 162-163 (resol. 4). Diana tends to end with the opinion that he regards as more persuasive. However, he gives no explicit endorsement of either position in this case.

annually, the mute are like other Christians, even though this requires them to use an alternative means (i.e., nodding and signs). However, if the means in question—in this case, writing—creates an excessive risk or burden, it is not required, even though writing *per se* is not usually onerous and the clarity of a written confession will exceed the intelligibility of a confession made through gestures. This conclusion suggests that, while disabled persons share basic Christian obligations, and even have a duty to pursue them by alternative means, they have no obligation to pursue them by heroic means.

Diana invokes the obligation of deaf-mutes to confess through signs as a precedent for solving another case—one that he reports that he has not found debated among the doctors. Can mute persons who were born deaf receive the Eucharist throughout their lives (i.e., at times other than when their imminent death is expected)?[89] Diana precedes his analysis by considering a narrower case regarding deathbed communion for persons with these disabilities. Here, he quotes without commentary several paragraphs from Jacobus Marchantius, who advocates administering Viaticum to those born deaf, but hesitates to give them the Eucharist under ordinary circumstances. The problem is again one of communication: how can a pastor be sure that a person who has never been able to hear a teacher or a preacher grasps the mystery of the sacrament sufficiently? Marchantius recognizes both theological and practical objections to this argument, including an appeal to the effects of the grace conferred in baptism and the impact of witnessing others' reverence for the Eucharist. As a pastor, he had seen a deaf-mute parishioner's gestures of devotion during the consecration and had concluded that this person perceived the Eucharistic mystery, at least in some limited way. Yet, when the parishioner asked to receive the sacrament, Marchantius hesitated to agree, especially since earlier pastors had refused. It was simply too difficult, he explains, to judge whether the parishioner's disposition, reverence for the sacrament, and understanding of the Church's command were sufficient.[90]

Diana, by contrast, regards administering the Eucharist to lifelong death-mutes only on their deathbeds as far too restrictive. For those born deaf who can read and write, the issue is simple: such persons have a means to learn about the sacrament and to express their comprehension of basic Christian doctrine. However, Diana believes that a pastor acts prudently in administering the sacrament to the illiterate as well. Theological consensus holds that deaf-mutes must confess their sins through signs and gestures, if they are able to do so. If those born deaf are required to confess, it must be because they can learn what they need to know in order to make good confessions. What

---

[89] Diana, *RM 5*, 163 (resol. 7).
[90] Diana, *RM 5*, 163 (resol. 6).

a penitent needs to know about sin, conversion, and satisfaction is no less challenging than Eucharistic theology. In practical terms, it is easier to teach the disabled to observe the Eucharistic fast than to instill sorrow for their sins. Therefore, Diana argues, if those born deaf are capable of confession, they must be capable of receiving the Eucharist as well.[91]

Diana finds a second precedent for his conclusion in the treatment of the intellectually disabled. There is no blanket denial of the Eucharist to the intellectually impaired, so there is no logical reason to exclude those born deaf, who may approach the sacrament with greater understanding. (Earlier in the argument, Diana had acknowledged the mental acuity of many deaf-mutes, as evidenced by their ability to communicate through signs.) While he does not invoke the term *justice* explicitly, Diana does make the inclusion of one group of disabled persons the warrant for inclusion of the other.

In both claims, Diana's method is consistent with Jonsen and Toulimin's explanation of the structure of casuistry, in that he solves one case by comparing it to another, more settled case resolution.[92] However, it is important to notice the difference between the two precedent cases (i.e., confession through signs and Eucharist for the intellectually disabled). The obligation to confess through signs is one of the cases that the tract considers directly, even though the *resolutio* indicates that there is no controversy regarding this duty. By contrast, the tract never asks whether the intellectually disabled should receive the Eucharist—this is simply a practice of the Church that is taken for granted. The intellectually disabled are a foil for an argument, rather than a subject of analysis within the tract as such.[93] Diana mentions them here only to bolster his defense of administering the Eucharist to deaf-mute Christians.

Finally, Diana's tract includes several cases about the continuing responsibilities of clergy and religious whose disability developed after their ordination or religious profession. All concern the ongoing duty to recite the divine office (also known as the liturgy of the hours) in the face of deafness or blindness.[94] This was an important practical question for those holding Church offices to which an income was attached, since the Fifth Lateran Council had established deprivation of one's revenues or even loss of such an office (i.e., a benefice) as a penalty for neglecting these prayers of the Church.[95] One can trace the

---

[91] Diana, *RM 5*, 163-164 (resol. 7).
[92] Jonsen and Toulmin, *The Abuse of Casuistry*, 35.
[93] Diana, *RM 5*, 164 (resol. 7). Obviously, there is much to criticize in the description of the intellectually disabled in this passage—not least the racist association of intellectual weakness with certain "Aethiopes"!
[94] Diana, *RM 5*, 166 (resols. 14, 15, 16).
[95] See Fifth Lateran Council, Session 9, 5 May 1514, *Bulla reformationis curiae,* sect. "Reformationis curiae et aliorum," in *Decrees of the Ecumenical Councils*, Vol. 1,

popular interest in the issue by noting how often Diana returns to these cases in various installments of the *Resolutiones morales*. His consideration of blindness and the liturgy of the hours begins as a side issue to a different case in Part II, before he posits a specific case on the topic in Part IV. The tract in Part V considers both blindness and deafness and the obligation to recite. Issues related to the divine office and both disabilities appear again in Parts VII, IX, and X.[96] (In the tenth volume, Diana mentions that he had recently been involved in a great argument with a curial official over the responsibilities of the blind regarding these prayers of the Church.)[97]

Within Diana's treatment of these cases, the questions concerning the responsibilities of the deaf are primarily theoretical, while the questions regarding those of the blind are practical. Since a deaf cleric or religious can still read and speak, such a person remains capable of reciting the prayers and readings, and Diana has no doubt that he or she has obligation to do so.[98] The theoretical question concerns religious who recite the offices in common. Does a person who cannot hear the community's responses really participate in *choir*? Is hearing as well as speaking part of the essence of this ministry? Diana believes that it is not, but, in Part IX, he cites an argument for the other position at some length, describing it as probable, the same classification that he applies to his own conclusions.[99] In this case, however, what is at stake is how the deaf religious's recitations should be interpreted, not whether he or she should perform them.

By contrast, Diana's questions about the cleric who has lost his sight are practical, and he develops them in greater detail in later volumes of the *Resolutiones morales* than in this tract from Part V.[100] Clearly, Diana argues one can have no obligation to read what one cannot see. Because parts of the office change from day to day, the blind person will be unable to recite the entire office from memory. On the other hand, if he has been reciting the office for years, it is quite likely that he has memorized parts of it, such as the Psalms. Conceivably, the blind person could recite the divine office with a friend, who would read the lessons and prompt him, if necessary, on the Psalms. Is there an obligation to recite what one can from memory,

---

Nicaea I to Lateran V, ed. Norman P. Tanner, S.J. (London: Sheed and Ward, 1990), 623. For a definition and explanation of the concept of a benefice, see Joseph Bergin, *Church, Society and Religious Change in France, 1580-1730* (New Haven: Yale University Press, 2009), 54-55.

[96] Diana, *RM* 2, 14 (resol. 43); Diana, *RM* 4, 87 (resol. 11); Diana, *RM* 7, 230-231 (resols. 3 and 6); Diana, *RM* 9, 342-343 (resol. 28); and Diana, *RM* 10, 430-431 (resol. 45).

[97] Diana, *RM* 10, 430-431 (resol. 45).

[98] Diana, *RM* 5, 166 (resol. 15).

[99] Diana, *RM* 9, 342 (resol. 28).

[100] The short discussion in this tract appears in Diana, *RM* 5, 166 (resol. 16).

if blindness makes it impossible to recite the whole? Is there an obligation to bring in a friend to assist with the recitation?[101] The arguments on both sides involve this question: are these alternative means to fulfill the Church's precept or are they excessive burdens upon the blind? The latter is not required. Antonio Escobar, whom Diana cites at some length in his return to this question in Part IX, uses the terms *ordinary* and *extraordinary means* [*mediis ordinariis ... extraordinariis*] to make this distinction.[102] Thus, the arguments about the responsibilities of the blind ecclesiastic parallel those concerning the deaf-mutes and confession in writing.

The tract "On the Mute, Deaf, and Blind" thus supports the claim the seventeenth century Roman Catholic casuistry recognized, and indeed, insisted upon the ecclesiastical responsibilities of the disabled. In a sense, this conclusion flows logically from the tract's acknowledgement of their capacities, since obligation presupposes the possibility of moral agency. However, the tract also highlights a useful principle for evaluating the options theoretically available to the disabled in fulfilling their obligations, i.e., the distinction between an alternate means and an excessively burdensome means. If casuists like Diana acknowledged the capacities and emphasized the ecclesiastical responsibilities of the disabled, they also recognized that their circumstances raised difficulties distinct from those associated with conventional forms of Christian practice.

Accommodations for the Mute, Deaf, and/or Blind

Interestingly, the tract devotes much less attention to accommodations for disabled persons than to their capacities and responsibilities. Regarding the ecclesiastical sphere, Diana considers three distinct cases. In the first, he simply reports decisions of central Church authorities. *Resolutio* 14, which discusses the financial rights of deaf or blind canons unable to participate in choir, had been settled in the canons' favor by precedents established in the Sacred Congregation on the Council.[103] A second case addresses the responsibilities of a confessor toward a deaf penitent. Here, Diana's source indicates that the confessor should administer the sacrament in a private part of the Church (since the penitent may have less skill in moderating his/her voice than a hearing person) and should abbreviate his interrogations to protect the penitent from fatigue.[104] Yet perhaps

---

[101] See Diana, *RM* 7, 230 (resol. 3); Diana, *RM* 9, 342-343 (resol. 28); Diana, *RM* 10, 430-431 (resol. 45).

[102] Diana, *RM* 9, 343 (resol. 28). While we typically associate this distinction with medical interventions, it had broader applications in the Early Modern Period. See Julia Fleming, "When 'Meats Are Like Medicines': Vitoria and Lessius on the Role of Food in the Duty to Preserve Life," *Theological Studies* 69, no.1 (2008): 99-115.

[103] Diana, *RM* 5, 166.

[104] Diana, *RM* 5, 163 (resol. 5).

the most striking ecclesiastical case involves the denial of a need for an accommodation, specifically regarding the administration of Extreme Unction to those born mute, deaf, or blind. The question that Diana poses is this: since such persons have never used their senses in a sinful way, why anoint their ears, eyes, etc., as death approaches?[105] Diana's sources point out that the disabled share the same internal powers as those able to see and hear: sin comes from the misuse of these internal capacities, not from the eyes or the ears *per se*. Like other Church members who can see and hear, those born deaf or blind are capable of sin and need divine mercy in the face of death. Their reception of the sacrament requires no special accommodation, since it reflects their human condition rather than their disability.

In his treatment of secular accommodations, Diana mentions Roman law's concessions for some deaf, mute, or blind persons as so-called *miserabiles personae* under the Code of Justinian, a status that allowed them special flexibility regarding the tribunals in which their cases were tried, as well as immunity from certain civic obligations.[106] Both sets of benefits accrue to the completely blind and deaf, as opposed to those who are only partially disabled.[107] Diana also discusses whether deaf-mutes and the blind are subject to ordinary punishments for crimes and to torture to elicit their confessions.[108] His authorities agree that deaf-mutes, assuming they are not also intellectually disabled, can be interrogated and can be required to respond to their questioners through signs or in writing. A literate deaf-mute can even be tortured to obtain a confession, if there is sufficient evidence. However, an illiterate person's confession made through signs requires corroborating testimony, given the risk of mistakes in its interpretation.[109] While Diana's sources conclude that a blind person can confess to and suffer punishment for murder, the Theatine makes torture of the blind the subject of a separate resolution, where he asserts that they are immune from such coercion. Perhaps because this is a matter of secular law, Diana simply points his reader to his source on the question (the jurist Nicola Gizzarelli) without

---

[105] Diana, *RM 5*, 165 (resol. 11). Diana appears to posit this as a hypothetical question, since he cites no author opposed to administering the sacrament in the conventional way.

[106] Diana, *RM 5*, 170, 171 (resols. 30, 33). For the text from the Code of Justinian, 3.14, see S.P. Scott, ed., *The Civil Law, Including the Twelve Tables, The Institutes of Gaius, The Rules of Ulpian, The Opinions of Paulus, The Enactments of Justinian, and the Constitutions of Leo*, 17 volumes (Ohio: The Central Trust Company, 1932), 12:280. See also Giovanni Maria Novario, *Praxis novissima et amplissimus, absolutissimusque tractatus de electione, et variatione fori,... pars prima* (Venice, Apud Paulum Balleonium, 1670), 46. Digitized by Google.

[107] Diana, *RM 5*, 170, 171 (resols. 30, 33).

[108] Diana, *RM 5*, 170-171, 172 (resols. 31, 37).

[109] Diana, *RM 5*, 170-171 (resol. 31).

explaining why the blind deserve greater accommodation than the deaf.[110]

Diana's brief discussion of these accommodations raises as many questions as it answers, but it also supports the argument that the tract approaches the disabled primarily as community members, whose special circumstances may or may not require adaptations in standard practice.[111] The subtext for this analysis is clearly the status of the disabled within their communities, whether as Christians in need of anointing at the time of death, or as subjects eligible for certain protections under civil law.

CONCLUSION: IMPLICATIONS FOR THE PRESENT

The preceding analysis has focused upon situating Antonino Diana's tract "On the Mute, Deaf, and Blind" within its historical context, and upon interpreting this text as evidence for several general conclusions regarding the approach to persons with these disabilities in seventeenth-century Roman Catholic casuistry. Diana's text is most useful to modern Roman Catholic ethics as an illumination of its history and as evidence of interest in ethical questions surrounding these disabilities in Early Modern Catholicism.

However, any historical investigation is almost inevitably, the product of questions about the present. Thus, I would like to end the paper with three very brief observations about the implications of Diana's tract for contemporary reflections on disability. My suggestions are intended only to spark a continued dialogue between contemporary disability ethicists and Diana's Early Modern contribution to the subject. These observations concern the significance of individual circumstances and histories for disability ethics, the distinction between an alternative means and an extraordinary means in evaluating the responsibilities of the disabled, and the value of the situation of the disabled as a lens for theological analysis.

If one can draw any general conclusion from Diana's collection of cases, it is surely that circumstances and personal histories play a particularly important role in addressing ethical questions regarding the disabled. The tract is not a study of disability *per se* but of situations involving persons with three particular disabilities (or

---

[110] Diana, *RM 5*, 171, 172 (resols. 31, 37). Gizzarelli's analysis concerns a defendant blind from birth, in a case involving the debasement of coinage. See Nicola Gizzarelli, *Aureae decisiones sac. reg. cons. Neap. Nicolai Antonii Gizzarelli* ... 2 vols. (Naples: Ex typographia Francisci Savii, 1632), 1:108-110. Digitized by Google.

[111] It would be interesting to know, for example, why Diana includes these last cases regarding the rights of the disabled under civil law. Is this an illustration of his thoroughness? Is the information intended to aid pastors and families in acting as advocates for the disabled? Does he intend to instruct the confessors of magistrates, who would have encountered the disabled in their courts?

combinations of the three). In most cases, the answer to the ethical question under consideration depends upon factors other than the disability itself, including the subject's intelligence, education, and facility in communicating. How the disability fits into a person's history is also significant, especially in terms of his/her age and status at the time when the disability developed. Many cases consider the degree of the subject's disability, since losses of vision, hearing, or the ability to speak fall along a continuum. Diana's cases remind us, therefore, that the disabled are *persons* affected in various ways and at different stages in their lives, by disabilities, to which they respond in light of their individual characters and through the resources they either have or are in a position to acquire. Ethical reflections on disability must not lose sight of this personal context.

Diana's tract also highlights an important ethical principle for addressing some cases involving disability: the distinction between an alternate means and a heroic means. As his analyses of confession in writing for the mute and recitation of the canonical hours for the blind reveal, Diana argues that the disabled need not use excessively burdensome means to fulfill their obligations, even though they can reasonably be asked to use alternative means. One can imagine some obvious applications of this principle for contemporary issues surrounding disability accommodations. How can a state, for example, best enable disabled persons to provide proof of identity? How can a government agency or employer verify disability without imposing excessive burdens upon the claimant? How should a professor respond to a disabled student whose needs exceed the limits of institutionalized accommodations? Such examples suggest that the distinction between an alternate means and an overly burdensome means may prove to be a useful tool for contemporary reflections on disability, just as it served the needs of Early Modern casuists.

Finally, Diana's tract reminds us that the experience of the disabled can serve as a lens for theological reflection, especially about the meaning of Christian practices. In considering the anointing of senses for the disabled within Extreme Unction, the obligation to "hear mass" for those both deaf and blind, or even the validity of a tandem baptism performed by a mute person (who pours the water) and a physically incapacitated person (who recites the formula), Diana and his sources are really analyzing the essence of these sacraments, in light of the liminal experiences of the disabled.[112] Theological reflection on foundational Christian practices can only benefit from looking through this alternative window into their meaning.[113]

---

[112] Diana cites Aquinas as a source for the baptism case, see *RM* 5, 161-162 (resol. 2).
[113] See, for example, Shane Clifton, "Theodicy, Disability, and Fragility: An Attempt to Find Meaning in the Aftermath of Quadriplegia," *Theological Studies* 76, no. 4 (2015): 765-784.

Diana and his colleagues lived in an age that emphasized the catechesis of ordinary Christians, and accordingly gave great weight to explicit knowledge of dogma.[114] The controversies over administering adult baptism and Eucharist to those born deaf reflect a tendency to conflate faith with the acquisition of doctrinal knowledge. This is true even in the arguments favoring sacramental administration to adults born deaf, since some of Diana's sources appeal to special revelation to get around the problem of familiarity with Christian teachings. This emphasis upon the understanding of doctrine also explains the sharp distinction in some case resolutions between those who are both intellectually and physically disabled and those with physical disabilities alone. Yet Diana's sources occasionally acknowledge that faith can be nurtured in Christian practice and experience rather than verbal catechesis, especially when they see evidence of grace in wordless gestures of reverence and contrition. This insight suggests an approach to the experiences of the disabled—especially the intellectually disabled—that escapes the tract's narrow association of faith with knowledge of doctrine. In the face of contemporary projections regarding Alzheimer's diagnoses, interpreting faith in the context of disability will be a challenge shared by this century's moral theologians. Perhaps Diana's tract can suggest both a salutary warning against and an intriguing alternative to the conflation of faith with doctrinal familiarity.

Diana's tract, therefore, is a historical artifact, but it is not simply a historical curiosity. While recognizing its limitations, perhaps we can draw upon this seventeenth-century work as one point of departure for our own ethical analyses, especially in terms of its sensitivity to the varied histories, circumstances, and experiences of disabled persons. In its consideration of the capacities and ecclesiastical obligations of individuals with particular disabilities, the tract reminds us that moral agency is by no means limited to those who can speak, hear, or see. To be a moral agent, with or without disabilities, is to face ethical challenges and to stand in need of grace. Diana acknowledges this human experience of finitude and temptation in the tract's final sentence: "May God grant that we, in respect to speaking, hearing, and seeing evil, may become mute, deaf, and blind."[115] M

---

[114] See, for example, Robert Bireley, *The Refashioning of Catholicism, 1450-1700: A Reassessment of the Counter Reformation* (Washington, DC: The Catholic University of America, 1999), 96-104, 121-125; Bergin, *Church, Society and Religious Change in France*, 277-309; and Patrick J. O'Banion, *The Sacrament of Penance and Religious Life in Golden Age Spain* (University Park, PA: Pennsylvania State University Press, 2012), 55-57.

[115] Diana, *RM* 5, 172 (resol. 37). The translation is my own.

Blessed Silence: Explorations in Christian Contemplation and Hearing Loss

Jana Bennett

A BROAD RANGE OF SCHOLARS REPRESENTING fields from philosophy to education to technology, each of whom writes about deafness, recently published an important collection of essays, which they called *Deaf Gain*.[1] "Deaf Gain" is a term that comes from sign language, but it is also meant to stand in stark and direct contrast to "hearing loss." Rather than seeing deafness as a loss, the scholars work to understand deafness as a gain for both the individual and society. The book's central premise is that people need to reconceive deafness and see it not as a loss but as something that adds to the diversity of human life.

Seeing deafness as a gain argues against the often-maligned "medical model" of disability that has been strongly operational for human beings since at least the nineteenth century. The medical model assumed a standard of normalcy against which all people were to be measured. On this view, those with disabilities needed to be "fixed" especially by medical and technological means. A medical model of disability is further supported by theological ideas of disability that were then, and sometimes remain today, related to sinfulness. Deaf Gain, on the other hand, operates within a "social model" of disability, a model that sees society as either diminishing or enhancing human life, including the lives of people with disabilities, depending on the ways society forms such diverse things as its architecture (as in ramps for wheelchairs and loops for the deaf), legal protections of people with disabilities, and the language used to speak about disabilities.

The "Deaf Gain" collection did not include a theologian's voice, but the concept is intriguing for theology. Seeing deafness as a gain runs counter to some dominant theological understandings in Christianity about the Word, and Jesus as the Incarnate Word of God, needing to be heard. As Thomas Oden notes, citing the ninth century theologian Prudentius, "Speaking and hearing are crucial to the Gospel, which is news to be spoken and heard. This is why Jesus opens

---

[1] H-Dirksen L Bauman and Joseph J. Murray, eds. *Deaf Gain: Raising the Stakes for Human Diversity* (Minneapolis: University of Minnesota Press, 2014).

ears and loosens tongues."[2] Prudentius's words about the deaf suggest negativity: "Deafened ears, of sound unconscious / Every passage blocked and closed, / At the word of Christ responding, / All the portals open wide, / Hear with joy friendly voices and / The softly whispered speech."[3] The Word, spoken and proclaimed, is a strong image – even a dominant image – in much of Christian thought. Jesus the Word himself becomes a stumbling block for those who cannot hear. Further, the emphasis in Jesus's miracles on healing people with disabilities, including deafness, can suggest that hearing loss is meant not to exist in God's good world.

The dominant and largely negative image of the Word, Christ, juxtaposed with the concept of Deaf Gain, invites theological consideration of deafness. This essay seeks to extend the discussion of Deaf Gain conversation occurring in secular disability studies by thinking about the possibilities of Deaf Gain as theological and as a good contribution to disability ethics conversations. I focus on the Christian practice of silent contemplation as one possible contribution for Deaf Gain. I argue that silent contemplation as a means of "Deaf Gain" is a helpful way for theologians and others working in disability studies to rethink hearing loss and theology of disability, as well as a crucial aspect of doing moral theology well. Yet, "Deaf Gain" can also seem boundary-less. In its search to show that deafness is beneficial to humanity in a range of ways, Deaf Gain ignores boundaries, especially the boundaries of physical bodies. That is, deafness is not a free-standing, infinite gain but one that must be embodied and therefore come with limits. Accordingly, while most of my argument articulates the importance of physical silence – both deaf and non-deaf – for rightly understanding moral thought and disability – my argument concludes that what we learn from silence and contemplation is not only an appreciation of deafness but also an appreciation for the limits of our bodies and our senses, deaf or not.

I make my argument first by naming how deafness has been principally understood as a loss, rather than a gain, in both theological and non-theological accounts of deafness, especially because of the silence that hearing loss induces. In this part, I raise some of the theological and ethical problems that arise with the propensity to see deafness as a loss, especially in relation to a medical model of disability. Then I turn to thinking about silence as a means of Deaf Gain, by discussing the silence of contemplation. Deaf Gain participates in a social model of disability, a model that shows that it is society that fosters disabling conditions. I show how silent contemplation can mirror the experiences of hearing loss, and how silent contemplation forms a necessary, if little recognized, aspect of

---

[2] Thomas C. Oden, *The Good Works Reader* (Grand Rapids: Eerdmans, 2007), 170.
[3] Oden, *The Good Works Reader*, 170.

Christian moral life. This means that deafness can and should be recognized more fully for its contributions in Christian life, which is precisely the kind of work that that authors of *Deaf Gain* hope to foster. However, at the conclusion of the essay, I offer a theological critique of Deaf Gain, via my focus on contemplation. I suggest that Deaf Gain must be tempered by knowledge and even embrace of embodiment and bodily disabilities, precisely so that the Holy Spirit can enter into our lives.

It is standard in discussions of deafness to clarify the term. In this essay, I use "deafness" to refer to all people who have hearing impairment, including but not limited to people who use sign language or are part of the Deaf Culture linguistic group. "Deaf" with an uppercase D refers to the Deaf community of people who sign and who form unique languages, not unlike English or French, and a set of language-related customs. "Hard-of-hearing" and hearing impairment also appear occasionally in this essay. Both terms refer generally and broadly to people with hearing loss in the ways that a (hearing) medical community might typically understand.

"Hearing Loss Fails to Silence…"[4]

Hearing loss, as the phrase suggests, is most often seen as a loss rather than a gain. It is perceived as a *problem* largely because of its silence. Hearing loss is counted as a social disability because a deaf person's silent world can limit or prohibit participation in social conversations and activities. Marriages where one person has a hearing loss and the other does not have higher rates of divorce than in the general population, due to the fact that at least one member of the couple does not feel heard. People with hearing loss lose participation in social events because they are often unable to hear in noisy restaurants, parties, or even relatively small gatherings of people. The collegial lunch, the after-work cocktail hour, and the large meeting conference room can each be isolating for people with hearing loss, and can affect a person's career trajectory and working relationships. Similarly, the dinner party (even a small one), the music in the background at a coffee shop where one has gathered with friends, and attendance at a play, concert, or movie theater all can be simply uncomfortable to nearly impossible with hearing loss. It should

---

[4] The pun is a common one in use in contemporary headlines for stories featuring athletes, musicians, dancers, and scholars who are hearing impaired. See, for example, Amy Scribner, "Hearing Loss Fails to Silence Allison Biggs' Talents," *The Spokesman Review*, May 27, 1999; Marc Shugold, "Beyond Silence: Profound Hearing Loss No Hindrance to Lass Who Lives by Rhythm," *Rocky Mountain News*, November 13 2002; Robert Croan, "Musician Hasn't Allowed Hearing Loss to Silence Her," *Pittsburgh Post-Gazette*, April 3, 1997; Blake Sebring, "Hearing Loss Can't Silence These Skills: Grant Isenbarger, 11, Hasn't Let Disability Keep Him Off the Hockey Rink," *The News Sentinel* (Fort Wayne, IN), February 16, 2005.

be no surprise, then, that at least one study has identified a correlation between degrees of loneliness and having hearing loss.[5]

Narrating his experience of deafness, computer programmer David Peter writes, "Deafness means I don't understand anyone. When someone talks at lunch, I want to know what they say. I miss out on the daily conversation, the back-and-forth, the friendships made after propinquity. And the worst part is that I don't have a choice in the matter."[6] His sense of social isolation is palpable. Peter goes on to describe the difficulty with being in an open office, where people casually share programming tips but where he misses every tip, off topic conversations that make for a friendly work environment, and even the stuff of meetings. While his workplace is helpful in hiring transcribers, it is difficult to overemphasize how much a deaf person might miss in daily interactions.

Medical reviews of deafness speak of fixing a world of silence via various forms of hearing aids and cochlear implants. The aim of these technologies is to bring sound into the life of a hearing impaired person. This is a laudable quest, especially given the forms of silence and isolation described above. Such technologies can backfire, however. "Fixing" a hearing loss with hearing aids or cochlear implants does not restore hearing to the level of a "normal" person, in the way that glasses, contact lenses, and LASIK surgery restore eyesight for many people who had been "sighted" before. Even a "normal" person who grew up without hearing loss during childhood, who loses hearing as an adult, and receives a cochlear implant in their 50s, will not experience their pre-loss hearing restored. The sounds will be different with these devices and implant recipients have to undergo training in order to identify sounds they hear with the implant.

A similar process can take place every time a hearing aid user switches to new hearing aids. In addition, feedback from hearing aids can prevent hearing, and the sounds via hearing aids can be so strange that a user gives up on hearing with them. Hearing aids and implants cannot always diminish background noise and may amplify exactly the wrong sounds for a given situation. Having hearing aids does not mean that every sound will be heard or that a person with hearing loss will stop saying "What?" or "Pardon me?" Fixing a hearing loss with medical devices therefore offers only a partial gift, a chance to participate a little more often in the particular social world of the hearing. (Such a view of fixing hearing loss tends to omit the fact that Deaf culture is also a very social world, but in a different language.)

---

[5] Ellen Christian, et al, "Sounds of Silence: Coping with Hearing Loss and Loneliness," *Journal of Gerontological Nursing* 15, no. 11 (1989): 4.
[6] David Peter, "Being Deaf: How Different the World Is Without Hearing," *Gizmodo*, gizmodo.com/5912623/being-deaf.

The desire to fix hearing loss, to overcome its silence and its results, plays strongly in contemporary media. Overcoming the silence of hearing loss features in numerous articles focusing on deaf athletes, musicians, and others. One article touts that a hockey player does not let silence prevent him from playing hockey—"Hearing loss can't silence these skills"—despite that skill in skating wouldn't seem to have much to do with whether a person hears. (Hearing loss will probably affect a person's ability to play in a game, however.)[7]

Theologically, the silence associated with hearing loss is a problem as well. Scripture proclaims, again and again, that in God's reign, the deaf shall hear! "On that day, the deaf shall hear the words of a scroll" (Isaiah 29:17-24). Deafness gets counted as one among many impoverished conditions that God will overturn: blindness, lowliness, lameness. Hearing loss is a definite loss in scripture. God is often portrayed as a God who hears, the God of the hearing. For example, theologian Wayne Morris exegetes Exodus 3:1-6, the story of Moses and the burning bush, by describing how impossible it would be for a deaf person to hear the voice of God from the bush and to cover their eyes (since eyes are one of the main ways that deaf people interpret the world around them).[8] If a deaf person could not communicate with God in this story, nor imagine what it would be like to be present in the story, it seems evident that God is a God of the hearing.

This is not the only story about deafness. God is also named as a champion and protector of people with deafness. In Exodus 4:11, in response to Moses' complaint that he does not speak well, God fires back, "Who gives one person speech? Who makes another mute or deaf...? Is it not I, the Lord?" God is the one who gives these characteristics. God can use them in whatever way God chooses, including by choosing Moses to lead the Israelites from slavery in Egypt. When God gives the law, part of what is included is injunctions against "insult[ing] the deaf" (Leviticus 19:14).

Yet, the more dominant images of deafness are ones that depict God as not hearing the cries of the people or that, out of frustration and need, implore God to hear: "To you, Lord, I call; my Rock, do not be deaf to me" (Psalm 28:1).[9] Deafness and the silence that come with it are experienced not as good, but as negatives, as indications that God simply is not present (or more problematically, ignoring requests). Deafness therefore implies the absence of God. Thus, Micah proclaims confidently, "I will wait for God my savior; my God will hear me" (Micah 7:7). If there is silence, it cannot be that there is any

---

[7] See above, footnote four for these references.
[8] Wayne Morris, *Theology Without Words: Theology in the Deaf Community* (Burlington: Ashgate Publishing, 2008), 96-7.
[9] See also Psalm 39:13 and Psalm 83:2.

real deafness present but only because we must wait for God to speak so that we may hear.

It follows, then, that the God of the hearing must require the deaf to become hearing. Prophetic scriptures speak about the good things God will do, which often recount how God will make the deaf hear. In Isaiah 35, for example, the prophet enumerates all the ways Israel will be redeemed from her time in captivity. Redemption includes: "Then the eyes of the blind shall see, and the ears of the deaf shall be opened" (Isaiah 35:5). Other scriptures have this focus on redemption via hearing: "On that day, the deaf shall hear the words of a scroll" (Isaiah 29:18).

Perhaps because of the way hearing is associated with the jubilee, deafness becomes a shorthand way to describe all that has gone wrong in peoples' relationship with God. For example, the prophet Micah says that when God comes to save the people, "The nations will see and will be put to shame, in spite of all their strength; They will put their hands over their mouths; their ears will become deaf...." (Micah 7:16). Deafness becomes a way to speak about Israel's refusal to listen to God. In Isaiah 42:18-20, the prophet admonishes the deaf to hear and the blind to look and see, but then says, "You see many things but do not observe; ears open but do not hear." Deafness (and blindness) are characteristics of the people who have turned away from God, who do not take heed of God's call to the people to live in better ways.

Deafness takes on a still different meaning with Christ's coming. Deafness is healed, and because deafness is healed, people see that Jesus really is Good News. So, in Matthew 11, Jesus can proclaim that the day of salvation has come in him, because the deaf shall hear (and the blind see, the lame walk, etc.). Even more, the good news is proclaimed by showing that the deaf can hear. As Morris suggests, "The recovery of hearing for Deaf people is seen as a sign of the Kingdom of God."[10] In Mark 7, Jesus heals a deaf man, and the people are astonished and say in response that Jesus "has done all things well" (Mark 7:37). Doing all things well means, of course, fulfilling the prophecies that have been told: whoever the Messiah is, the Messiah will be recognized as someone who causes the deaf to hear.

In Morris' hearing and the Protestant church world, a pastor might ask from the pulpit: "Can I have a word from the Lord?" The phrase suggests that God and God's Word are depicted as voices people can hear. An equivalent in Roman Catholic or similar liturgies might be the proclamation lectors say at the conclusion of the lectionary readings: "The Word of the Lord." While in the hearing world, it is understood that hearing God's voice is metaphorical for most,[11] Morris also helps theologians understand that in deaf context, deaf

---

[10] Morris, *Theology Without Words*, 99.
[11] With the exception of rare locutions, such as the one that Mother Teresa heard.

people wouldn't see these kinds of phrases as metaphorical. Morris recounts deaf people asking him, "What does God's voice sound like?" Clearly, as the tradition has it, God is most definitely a God of the hearing, someone who speaks to those "who have ears to hear."

Given this scriptural witness, it is no surprise that many Christian theological strands emphasize the need for hearing to be sound or restored when lost. In some strands of theology about disability, hearing loss along with other impairments is seen as a sign of sin. The sign of taking away the sin is therefore that the person is healed.[12] Hearing loss is also often treated with pity, as something that Christians need to respond to or provide for. Such a view always makes people with hearing loss objects rather than persons and does not recognize deaf peoples' contributions to church or society.

Liturgical practice similarly reflects the needs and experiences of the hearing and thereby also marginalizes those with hearing loss. Songs sung slowly and closed eyes during prayer make worship isolating for those who cannot hear. "The Word of the Lord" and "Lord, hear our prayer" are two common liturgical statements in many denominations' worship services that presume hearing. Further, in practice, Christians have sometimes been disturbed by the silence occasioned in deafness. In Roman Catholic practice, deaf people frequently were not permitted to receive communion or to enter into marriage contracts because they could not verbally express understanding of what was happening at the Eucharist nor verbally express consent for marriage. This denial was despite clear legal allowances for the deaf to receive the sacraments.[13] In a context where deafness is so much maligned, it makes sense that the church's emphasis would be on healing and restoration – on making deaf people hear just like the hearing so that they, too, can participate in the church and be one of God's people.

Of course, the fixes that a medical model offers and a hearing society extols have been the subjects of debate among those who are deaf. Cochlear implants have become a political issue, a much-publicized debate, and a clash about whether the implants destroy Deaf community. In correcting deafness via cochlear implants, the Deaf community loses a person that might learn its unique language and customs. That is, while it is the case that hearing loss affects a person's ability to participate in a hearing community and its social nature, deafness may be an entrée into deaf communities and a distinctive way of being social. Deaf culture features a language and a

---

[12] See Morris, *Theology without Words*, chapter 5 ("Anyone who has ears, let them hear... But what about Deaf people?").
[13] The First Council of Orange in 441 makes mention of receiving communion. Canons 1101 and 1104 discuss marriage. See Marcel Broesterhuizen, "Faith in Deaf Culture," *Theological Studies* 66, no. 2 (2005): 307.

particular way of life. When cochlear implants first arose on the scene, that culture seemed at risk of extinction.[14] A similar critique can be made of the hearing church that so focuses on hearing that people often do not see that deafness might in fact be a valuable part of the Body of Christ. Deaf culture as well as contributions of the deaf more generally are vibrant and vital aspects of the church. It is to that question I now turn, with a particular look at the experience of silence as a contribution that deaf people make to the church.

DELIBERATE SILENCE

In contrast to the medical model of disability, a Deaf Gain view articulates a social model of disability, a model that sees society as the major factor limiting full participation of people who have abilities that differ from the so-called norm. One of these norms is that silence is odd, as evidenced in the above section. In this section, however, I discuss ways that silence – including the silence of deaf people – should not be odd, especially in relation to Christian tradition.

For many Christians, silence seems a small way to encounter God. The vow of silence taken by some monastic groups, such as Cistercians and Carthusians, is by turns awe inspiring, compelling, or perplexing (and even repellent). It is precisely because humans often reject silence that it becomes an important way to encounter God. In scriptures, God and God's love so often becomes revealed through the small and the rejected: the mustard seed, the sparrow, the widow's mite. Silence offers another small, forgotten, even rejected state of being for many, a state which actually sows spiritual benefits. This Christian tradition offers a different view of hearing loss and its accompanying silence, a view that does not reject silence but embraces it. The potential parallels between hearing loss and silence are important because, while hearing loss is seen as detrimental to human flourishing, contemplative silence is often seen as *necessary* for human flourishing.

Deaf people often seek out and crave silence. Christina Hartmann writes:

> Silence is far more peaceful and soothing for me. There's a part of me that has to brace itself every morning when I turn on the CI [cochlear implant] and face the barrage of noise of the world around me. Most of these noises aren't pleasant: dogs barking, car starting, amidst the

---

[14] Much of the debate about cochlear implants occurred in the late 90s and early 2000s. See, for example, Bonnie Poitras Tucker, "Deaf Culture, Cochlear Implants, and Elective Disability," *Hastings Center Report* 28, no. 4 (1998) 6-14. That said, the issue is often still mentioned in contemporary writing, even if cochlear implants themselves are not the main subject of an article or book.

tumultuous world, it's nice to know that I can carve out some tranquility.¹⁵

Sara Novic observes similarly, "I like being deaf. I love the feeling of quiet and comfort I have even while living amid the noise and crowds of New York City."¹⁶ Hartmann and Novic use words like "tranquility," "quiet," and "comfort" to describe the presence of silence. These words provide contrasts to the world of noise each experiences when hearing.

The well-known author and practitioner of contemplative prayer Martin Laird describes the importance of physical silence for contemplative prayer. He says,

> Without doubt, regular periods of physical silence play a crucial role in the spiritual life. It must be cultivated and reverenced. We don't make retreats alongside highways. Places of retreat, centers of recovery and healing, even some religious communities purposely cultivate physical silence in service of something else. Stretches of physical silence and contemplation, especially on a daily basis, help destress the nervous system.¹⁷

Silence is physically and physiologically necessary for Christians. We cultivate silent spaces on purpose. We note how silence helps our bodies, and the construction of special spaces for silence aids in Christians' desires to remain undistracted by both outer and inner noises.

The contrast of welcoming this form of physically constructed silence but condemning the silence of the deaf is striking. Silence of the deaf is physical too. Just as people construct cathedrals, monasteries, and places of retreat with silence in mind, so deafness constructs a physical space and reality in which being silent is one probable default mode of encountering the world.¹⁸ While the hearing cannot quite construct their bodies to experience and encounter silence in this way, perhaps the hearing can learn about the benefits of silence from those who are deaf. Learning about silence's benefits might be especially important in a technocratic culture like ours, where noise and distractions are default experiences for hearing and deaf people alike.

---

[15] Christina Hartmann, "What is it like to be deaf from birth?" *Quora*, www.quora.com/What-is-it-like-to-be-deaf-from-birth.
[16] Sara Novic, "I'm Deaf and I'm Totally Cool With It, Thanks," *XO Jane*, www.xojane.com/issues/im-deaf-and-i-like-it.
[17] Michael Laird, OSA, *A Sunlit Absence: Silence, Awareness, and Contemplation* (New York: Oxford University Press, 2011), 45.
[18] It is worth noting, however, that often deaf peoples' encounter with physical deafness is filled with the particular noise of tinnitus – clicking, buzzing, static noises that can likewise be distracting.

The irony that the silence of deafness is not celebrated goes deeper, however. Silence is not merely an important aspect of Christian spaces. It is not merely integral to the Christian act of contemplation that Laird and others argue ought to take place each day. Silence is also integral to developing a whole relationship with God. Scripture, in fact, sometimes witnesses to the importance of silence.[19] Silence brings peace and salvation, as Psalm 109 instructs:

In their distress they cried to the LORD,
who brought them out of their peril;
He hushed the storm to silence,
the waves of the sea were stilled.
They rejoiced that the sea grew calm,
that God brought them to the harbor they longed for.
(Psalm 107:28-30)

Silence permits a harbor of rest, a sign of rescue from trouble. Still, more often than not, references to silence are negative, however, as in the passages mentioned in the above section. Even passages that might seem favorable to silence and deafness—like the famous one in which Elijah hears God in a whisper (1 Kings 19:11-13)—are not, for deaf people, positive. Whispering is frustrating for deaf people because it is not, properly speaking, silence, and yet it is also not hear-able for those who have some ability to hear.

So, it is interesting that despite scripture's relative silence on silence, numerous holy people in the Christian tradition have declaimed on the benefits of silence. Saint John of the Cross preaches that, "The Father spoke one Word, which was his Son, and this Word he speaks always in eternal silence, and in silence must be heard by the soul."[20] Whereas in traditional Christian understanding (both deaf and non-deaf), the Word is a speaking and hearing word, Saint John of the Cross proclaims that the Word is silent, eternally so. If we are to encounter this silent word, we must still use our own bodies to "hear" that silence.

One of the central motivations for silence – both physical and interior – is that it is a way of "praying without words."[21] Praying

---

[19] With emphasis on "sometimes." In scripture, silence is often treated with similar kinds of derision as deafness. God will "silence" enemies.
[20] Saint John of the Cross, *Maxims on Love 21* in *The Collected Works of St John of the Cross*, trans. K. Kavanaugh and O. Rodriguez (Washington, DC: Institute of Carmelite Studies Publications, 1979), 675. Cited in Martin Laird, *Into the Silent Land: A Guide to the Christian Practice of Contemplation* (Oxford: Oxford University Press, 2006), 2.
[21] Justin Langille, "Nothing Between God and You: Awakening to the Wisdom of Contemplative Silence," in *Spirituality, Contemplation, and Transformation: Writings on Centering Prayer*, ed. Thomas Keating and Paul David Lawson (Brooklyn: Lantern Books, 2008), 57-80, 68.

without words offers a way to allow nothing, including language, to come between self and God. As contemplative Justin Langille puts it, "Praying without words is not something I do for God; it is rather doing *nothing* in the service of love."[22] Nothing comes between God and me, so *nothing* becomes my prayer. At its best, contemplative prayer enables nothing to stand in the way of God. In silence, I divest all my pride, faults, wrongdoings, but also my goods, my bests, the activities I do well. "To pray without words puts the emphasis on being rather than doing."[23] Silence in this context enables an awareness of the world and one's self that often becomes obscured by the distractions of noise and words.

From that place of silence, we come face to face with God. Thomas Merton, the well-known Cistercian monk who wrote frequently about the benefits of silence, says of God, "It is necessary to name Him Whose silence I share and worship, for in His silence He also speaks my own name."[24] God's speaking of Merton's name in silence is truthful. By contrast, Merton realizes that his own poor attempts to speak result in darkness and death: "My own voice is only able to rouse a dead echo when it calls out to itself. There will never be any awakening in me unless I am called out of darkness by Him Who is my light."[25] The noise of Merton's own voice does not lead to God. It only leads back to himself. Noise from a world that is predominantly a hearing world suffocates because it is merely an echo chamber in which we hear ourselves and others, for the sake of ourselves and others but not for God.

When we are silent, however, Merton suggests that we are able really to "hear" God. "My life is a listening, His is a speaking. My salvation is to hear and respond. For this, my life must be silent. Hence, my silence is my salvation."[26] Merton still uses listening and hearing in ways that Wayne Morris and his Deaf Community Churches might find problematic because they are metaphorical uses of listening and hearing that those with hearing loss may not be able to grasp, precisely because metaphor is part of a particular linguistic community. The Deaf community is its own cultural linguistic community with its own metaphors. Even with that caveat, however, I note the distinction between Merton's metaphorical use of listening and silence compared with the predominant metaphorical uses of listening and hearing in scripture and liturgy. Scripture and Liturgy emphasize the Word as spoken and yet heard only internally in really

---

[22] Langille, "Nothing Between God and You," 76.
[23] Langille, "Nothing Between God and You," 76.
[24] Thomas Merton, *Thoughts in Solitude* (New York: The Noonday Press/Farrar Strauss and Giroux, 1956), 73.
[25] Merton, *Thoughts in Solitude*, 73-74.
[26] Merton, *Thoughts in Solitude*, 74.

a silent way. Merton, however, names specifically that speaking is a silence that we impose on God. We cannot really hear God without silence. In saying this, Merton is more truthful, at least for those with deafness, than the liturgy is.

Moreover, Merton suggests that silence is the beginning from which words flow. Silence, rather than words, noise, and hearing, is the default way of encountering the world. When we have acknowledged the importance of silence in our lives, then noise, speaking, and human words take their rightful place and do not separate us from God. However, we often fail to recognize this in our constant speaking and desire for noise. As Merton writes,

> Words stand between silence and silence: between the silence of things and the silence of our own being. Between the silence of the world and the silence of God. When we have really met and known the world in silence, words do not separate us from the world nor from other [people], nor from God, nor from ourselves because we no longer trust entirely in language to contain reality. Truth rises from the silence of being to the quiet tremendous presence of the Word.[27]

Being hasty about our words and a constant pressure to generate words and noise actually separate us from God, others, and ourselves, because we trust too much in the production of that noise. The noise of the hearing world becomes an idol that obscures God from us.

Martin Laird helps us understand Merton's point further. Laird remarks that noise constantly makes us aware of external objects, while part of the point of silence and contemplation is to focus on what cannot be objectified, namely God. God "is not an object in the way these things are objects."[28] We learn more about who God is precisely because we stand in silence. Theologically, then, physical silence has the potential to help people acknowledge what Thomas Aquinas and numerous others have acknowledged about God. God is not and cannot be any part of the existing created universe, except, of course, in Jesus, the Incarnate Word of God.[29] Sometimes particular ways of being embodied – such as hearing – can obscure encounters with God because they cause us to look in all the wrong places. It should be said that silence is not the whole of contemplation and that there are different types of silence. Still, physical silence, especially in a culture where physical silence is ever more rare, enables access to other forms of silence.

---

[27] Merton, *Thoughts in Solitude*, 86.
[28] Laird, *A Sunlit Absence*, 45.
[29] Meditating on Thomas Aquinas's *Prima Pars* of the *Summa Theologica*, especially questions 1-10, aims at this point. Theologian Herbert McCabe, a Blackfriars Thomist, also makes this point over and over again in his book *God Matters* (London: Mowbray, 2000).

The idea that silence engenders a deep relationship with God stands in striking contrast to the "God of the hearing" as described in the first part of the essay. When we focused on deafness and its problems as interpreted in the medical model, God was patently a God of the hearing, whose Word remained isolated from those who cannot hear the Word of God. Yet, when the focus shifts to silence, God is no longer isolated from the experience of the deaf – especially in the silence of being deaf.

While the silence of contemplation is a necessary physical aspect of Christians' relationship with God and provides a potentially more truthful account of God's being and activity, Christian tradition has also often connected the silence of contemplation with good moral action. It is contrasted with speech and hearing, as in Isaiah who writes:

> For the fool speaks folly,
>   his heart plans evil:
> Godless actions,
>   perverse speech against the LORD,
> Letting the hungry go empty
>   and the thirsty without drink.
> The deceits of the deceiver are evil,
>   he plans devious schemes:
> To ruin the poor with lies,
>   and the needy when they plead their case.
> But the noble plan noble deeds,
>   and in noble deeds they persist. (Isaiah 32:6-8)

Words become perverse speech able to deceive, and moreover to bring about "devious schemes" that ruin the poor and that perpetuate injustice. Yet, Isaiah continues in verse 14, "the noisy city [will be] deserted," and the people will go to the wilderness, which will become a garden. In that garden, "My people will live in peaceful country, in secure dwellings and quiet resting places" (Isaiah 32:18). Perhaps the noble people who plan noble deeds, then, are the ones who refrain from "perverse speech" by being silent, by acknowledging the peacefulness, quiet, and justice of silent resting spaces.

Silence and the practice of peace and justice thus become interconnected. In his exposition of Psalm 139, Augustine speaks at length about the deceit and injustice of those who speak with "smooth talk" and "malicious hearts."[30] Augustine suggests that the antidote to speaking unjust words, animosity, and hatred is silence. "A talkative

---

[30] Augustine, "Exposition of Psalm 139," in *Exposition of the Psalms*, A Translation for the 21st Century (Hyde Park, New York: New City Press, 2004), §5.

man loves lies. What gives him pleasure? Only talking."[31] Augustine therefore counsels,

> Let your enjoyment be in listening to God and your speaking be prompted only by necessity; then you will not be a chatterbox at risk of not being guided aright. Anyway, why do you want to speak and not want to listen? You are always rushing out of doors but are unwilling to return to your own house. Your teacher is within …. It is inside that we listen to truth.[32]

In silence, as Augustine writes, we are guided by truth, in silence we learn from God. Hearing and speaking are, in fact, detrimental to moral activity.

The result of such silence is related to justice. Augustine writes, quoting the psalm, "I know that the Lord will see justice done for the needy." Then he expounds, "This needy person is not talkative, for anyone who is talkative aspires to wealth and is a stranger to hunger."[33] Augustine links talkativeness to selfishness and injustice and admonishes teachers not to speak unless it is truly necessary. He ends his exposition noting that God will be present for the needy, for the ones who see "the face of Christ" because they are pure-hearted and devout, not the ones who have learned to speak deceitful lies.[34] A contemporary deaf pastor puts Augustine's admonitions into the words of contemporary pastoral practice,

> Let me tell you what God has really done for me in my 'defective state.' He has created me with ears that hear what people REALLY say, for in my intensity to hear I listen not just with mechanically assisted hearing. I listen with my whole body. My eyes see the joy, pain and sorrow sometimes hidden in the words as the ears of my heart listen and read the body language of the speaker.[35]

In not rushing to speak, in maintaining silence, this pastor is able to love her neighbor by sharing joys and sorrows.

Moreover, what this deaf pastor describes about listening with her "whole body" can help those with hearing understand the detrimental aspects of multi-tasking. While research on multitasking over the past two decades consistently shows a negative impact, it remains difficult for people to step away from doing many things at once because our

---

[31] Augustine, "Exposition of Psalm 139," §15.
[32] Augustine, "Exposition of Psalm 139," §16.
[33] Augustine, "Exposition of Psalm 139," §17.
[34] Augustine, "Exposition of Psalm 139," §18.
[35] Elizabeth Von Trapp Walker, "Is Disability A Gift from God?" www.satcom.net/mariposa/gift_or_nov.html. Cited in Broesterhuizen, "Faith in Deaf Culture," 313.

technocratic society so emphasizes multitasking.[36] For a deaf person, listening and writing are not activities that can be done well simultaneously. (This is why deaf people often request note takers in academic and conference environments.)

Much more, of course, could and should be developed on the importance of silence and contemplative voice. In this section, I have aimed to offer a taste of the importance of silence for knowing God and for just moral action in relation to the silence of deafness. Such silence therefore appears as a Deaf Gain. Silence, I suggest, needs to be recovered and discussed in much more detail, as part of what deaf people bring and contribute to a church that stands in need of more and better silence. This is not to say that deaf people always experience or use silence well, nor that silence always becomes contemplative. It is, however, to put the silences of both deafness and contemplation in stark contrast to the problems of silence that the medical model and mainstream theology articulate.

For all that silence is a good in Christian tradition, it is still a limited good. Indeed, the very practice of contemplative silence itself demonstrates the ways the goods of our earthly existence are limited goods. Contemplative silence helps people be aware of bodily limits (deafness, as well as other kinds of limits), and, in becoming aware of our limitations, we may become even more able to respond to and receive God. In the next section, I conclude with a discussion of the caveats of understanding the benefits of silence as Deaf Gain.

THE LIMITS OF DEAF GAIN: EMBODIMENT AND THE WORKING OF THE HOLY SPIRIT

Predominant models of thinking about disability, the medical model discussed in the first section as well as the social model discussed in the above section, are troubling from a theological point of view. A medical model presumes that normalcy, as humans have typically defined it, equates with what God understands as "good." Yet, normalcy would seem to be precisely that which God critiques in scripture and tradition. It is not the normal, and especially the supernormal, whom God champions, but rather the poor, the meek, and the lowly.

The social model of disability has much to recommend it. Deaf Gain helps us see the importance of silence, both for deaf people and for the Christian tradition. Yet, the social model, which suggests that disability exists primarily where societies refuse to provide

---

[36] See, for example, Mareike D. Wieth and Bruce D. Burns, "Rewarding Multitasking: Negative Effects of an Incentive on Problem Solving Under Divided Attention," *Journal of Problem Solving* 7, no. 1 (2014): 60-72. The authors provide an overview of previous literature as well as demonstrate in their own study how multitasking continues to be an issue.

accommodations for those with disabilities, also falls short theologically. While social models rightly critique society's lack of responsiveness in building ramps or accessible bathrooms or other design features, social models often ignore or bypass a disabled individual's experience with disability by focusing so intently on making social changes. In promoting social barriers as a main reason for why people with disabilities encounter problems and difficulties, disability itself becomes included in the realm of what ought to count as normal. A social model enables and embraces people of all abilities and says that pretty much all abilities ought to be taken as goods. The proponents of Deaf Gain fit very well in the social model vision, taking a view of deafness as an unmitigated good that all people should welcome.

Theologian Deborah Creamer describes well some of the theological problems with the social model of disability. She suggests that the social model creates a "new normal" that appropriates deafness, for example, as a de facto good. In creating this de facto good, however, there is the negative effect of making any people who experience discomfort, pain, or unhappiness with their disabilities feel excluded.[37] Ironically, the social model's good impulses to embrace others who are different also creates barriers of acceptance – especially acceptance of the idea that deafness is not an unmitigated good. In turn, this prevents a fuller development and articulation of important theological concepts in relation to disability. For example, standing with those who are suffering is one way of practicing mercy and love. Suffering is also understood in some theological traditions as linked to the suffering of Christ, which can lead to some quite deep theological concepts about Christ, suffering, and life and death.

Creamer's alternative is a concept she calls "embodied limits."[38] Embodied limits stand, for Christians, as an alternative to either medical models of disability or to social models of disability that seek to include people with disabilities in mainstream society. Embodied limits enable all of us, disabled or not, to recognize the truth of what it means to be human: that we are embodied and that very embodiedness includes and creates limits. Limits can be painful and engender suffering. Limits mean that disabilities, including deafness, are not unmitigated goods, however much we might like them to be, but rather are "goods" only insofar as they are recognized as pertaining to everyone.

When it comes to critiquing Deaf Gain as a social model and offering an alternative, the silence of contemplation presents a help for

---

[37] Deborah Creamer, *Disability and Christian Theology: Embodied Limits and Constructive Possibilities* (New York: Oxford University Press, 2008), 27.
[38] Creamer especially describes embodied limits in *Disability and Christian Theology*, chapter five.

Christians. First, the very fact of our silent contemplation will quickly mean that we come face to face with our own goodness and woundedness. We will recognize our embodied limits. Recognizing those limits, however, can be, and usually is, very painful. We confront the fact that disability is not an absolute good, even as the disability of deafness can offer speedy entry into spiritual life with God. Martin Laird writes extensively on this aspect of the contemplative life.

> The doorway into the silent land is a wound. Silence lays bare this wound. We do not journey far along the spiritual path before we get some sense of the wound of the human condition, and this is precisely why not a few abandon a contemplative practice like meditation as soon as it begins to expose this wound; they move on instead to some spiritual entertainment that will maintain distraction. Perhaps this is why the weak and wounded, who know very well the vulnerability of the human condition, often have an aptitude for discovering silence and can sense the wholeness and healing that ground this wound.[39]

It is not a given that people will participate in silence, nor embrace the silence of contemplation, even if it is the condition of their physical lives in deafness. Those who are deaf do not necessarily willingly embrace deafness and the silence that goes with it. While we saw ways in which the silence of deafness can be tranquil, we cannot avoid the pain of deafness as exclusion. The silence of deafness separates the deaf from the social life of the hearing. That separation can be excruciatingly painful.

Laird presumes a hearing audience, an audience whose wounds appear to become no less excruciating when exposed to silence, even if that silence is not physically imposed in deafness. Yet, where those who are not deaf are free to leave aside contemplation in search of "entertainments," those who are deaf do not have such freedom. For Laird, this is positive, and he even goes on to suggest that the weak and wounded "often have an aptitude" for contemplation. That aptitude is not a given. Whether people receive silence willingly or unwillingly, they must at least be willing to confront wounds and suffering, even to embrace wounds as suffering as Jesus did on the cross.

Christian contemplation has a long tradition of contemplating God's broken and bruised body on the cross. In that contemplation, we marvel at how God has taken on human suffering – a marvel that can only be had if we trudge through the truth of our own embodied limits and suffering. Laird notes, "Because of the death and resurrection of Jesus, wounds, failure, disgrace, death itself all have a

---

[39] Laird, *Into the Silent Land*, 117.

hidden potential for revealing our deepest ground in God. Our wounds bear the perfumed trace of divine presence."[40] Silence does not avoid wounds or suffering, it runs straight toward them, especially in the Christian's focus on Christ's own life. We thus delve into the mystery of how death becomes life. Saint John of the Cross writes in *The Dark Night of the Soul*, "O sweet cautery,/ O delightful wound!/ O gentle hand! O delicate touch/ That tastes of eternal life/ And pays every debt!/ In killing you changed death to life."[41] The saint goes on to describe how the Holy Spirit is the cautery and the wound that leads us to God himself. God is encountered in our embodied limits.

Contemplation is not exclusive of other ways of meeting Christ that do not focus on such suffering. Part of what can be learned from this particular means of contemplation is that the wounds of Christ enable a different vision of hearing loss/Deaf Gain. Just as contemplative silence pointed us toward seeing the goodness of the physical silence encountered in hearing loss, so too the knowledge of contemplative silence points us toward the limits of physical silence, and the limits of being deaf. Put more boldly, contemplation itself asks Christians to confront their own limits, not by necessarily calling those limits good, but by allowing those limits simply to be there. Thus, Deaf Gain becomes rightly positioned as a relative gain, a gain that offers an important corrective to medical models of deafness that constantly seek to fix hearing loss. Deaf Gain, as a pattern of thought, understands the goodness that can come from various aspects of hearing loss as well as the manifold ways in which humans are limited.

Contemplation, however, takes people still further than the goods afforded by Deaf Gain suggest. Contemplative prayer, typically done in silence, understands that the silence of deafness cannot and should not always be seen as a good. Sometimes, people will simply not recognize silence as a gift, especially that which results from hearing loss. More significantly, silence can wound. It can be the cause of disruptions of relationships, of hurt, of misinterpreted conversations and lost meanings.

Instead, contemplative prayer asks practitioners to take an approach that acknowledges wounds, pain, disruption, but "to move through struggle; and the only way through is through – not around, over, under, or alongside, but through."[42] Thus, in contemplative practice, people can both embrace some of the beauty and blessedness that silence can bring, as well as acknowledge that silence can harm and hurt. Silence can cause separation between people, socially disrupt

---

[40] Laird, *Into the Silent Land*, 120.
[41] Saint John of the Cross, *The Dark Night of the Soul* (Westminster, MD: Newman Press, 1953), Stanza 2.
[42] Laird, *A Sunlit Absence*, 123.

lives, and lead to the detrimental aspects of health considered in section one.

It is important, too, to note that physical silence is meant to be a beginning point in the spiritual life. Physical silence is not the point of contemplative prayer, even though much of the tradition deems physical silence to be necessary especially when a person begins the practice. Thus, some of those who practice silence hope to progress in their prayer lives to the point that noise ceases to become a distraction, such that people can be with others, even noisy others, and attend to those others' needs without losing the practice of the presence of God. However, physical silence is not an end in itself but part of the means of contemplative prayer. In understanding this aspect of contemplative prayer, we can also see how the physical silence of deafness is a limit. It can provide an entry into silent contemplation. Those who are deaf can help others learn how to embrace the physical silence that can be so uncomfortable to those who hear.

One of the most celebrated contemplatives, Teresa of Avila, when writing her famous *Interior Castle*, a description of contemplative prayer and its stages, describes her head being full of noise. Teresa suffered from tinnitus, a condition that causes ringing and other noises in the ears. It is also a condition strongly linked to hearing loss. Teresa describes, "As I write this, the noises in my head are so loud that I am beginning to wonder what is going on in it. As I said at the outset, they have been making it almost impossible for me to obey those who commanded me to write. My head sounds just as if it were full of brimming rivers, and then as if all the water in those rivers came suddenly rushing downward."[43]

She observes all the noise in her head with a kind of detachment, however, and with a view toward incorporating even the turmoil of her tinnitus with her union with God. She writes, "I should not be surprised to know that the Lord has been pleased to send me this trouble in my head so that I may understand it better, for all this physical turmoil is no hindrance either to my prayer or to what I am saying now, but the tranquility and love in my soul are quite unaffected, and so are its desires and clearness of mind."[44] For Teresa, God is present in the turmoil of the tinnitus. She wonders if perhaps God is even especially speaking to her in her tinnitus. Her awareness of her physical condition does not prevent a relationship with God, nor prevent her prayer, nor cause her to pray for the removal of tinnitus. Rather, the tinnitus simply exists, and she constantly aims toward God no matter what her physical state is. Thus, physical silence may not remain permanent, but a person ought to be able to cultivate the

---

[43] Teresa of Avila, *Interior Castle*, IV.1. *The Complete Works of St. Teresa of Avila*, ed. Allison Peers (New York: Burns and Oates, 2002).
[44] Teresa of Avila, *Interior Castle*, IV.1.

benefits of silence even in the midst of the busy world. Or, as Martin Laird observes: "We learn to meet sound that displeases with the same stillness with which we meet the sounds that please us...."[45]

CONCLUSIONS

Meditation on deafness as Deaf Gain should rightfully cause us also to meditate more on a key aspect of deafness that Christian tradition has overlooked: the presumed problem with deafness (its silence) is also the seat of contemplative Christian practice. Silence is important. However, contemplation does not lead us to see deafness as an unmitigated good but to place deafness in relation to Christ's own life.

There are implications for Deaf Gain, and especially for the silence of both deafness and contemplation, on the fields of Christian theology of disability and moral theology. A Christian theology of disability might uncover surprises when it investigates disability not chiefly as a loss. but as a gain, just as a discussion of the silence of hearing loss deepens into a meditation on contemplation as a practice toward which all Christians should aim.

In relation to moral theology, my discussion of contemplation raises some intriguing questions about links between contemplative silence and the practices of justice and truth, as well as what it means to love our neighbors as ourselves. I have here only begun to develop this angle. More work needs to be done in describing more fully how moral life and contemplative silence might be linked and, in turn, what that means for Christians as they seek to live lives of justice in the contemporary world.

---

[45] Laird, *A Sunlit Absence*, 49.

Becoming Friends: Ethics in Friendship and in Doing Theology

Lorraine Cuddeback

For the first time in a decade, I would be attending prom. Not a high school event, but the annual prom hosted by a local center for adults with intellectual and developmental disabilities. The event was eagerly anticipated for weeks, maybe months, ahead of time, chattered about in the arts and crafts class where I volunteer and observe. My decision to attend was fairly last minute. I'd been asked repeatedly by the clients, with whom I work at the center, whether I was coming.[1] When I finally announce that, yes, I would be volunteering that night, the two women I'm helping at the moment (we were making Mother's Day cards) become visibly excited.
"Awesome," says Jess.[2]
"Great!" This is Kara, one of Jess's best friends. "I'm going to take a picture with you," Kara continues. I'm caught by surprise. *She wants a picture of us together?* But I never ask a follow-up, and Kara and Jess move on, talking about pre-prom plans with their dates.

ACROSS THE FIELD OF CONTEMPORARY theological work on disability, "friendship" is certainly one of the most common and consistent themes employed by scholars. Along those lines, almost every major theological work on intellectual disability in recent years has included some form of personal narrative about the author's friendship with a person who has an intellectual disability—Jean Vanier's intimate reflections on L'Arche and the formal theological work of Hans Reinders are prime examples.[3]

---

[1] The term "client" is the center's terminology for the people with intellectual disabilities that it serves, which I have adopted out of respect to the environment I'm depicting.
[2] All names of persons and locations have been changed to preserve privacy of those participating in my fieldwork.
[3] Regarding language, in this essay I am abiding by the "person-first" convention, thus using the descriptor "a person with a disability" rather than "a disabled person." With some exceptions, this is the broadly accepted convention among disability advocates. I use the term "intellectual disability" to encompass a range of conditions that impact intellectual development and limit social adaptation. The broadness of this definition is designed to reflect my field site, as most of the clients I work with have multiple disabilities, physical and intellectual (and in a few cases, mental illness, as well), and few have disclosed the precise diagnosis of their intellectual disabilities to me. Use of

Friendship is cast as one of our principal ethical obligations to people with intellectual disabilities as an antidote to a thin, legalistic understanding of "inclusion," as a way beyond the simple provision of access or resources, and as a movement toward true belonging and community integration. Even as I support these ends, there is something more that needs to be said about friendship and intellectual disability.

Friendship is complex, fraught with risk, exposure, and moral challenge. In general terms, few theologians would dispute this description of friendship. However, when the topic is friendship and intellectual disability, theologically situated moral appeals for the good of friendship with people who have an intellectual disability tend to fall short on two significant counts. First, there is an unreflective tendency to focus on friendships between people without intellectual disabilities and people who have an intellectual disability—and this neglects the friendships that exist among people with intellectual disabilities themselves. This tendency is the result of praiseworthy efforts to focus on a shared humanity rather than aspects of human difference. This tendency, however, leads to a second problem: such theologies are liable to gloss over difference in a way that obscures the risks and vulnerabilities of friendship. Without recognition of these challenges, appeals to friendship (and, particularly, personal narratives about friendship and intellectual disability) risk the kind of instrumentalization of people with intellectual disabilities that should be avoided.

In this essay, I describe a strategy for giving proper, method-grounded attention to the friendships that exist among people with intellectual disabilities—and I do so through discussion of ethnographic fieldwork I have been doing in a non-profit organization that serves adults with various kinds of intellectual disabilities. Through this ethnographic work, I raise a critical question concerning the theological appeals to friendship that have been held forth as solutions to the problem of inclusion. This rejection of the 'inclusion paradigm' rests on the paradigm's tendency toward an unwarranted division between justice and love. Instead, I argue that justice is a necessary part of our friendships, not because of a liberal vision of equality, but because of the differences that mark human relationships. To this extent, I critically engage the role that friendship plays in Hans Reinders's theological anthropology. Reinders's desire for a universal definition of humanity causes him to problematically neglect how difference engenders risk and vulnerability in friendship. Thomas Reynolds's work on difference and vulnerability offers a corrective to Reinders, as well as a way of understanding the role that justice may

---

the term "disability" without the modifier "intellectual" will be reserved for points that encompass a larger range of physical, intellectual, or emotional disabilities.

play in friendship. I conclude with an argument for careful reflexivity in our appeals to friendship with people with intellectual disabilities — a reflexivity that I will also perform throughout the essay.

THE MEANING OF INCLUSION

I've been attending the arts and crafts class as a participant observer for two years now, and, in that time, I've watched the friendship between Jess and Kara evolve. They've worked together for some years in a workshop, run by the center, where many clients work to earn money, but mostly to occupy their day.[4] The narrative they tell of their friendship begins around the time I met them. "Kara came to my pool party when no one else did," Jess says, going into detail about the arrangements she had made (which everyone except Kara missed out on). "I'm not going to have another one," she threatens, disappointed with her other friends, "but Kara can come over, still."

As best friends go, Jess and Kara are almost comedic opposites, the kind you might see in a sitcom. Jess is short, heavyset, with a bob of brown hair that she and her mother often dye together — currently reddish brown, not far from a color I use on my own hair. Jess is a bubbly talker, loves the color pink and "Hello Kitty," and takes pride in making glittery crafts she passes on to friends. She lives with her family and is something of a gossip. At times, I admit I get a sense of something like a "mean girl" streak in her possessiveness over friends and preoccupation with status symbols, which can include both Build-A-Bear stuffed animals and a Kindle Fire.

Kara, meanwhile, is tall to Jess's short, with salt and pepper hair consistently trimmed close to her head. She wears somber colors and plain cotton t-shirts, and lives on her own with help from daily staff. Kara talks a lot less than Jess, and Jess is very capable of filling the silence. Where Jess has cycled through numerous boyfriends (and some more than once) in the time I've known the pair, Kara has been dating one close friend of hers for close to two years. She is always willing to accept invitations but is also reserved about them. She is subject to frequent seizures and often has to miss the social events that she is most excited about.

In the months leading up to Prom, it became increasingly apparent to me that I am seen as included in their social circle. Questions about

---

[4] The workshop was a former "sheltered workshop," a model which employs people with disabilities in order to complete basic tasks, such as filling bottles or applying labels. The workers with disabilities earn a low-piece rate for their work, often only a few cents per bottle or label. This model has mostly fallen out of use, in favor of community-based employment at an hourly wage and with supports, which the center where I do my research is in the process of establishing. Still, some sheltered workshops remain because of family and client preferences for a relatively private, predictable working space, and in no small part because of the relationships they can engender. See Alberto Migliore, Teresa Grossi, David Mank, and Patricia Rogan, "Why Do Adults with Intellectual Disabilities Work in Sheltered Workshops?" *Journal of Vocational Rehabilitation* 28, no. 1 (2008): 29–40.

what other events I would be attending became more common (such as other dances, or an annual overnight camping trip), and their disappointment more explicit when I said no. This was typically followed by a stronger insistence that "next year" I should go. If I'm late to class, Kara points it out. If I miss and don't tell them beforehand, I'm asked about it next time I see them.

And I've been resistant to their questioning. I'm a volunteer —but I'm also a researcher. Both Jess and Kara know my position. They signed consent forms, willingly and eagerly, when I explained that I will be incorporating their stories in my schoolwork and writing. For me, the knowledge that the time I spend in their art class is in service of another goal is always at the forefront of my mind. Often, it makes me feel dishonest, disingenuous. Am I really engaging in the mutuality of friendship if all the time I spend with these women will be mined for my academic work? For the past couple of years, I have strictly enforced the spatial and temporal boundaries of my relationship with them: only these couple of hours, only in this space. Such boundaries give me comfort that I am not building up expectations I cannot fulfill.

Inclusion and Being "Normal"

The important role of friendship and inclusion in the lives of people with intellectual disabilities is a growing point of discussion within social science literature, which indicates three interrelated challenges that need to be addressed: social segregation and isolation, shallowness of community encounters, and the ideology of "normal." The problem of social isolation and exclusion on a broad scale is well-documented, as Roy Baumeister's overview indicates.[5] Baumeister illustrates that long-term experiences of exclusion can inhibit emotional growth and empathy across demographics. While there have been significant societal improvements in physical access to space and resources, authentic, relational inclusion is still a struggle. The everyday lives of people with intellectual disabilities are often highly structured and micro-managed. They are directed, often literally driven by caretakers and family members to a variety of programs, appointments, and institutional locations that serve only other people with intellectual and developmental disabilities.

A 2009 study of social practices of inclusion in New Zealand gives further detail to the problem of isolation for people with intellectual disabilities by describing how their community encounters feel shallow and inadequate.[6] The problem was not that participants had no access to community spaces but rather that their interactions with

---

[5] Roy F. Baumeister, "Effects of Social Exclusion and Interpersonal Rejection: An Overview with Implications for Human Disability," in *The Paradox of Disability: Responses to Jean Vanier and L'Arche Communities from Theology and the Sciences*, ed. Hans S. Reinders (Grand Rapids: William B. Eerdmans Publishing Co., 2010).

[6] P. Milner and Bernadette Kelly, "Community Participation and Inclusion: People with Disabilities Defining Their Place," *Disability & Society* 24, no. 1 (2009): 47-62.

other community members rarely happened on the terms that people with disabilities desired. One participant, named Kelly, described how time in the community was limited by rules set by her professional staff: "Well, basically you go out, or if you don't do what you're told, you get told off, but no, they basically want you out in the community."[7] Indeed, spatial inclusion is insufficient without relationship, which leads to the third problem: inclusion often presumes the dictum of "normalization." Though developed as a way to empower people with disabilities to have "normal" lives, today's version of the concept tends to expect assimilation: i.e., that relationships may flourish only insofar as people with disabilities can pass as "normal."[8]

This final problem of assimilation to the "normal" points to a particularly insidious obstacle for inclusion. Authentic inclusion of people with intellectual disabilities often requires challenging the values of the surrounding society, challenging what we presume to be "normal." Lennard Davis's definitional work in disability studies, *Enforcing Normalcy*, argues that "normal" is an inescapably value-laden term, which operates in a social hegemony of normalcy.[9] In fact, the word "normal" itself is a development of the mid-nineteenth century. Prior to the concept of normalcy, one might have spoken of an "ideal," but an ideal was by definition unreachable. Even if the ideal was in some sense aspirational, it was not prescriptive. Normal, by contrast, came to be prescriptive in large part because of its cooption by the eugenics movement of the early twentieth century, a time when

---

[7] Milner and Kelly, "Community Participation and Inclusion," 51.

[8] "Normalization" has undergone significant shifts and development as a concept. Initially developed in Sweden by Bengt Nirje in the 1970s, normalization meant making available the kinds of opportunities and experiences to people with disabilities to which people without disabilities have ready access. Wolf Wolfensberger championed the concept in the United States but eventually changed the terminology to "social role valorization." See Wolf Wolfensberger, "Social Role Valorization: A Proposed New Term for the Principle of Normalization," *Intellectual and Developmental Disabilities* 49, no. 6 (December 2011): 435–40. This was shortly after Wolfensberger and Nirje parted ways on the concept, with Nirje expressing concern that Wolfensberger was using "normalization/social role valorization" as a way of reinforcing the status quo regarding social stratification, rather than challenging it. Wolfensberger refuted this charge, arguing that the "empowerment" Nirje's version promoted was less important than the ability to offer practical, empirically-verifiable means of improving the lives of people with intellectual disabilities. See Wolf Wolfensberger, "Social Role Valorization And, or Versus, Empowerment," *Intellectual and Developmental Disabilities* 49, no. 6 (December 2011): 469–76. Yet, the debate about whether normalization helps or further restricts continues. See Sheridan Forster, "Age-Appropriateness: Enabler or Barrier to a Good Life for People with Profound Intellectual and Multiple Disabilities?" *Journal of Intellectual and Developmental Disability* 35, no. 2 (June 2010): 129-131.

[9] Lennard Davis, *Enforcing Normalcy: Disability, Deafness, and the Body* (New York: Verso, 1995).

the United States was rapidly changing and the predominantly white middle class felt threatened. Sir Francis Galton, both an early statistician and a eugenicist, developed the statistical bell curve into a "normal distribution curve," essentially making one end of the curve desirable, and the other undesirable, the result of deficiency or failure. By applying value across the curve, Galton redefined "ideal" into a location within the statistical distribution: "The new ideal of ranked order is powered by the notion of progress, human perfectibility, and the elimination of deviance."[10] The eugenic desire to eliminate deviance was ultimately a desire to eliminate difference, to make society "normal," with a definition that favored white, middle class culture and values.[11]

Our expectations for normal are never merely descriptive but grounded in a particular set of values and expectations. Passing for normal will not be possible for many people with disabilities. Rather than pushing people with disabilities towards assimilation, moral philosopher Eva Kittay suggests that a caretaker, professional or otherwise, must prepare society to accept her dependent just as much as, if not more than, she must prepare her dependent for socialization.[12] Current practices with the aim of community inclusion encounter a number of problems in this area.[13] These practices tend to emphasize the frequency of community encounters rather than the quality or intimacy those encounters may occasion. These practices fail to encourage the staff, professionals, and caretakers (inevitably responsible for facilitating inclusion) to challenge the presumptions of a hostile society. Finally, normalization privileges the cultivation of relationships between people without intellectual disabilities and

---

[10] Davis, *Enforcing Normalcy*, 35.
[11] Davis, *Enforcing Normalcy*, 27. Davis actually notes a slight difference between the celebration of the middle class as the rational mean and Galton's contribution of ranking. Davis considers Adolphe Quetelet to be the statistician who first developed the concept of *l'homme moyen*, and therefore *les classes moyens* as "the exemplar of the middle way of life" (26-27). Quetelet's concept would have seen both ends of deviance from the statistical median as problematic, whereas Galton's version only sees one end as such. Allison Carey's work on the development of rights for people with intellectual disabilities also addresses the link between eugenics and the desire for a bourgeois cultural hegemony, in much greater detail than Davis. See Allison Carey, *On the Margins of Citizenship: Intellectual Disability and Civil Rights in Twentieth-Century America* (Philadelphia: Temple University Press, 2010), 52-82.
[12] Eva Feder Kittay, *Love's Labour: Essays on Women, Equality, and Dependency* (New York: Routledge, 1999), 33. Kittay's stress on the dual direction of preparing both society and a dependent for socialization is her adaptation of philosopher Sarah Ruddick's concept of "mothering."
[13] Tim Clement and Christine Bigby, "Breaking Out of a Distinct Social Space: Reflections on Supporting Community Participation for People with Severe and Profound Intellectual Disability," *Journal of Applied Research in Intellectual Disabilities* 22, no. 3 (May 2009): 264–75.

people with intellectual disabilities. The result is that relationships among the latter community are rendered invisible in the debate.[14]

Debates about Inclusion within Theology

Much of the dissatisfaction with the merely spatial inclusion described above has also been named among theological ethicists, which generates their turn to friendship as the proper theological response. Both Hans Reinders and John Swinton have written critiques of inclusion as a political paradigm. Swinton locates the concept of inclusion within the realm of law (as a goal that legislation like the Americans with Disabilities Act would pursue) but argues that Christians are instead called to offer people with disabilities a place of belonging.[15] He expresses concern that social or minority models of disability (on which the ADA is based), which define the experience of disability as one of oppression and injustice, render people with disabilities too thinly by ignoring the differences that mark the heterogeneous category of disability. At the same time, simply marking disability as "difference" is also problematic. Though Swinton does not cite Davis, he shares the same concerns about seeing disability as a deviation from "normal" and invokes the relationship of statistical norms and eugenics in the United States. Rather, Swinton argues, "the only real norm for human beings, even at a genetic level, is difference."[16]

Swinton claims that both deviance and social models for disability lack the moral torque to draw people into relationship with one another.[17] Swinton's proposal is to encourage "thick" understandings

---

[14] Even with a generous read of the potential for Wolfensberger's work on normalization and social role valorization to challenge the status quo, he makes it clear that "deviant individuals should have maximal exposure to the nondeviant, and minimal exposure (or juxtaposition) to workers, volunteers, or other individuals who are perceived deviants themselves." See Wolf Wolfensberger, *The Principle of Normalization in Human Services* (Toronto: National Institute on Mental Retardation, 1972), 35. The reasoning is that the perceived value of people with intellectual disabilities will only be improved if they associate with people who already have social value (that is, people without disabilities).

[15] John Swinton, "From Inclusion to Belonging: A Practical Theology of Community, Disability and Humanness," *Journal of Religion, Disability & Health* 16, no. 2 (2012): 172–90.

[16] Swinton, "From Inclusion to Belonging," 179.

[17] The social model or minority model of disability argues that having a disability is not a deficiency, but rather a result of systems of exclusion that limit the participation of people with certain bodily, intellectual, or emotional impairments in society, particularly their access to rights such as employment or housing. Swinton is operating within the UK definition of the social model, though he holds it close to the version developed in the United States. Swinton understands the minority model to claim that it is the "shared experience of oppression rather than the particularity of experiences (e.g., autism, paraplegia, schizophrenia, hearing impairment) that forms the category

of people with intellectual disabilities, by being in relationship with them.[18] To make this point, he describes the experience of a man named Kevin in a church community.

> After much debate the staff group decided to take Kevin to a local faith community. They viewed this purely as a social opportunity as they did not feel justified taking him on religious grounds. Nevertheless, they recognized this as an important dimension of Kevin's life and were keen to help him explore it. During the three months he attended, not one person spoke to him. One person patted him on the head in passing but that was it!... Kevin was perceived by the church as disabled—a thin person; someone (it seems to have been presumed) without a personality or the longings and desires that so called normal people take for granted. He was a stranger, a member of that odd group of people we call the disabled. Kevin was *included*, but he did not *belong*.[19]

We see in this anecdote some of the problems named by social scientists. Kevin was granted physical access to the church but no relationships resulted. His support professionals viewed his time in church as a general social benefit, but there is no indication they tried to help facilitate these relationships (nor that they would have known how to, if the religious community was foreign to them). The problem, Swinton argues, is that "while law can change structures it simply cannot change hearts."[20] Swinton's basic insight is accurate: the law is not designed for conversion. Nonetheless, he risks putting too large of a wedge between the role of law and love in shaping practices of either inclusion or belonging. By underestimating the importance of laws like the ADA, which are explicitly concerned with promoting justice and combatting injustice, Swinton also reveals a "thin" understanding of the importance of justice within relationships, within love.

---

of disability and binds people with a variety of impairments together as a political movement." Swinton, "From Inclusion to Belonging," 175-176.

[18] Swinton make this claim with reference to anthropologist Clifford Geertz's famed "thick description." As Swinton defines the concept: "A thick description of a situation focuses not simply on the bare bones of the phenomenon under observation, but also its context and the deep and meaningful activities that participants engage in. So, for example, if I wink at someone, at one level I am simply closing my right eye. However, the meaning behind this gesture and the cultural context from which it emerges and into which it speaks, means that the simple gesture of quickly opening and closing my eye has a whole range of meanings and indicates a range of emotions and social possibilities: amusement, deceit, friendliness, farewell, and so on. Thick descriptions strive to see the whole of a thing." Swinton, "From Inclusion to Belonging," 180.

[19] Swinton, "From Inclusion to Belonging,"180-181. Emphasis original.

[20] Swinton, "From Inclusion to Belonging," 182.

Reinders offers a similar critique of inclusion, though he does not render love and law in quite as exclusive categories as Swinton.[21] Instead, Reinders argues for an "ecological" vision of inclusion, one that is "distinct from—not opposed to—a political approach."[22] An ecological approach to inclusion would recognize that each person has particular needs, a natural environment in which that person may flourish. Here, Reinders is subtly playing on the notion of difference, since each person's "ecology" would vary by different needs and capacities. Part of everyone's ecology is the need to be chosen for friendship, or colloquially, "being the apple in someone else's eye."[23] Here, Reinders offers the story of Larry, a man with an intellectual disability, who would frequently and loudly scream at home. Eventually, Larry started to attend a men's volleyball game, where the team "took him in, screaming and all, as their number one fan, which made him a lot of friends. And, of course, after a while Larry virtually stopped screaming at home."[24]

The stories given by Reinders and Swinton offer friendship as a necessary corrective to shallow understandings of inclusion, with which, as noted above, the social science literature struggles. Friendship with people with intellectual disabilities prompts the conversion of heart for which Swinton argues and could in turn prompt the challenge to society's "normal" that is so badly needed. Yet, in the anecdotes that Swinton and Reinders offer, the necessary friendships are those between people with intellectual disabilities and people without them. Both want to avoid essentializing disability while, at the same time, they want to bring the commonalities between people with and without intellectual disabilities to the fore.

Yet, in their desire to promote these kinds of friendships, both Reinders and Swinton neglect how people with intellectual disabilities are already navigating their relationships with others, nondisabled and disabled alike. Part of what is at stake, both in theology and in the social sciences, is an epistemological position. If, as Swinton calls for, we need to see people with intellectual disabilities in a "thick" sense then we need to place ourselves in a position to seek all the layers, contexts, and meanings in their relationships. Yet, as I am learning through my fieldwork, placing ourselves in the thick of things raises a question of accountability. Which meanings come to the fore? Whose voices are we letting through?[25] Swinton, an established

---

[21] Hans S. Reinders, "The Power of Inclusion and Friendship," *Journal of Religion, Disability & Health* 15, no. 4 (2011): 431-436.
[22] Reinders, "The Power of Inclusion and Friendship," 434.
[23] Reinders, "The Power of Inclusion and Friendship," 434.
[24] Reinders, "The Power of Inclusion and Friendship," 435.
[25] This epistemological move is indebted to the work of moral philosophers Eva Kittay and Licia Carlson. Kittay's work concerning her experiences as mother to Sesha, her daughter with a profound intellectual disability, calls for philosophy to hold both an

qualitative researcher, knows this and gives his story in the role of a researcher, on the outside of the relationships and events he is recording. Similarly, Reinders's story of Larry is third-hand, given from a distance (but as will be discussed below, this is not the only time Reinders invokes friendship). In narrating from the outside, both men implicitly assume that people with intellectual disabilities cannot directly contribute to our understandings of friendship, of inclusion, or of doing theology itself.

THE VALUE OF FRIENDSHIP

The theological value of friendship is intertwined with the Christian understanding of the human relationship with God. Reinders's work on friendship with people with intellectual disabilities relies on such a connection between God's friendship with us and our friendships with others. In *Receiving the Gift of Friendship*, he seeks a theological anthropology that is universal enough to account for the existence of people with profound intellectual disabilities, naming in particular a micro-encephalic woman named Kelly.[26] While Reinders is not trying to dismiss the reality of human difference, his fear that such difference would define someone like Kelly out of humankind prompt him to argue that we must look at "sameness" before we turn to difference. Indeed, contra the

---

"epistemic responsibility" (to have an adequate understanding of intellectual disability) and "epistemic modesty" (regarding the extent of their authority on interpretations of intellectual disability). See Eva Feder Kittay, "The Personal is Philosophical is Political: A Philosopher and Mother of a Cognitively Disabled Person Sends Notes from the Battlefield," in *Cognitive Disability and Its Challenge to Moral Philosophy*, eds. Eva Feder Kittay and Licia Carlson (Malden: Wiley-Blackwell, 2010): 393-413. Carlson further develops this thread in her own work, criticizing the discursive practices of most philosophers for distancing themselves from the particular realities of people with intellectual disabilities and for acting as gatekeepers in the subject. Carlson comments: "Whose perspectives are absent from philosophical discussions of intellectual disability? The most profound silence surrounds persons with the disabilities themselves. While individuals with profound and severe intellectual disabilities may be incapable of entering into the conversation, there is a paucity of work that includes the voices of those with mild intellectual disabilities" (121). Generally, the phenomenon that Carlson describes for philosophy applies to the broader state of the literature on intellectual and developmental disability within theology, as well. See Licia Carlson, *The Faces of Intellectual Disability: Philosophical Reflections* (Bloomington: Indiana University Press, 2010), 105-130.

[26] Micro-encephaly is a condition in which a person has an extremely underdeveloped brain. Reinders describes Kelly as missing "a significant part of the normal human brain," and characterizes her profound disability as "meaning that for all the important activities that characterize our lives — health, safety, relationships, communication, and so on — she will be entirely dependent on others .... Kelly's condition does not allow her any 'interior space,' by which I refer to the inner life, that part of me where I am with myself." See Hans S. Reinders, *Receiving the Gift of Friendship: Profound Disability, Theological Anthropology, and Ethics* (Grand Rapids: William B. Eerdmans Publishing, 2008), 21.

postmodern emphasis on difference, Reinders argues that "difference can be celebrated only because it has no theological significance."[27] Yet, his turn to "sameness" ultimately fails to take account of how differences shape the way we both experience and respond to the offer of God's grace.

To begin with, friendship plays a significant role in Reinders's theological anthropology. In order to make sure Kelly is included as a person, Reinders refuses any reliance on intrinsic human capacities, such as reason. Instead, he defines "person" solely on the extrinsic quality of God's gratuitous love for us. We experience God's offer of grace in this life as friendship with God's own self, knowledge of which is made possible by our friendships with others. However, Reinders's eschewal of human agency impacts how we understand the role of friend. He argues against an Aristotelian understanding of friendship that relies on equality, or mutual beneficence, aspects that are difficult to identify in friendships between those with and without intellectual disabilities.[28] In a typically Aristotelian friendship, a friend first gives in order that the friend might one day receive. For Christians, however, our nature is founded on gift. Our primary relationship comes from God's gift of friendship. Therefore, the act of *receiving* should have priority, not the act of giving. Reception is where Reinders locates the value of friendships because it is important that "knowing how to receive is necessarily prior to knowing how to give."[29] People with intellectual disabilities provide a witness to what it means to receive and to trust in God.

Reinders is aware of the risks of these claims. In speaking of being friends with people with intellectual disabilities, we must be careful not to either romanticize or instrumentalize such relationships. Reinders works against the romanticization of friendship with people with intellectual disabilities by drawing on the work of Jean Vanier and other personal accounts of those who have worked as assistants in L'Arche communities, in which friendship, vulnerability, and mutuality are permeating themes. Reinders describes the process of becoming friends with someone with an intellectual disability as a difficult process of conversion, of sacrificing a sense of superiority and virtue in the "choice" to serve this community, highlighting Henri Nouwen's biographical account of his time spent in L'Arche, *Adam*, as an exemplar of this process.[30] By caring for the core members of a L'Arche community, an assistant like Nouwen will be confronted by his own fragility, by the limits that are inherent across all human lives, not just those with disabilities. Eventually, through friendship, all

---

[27] Reinders, *Receiving the Gift of Friendship*, 283-84.
[28] Reinders, *Receiving the Gift of Friendship*, 360.
[29] Reinders, *Receiving the Gift of Friendship*, 318.
[30] Henri Nouwen, *Adam, God's Beloved* (Maryknoll: Orbis Books, 1997).

(regardless of whether they have a disability) will become able to see ourselves as God sees us.[31]

Yet, celebrating what we who are without intellectual disabilities may learn through friendships with people with intellectual disabilities points to the problem of instrumentalization, to which Reinders objects because it places the human value of people with intellectual disabilities within the problematic "contributory model" critiqued by David Pailin.[32] Reinders tries to distance himself from this charge with two strategies. First, Reinders engages Pailin's Kantian argument against instrumental value while also arguing that Kant's system is inherently disordered because it leaves God out of the framework. The Kantian moral logic is ordered only to our own good and the good of the other. By contrast, Reinders proposes a logic of three, that we (one) treat the other (two) in light of our true moral object, God (three). The question is not how to treat the other but how to treat the other as a response to how we are treated by God. This leads to the second strategy. Within this three-way relationship, we return to the claim that receiving is prior to giving. Friendship is a response, is a result of "paying forward" the gift of friendship that God has already offered to us.[33]

This solution, however, is tenuous. Reinders insists that "friendship is its own reward," and our calling as people without intellectual disabilities is to be friends with those who have intellectual disabilities (as much as those without) "for their own sake."[34] Moreover, he asserts that "true friendship is about committing ourselves to those who are despicable in the eyes of the world."[35] Though we do not originate the gift, it matters to whom the gift is offered, namely those "despised" by the world of normalcy, people with intellectual disabilities. At the same time, at any moment that any

---

[31] Reinders, *Receiving the Gift of Friendship*, 335-344.

[32] Reinders examines and generally accepts the critiques of the "contributory view of worth" in Pailin's work (Reinders, *Receiving the Gift of Friendship*, 206-216). See David Pailin, *A Gentle Touch: From a Theology of Handicap to a Theology of Human Being* (London: SPCK, 1992). Though Reinders celebrates the lack of romanticization in the L'Arche accounts, in using them as exemplars, he does not address the multiplicity of ways in which Vanier and Nouwen both potentially instrumentalize core members of L'Arche precisely by emphasizing how they expose "a hidden sense of superiority," or prompt each other "to face the truth about themselves" (Pailin, *A Gentle Touch*, 339-340). That being said, Vanier's tone, at least, varied widely depending on audience and goal, and it is very possible his instrumentalizing narratives were used to appeal to a particular kind of reader. For a general overview of Vanier's biography, insights and writings on L'Arche, see Jean Vanier, *Jean Vanier: Essential Writings,* trans. and ed. Carolyn Whitney-Brown, (Maryknoll: Orbis Books, 2008).

[33] Reinders, *Receiving the Gift of Friendship*, 316-318.

[34] Reinders, *Receiving the Gift of Friendship*, 349.

[35] Reinders, *Receiving the Gift of Friendship*, 365.

of us have friends, it is because we have been chosen by others (similar to the way we have been chosen by God): the "important thing in friendship for me is what the other person does...by *claiming me as a friend.*"[36] Reinders offers his own relationship with Ronald, a friend who has an intellectual disability, as an example. However, he makes this claim with language that cannot avoid describing something like agency: Ronald "found" Reinders. We do not choose but are chosen *by someone*.

Despite his efforts, Reinders has a hard time escaping the logic of agency in its entirety. This is not to say his warnings about hubris are not insightful or needed. My own fears about the authenticity of my relationship with Jess and Kara are founded on precisely the worry that, as long as I am using my time with them for the alternative purposes of research and writing, there can be no genuine friendship. Boundaries, the capacity for me to choose when I come and go, may well be a "strength" in which I am "hiding," to borrow Reinders's phrasing.[37] I chose to do fieldwork as a part of my research precisely because I wanted to write "thick descriptions," as Swinton called for. I did not want to fall victim to the temptation of *writing about*, rather than *being with*, a temptation Reinders himself confesses. He also warns that this decision bears the risk of trying to legitimize my words and my thinking on intellectual disability with an appeal to a friendship: another kind of instrumentalization which I fear.[38]

Nonetheless, though I have made my research known, though I remind Jess and Kara of my work, and though I draw boundaries, *I have been claimed* by them as a friend. My concerns about this claiming reflects another question that Reinders raises: how can I be certain of an authentic friendship?[39] Reinders asks this question to remind people without intellectual disabilities of how sin affects all relationships and hides all the ways one might fail as a friend. This reminder is not unwarranted, but it is limited and is precisely where he runs into the problem of difference. Using the story of the man born blind in John 9, Reinders indicates that it is only through God's forgiveness that we can learn to "see" properly, to see everyone, especially people with intellectual disabilities, the way God sees all of us. The agency to forgive belongs to God, but the agency for sin and conversion belongs to us. Yet, Reinders never asks if people with intellectual disabilities need to undergo this conversion process, as well. Reinders rightly uses John 9 to put distance between the assumption that disability and sin have a causal relationship.[40] I cannot

---

[36] Reinders, *Receiving the Gift of Friendship*, 366, emphasis in the original.
[37] Reinders, *Receiving the Gift of Friendship*, 342.
[38] Reinders, *Receiving the Gift of Friendship*, 356.
[39] Reinders, *Receiving the Gift of Friendship*, 364.
[40] Reinders, *Receiving the Gift of Friendship*, 327.

emphasize enough that he, and others, are correct to do so. Nonetheless, in issuing this warning against a sinfulness that people with intellectual disabilities seem to have no part of, Reinders reveals how unilateral his conception of friendship really is. People with intellectual disabilities can *claim* friends—demonstrating a necessary agency that Reinders seems to otherwise want to avoid—yet he does not *explicitly* recognize in people with intellectual disabilities their own capacities to use these friends, to hide in their own particular kinds of strength.[41] Rather, as will be seen below, this difference remains implicit, seen in his narrative about Ronald, but never wrestled with in a theological sense. Despite a claim that human difference is insignificant, Reinders inadvertently renders a difference between people with disabilities and those without that is unavoidably theological and significant.[42]

DIFFERENCE AND VULNERABILITY IN FRIENDSHIP

> It has been a hard winter for Jess and Kara. On an afternoon in late January, waiting for instructions on that week's craft, I hear Jess tell Kara, "Guess what I have to do Wednesday?" Jess's voice drops, like when she tells gossipy stories, her can-you-believe-it stories. I hear only a few words: the name of a nearby town, and "she needs this." Eventually, Kara noticed my interest in the conversation. She looks over and tells me, "We had a problem this week."
> "Oh yeah?" I ask, expecting the regular problems: relationship drama, accusations of theft, someone getting fired. These were common topics of gossip.
> "A wake and a funeral on Monday." From there, the story spills from Jess and Kara in overlapping fragments. Liza was her name, and she was a co-worker. She had started a community job some months earlier, so she wasn't around as much, only spending one day a week at the workshop. Later, Jess tells me Liza volunteered at the humane society with her. The two women describe their friend as generous, sharing whatever she didn't want.
> "She used to talk to me a lot," says Kara, "and you know with some of these people...." She drops off for a moment, before finishing: "I don't have a lot of friends."

---

[41]Reinders does address the history of attributing intellectual disability to moral disorder, specifically in Wolf Wolfensberger's work. Reinders seems to be wary of the claim, though he does appreciate that Wolfensberger renders the relationship of the will to intellectual disability in a way that limits moral culpability, or at least makes it ambiguous, although ultimately Reinders finds the question of moral accountability irrelevant to understanding ethical obligations of the nondisabled. Reinders, *Receiving the Gift of Friendship*, 302-307; see also Wolf Wolfensberger, "An Attempt to Gain a Better Understanding from a Christian Perspective of What 'Mental Retardation' Is," in *The Theological Voice of Wolf Wolfensberger*, ed. William C. Gaventa and David L. Coulter (New York: The Haworth Press, 2001), 71-83.

[42] Wolfensberger, "An Attempt to Gain a Better Understanding," 284.

"Except me," asserts Jess.

"Well, yeah," Kara agrees, "but I mean of those folks," her co-workers.

The conversation continues as Jess and Kara unpack the events that immediately preceded her death. Liza had felt unwell at work and went to the emergency room that night. Doctors found a blood clot, which moved quickly to her lungs. She died the next day.

"How did you find out?" I asked Jess, who told Kara and their other friends.

"Facebook." Jess says, with a withering look.

"Wow." The indignity of it understood, I feel hurt on Jess's behalf.

"At 5:30 in the morning," she continues, "I bawled my eyes out to my Dad and told him." Then she went to work and spread the news. At this point, their story becomes more fragments than narrative, but I learn that Kara and Jess went to the funeral together. Jess says, of Liza, "We were best friends. You know how I am. We were like sisters."

That night, I go to a coffee shop to write up my field notes. In my listening, in my jotting, I never told Jess or Kara how well I understood their loss. They don't know that I have also lost someone I loved, someone who had an intellectual disability and died suddenly. I never said that I am still working out in my theology what it means to love and be loved by someone with an intellectual disability, but, as I sit and write that night, I feel the old wounds, old grief resurface. I open my phone and call for a friend to join me.

Although Reinders recognizes human insufficiency, interdependence, and vulnerability, it is Thomas Reynolds's work in *Vulnerable Communion* that more deeply delves into the tragedies that inevitably accompany encounters with human finitude and the fearful reaction each of us has to that instability. On a basic level, Reynolds and Reinders agree that our existence, our human nature, is primarily defined by gift, that it is God's gift to us. Where they part is in the role that difference plays. Where Reinders seeks a definition predicated on "sameness," Reynolds sees difference as an integral part of that definition. Difference is a part of God's plan for creation: "Finitude involves fundamental limitations that not only set beings apart from God but also from one another…the universe is blessed as a milieu of astounding abundance and staggering complexity and diversity."[43] Yet the beauty of this diversity, of God's creative power to generate difference, is "marked from the start by an accompanying instability."[44] In a world marked by limits, contingent beings will need each other, and be made vulnerable by that need. It is in these relationships that we are most at risk, where tragedy—man-made or otherwise—may strike. It is our fear of difference, of tragedy, that has

---

[43] Thomas E. Reynolds, *Vulnerable Communion: A Theology of Disability and Hospitality* (Grand Rapids: Brazos Press, 2008), 160.
[44] Reynolds, *Vulnerable Communion*, 161.

generated what Reynolds names the "cult of normalcy." Here, Reynolds develops Davis's concept of normalcy in a theological register. The cult of normalcy, Reynolds argues, generates a distorted view of the gift of creation and links disability with pain, suffering, and sin. What must be stressed, however, is that the cult of normalcy is not simply about who is abled or disabled but originates in a fear of *difference*, broadly speaking.

Theological works that describe friendship with people with intellectual disabilities may pay nominal attention to difference, but they are still at risk of playing into normalcy when they prioritize friendship between people with and without intellectual disabilities. Furthermore, they fall suspect to the cult of normalcy when they try to overwrite difference with sameness. "Normal" in these works may shift from being Aristotelian magnanimity or liberal autonomy to being mutual vulnerability, but it still seeks to smooth out difference. Dependency can be wielded as lethally as autonomy and end up limiting the kinds of authentic vulnerable relationships that we would otherwise seek.[45]

Like Reinders, Reynolds also calls for a process of conversion, but it comes through rejecting the cult of normalcy and turning towards Jesus as our example of what it means to be *imago Dei*.[46] Jesus, in his friendships, was also vulnerable to the tragic—he, too, wept for the death of his friend Lazarus—but nonetheless continued to show us what it means to be relational, creative, available beings. Jesus models how we are to love each other and work for a common good that allows all persons, in all their contingencies, to flourish.

Unlike Reinders, Reynolds makes justice an integral part of this task, embedded within the framework of love.[47] Reinders dismisses the role of justice in friendship, at least as Aristotle describes it, believing that justice requires an equality that would exclude people with intellectual disabilities.[48] One key concept marks the difference between Reinders and Reynolds: *dependency*. Although Reinders intermittently gestures towards human interdependence, he does not give attention to the inequalities that can mark dependence and vulnerability. Reynolds draws on the work of both Kittay and Alasdair MacIntyre, who offer ways to distinguish between our shared, mutual vulnerability and the particular vulnerability of long-term

---

[45] Reynolds, *Vulnerable Communion*,193-95. As seen above (7), Swinton makes a move that echoes Reynolds, when discussing "disability as difference"; what sets Swinton apart is that his claim that "the only real norm for human beings...is difference," is meant to justify ignoring "difference." See Swinton, "From Inclusion to Belonging," 180. Reynolds, by contrast, makes difference a "universal" attribute, but one to which we must pay attention.
[46] Reynolds, *Vulnerable Communion*, 209.
[47] Reynolds, *Vulnerable Communion*, 104-131.
[48] Reinders, *Receiving the Gift of Friendship*, 359-361.

dependency. Accepting MacIntyre's assertion in *Dependent Rational Animals* that dependence is a part of our way of being, Reynolds stresses that each person's way of being vulnerable, of being dependent is unique.[49] Kittay bolsters this assertion about our "inevitable dependencies" but also clarifies the differences between times when our dependence may be reciprocal and the particular kind of dependence that comes when a charge is unable to reciprocate (as would be the case for someone with a profound intellectual disability).[50] Kittay's clarification brings forward the kinds of differences that we must keep in mind when discussing vulnerability, such as differentials of power and resources that commonly exist between people with and without intellectual disabilities. As Reynolds observes, "Vulnerabilities are unequal; some bear the burden of vulnerability more than others."[51]

In light of these differences in our vulnerability, justice actually becomes essential. Again drawing from MacIntyre, Reynolds argues that, if we are dependent on relationships and embedded in a community, the just work of a community is to pursue the common good of all and to protect each other in all our different kinds of vulnerabilities.[52] Critiques of inclusion that pull love and justice apart miss how integral both components are to each other. Inclusion without relationship, without love and "belonging" (as Swinton holds) will be hollow. Yet Reynolds warns us that love without justice is "sentimental and cheap, or worse, a tool for domination and exploitative imperialism that merely pretends to have the good of others in mind."[53]

---

[49] See Alasdair MacIntyre, *Dependent Rational Animals* (Chicago: Open Court, 1999). MacIntyre offers a corrective to his previous work on virtue, by developing a Thomistic-Aristotelian account of virtue that develops a stronger connection to our biological, animal nature and all the embodied variations that can entail. Indeed, it is surprising that Reinders does not invoke MacIntyre in *Receiving the Gift of Friendship*, given MacIntyre's influence on his other books, and Reinders's engagement with both Thomistic accounts of personhood and an Aristotelian account of friendship in the text.

[50] Kittay, *Love's Labor*, 30-32. Kittay's project concerning dependency work ultimately makes an intervention in Rawlsian principles of justice by rewriting presumptions of equality as an individual attribute and shifting to a "connection based equality," defined as: "to each according to his or her need for care, and from each according to his or her capacity for care, and such support from social institutions… so that all will be adequately attended in relations that are sustaining" (Kittay, *Love's Labor*, 113).

[51] Reynolds, *Vulnerable Communion*, 130.

[52] In *Dependent Rational Animals*, MacIntyre preserves the role of people with significant intellectual disabilities in discerning the common good through the process of "proxies," or friends who are charged with making a prudent, practical judgment about how their friend with a disability would judge decisions to be made regarding the common good. See MacIntyre, *Dependent Rational Animals,* 119-155.

[53] Reynolds, *Vulnerable Communion*, 130-131.

Becoming Friends

The justice that emerges in Kittay, MacIntyre, and Reynolds is demanding and requires a tireless kind of attentiveness. For Kittay, this is attunement to the unique needs of a dependent charge. For MacIntyre, it is learning to be truthful and constantly deconstructing the errors of judgment that friendships with people with intellectual disabilities bring forward.[54] In a sense, we might return to Reinders's question about knowing the authenticity of our friendships: how do we know we are being attentive to the right things? I posit that we must begin, at least, not in sameness but in recognizing difference. My friendship with Kara or Jess is different from their friendship with one another, from each of their friendships with Liza, and from each of the others' friendship with me. The obligations that exists between all of us will vary. Yet, what I have been able to witness of Kara and Jess's friendship is an ongoing, inevitably imperfect process of learning the differences and limits between and among friends.

REFLEXIVITY AND NARRATING FRIENDSHIP

> I watch Jess and Kara connect and disconnect over the following few months, as Liza's death looms heavily over them, particularly over Jess. Jess tells about me how her boyfriend supports her, or how a friend from Ohio called to speak with her. Each week, Jess announces how long it has been since Liza died. "She died three weeks ago, today," or "You know who died seven weeks ago today?" Fights break out between Jess and her friends (which I hear about secondhand). Jess tells me about how a mutual friend, someone who also knew Liza, becomes angry with her, quick to yell, or is going days without speaking to Jess. I ask Jess if she thinks this friend is also having a hard time grieving for Liza.
> "Sure," Jess says, easily, "but that doesn't mean you get to take it out on me."
> Meanwhile, Kara's seizures are getting worse and her temper shorter. She isn't able to participate in recreation events as often, and this frustrates her. Jess's mourning is a public process; Kara's personal struggles are hidden and distract her from Liza. Neither woman seems quite attuned to the other's need.
> Despite their disconnection, I never hear Jess or Kara complain about one another. I never hear Kara give a harsh word to Jess, but I often hear her snap at Jimmy, a fellow client known for being aggressively loud and repeating the last phrase that he hears. And when Kara is being silent and gloomy, Jess chatters on, undeterred by her friend's bad mood.
> Nine weeks after Liza's death, it is the week before the clients' annual camping trip. The first thing Jess tells me that day is about how earlier in the week some of Liza's belongings had been passed out to her

---

[54] MacIntyre, *Dependent Rational Animals*, 137-138; Kittay, *Love's Labor*, 169.

friends in the workshop. Jess received two small horse figurines. To Kara, Jess asks, "Did you get anything?"

"I don't get anything," Kara responds, rather cantankerously. Beyond the table, I hear Jimmy talking about the bus arrangements to camp with other clients. There is a general but loosely-enforced rule against talking across tables during class, but that afternoon, the conversations were hard to keep in check because of how excited the camp trip made everyone. Jimmy became louder, though I have gotten used to him enough that I no longer notice the repeating. Kara is agitated. "Jimmy, shut your mouth!"

I jump in to de-escalate. "Hey, hey, conversation at the table, right guys?" It only sort of works, though Kara looks down and silently glowers at her craft.

A staff member comes over, and Jess looks up at her, asking, "You know who this reminds me of…?" Not getting the staff's immediate attention, Jess reiterates the question. "Who died nine weeks ago today?"

That prompts the response Jess wants from the staff member: "Oh, I know, it will be weird without her this year," meaning, without Liza on the camp trip. Mostly, the staff have not talked about Liza's death. They are more aware of, perhaps more adjusted to the many fragile parts of clients' bodies and health.

As Jess reminisces about Liza, I notice Kara has become very quiet. I look over at her, compliment the way she's been painting.

"I'm sorry I'm not very talkative," she says to me, quietly, so no one else can hear. "I don't like what they're talking about."

"Camp?" I ask.

"…I don't think I'll get to go."

I know what this means, maybe. "You won't feel well?"

"I feel my seizures…I can't talk about it…" The sentence drifted off, and I don't press her for more.

It should be said, however, that the argument I want to make about recognizing the value of friendships among people with intellectual disabilities is made complicated by my own presence in the story. I am only able to witness the friendship of Jess and Kara because of the time I spend with them, maybe as a friend myself. MacIntyre writes that truthfulness is one of the primary virtues we owe to our friends, that truthfulness "is one of the virtues of acknowledged dependence."[55] Yet MacIntyre's list of offenses against truthfulness focuses on ways of disguising truth from others. I would add another element: truthfulness to self. For this, we require an ethnographer's reflexivity.

The fraught dynamics of relationships between the ethnographer and the informant is an old problem. Paul Rabinow describes this in his reflexive work on ethnography, *Reflections on Fieldwork in*

---

[55] MacIntyre, *Dependent Rational Animals*, 151.

Morocco.⁵⁶ Near the end of *Reflections*, Rabinow relates how he developed a close friendship with his host, Ben Mohammad, but he is clear that this friendship was only able to emerge because Ben Mohammad refused informant status. Where Rabinow and many other ethnographers would be more cautious in their interactions with informants, whether in observation or interviews, without the structure of professional boundaries in place Rabinow finds himself seeking out support, even a kind of emotional intimacy from Ben Mohammad. In reflecting on this, Rabinow relies on rendering Ben Mohammad as an equal: "In his own modest way, [he] was an intellectual, but he was one of those who still looked to Fez rather than Paris for his inspiration. This provided a crucial space between us."⁵⁷ With recognition of a kind of intimacy, a fundamental equality but disparate social contexts allowed the creation of a middle space where Rabinow felt he could press Ben Mohammad in ways that he would not have done otherwise, such as challenging the cultural racism that Rabinow had heard from other informants, or difficult-to-interpret passages from the Qur'an. This honesty was the foundation of their friendship, a friendship of virtue and character in the tradition of Aristotle.

Yet the fundamental assumption of equality between ethnographer and informant is something to be careful in asserting. In fact, the discussion above should make us hesitant to ever assume friendship generates a simple equality. The tool we researchers use in navigating these fraught boundaries is reflexivity, a self-critical analysis taken up by the ethnographer-theologian that calls awareness to the disparities between the researcher (or theologian) and the community in which she works. It allows research in the field to remain flexible and responsive, and — more importantly — calls for ethical accountability. Natalie Wigg-Stevenson has argued that theologians who use ethnography should push this posture further, beyond the role of ethnographer and into the discipline of theology as a whole.⁵⁸ The production of texts in academic theology should be subject to ethical reflection on its portrayal of the communities written about.⁵⁹ For theologians who want to use narratives of friendships, whether their own or of others, in theological texts, reflexivity may be a necessary virtue to cultivate, not only in the process of engaging our friends, but within the texts themselves. Rabinow's work, about which he half-jokingly says violated "clan taboos" within the academy, laid bare the difficulties and hazards of doing ethnographic work.⁶⁰ Perhaps it is

---

⁵⁶ Paul Rabinow, *Reflections on Fieldwork in Morocco* (Berkeley: University of California Press, 1977).
⁵⁷ Rabinow, *Reflections on Fieldwork in Morocco*, 143.
⁵⁸ Natalie Wigg-Stevenson, "Reflexive Theology: A Preliminary Proposal," *Practical Matters* 6 (2013): 1-19.
⁵⁹ Wigg-Stevenson, "Reflexive Theology," 4.
⁶⁰ Rabinow, *Reflections on Fieldwork in Morocco*, 4.

also time to do the same for theology and for how theology reflects on intellectual disabilities and people with (and without) them.

Significantly, Reinders incorporates personal anecdotes, honest and reflexive in their own way, of his relationship with Ronald as a part of *Receiving the Gift of Friendship*. However, he stops short of integrating his relational insights into his theology. Describing Ronald, Reinders writes, "Buying things is an obsession for him. CDs, videos, watches, and pens are his favorites. He usually does not have enough money to buy what he wants, but he has no problem relying on the fact that I do." Reinders admits, "I didn't like that, of course. I felt used."[61] These anecdotes are precisely why Reinders dismisses the role of justice in friendship: justice requires equality, and the give and take of their particular friendship must inevitably result in Reinders giving more and Ronald taking more. The narrative is crafted to illustrate a point, that the value of friendship with a person cannot be based in mutual exchange. This point leaves the impression that Reinders is friends with Ronald purely out of a sense of obligation. More importantly, it gives no indication that Ronald is friends with him *for Reinders's own sake,* that is, that Ronald in any sense takes up the ethical posture of receiving the gift of friendship that Reinders asks of all of us. These moments of reflexivity do not extend far enough to dislodge a hidden presumption that their friendship is a gift—in another sense, a luxury—for Reinders but a necessity for Ronald. Furthermore, it reiterates the focus on the partner without an intellectual disability in these friendships: the assistants over the core members of L'Arche, Nouwen over Adam, and Reinders over Ronald.

What of myself, over Jess or Kara? I have tried to use ethnography to overcome this problem, but I admit it is imperfect. I cannot avoid being a character, a catalyst in these stories. I am still wrestling with the paradox of which Reinders spoke: resisting the temptation to *write about* rather than *to be with* people with disabilities. Further, we must also resist temptation to instrumentalize these relationships for legitimacy and authority. I have tried to navigate this challenge, and I will continue to do so, both on paper and off. I tell Jess and Kara, and others, when I am presenting and using stories about them in my work. I have told them that I wrote this article, and their only reaction was to ask, "Will your other school projects keep you busy, too?" Too busy, that is, to go on the camping trip or attend the next dance. To be perfectly honest, they generally do not seem to care about my research or how that shapes our relationship. The life I lead in the academy is very far from the life in which they know me, where I wash paint brushes and help them flip papier-mâché bowls. They see me as a friend, first. I must learn to accept that I have been chosen, but I must also be careful to recognize the new kinds of vulnerabilities that being

---

[61] Reinders, *Receiving the Gift of Friendship*, 357.

chosen raises among us. I want to rightly and justly fulfill the kinds of obligations that follow in both act and word. I want to be responsive, but I know I am not available. Keeping my distance seems like the safer way to be their friend. As I close this essay, I leave with one last story, a final ambiguous example of whether I live up to the demands that *being claimed* makes.

> The week after prom, we are finishing up a painting project when Jess starts showing us some photos from the dance that she has on her iPod. She calls over staff members, other clients, and speaks animatedly about her plans to rent a limo next year, which Kara and her boyfriend will be invited to, as well.
> "We have so much fun together," Jess exclaims, swiping through the photos. Even Kara seems amused.
> I smile to myself as I listen, while I clean up the large sheet of butcher paper on the table, left to protect it from inevitable paint spills during the project. Kara stops me for a moment. "Before you clean up and leave, could you write your name down on a paper for me?"
> I balk without thinking, asking sharply, "why?" They have my name and email on the copies of the consent and assent forms I returned to them, though I am also sure that most clients have probably lost those into their overflowing backpacks and lunch bags, or shuffled the forms in with the art projects we did the day they signed them. Jess and Kara have talked about their use of social media, and I occasionally get a question about whether I was on this or that site. I have done my best to defer those questions, talking about how strict my privacy levels are, preventing students from finding me. They have mostly accepted this, but, in the moment Kara asks for my name, I worry that she'll search for me, find a profile I thought I had hidden. Kara looks hurt, wounded. "Well, because I took that picture with you and I want to be able to know who…." She trailed off. I know the end of that sentence: to remember who I am, after I leave. My leaving is inevitable; staff and volunteers move through their lives with much ease and little thought. Kara knows my time is temporary, and yet I—and the rest of the volunteers who come—are still called "friend."
> "Okay, sure." I write my first name and last initial only on a corner of the butcher paper, tear it off and hand it to Kara. I watch as she places it carefully in her wallet. Ⓜ

The Slow Journey towards Beatitude: Disability in L'Arche, and Staying Human in High-Speed Society

By Jason Reimer Greig

SOMETIMES IT CAN APPEAR IN LATE MODERNITY that the pace of life is increasing to the point of leaving persons breathless. The metaphor of being caught up in the "hamster wheel" of social acceleration, which binds persons in a race not to get left behind, more and more captures people's feelings and intuitions about striving for the good life in the contemporary world.[1] Whether it concerns the proliferation of "educational" toys trying to get children to learn at earlier ages or the drive for ever and ever faster internet connections, speed lies at the core of morality and politics in late modernity.

How does this acceleration affect a culture's basic views on being human? What does the moral life look like in this kind of temporality? The time needed to reflect upon these questions increasingly eludes citizens, leaving most running merely to catch up, generally too busy to reflect upon their participation in the societal "rat race." But is this good enough for late modern Christians? If not, what does it mean to try to follow Jesus in high-speed society? What might be a truly liberating anthropology in a time when speed sometimes makes it hard to feel human? Where are examples that embody the good life in an accelerating world?

---

[1] For a sample of works reflecting upon social acceleration, see Hartmut Rosa and William E Scheuerman, eds., *High-Speed Society: Social Acceleration, Power, and Modernity* (University Park: Penn State University Press, 2009); James Gleick, *Faster: The Acceleration of Just about Everything* (New York: Pantheon Books, 1999); Stephen Bertman, *Hyperculture: The Human Cost of Speed* (Westport: Praeger, 1998); John Tomlinson, *The Culture of Speed: The Coming of Immediacy* (Thousand Oaks: SAGE, 2007); Mark C. Taylor, *Speed Limits: Where Time Went and Why We Have So Little Left* (New Haven: Yale University Press, 2014); Hartmut Rosa, *Social Acceleration: A New Theory of Modernity*, trans. Jonathan Trejo-Mathys (New York: Columbia University Press, 2013); Hartmut Rosa, *Alienation and Acceleration: Towards a Critical Theory of Late-Modern Temporality* (Malmö, Sweden: NSU Press, 2010); Thomas Hylland Eriksen, *Tyranny of the Moment: Fast and Slow Time in the Information Age* (London: Pluto Press, 2001); Robert Hassan, *Empires of Speed: Time and the Acceleration of Politics and Society* (Boston: Brill, 2009).

This essay argues that the speed inherent in late modern conceptions of time creates false anthropologies which derail and deform persons' journeys to becoming human. These visions of the person alienate people from God and themselves, while also creating "wasted" persons unable to meet human status. The latter applies particularly to those labelled intellectually disabled, who embody the very antithesis of the characteristics needed for personhood in high-speed society. A more authentic and truthful anthropology lies in French Roman Catholic personalism and its appropriation of Catholic social teaching. These visions of the human person, as persons created by God for communion with him, serve as a font for the thought and praxis of Jean Vanier and the communities of L'Arche. Vanier's life with persons considered by late modernity as "useless" led him to discover them as teachers in becoming human. As potential centers of alternative communities, persons with cognitive impairments live slowed-enough to become friends with God and one another. In this way, communities like L'Arche participate in the church's mission to redeem all creation toward the beatitude of God's liberating *shalom*.

THE TRIUMPH OF CLOCK AND NETWORK TIME: TOWARDS A HIGH-SPEED ANTHROPOLOGY

The acceleration of society which has accompanied modernity has brought with it a profound change in basic notions of time. The individual and societal relationship with temporality since the Enlightenment has likewise undergone radical transformation, even if on a deeply implicit level. The speed at the heart of the late modern project has profoundly penetrated the western social imagination, through its economic, political, and education institutions.

A crucial innovation of modernity was the advent of a machine that standardized and universalized time: the mechanical clock. The ensuing development (and eventual dominance) of "clock time" promised to make the "telling of time" more reliable and objective as well as assisting the ascending merchant class of late medieval Europe in making their trade more efficient and productive. As Robert Hassan suggests, "The clock is a technology of speed that has only one speed, but it created or helped give the force of organizational logic to the interrelated projects of Enlightenment and modernity."[2] Clock time specialized in instrumentalizing and breaking down time into measurable units, taking the particular of the moment and abstracting it into a controllable object. This temporality worked great for the successes of modernity – empirical science, the development of technology, rational forms of management, efficient factory production – but less well for actual persons. The dominance of clock time alienates persons from their environment and reduces them to

---

[2] Hassan, *Empires of Speed*, 52.

their material and productive functions. In the words of Gabriel Marcel, this "functionalized world" equates people's identities with their functions and reduces time into an object to be "used" and eventually commodified.[3]

Teresa Reed contrasts clock time with the "lived time" of human experience, along with the "spiritual time" of religion and the church. For Reed "lived time" is "the time of actual human experience in the real world, experience which varies qualitatively according to that which is experienced."[4] Thus, lived human experience can never be standardized or broken down into segments but must be lived wholly and relationally. Intense experiences like giving birth or accompanying someone's death manifest the unevenness and inability to schedule lived time. Related to lived time is what Reed considers "spiritual time": "a distinctive form of lived time in which human activity is directed toward eternity and opens itself to the presence of God."[5] Sacred time hosts the intersection of the temporal and spiritual and directs the ordinary life of persons to their ultimate end, the good of eternal life. Modernity's reduction of the material to the objective and controllable, however, pushed the spiritual outside of the temporal and reduced God's presence in the world to the unreliable, "subjective" private lives of individuals. According to Reed, this reduction resulted for human persons in alienation and fragmentation from God, world, and self.

Yet, as much as clock time has come to dominate western notions of time, the meteoric rise of computers and information technology brings with it a new temporality. Hassan contends that the new temporal normal in late modernity is "network time," emerging from a "network society" whose orientation is nothing less than "pure speed."[6] On the surface, network time seems to offer the promise of connection and solidarity with others, thus ending the alienating influence of clock time. However, a closer look reveals that network

---

[3] Gabriel Marcel, "Concrete Approaches to Investigating the Ontological Mystery," in *Gabriel Marcel's Perspectives on the Broken World*, trans. Katharine Rose Hanley (Milwaukee: Marquette University Press, 1998), 173.

[4] Teresa I. Reed, "Time and the Human Person," in *Maritain and America*, ed. Christopher M. Cullen and Joseph Allan Clair (Washington, DC: American Maritain Association, 2009), 166. See also Teresa I. Reed, "Time in Relation to Self, World, and God," in *Faith, Scholarship, and Culture in the 21st Century*, ed. Alice Ramos and Marie I. George (Washington, DC: The Catholic University of America Press, 2002), 166–77.

[5] Reed, "Time and the Human Person," 167. Reed also draws on the thought of Mircea Eliade here. See *The Sacred and the Profane: The Nature of Religion*, trans. Willard R. Trask (New York: Harcourt, Brace & World, 1959) and *Cosmos and History: The Myth of the Eternal Return*, trans. Willard R. Trask (New York: Harper, 1959).

[6] Hassan, *Empires of Speed*, 67. Hassan borrows the term "network society" from Manuel Castells, *The Rise of the Network Society*, 2nd ed. (Hoboken: Blackwell Publishers, 2000).

time acts less as a counter to modern temporality than merely its sped up version. Digital media's radical open-endedness and its pervasiveness of "real time" creates its own environment that totalizes and brings all persons and ways of thinking under its control. In the annihilation of space accompanying time at the speed of light, French social theorist Paul Virilio also sees a movement toward a dematerialization that sees bodies as obstacles to the growth of a disembodied self. In a culture which prefers the virtual to the concrete, bodies only get in the way and become new targets of technological renovations that increasingly turns flesh into sleeker, faster machines.[7] Network time may claim to free persons from the shackles of scheduled modernity, but it does not necessarily let God back in the world. Instead, network time stands as the ultimate closing in of the human person upon herself. Theologian Johan Baptist Metz sees in late modernity a vision of time as "an empty infinity without surprises," promising only an "eschaton of boredom and apathy."[8] Despair and fanaticism flourish in this temporality, where persons look forward only to a predictable more of the same.

Any concept of time helps to create and support a particular vision of the human person and the human good. Thus, both clock and network time project onto a culture what Brian Brock calls "best-case anthropologies": the icons of human being presented as worthy of value and emulation.[9] The successful person of clock time is efficient, productive, rational, autonomous. Network time promotes the quick-thinking multitasker, infinitely mobile and flexible, ever ready to refine and renovate his identity to his liking. Clearly persons considered intellectually disabled, particularly those whose embodiments include severe impairments, do not and can never meet the iconic dimensions in these temporalities. As Reed mentions, "In the clearly instrumental view of the human being" promoted by clock time, "failure to carry out one's function means that one becomes useless."[10] The inability to move or think at the speed of network time leaves little to no room for those who reason more with their bodies than with a disembodied mind. Thus, in both of these forms of time,

---

[7] As a "thinker of speed," Virilio's *oeuvre* on social acceleration is legend. For a sample, see Paul Virilio, *Speed and Politics: An Essay on Dromology*, trans. Mark Polizzotti (Los Angeles: Semiotext(e), 2006); Paul Virilio, *Open Sky*, trans. Julie Rose (Brooklyn: Verso, 1997); Paul Virilio, *Negative Horizon: An Essay in Dromoscopy*, trans. Michael Degener (London: Continuum, 2005); Paul Virilio, *The Virilio Reader*, ed. James Der Derian (Hoboken: Blackwell Publishers, 1998).

[8] Johann Baptist Metz, "The Second Coming," in *Love's Strategy: The Political Theology of Johann Baptist Metz*, ed. John K. Downey (New York: Continuum, 1999), 154.

[9] Brian Brock, "Introduction: Disability and the Quest for the Human," in *Disability in the Christian Tradition: A Reader*, eds. Brian Brock and John Swinton (Grand Rapids: Eerdmans, 2012), 1.

[10] Reed, "Time and the Human Person," 174.

people with cognitive impairments become highly regrettable and what Zygmunt Bauman calls "wasted lives."[11] Perceiving these persons as "wrongful" appears logical in this context, with the technological advancements of prenatal testing serving as an apt tool to diagnose and terminate potential wasted lives.[12] The prospect of being so radically left behind in the high-speed society represents such a life of burden that termination appears completely rational.

Another vision of time exists, however, which can challenge the anthropological and moral assumptions of clock and network time. The work of Roman Catholic philosopher Jean Vanier and the practices of the L'Arche communities he helped found offer a temporality and understanding of the human person which perceive people considered intellectually disabled in a radically different light. Vanier and L'Arche offer a living philosophy which recognizes no one as superfluous. A font for this vision lies in French Catholic personalism, and its subsequent appropriation in Catholic social teaching. Before turning to Vanier and L'Arche's insights about disability and being human in high-speed society, a discussion of this personalist philosophy and its articulation in the church's social ethics is needed.

MARITAIN, MOUNIER, AND INTEGRAL PERSONALISM

Although Vanier placed much emphasis on the intuitive and existential nature of his beginning L'Arche, his context reveals the presence of a tradition informing his action. Vanier's founding of communities of persons considered disabled and nondisabled comes not *ex nihilo* but remains firmly nestled within a tradition, even while he sometimes re-interprets and re-directs it. In particular, Vanier

---

[11]Zygmunt Bauman, *Wasted Lives: Modernity and Its Outcasts* (Cambridge: Polity Press, 2004). While Bauman categorizes the burgeoning global underclass as the redundant fallout of modernity, persons considered intellectually disabled could well fit the same taxonomy.

[12] On the prevention of potential children with genetic abnormalities being at the heart of prenatal testing, see anthropologist Rayna R. Reiter, *Testing Women, Testing the Fetus: The Social Impact of Amniocentesis in America* (New York: Routledge, 1999), as well as David A. Savitz, "How Far Can Prenatal Screening Go in Preventing Birth Defects?," *Journal of Pediatrics* 152, no. 1 (2008): 3–4; Ilana Löwy, "How Genetics Came to the Unborn: 1960-2000," *Studies in History & Philosophy of Biological & Biomedical Sciences* 47 (2014): 154–62; N. Neely Kazerouni et al., "Ancillary Benefits of Prenatal Maternal Serum Screening Achieved in the California Program," *Prenatal Diagnosis* 30, no. 10 (2010): 981–87. On the cases of parents of children with disabilities suing physicians under the banner of "wrongful life," see Rosamund Scott, "Reconsidering 'Wrongful Life' in England After Thirty Years: Legislative Mistakes and Unjustifiable Anomalies," *Cambridge Law Journal* 72, no. 1 (2013): 115–54; Daniel W. Whitney and Kenneth N. Rosenbaum, "Recovery of Damages for Wrongful Birth," *The Journal of Legal Medicine* 32, no. 2 (2011): 167–204; "Wrongful Birth and Wrongful Life: Basic Questions," *Journal of European Tort Law* 1, no. 2 (2010): 125–55.

consistently acts out of French Roman Catholic personalism of the early twentieth century as articulated by Jacques Maritain and Emmanuel Mounier. While these important French intellectuals differed in style – Maritain the metaphysically inclined, Neo-Thomist philosopher versus the more existentialist and communitarian Mounier[13] – they each intuited that the fall of western civilization into nihilism and individualism required a return to a truer view of the human person, an integral personalism.

Worked out amidst and between two devastating wars, French Catholic personalism arrived as an attempt to account for as well as try to resurrect the ruins of modern Europe. Reform was not enough; only the transformation of culture into a "new civilization" would be sufficient. Thus, for both Mounier and Maritain, personalism represented not so much a strictly ordered metaphysical system but more a practical philosophy which could act as a lens for Christian action in the world. Fundamental to that hermeneutic would be the person at the center of any potential solutions to the problems of the time. The articulators of integral personalism saw the end of the human in the systems of both bourgeois liberalism and totalitarianism, whether of the fascist or communist variation. Both liberal and collectivist societies assumed people not as persons but as "individuals," the modern reduction of the person into a nameless, replaceable statistic with no horizon beyond the temporal and material. The individualism inherent in modernity expressed itself through bourgeois capitalism's purely self-interested individuals, devoid of social bonds and left to fend for themselves. Yet, this same impulse also gave birth to collectivist movements which tried to restore liberalism's error through a totalization of the state and the subjugation of individuals to its good. Both systems either confined individuals' spiritual identity to the "private" realm or denied any eternal end altogether, effectively locking humans into a solely material horizon. In Maritain's words, an integral personalism had to counter this social imaginary and "re-make anthropology, find the rehabilitation and the 'dignification' of the creature not in isolation, in a closed-inness of the creature on itself, but in its openness to the world of the divine and super-rational; and this implies in practice a work of sanctification of the profane and the temporal."[14]

---

[13] Bernard Gendreau categorized the French personalism created in the 1930s as "integral," based on the complementarity of Maritain and Mounier. See Bernard A. Gendreau, "The Role of Jacques Maritain and Emmanuel Mounier in the Creation of French Personalism," *Personalist Forum* 8, no. 1 (1992): 97–108. Related here is also Maritain's "humanisme integral." See his *True Humanism,* trans. Margot Adamson (London: Scribner, 1950).

[14] Jacques Maritain, "Integral Humanism and the Crisis of Modern Times," *The Review of Politics* 1, no. 1 (1939): 7.

Yet it is not enough to simply bring individuals back into the center of moral reasoning and then call them "persons." More importantly, one must begin with a correct understanding of who persons are, which includes their vocation and end. As distinct from a modern individual, a human person can never be replaced or duplicated but stands as a unique creation made in the image of God. In this creation rests each person's inalienable dignity and rights to human fulfillment, as well as his or her human *telos*. For as creatures created by God, persons will only find their ultimate happiness in God and are therefore destined for eternity. Materialist reductions of humans to purely temporal individuals cannot truly account for persons but, in fact, alienate them from their source and end. Due to being made by and ultimately for God, persons have an innate desire for transcendence.[15] Thus, integral personalism insists that, while the temporal and material life of persons matters and truly makes up a part of persons, the spiritual dimension of life has primacy of place. This does not mean that violations of human rights and abject poverty in earthly life must be passively accepted as "one's lot in life." Destitution as a "hell on earth" must be vigorously countered by Christians, not only because it violates a person's fundamental dignity but because it can turn people against God and thus alienate them from their spiritual identity.[16] Only by looking at the integral person, namely as a material creature with a spiritual core and end, can cultures provide the milieu where the whole person can develop in their human vocation.

As creatures created by and for God, persons have a seed of transcendence within them that endows them with something of the ineffable. In the personalist universe, persons can never be fully categorized because of their graced link with the indescribable and undefinable God. Persons are essentially *mysteries* that can never be totalized without violating their human dignity. As Mounier writes, "The person is not 'something' that one can find at the end of an analysis, nor is it a definable combination of characteristics....It is a *presence* rather than a being, a presence that is active, without

---

[15] Jacques Maritain, "The Thomist Idea of Freedom," in *Scholasticism and Politics*, trans. Mortimer Jerome Adler (New York: Macmillan, 1940), 106.

[16] "As long as modern societies will secrete destitution as an ordinary product of their functioning, there cannot be repose for the Christian" (Jacques Maritain, "Catholic Action and Political Action," in *Scholasticism and Politics*, 161). Maritain never wishes to deny the material part of the person, that which makes them an "individual." Even as he re-prioritizes the spiritual dimension of the person, he still maintains the ontological validity of material existence. See Jacques Maritain, *The Person and the Common Good*, trans. John J. Fitzgerald (New York: C. Scribner's Sons, 1947), 45–6.

limits."[17] The continuity of personal being consists not in repetition but in "super-abundance," where a person "overflows any conceptions meant to contain it."[18] Modernity's reductionist and instrumentalist impulses had denuded life of mystery and thus made all things (including persons) into objects, means to use for one's own self-interest. To treat and see another personally, one must recognize in the other "a presence – which is to recognize that I am unable to define or classify him, that he is inexhaustible, filled with hopes upon which he alone can act."[19] In this meeting of two created mysteries, a true dialogue happens where each is received by the other, which involves both a gift of welcome as well as a giving of self. Through seeing one another as unique manifestations of God's creation rather than instrumental and replaceable objects, persons truly communicate with one another and live authentically in their being as creatures who naturally tend toward communion.

As persons made for communion, integral personalism recognizes the fundamental human need to be a member of society. Maritain understands this need as being centered in the person's fundamental desire to communicate love and knowledge to others. "In its radical generosity, the human person tends to overflow into social communications in response to the law of superabundance inscribed in the depths of being, life, intelligence and love."[20] Persons must encounter and live with others because their being and end are wrapped up with God their source, the one who, as both immanent and economic Trinity, seeks to communicate love and grace to all creation. Yet, persons seek the company of others also because they can never achieve fullness alone. As creatures made for eternity but still living amid the wounds of the human condition, persons inhabit a vulnerability which requires the presence of others. "It is not by itself alone that [a human person] reaches its plenitude but by receiving essential goods from society."[21]

Because of the person's social being, integral personalism recognizes the purpose of social institutions as serving the common good and providing the goods – whether they be economic, political, or cultural – necessary to advance the human person in his or her particular vocation. At the same time, those institutions must not overstep their bounds and displace the primacy of the person in society. Societies exist for the growth and fulfillment of persons, not the reverse. Persons recognize their inherent need for communication

---

[17] Emmanuel Mounier, *Personalism*, trans. Philip Mairet (London: Routledge & Kegan Paul, 1952), 35.
[18] Mounier, *Personalism*, 67.
[19] Mounier, *Personalism*, 23.
[20] Maritain, *The Person and the Common Good*, 47–8.
[21] Maritain, *The Person and the Common Good*, 48.

with other persons and thus seek to create and foster communities which reflect the freedom and dignity of friends of God. "The primary action of the person, therefore, is to sustain, together with others, a society of persons, the structure, the customs, the sentiments and the institutions of which are shaped by their nature as persons."[22] Only a society of free persons can steer a course away from the corrosive effects of liberal individualism, as well as avoiding the collectivist excesses which absolutize the state and its institutions.

Both Mounier and Maritain mention that Christians cannot restrict themselves to sectarian communities of the pure. Fundamental to the Christian call to become a person lies a vocation to participate in civil society, living one's personhood in such a way as to become instruments of transformation for the whole social order. Integral personalism always remained committed to the church yet did not seek a return to a triumphalist and "politically responsible" church as a solution to the crisis of western civilization. "It is not the direct and proper function of Catholic action to solve the social problem, but to make the vivifying inspiration of the Kingdom of God and His justice penetrate the social matters themselves."[23] This call to penetrate the civil life with the lived Gospel means not a need for a spiritual elite but the "super-ordinariness" experienced by all Christians in everyday life.[24] As creatures made for eternity, Christian persons bring God's future into the realm of ordinary life, participating with God in the sanctification of the earthly and the temporal. Therefore, the Body of Christ gives its allegiance, and thus mode of acting, not to a leader of war but to the "King of Grace and Charity."[25] Just as a Christian integrates and recognizes the place of creatureliness and eternity in his being, so the church embodies the same reality to the world. The personalist universe recognizes in the church's loss of social position its slow return to its "first position": "renouncing government upon earth and the outward appearance of sanctification to achieve the unique work of the Church, the community of Christians in the Christ, mingled among all men in the secular work, — neither theocracy nor liberalism, but a return to the double rigours of transcendence and incarnation."[26]

THE PERSONALIST ANTHROPOLOGY OF CATHOLIC SOCIAL TEACHING

The influence of personalism, particularly as articulated by Jacques Maritain, cannot be overestimated in Catholic social teaching. During

---

[22] Mounier, *Personalism*, 21.
[23] Maritain, "Catholic Action and Political Action," 162.
[24] Mounier, *Personalism*, 46.
[25] Maritain, "Catholic Action and Political Action," 169.
[26] Mounier, *Personalism*, 122.

the papacy of John XXIII and Vatican II, Catholic social teaching turns towards the human through an emphasis on the principles of human dignity and the social nature of persons.[27] Maritain's influence at the Council is well attested, culminating in Paul VI presenting him the closing "Message to Men of Thought and Science" document.[28] Maritain's articulation of "integral humanism" is subsequently quoted by Popes Paul VI, John Paul II and Benedict XVI, all revealing the personalist thrust that would accompany much of the Church's social teaching. In fact, John Paul II claims in *Centisimus Annus* that the guiding principle of Catholic social teaching "is a correct view of the human person and of the person's unique value" (no. 11).

John XIII recognizes human dignity as a "fundamental principle" in *Pacem in Terris*, where he emphasizes that "each individual man is a person" (no. 9). *Gaudium et Spes* prioritizes anthropology by placing it before pressing social issues, confirming a need to understand persons first before proposing solutions for social problems.[29] The document begins chapter one by stressing the dignity belonging to each person by being made in the image and likeness of God (*Gaudium et Spes*, no. 12) and later sees this view confirmed more universally in the "growing awareness of the exalted dignity proper to the human person, since he stands above all things, and his rights and duties are universal and inviolable" (no. 26). In *Populorum Progressio,* Paul VI consistently calls attention to the violations to human dignity which come from poverty and injustice committed against persons (nos. 6, 37, 71). John Paul II took up the call to annunciate and protect the fundamental human dignity of persons, understanding this vocation as the very object of the church's social teaching. As creatures made by and for God, all persons can recognize

> The sacred value of human life from its very beginning until its end, and can affirm the right of every human being to have this primary good respected to the highest degree. Upon the recognition of this right, every human community and the political community itself are founded. (*Evangelium Vitae*, no. 2)

The Church as the community of believers holds the Gospel story of life and human flourishing, which proclaims fullness of life and an untiring hope through communion with God in the Spirit. Through its proper understanding of the human person, believers see that the

---

[27] Charles E. Curran, *Catholic Social Teaching, 1891-Present: A Historical, Theological, and Ethical Analysis* (Washington, DC: Georgetown University Press, 2002), 135.
[28] "Pope Paul VI, Discourse and Messages at the Close of Vatican II," in *Reassessing the Liberal State: Reading Maritain's* Man and the State, ed. Timothy Fuller and John P. Hittinger (Washington, DC: American Maritain Association, 2001), 243.
[29] Curran, *Catholic Social Teaching*, 128.

"Gospel of God's love for man, the Gospel of the dignity of the person and the Gospel of life are a single and indivisible Gospel" (*Evangelium Vitae*, no. 2).

A dimension of this Gospel of life rests in recognizing persons as whole beings, which include their vocation to transcendence. In this regard, the "integral humanism" of Jacques Maritain shows the influence it has played in subsequent social teaching. Paul VI first used the expression in *Populorum Progressio* to emphasize how the quest and goal for development cannot only consist in focusing on the material dimension of persons. Instead, development must also take into account the spiritual aspect of persons, whose destiny is eternity. "The development we speak of here cannot be restricted to economic growth alone. To be authentic, it must be well rounded; it must foster the development of each man and of the whole man" (*Populorum Progressio*, no. 14).

The goal of a "full-bodied humanism" must account for the transcendent destiny of persons and recognize that "Man becomes truly man only by passing beyond himself" (*Populorum Progressio*, no. 42). Any other anthropological system which closes persons off in a strictly temporal *telos* cannot lead to human flourishing and life. John Paul II repeats, in *Sollicitudo Rei Socialis*, the need not only to focus on the economic and material development of persons but also to pay attention to the immortal vocation of and spiritual destiny of persons (no. 29). A too strong attachment to the former leads to a kind of "superdevelopment" which can result in the kind of "pure consumerism" pervasive in western society. Drawing on Gabriel Marcel's distinction between "being" and "having," John Paul II sees in many western ideologies of development a "cult of having," which distracts people from their journey to being, while at the same time depriving others of the necessary material goods needed to realize their human vocation (*Sollicitudo Rei Socialis*, no. 28).

Benedict XVI also recognizes the insight that development must concern the whole person in all her dimensions. Life understood merely on the temporal and material plane can never satisfy human persons because it keeps them from their source and end.

> Without the perspective of eternal life, human progress in this world is denied breathing-space. Enclosed within history, it runs the risk of being reduced to the mere accumulation of wealth....Such development requires a transcendent vision of the person, it needs God: without him, development is either denied, or entrusted exclusively to man, who falls into the trap of thinking he can bring about his own salvation, and ends up promoting a dehumanized form of development. (*Caritas in Veritate*, no. 11)

Persons trapped in modernity's temporality – either in clock or network time – can never grow in their vocations, no matter how powerful the means or impressive the technology, because it denies full human nature. There is an ineffable and miraculous aspect of life, Benedict claims, that always brings us to a height over and beyond what we could ever imagine or conceptualize.

> The development of individuals and people is likewise located on a height, if we consider *the spiritual dimension* that must be present if such development is to be authentic. It requires new eyes and a new heart, capable of *rising above a materialistic vision of human events*, capable of glimpsing in development the 'beyond' that technology cannot give. (*Caritas in Veritate,* no. 77)

By acknowledging that persons cannot develop alone but need a community of persons to fully develop, Catholic social teaching also affirms the inherently social nature of the person.

> Man's social nature makes it evident that the progress of the human person and the advance of society itself hinge on one another ....Since this social life is not something added on to man, through his dealings with others, through reciprocal duties, and through fraternal dialogue he develops all his gifts and is able to rise to his destiny. (*Gaudium et Spes*, no. 25)[30]

Paul VI and John Paul II emphasize solidarity as a particular characteristic of the church's social teaching. A greater universal acknowledgement of belonging to the same human family – by virtue of being created in the image of the same God and thus having the same source and end – means also a growing awareness of the injustices committed against people around the world.

> When interdependence becomes recognized in this way, the correlative response as a moral and social attitude, as a 'virtue,' is solidarity. This then is not a feeling of vague compassion or shallow distress at the misfortunes of so many people, both near and far. On the contrary, it is a firm and persevering determination to commit oneself to the common good; that is to say to the good of all and of each individual, because we are all really responsible for all. (*Sollicitudo Rei Socialis,* no. 38)

As social creatures, persons have a responsibility for the other, as well as needing the other for their own fulfillment. As opposed to liberal individualism, which posits autonomous monads closed in upon

---

[30] *Gaudium et Spes*, no. 25 also points out how institutions are meant to serve persons and not the reverse: "For the beginning, the subject and the goal of all social institutions is and must be the human person."

themselves and responsible only for their own being, the church announces a more truthful anthropology of interdependence and relationality.

> As a spiritual being, the human creature is defined through interpersonal relations. The more authentically he or she lives these relations, the more his or her own personal identity matures. It is not by isolation that man establishes his worth, but by placing himself in relation with others and with God. (*Caritas in Veritate*, no.53)

L'ARCHE AS CHRISTIAN ALTERNATIVE TO HIGH-SPEED SOCIETY

Before discussing Jean Vanier's appropriation of integral personalism and Catholic social teaching, it is important to begin with a brief retelling of L'Arche's story. Stories interrupt attempts at conceiving of life in abstract terms with the radical particularity of human experience. Vanier has always seen narrative as a profound way of expressing the truth of "lived time." His work is peppered with the stories of real men and women with and without intellectual disabilities whom he has shared life with in L'Arche. Retelling stories imparts meaning to people's histories and recognizes God's place at the center of person's lives. Thus, story-telling in L'Arche also stands as a kind of "sacred time" that sees God in the midst of lives and the world. In this way, narrative represents a pathway to eternity and to another vision of time where friendship rather than speed facilitate beatitude and communion.

Beginning with Vanier's telling of L'Arche's story also reveals the impact of community life on his philosophy. In particular, Vanier's relationships with people considered intellectually disabled formed his basic convictions in a way he found truthful and in tune with the Gospel. Like Maritain and Mounier, who wished to confront rather than hide from the tumultuous social issues of their time, Vanier received his Christian faith and attempted to respond to the world, not only with his mind but also with his body and his heart. Thus, Vanier's personalism cannot be understood without looking at the crucible which shaped his anthropology.

In August 1964, Jean Vanier, son of respected French-Canadian diplomat Georges Vanier, embarked on an adventure of faith which would radically transform his life and vision of the good life. Through his naval and academic training, Vanier was formed in the logic of modernity: speed, efficiency, instrumental reason.[31] Yet, for all his achievements in climbing the ladders of success, Vanier knew that his

---

[31] For biographical information on Vanier, see Kathryn Spink, *The Miracle, the Message, the Story: Jean Vanier and l'Arche* (Toronto: Novalis, 2006). For more on the story of L'Arche, see Spink's book, as well as Jean Vanier, *An Ark for the Poor: The Story of L'Arche* (Toronto: Novalis, 1995), and Jean Vanier, *Our Life Together: A Memoir in Letters* (Toronto: HarperCollins, 2007).

formation missed something essential. The sense of competition and speed in modern culture seemed to destroy rather than accompany a world striving for peace.

Uncertain of how to live his desire to follow Jesus and live the Gospel, Vanier's spiritual director, Thomas Philippe, O. P., advised Vanier to come and meet some of his new "friends." Philippe was chaplain at the Val Fleuri, an institution for men with cognitive impairments in Trosly-Breuil, a small village about 75 km northeast of Paris. In December 1963, Vanier visited the institution and was deeply moved. While the men said very little, Vanier still heard them question him: "Will you come back? Do you love me? Will you be my friend?" Vanier began to visit other institutions, increasingly appalled by what he saw. The inhumane and degrading conditions of a mental hospital on the outskirts of Paris shocked him to his core. Here lay the men whom modernity could not countenance, seen as useless and segregated into institutions that served more like prisons. At the same time, Vanier discovered in the midst of the squalor a compelling presence of God alive in the men called disabled. Even amidst so much rejection and suffering, God made himself known in the lives of these men. Philippe gently suggested that perhaps Vanier could begin "something" as an attempt to alleviate this profound injustice.

Vanier's response was to buy a small house in rural France and welcome two men labelled as having intellectual disabilities, Raphaël Simi and Philippe Seux, to share life and faith with him. This "L'Arche," the French word for Noah's "Ark," would serve as a sanctuary for these men and the many others who would later be welcomed. Like so many other people with cognitive impairments, these men were considered "wasted lives" and thus confined to institutions and asylums. Raphaël and Philippe represented everything modernity attempted to conquer: unproductivity, immobility, non-rationality. Vanier understood how an accelerating society left behind people labelled intellectually disabled. In a culture increasingly impatient with anything slow, those who could not keep up with the train of progress became deeply regrettable. L'Arche would exist as a new form of community where these persons could experience family, where they could truly grow and reclaim the humanity modernity had denied them.

While many perceived L'Arche as a charitable exercise in showing mercy to the defective poor, life together with Raphaël and Philippe began to give Vanier a very different perception of persons labelled disabled, one which challenged the dominant anthropology of modernity. While the logic of speed consistently produced alienation, Vanier found that Raphaël and Philippe had a gift for relationship that brought people together. Friendship rather than domination characterized the orientation of these men, one which took the time to be present with the other rather than continually attempt to outrace the other. Only by living in a more contemplative temporality could this gift for friendship be recognized.

> I discovered the great capacity for relationship of these men and [subsequently] women who were very limited on the rational and verbal level. They were extremely poor intellectually, but tremendously rich in qualities of the heart. For us to perceive all the treasures of their hearts, we ourselves must become poor; we have to move into a slower pace of life, be more attentive, more centred and more contemplative. They invite us to an interior silence in order to welcome them within their silence.[32]

In this regard, those whom late modernity considers superfluous become moral exemplars and teachers in the art of being human. While the military and academy formed Vanier in a modern logic based on speed and efficiency, his new "friends" in L'Arche were shaping him in a more capacious and Christian anthropology.

As L'Arche began to grow and expand both physically as well as spiritually, communities began to build structures to bring an often chaotic life into something of an order. Vanier approved of this institution building yet also continually voiced the need for the community to always serve the persons in it rather than the reverse. "A community is always built around people; people should not be shaped to suit community."[33] When a community becomes not an end in itself but a place where people can grow into their own vocation, the power of the Holy Spirit transforms its members into ever more free human persons. Even more so, Vanier found that the driving change agents of community life were not so much nondisabled assistants but actually people with cognitive impairments. Out of this discovery comes L'Arche's bold and revolutionary insight: entering into relationships with persons whom late modernity considers useless can teach the world about being and becoming human. "Assistants begin to see in a new light people of whom they had been consciously or unconsciously been afraid, whom they had considered to be 'no persons.' Community members with learning disabilities begin to see as friends those who had frightened them, and furthermore to see themselves as people able to give life and joy to others. Each discovers himself as a blessing in the world. It is then that they begin to sense a new vision for humanity."[34]

---

[32] Vanier, *An Ark for the Poor*, 72.
[33] Jean Vanier, *Community and Growth*, 2nd rev. ed. (New York: Paulist Press, 1989), 215.
[34] Jean Vanier, "The Transforming Power of People with Disabilities," in *The Vocation of Theology Today: A Festschrift for David Ford*, ed. Tom Greggs, Rachel Muers, and Simeon Zahl (Eugene: Cascade Books, 2013), 353.

VANIER'S PERSONALIST ANTHROPOLOGY

Like the personalist tradition, Vanier saw a return of the person as crucial in facing the pressing social and ethical issues of the contemporary world. "If our society has difficulty in functioning, if we are continually confronted by a world in crisis, full of violence, of fear, of abuse, I suggest it is because we are not clear about what it means to be human."[35] Only a solution rooted in a truthful anthropology can bring peace, whether that peace be between nations or within individual persons. Living the microcosmic life of community continually affirmed Vanier in this insight: communal harmony could never arrive merely by legal and structural reform but always had to center on the lives and bodies of community members.

Vanier shares with personalism and Catholic social teaching the fundamental moral principle of the inherent and inalienable dignity of every human person. "[L]ife is a first principle: I believe in the sacredness of every human being and that each one is called to be fully alive."[36] Belonging to the human community comes from being born of a human mother, not through meeting capability requirements.[37] Thus all humans, no matter their ability or limitation, have the rights to the basic goods of the community which will assist them in becoming persons. Vanier would readily affirm that as creatures made in the image and likeness of God, human persons can never be treated merely as a means but always remain ends in themselves.

While firmly believing in the personalist affirmation of the inherent dignity of all, Vanier also offers a different interpretation of the essential attributes of the person. Roman Catholic tradition often stresses the capacities of reason and will, which respectively assist persons in discerning the truth as well as responding to God's grace. Vanier never disputes this view, but his reflections on what makes up the person never consider rationality and free will. Instead, Vanier continually points to the core of the human person as the *heart*, the center of all relationality and what is deepest in each person.

> We tend to reduce being human to acquiring knowledge, power, and social status. We have disregarded the heart, seeing it only as a symbol of weakness, the center of sentimentality and emotion, instead of as a powerhouse of love that can reorient us from our self-centredness, revealing to us and to others the basic beauty of humanity, empowering us to grow.[38]

---

[35] Jean Vanier, *Becoming Human* (Toronto: House of Anansi Press, 1998), 77–8.
[36] Vanier, *Becoming Human*, 114.
[37] See Jean Vanier, *Our Journey Home: Rediscovering a Common Humanity Beyond Our Differences* (Ottawa: Novalis, 1997), 147: "For me, a person exists from the moment of her conception. She exists even if, like Eric or Hélène, she has a profound handicap."
[38] Vanier, *Becoming Human*, 78.

Persons are far "more than the power or capacity to think and to perform" but more fundamentally hearts that love and seek communion with others in a spirit of solidarity.[39] The intellect remains an important aspect of being human, but, if it does not meet the heart, a person will never truly mature in their humanity.

Thus, the meeting of the heart and mind stands as a basic requirement of humans to become free persons. Vanier recognizes freedom as a fundamental requirement for becoming a person and a proper understanding of truth undergirds this freedom. For Vanier, though, truth does not consist in static and abstract concepts that persons must then freely accede to intellectually and then independently act upon. Truth means more to see and accept the bold givenness of reality laid before persons, rather than believe in a fantasy which conforms to an individual's self-made world.

> The big question at L'Arche is always how to welcome reality and not create or live in illusions, because it is reality that gives us freedom. To be free is to look reality in the face, whether it be the reality of suffering, the reality of death, the reality of people in their weakness or the reality of our own mistakes.[40]

This kind of welcome demands a personal struggle, particularly for those formed in an individualism which places self-sufficiency and competition as the highest values. Ultimately freedom comes as a gift, though, particularly when persons become open enough to recognize God as the source of all being. Free persons living in communion with God then discover "that the truth is not a set of fixed certitudes but a mystery we enter into, one step at a time. It is a process of going deeper and deeper into an unfathomable reality."[41] Encountering the ultimate mystery in God means learning how *to be* and how *to be true*, knowing that nothing is absolute in front of the Creator of the universe.

Communion with mystery connects persons with the ineffable and thus helps them understand their own lives, and indeed all of creation, as a mystery as well. Thus, every person carries a dimension of the holy that always leaves her outside any attempt to totalize and categorize her. Vanier's more than fifty years in community exposed him to modernity's labelling and classifying of people considered intellectually disabled as regrettable defectives. Modernity's subjection of persons with cognitive impairments to medical, educational, and institutional regimes too often assumed an omnipotent knowledge of these persons, rendering their disturbing difference controllable. Vanier consistently refuses to identify those

---

[39] Vanier, *Becoming Human*, 86.
[40] Vanier, *Our Life Together*, 546.
[41] Vanier, *Becoming Human*, 117.

considered disabled as the "sick and suffering." Instead, Vanier tries to see the mystery of every person he meets, whether it be a pope or persons profoundly disabled. The freedom that comes from communion helps persons see others as God sees them, namely as precious and indescribably beautiful. Contemplation characterizes this seeing of persons as persons, which values presence over competition.

That vision of the self and the other as mystery never denies the whole truth of reality, which also includes pain, vulnerability and weakness. If the purpose of life is to become ourselves in God rather than what others wish us to be, then this must include the fragility and contingencies of life. The freedom which comes from being in communion with mystery results not in an autonomous chooser or a muscular savior. Rather the free person in Christ receives "the freedom of vulnerability, the capacity to suffer with others, to listen to them so as to understand their pain."[42]

Vanier even takes the extra step of not only acknowledging the contingency of the human condition but also refusing to absolutely pathologize weakness. The nondisabled in L'Arche see every day how a high-speed culture cannot incorporate persons who cannot move and think in its logic of acceleration. In L'Arche's logic, however, the vulnerability and fragility embodied by community members represents less a pathology than an aspect of being human that slows persons down enough to become available to one another. Vanier sees this reflected in Jesus, his icon and ultimate model for becoming human. Jesus's kenotic journey into the pain and littleness of the human condition stands as a model for how persons must learn to embrace their vulnerability in order to welcome God, themselves, and the other. Vanier finds this summed up in Paul's claim that the wisdom of God comes not through great actions or rational knowledge but through "God's foolishness" (1 Cor. 1:25). Persons considered intellectually disabled in L'Arche embody for Vanier the bold insight that "God chose what is foolish in the world to shame the wise; God chose what is weak in the world to shame the strong" (1 Cor. 1: 27).[43]

When weakness is understood as a dimension of humanness (and not as pathology), the social nature of the person becomes ever clearer. For Vanier, humans cannot grow without others not only because

---

[42] Vanier, *Our Journey Home*, 168.
[43] Vanier often mentions the need for marginalized persons to be part of communities which assist in empowering them to greater freedom. Thus, he never tries to romanticize poverty so as to keep people in situations of destitution. Yet he also intentionally uses the word "weak" to describe his friends in order to counter the common cultural negative valuing of weakness. Denying the weakness of the human condition ultimately leaves many persons considered intellectually disabled, particularly those who will never transcend situations of dependence, outside of late modern moral systems of value. For Vanier's attempt to qualify his uses of "weakness" and "poverty," see Vanier, *An Ark for the Poor*, 14.

persons are never sufficient on their own but also because belonging is a fundamental human need. The social recognition which comes from feeling valued in a community rests as a building block for the integral development of all persons, something which can only come through being part of a body of other persons. "We do not discover who we are, we do not reach true humanness, in a solitary state; we discover it through mutual dependency, in weakness, in learning through belonging."[44]

According to Vanier, at the heart of belonging lies the reality that persons do not make their lives alone but fundamentally receive their existence from others. Persons are created by God and for God and also grow in their vocation through belonging to a community of free persons. Vanier saw this need most clearly in the persons labelled as disabled. While most people take their sense of belonging to a family, or group, or humanity for granted, persons with cognitive impairments often have few or none of these basic human needs, missing a valuable piece required for being and becoming a person. While people like Raphaël exhibit a particular need for belonging, the insight of L'Arche rests in seeing the fundamental social needs for *all persons*.

Recognizing belonging as important also puts into sharp relief late modern individualism and its corrosive effect on persons. Vanier would fundamentally agree with the personalist diagnosis of the pathologies of liberal individualism. Not only does an anthropology based on self-interest skew the perception of the human person, it also turns people against one another. In this social imaginary, life becomes a battle and competition that ultimately leads to violence and injustice.[45] The incessant mobility of network time promises freedom yet too often brings more loneliness than happiness. Vanier became more and more committed to community life as he saw the violence and alienation western liberalism created. "In order to discover the importance of community we have to realise somehow that individualism can lead to death."[46] Like Mounier, Vanier saw as part of the Christian vocation the need to build and foster alternative communities of free persons. These communities would supply the appropriate milieu of lived and sacred time to assist people in their own growth. In addition, these groups could witness to the larger society a more truthful and hospitable vision of being human. The orientation of these communities countered the logic of clock and network time with a more Christian temporality: "less speed and mobility and more interiority; less consumption and more relationships; less technology and more humanity; less dissipation and

---

[44] Vanier, *Becoming Human*, 41.
[45] Jean Vanier, *Man and Woman God Made Them* (Ottawa: Novalis, 2007), 52–3.
[46] Jean Vanier, "Power to Make Human," in *A Prophetic Cry: Stories of Spirituality and Healing Inspired by L'Arche*, ed. Tim Kearney (Dublin: Veritas, 2000), 130.

more unity; less competitiveness and more community; less individualism and more sharing and living together."[47] This witness could thus provide the fertile environment for personal growth as well as contribute to the personalist desire for the transformation of the entire social order.

PEOPLE CONSIDERED DISABLED AS TEACHERS IN A CHRISTIAN TEMPORALITY

The story and practice of L'Arche as discerned through Vanier's personalism includes an orientation to time which counters the logic of clock and network time. Modern temporalities closed persons up in a stifling materialism, alienating people from their own experience and driving them toward a perpetual violence of self against self. In contrast, people labelled as intellectually disabled revealed a different orientation to time, where the path to human flourishing lay with slowing down enough to become friends: friends with God, friends with one another, friends with life itself. Vanier's Aristotelian training had impressed upon him the importance of friendship, but it was people like his friend Antonio – a person considered profoundly intellectually disabled – who embodied for him friendship as the mode of peace and unity.[48] As opposed to high-speed society's impatience with and need to totalize time, those with cognitive impairments live a kind of temporality which forms non-disabled assistants in becoming more Christian persons.

> The assistants who feed, bathe and care for them have to do this, not at their own rhythm, but at that of the people with a handicap. Things have to go at a pace which can welcome their least expression.... [Assistants] become increasingly people of welcome and compassion. The slower rhythm and even the presence of the people with severe disabilities makes them slow down, switch off their efficiency motor, rest and recognise the presence of God.[49]

In the more contemplative orientation needed to live mutuality with persons like Antonio, the nondisabled assistants enter into a space where the authentic integration of their personhood can develop. By slowing down, assistants learn to understand themselves as human creatures invited into participation with the divine life.

Through leading assistants back down toward the ground of their being, Vanier discovered how much those considered "useless" by

---

[47] From an unpublished letter, quoted in Jean Vanier, *Jean Vanier: Essential Writings*, ed. Carolyn Whitney-Brown (Maryknoll: Orbis Books, 2008), 172.

[48] For his work on Aristotle's notion and ethics of friendship, see Jean Vanier, *Made for Happiness: Discovering the Meaning of Life with Aristotle* (Toronto: House of Anansi Press, 2001), 54–75.

[49] Vanier, *Community and Growth*, 187–188.

modernity can teach others about staying human in high-speed society. Persons in L'Arche have noticed and been transformed by a gift that many people labelled disabled have for living in the present moment and thus transforming others formed in the logic of modern and late modern time.

> They have no big plans for tomorrow. Plans are more for people who have greater autonomy and the capacity to lead their lives as they want. Those with disabilities do not cry out for power or success; their energies are used for seeking out the warmth of relationships. I notice how many of us have our eye on the clock, mindful of our next meeting, a talk to give, a deadline to meet. People with intellectual disabilities do not seem to be governed by time in the same way. They tend to live more fully in the present, sometimes enjoying themselves, sometimes angry, usually trusting in the presence of people who appreciate them.[50]

Vanier discovered in many persons considered disabled a freedom and spontaneity that eluded the totalizing thrust of clock and network time. Their freedom in turn witnessed to others a more loving and human temporality, as well as often exemplifying for the nondisabled a more authentic and Christian alternative relationship to time.[51]

Time in L'Arche teaches those trapped in the temporal logic of late modernity that patience rather than speed more fully opens one to experiencing reality as one of grace and welcome. Someone like Antonio's orientation to friendship embodies how God extends the same offer of friendship to humanity, a mutuality patiently offered in the fullness of time. Valuing and practicing patience shapes individuals into persons who learn how to wait for God in God's time. Just as Jesus took the time to become flesh through the Incarnation and remains ever patient through the presence of the Holy Spirit, Christians can witness against high-speed society's alienating anthropology. Living in God's time shows believers that speed often dulls experience rather than intensifies it. In the Christian logic of L'Arche, those persons considered "wasted" by late modernity often exemplify a contemplative trust in the present and make space for the slow friendships needed to realize the fullness of their humanity.

The freedom of integrated persons means not only becoming friends with other subjects but also with the body and all material

---

[50] Vanier, *Becoming Human*, 94.
[51] It is important to see how L'Arche's understanding of people with intellectual disabilities as "teachers" should not be construed as an attempt to explain away the difference of these persons as "special" or "holy innocents." Vanier's insight into the capacity persons like Antonio have to help transform people came not from seeing him as a kind of holy "object" or spiritual "visual aid." Instead, this discovery came through *being in relationship* with persons considered disabled and through sharing daily life with them in a spirit of friendship.

reality. While clock and network time continually try to conquer the limitations of the material world, L'Arche's temporality welcomes the truth of the body, even in its vulnerability and brokenness. Rather than the late modern impulse toward the virtual in which bodies increasingly disappear, the bodies of people with cognitive impairments inhabit space and refuse to be ignored. In network time, this utter resistance to speed acts as a danger and threat. Living in God's time, though, means receiving the grace of "real presence," not primarily as information but a person lovingly created by a good God, for God. Vanier never tires of pointing out how people like Antonio have taught others how to accept their bodies not only as a gift but also as a "temple of the Holy Spirit." The basic Christian conviction that material reality stands as crucial rather than peripheral to being human means that apparently slow and limited human bodies actually assist people in their human vocation. As a basic ground of all persons, physical bodies indicate the common destiny of everyone to befriend truth and receive God's friendship.

CELEBRATING AND BECOMING HUMAN IN GOD'S TIME

The importance of celebration in L'Arche became clear for Vanier upon sharing life in community. For persons like Antonio, generally considered in modernity as "useless," celebration was rarely connected with their lives. By celebrating these persons through simple things like birthdays and anniversaries, these rituals became profoundly evocative events, communicating the preciousness of many socially devalued persons. At the same time, Vanier grew to see celebration as a fundamental aspect of community for *all persons*, the nondisabled included. Celebrations represented opportunities to step out of the confines of clock and network time in order to thank God together for the gift of life and remember the presence of the Holy Spirit as the living flame of communal unity. By so doing, persons also deepen their vocation to communion and friendship as well as remember the inspiration which originally brought people together.

Taking the time to celebrate means intentionally entering into an eschatological mode of time where people enter the feast of God. One of Vanier's favorite images of the Kingdom of God is as a wedding banquet. Joy and gratitude predominate in this temporality. The common work of the people comes not as achievement but giving thanks for God's presence in the community's story, and it imparts a humble hope in God's future. Celebrating represents not an escapism from life but a longing for transcendence and communion. These events usher persons into the eschatological time of the Lord and represent "a moment of wonder when the joy of the body and the senses are linked to the joy of the spirit."[52] As sacred time, celebration

---

[52] Vanier, *Community and Growth*, 315.

makes the time for integrating the material and physical dimensions of persons, thereby developing the whole person within a larger Body of persons. Practicing celebration shapes persons in the Gospel of life, where time represents not a claustrophobic prison but the redeemed milieu where God reconciles the world and calls friends to the eschatological wedding banquet.

The Eucharist stands as a particularly apt practice both to express L'Arche's vision of being human and to form its members in becoming friends of truth. Vanier found that many of his friends in L'Arche sought not the disembodied "real time" of dematerialized social networks but the *real presence* of others. Thus, God's presence through the gathering of the people and the celebration of the life, death, and resurrection of Jesus resonates with their intuitive sense of being in relationship. Vanier's understanding of Jesus as Word-made-flesh included God's desire to reconcile the world to God's self through befriending creation. In the Eucharist, Jesus gives himself to his people and forms them ever deeper into their *telos* as friends of God.

Celebrating communion at the table of the Lord exemplifies how the journey of becoming human goes most fundamentally not through the intellect but through *the heart*, the part of the human where God dwells and beckons persons. Vanier speaks about Eric, a man considered profoundly disabled who had passed "through many hands that touched and handled him, often without real love or any real commitment."[53] Yet in the chapel during the Eucharist, people would notice how peaceful he appeared, even though he could not hear or see anything. Somehow, Eric lived from his heart and had a capacity to receive and open himself to the eternal mystery.

> People who have highly developed intellects often try to reach God through their minds and thoughts. People who have limited intelligence are more open to a simple presence, a heart-to-heart relationship of communion and love. They receive God in the peace of their hearts, although they are unable to put their experience into words. If Eric could have described what he lived during the eucharist, he would probably have said, "I was filled with deep peace and joy."[54]

Eric showed the way for others to experience a deep sense of communion and friendship with Jesus, the end and beatitude of human persons.

Against the view that the use of reason is the foundation of moral subjectivity, Vanier's recognition that persons who lack the use of

---

[53] Jean Vanier, *The Heart of L'Arche: A Spirituality for Every Day* (London: SPCK, 2013), 38.
[54] Vanier, *The Heart of L'Arche*, 39.

reason still experience a relationship with God helped him remember the centrality of the body in Christian life. The pervasively virtual nature of life at network time easily assists people in forgetting that persons not so much have bodies but *are* bodies. The desire that many people labelled intellectually disabled express for celebration showed Vanier the crucial place of the body in human experience as sacramental, as a medium for encountering the Source of life. Vanier found this insight revealed particularly intensely when people gathered together for the Eucharist.

> Being in l'Arche, I am very sensitive to the reality of the body. Many of our people cannot speak, but all express love and fear through their bodies. The body is more fundamental than the word. The Body of Christ is more fundamental than his Word. Many handicapped people cannot understand the Word but they can eat his Body. And they seem to have a deep understanding of what communion means.[55]

This understanding of communion applies not just for personal communion with Jesus through receiving the host but also for the unity within the larger Body. Many of those labelled as having intellectual disabilities intuitively understood more than nondisabled assistants that persons become human as a body within the larger Body of free persons in Christ.

The bodies of persons require not the productive and efficient bodies of clock time or the sleek and infinitely mobile bodies of network time. On the contrary, persons remember at the Eucharistic event that the glory of Christ is intimately integrated with his *broken body*, a body present in the rejected and most vulnerable persons. "The broken body of Christ in the Eucharist is only clearly understood when it is seen in relation to the broken bodies and hearts of the poor; and their broken bodies and hearts find meaning in the broken Body of Christ."[56] This kind of integration of glory and pain celebrated in the Eucharist, which models the journey of persons in bringing the material into the realm of the spiritual, appears unbearable to a late modern temporality. The Church, however, remembers Jesus's embodied identification with the most rejected, where persons celebrate and practice the Eucharist and the Eucharist shapes its participants in the radical patience needed to become friends. This form of *patientia* connotes not only a spacious waiting for other persons but also the capacity to bear with one another, even amid severe trials and periods of great suffering. Clock and network time simply have no time to suffer with others. The example of people like Antonio revealed to Vanier that communion with God does not mean

---

[55] Vanier, *Community and Growth*, 197.
[56] Vanier, *Community and Growth*, 198.

elimination of vulnerable persons for their sake and the community's sake; rather, the Eucharist as practice forms persons into friends often through those considered the most regrettable and "useless."

Persons like Antonio reside at the center of these communities of God's friends, showing high-speed society that, by slowing down enough to celebrate and to be fully present to one another, persons can grow into that beatitude for which they were created. For Vanier, what L'Arche most reveals to the world is that social renewal comes not necessarily through exercising political responsibility or the wheels of power but entering the happiness God desires for the whole world.

> We must not get caught up in the need for power over the poor. We need to be with the poor. That can seem a bit crazy because it doesn't look like a plan to change the world. But maybe we will change the world if we are happy. Maybe what we need most is to rejoice and to celebrate with the weak and the vulnerable. Maybe the most important thing is to learn how to build communities of celebration. Maybe the world will be transformed when we learn to have fun together. I don't mean to suggest that we don't talk about serious things. But maybe what our world needs more than anything is communities where we celebrate life together and become signs of hope for our world. Maybe we need signs that it is possible to love each other.[57]

As signs for the world of the slow journey towards beatitude, L'Arche communities give witness to an anthropological outlook where those seemingly most "wasted" can lead others in their full development as persons.

CONCLUSION

The pervasive power that clock and network time possesses in late modernity gives it the appearance of hegemony, but the communities of L'Arche stand as alternative sites of Christian resistance to this temporality. Grounded in integral personalism and Catholic social teaching, Jean Vanier and L'Arche present a more Christian and authentic anthropology, one that takes the time to become friends and live in God's time rather than clock or network time. The very atypical exemplars in L'Arche offer a contemplative temporality, leading its members in a more Christian relationship with time and the natural world. Jean Vanier's discovery of the gifts of those labelled intellectually disabled means that they cease to be "wasted lives." Instead, friendship with intellectually disabled persons opens opportunities to discover the authentic rhythm and pace of the Christian life, one that seeks not the "real time" of virtuality but the

---

[57] Jean Vanier, "The Vision of Jesus: Living Peaceably in a Wounded World," in *Living Gently in a Violent World: The Prophetic Witness of Weakness*, by Stanley Hauerwas and Jean Vanier (Downers Grove: IVP Books, 2008), 75.

slow and real presence of embodied, creaturely life. Vanier's friends like Antonio show that patience formed in relationship is a Christian habit, manifested by an attentiveness to other bodies in the Body, as well as at the eucharistic table of the Lord. At this table, the material and temporal meet, facilitating the beatitude for which those in high-speed society strive.

Celebration characterizes the joy and peace found when persons find the time to remember the Source and End of all life. L'Arche shows how the "civilization of love" hoped for in the personalist and Roman Catholic tradition comes not through a triumphalist and all-powerful institution but in countercultural communities of faithful persons joyfully witnessing to God's presence in the world. Thus, the image Vanier presents of the community of God's friends is not that of the "hamster wheel" but of the eschatological wedding feast. In the banquet of God, the slow and contemplative welcome the impatient to know their preciousness and dependence on God, others, and creation. These contemplative persons reveal real human being in high-speed society: free persons living from the heart, welcoming others in their mystery, patiently witnessing to the Gospel of life calling everyone to a pilgrimage gently taken.

The Goodness and Beauty of Our Fragile Flesh: Moral Theologians and Our Engagement With "Disability"

Miguel J. Romero

"The starting point for every reflection on disability is rooted in the fundamental convictions of Christian anthropology." – Pope Saint John Paul II, "On the Dignity and Rights of the Mentally Disabled Person," no. 2.

"It is essential that man should acknowledge his inherent condition as a creature .... Only by admitting his innate dependence can man live and use his freedom to the full. [S]uffering and death ... these are a part of human existence, and it is futile, not to say misleading, to try to hide them or ignore them." – *Evangelium Vitae*, nos. 96-97.

"God fashioned the human body in that disposition which was best, befitting [*optima dispositione secundum convenientiam*]...the soul and its operations." – St. Thomas Aquinas, *Summa Theologiae,* I q. 91, a. 3, co.

THE RECOGNITION THAT WE ARE COMPOSITE creatures, a spiritual and corporal unity, is basic to the Christian understanding of the human being. For this reason, Christian doctrine on our integral dignity has always included an affirmation of the goodness of the human body and, likewise, an affirmation that the innate vulnerability of our bodies coincides with the harmony of our specific place in the good order of God's creation.[1] In other words, Christians believe that the vulnerability and coordinate dependencies of the human body are essential creaturely goods, enduring aspects of our original nakedness, which are not in themselves a cause for shame.[2]

Those gifts are among the natural goods that predicate our greatest good and final perfection, as incarnate intellectual creatures formed in

---

[1] See, for example, Genesis 1:26-27, 2:7, 18-25; Psalm 8; *Gaudium et Spes*, nos. 12, 14; *Evangelium Vitae*, nos. 96-97; *Catechism of the Catholic Church*, nos. 1934-8.
[2] Pope Saint John Paul II, "The Presence of Evil and Suffering in the World," June 4, 1986, nos. 5-7; See John Paul II, *Man and Woman He Created Them: A Theology of the Body* (Boston: Pauline Books & Media, 2006), 154-156, 238-242.

the image and likeness of the triune God.³ In that vein, at the proclamation of St. Hildegard of Bingen (1098-1179) as *doctor ecclesiae* (2012), Pope Benedict XVI remarks on the understanding of the human being given in St. Hildegard's "eminent," "penetrating," and "comprehensive" theology:

> Hildegard's anthropology begins from the biblical narrative of the creation of man, made in the image and likeness of God...a unity of body and soul ... a positive appreciation of corporeity and providential value is given even to the body's weaknesses. The body is not a weight from which to be delivered ... human beings are weak and frail ... [and our] bodies, like the body of Christ, are oriented to the glorious resurrection.⁴

This distinctively Christian understanding of human nature and human dignity flows directly from the Good News of God's love for the world, revealed in and through Jesus Christ. That is to say, Christian theological anthropology is regulated by Christian belief in the origin, history, status, and destiny of the human being, amid the ongoing act of creation: the utter gratuity of our specific dignity, original innocence, original sin, the Fall, the Incarnation of God in Christ, reconciliation, bodily resurrection, and final beatitude.⁵

---

³ In the words of Aquinas, the human being is created a "mortal rational animal" (*animal rationale mortale*). Aquinas, *Sententia libri Metaphysicae* VII.5, 1378-9. This does not mean that the human being is *merely* a 'mortal rational animal,' nor does this mean our innate vulnerability and coordinate dependencies are *all that God intends* for the human being. Rather, it means that whatever our potential to exceed our nature and whatever God might intend for the human being, Christians believe that our natural corporeal vulnerability to impairment, illness, and injury is integral to the specific nature that is perfected and the creaturely dignity that is elevated.

⁴ Pope Benedict XVI, "Proclaiming Saint Hildegard of Bingen, professed nun of the Order of Saint Benedict, a Doctor of the Universal Church," October 7, 2007, no.5, w2.vatican.va/content/benedict-xvi/en/apost_letters/documents/hf_ben-xvi_apl_20121007_ildegarda-bingen.html. Throughout her eighty-one years of life, from her early childhood, St. Hildegard constantly experienced 'potent infirmities,' including debilitating migraines, synesthesia, seizures, chronic pain, partial blindness, periods of complete blindness, partial deafness, recurring bouts of severe paralysis (including thirteen years of complete paralysis). See Sabina Flanagan, *Hildegard of Bingen: A Visionary Life* (New York: Routledge, 2002), 146-161. See also Anna Silvas, *Jutta and Hildegard: The Biographical Sources* (University Park: Penn State University Press, 1999).

⁵ See *Gaudium et Spes*, nos. 12, 14: "Endowed with light from God, [the Church] can offer solutions...so that man's true situation can be portrayed and his defects explained, while at the same time his dignity and destiny are justly acknowledged .... Though made of body and soul, man is one. Through his bodily composition he gathers to himself the elements of the material world; thus they reach their crown through him, and through him raise their voice in free praise of the Creator. For this reason man is not allowed to despise his bodily life, rather he is obliged to regard his body as good and honorable since God has created it and will raise it up on the last day. Nevertheless, wounded by sin, man experiences rebellious stirrings in his body."

Considered by way of that revealed history, the various postlapsarian disclosures of our innate vulnerability are rightly regarded as privations of a relative corporeal good. Those "defects" and "infirmities," however, do not diminish our incarnate, creaturely dignity and cannot displace the fittingness of our composite nature.[6] Rather, in the light of the Gospel, as discussed below and following Aquinas, the "defects" and "infirmities" of the human body manifest the goodness of corporeality and the fitting beauty of our fragile flesh.[7] Our fragility is revealed as beautiful in the light of the truth of "wounded Beauty," where the defects assumed by Christ and the infirmities he bore summon us away from deception toward a beauty we must learn to see.[8] The Christian affirmation of our specifically incarnate intellectual dignity, the fittingness of our vulnerability, and the enduring goodness of corporeality in light of the Fall—these three doctrines—function as anthropological principles for distinctively Christian theological consideration of the integral good proper to the human being and moral theological descriptions of human happiness.

My interest in this essay is the way those three particular anthropological principles—our specific dignity, the fittingness of our vulnerability, and the enduring goodness of corporeality—are navigated in contemporary Christian theology. The particular, animating concern is a somewhat consistent, recurring tendency to avoid or muddle this constellation of anthropological principles in moral theological and Christian ethical discourse. Indeed, in some quarters of Christian theology, the suggestion that our corporeal

---

[6] See *Salvifici Doloris*, no. 7: "Christianity proclaims the essential good of existence and the good of that which exists, acknowledges the goodness of the Creator and proclaims the good of creatures. Man suffers on account of evil, which is a certain lack, limitation or distortion of good. We could say that man suffers *because of a good* in which he does not share…. He particularly suffers when he ought—in the normal order of things—to have a share in this good and does not have it. Thus, in the Christian view, the reality of suffering is explained through evil, which always, in some way, refers to a good."

[7] A preliminary point is called for concerning the distinctively Christian theological use of words like 'defect' (*de-* "away" + *facere* "to do, make") and 'perfect' (*per-* "complete" + *facere* "to do, make"): Even if there are *absolute* goods (concerning the whole of us) that follow from the privation (an absence of something expected) of a *relative* corporeal good (concerning only the bodily part of us), the relative corporeal 'defect' (an 'away-from-doing' that only concerns the body, in the semantic range of 'impairment') does not diminish the integral creaturely dignity or 'perfection' (the integral goodness of the whole person) of the person whose body is impaired nor does the relative corporal 'defect' redefine the corporeal good that is impaired. I'll return to this in section four, when I discuss impairment, healing, and the non-competitive transcendence of God.

[8] Joseph Ratzinger, "The Feeling of Things, the Contemplation of Beauty," August 2002, www.vatican.va/roman_curia/congregations/cfaith/documents/rc_con_ cfaith_ doc_20020824_ratzinger-cl-rimini_en.html. See also *ST* III q.14 & 15, where Aquinas treats the defects assumed by Christ in the Incarnation.

vulnerability is an essential and fitting creaturely good might be regarded as inconsistent with Christian doctrine on original sin and the Fall—supposing that the vulnerability of our bodies to external effects is a primeval curse which corrupts human nature and undermines human dignity.[9] In other quarters of Christian theology, the mention of "evil," "sin," or "defect" in relation to bodily impairment, illness, and injury might be regarded as having elitist and chauvinistic, if not dangerously eugenic implications, that threaten to undermine the dignity of persons who have some form of impairment—supposing that the Christian affirmation of our inalienable dignity remains intelligible when abstracted from the particulars of the Gospel.[10] The breadth and depth of this contemporary problem is struck in high relief when we consider how the topic of "disability" is theologically conceived and navigated, engaged and avoided, in contemporary Catholic systematic, moral, and ethical discourse.

My overarching contention is that persistent avoidance of or confusion about the three anthropological principles mentioned above can undermine the coherence and integrity of Catholic moral theology. More precisely, my contention is twofold. First, any theological account of the human good and human happiness is incomplete if it does not, and cannot, account for how that life is possible for the kind of beings that we are: intellectual creatures, composite beings, formed

---

[9] In response to that view, see *Summa Theologiae* (ST) I q. 96, a. 3, co., where St. Thomas Aquinas discusses the innate vulnerability and coordinate dependencies of the human body before the Fall: "We must needs admit that in the primitive state there would have been some differences [*disparitatem*].... There might also have been bodily disparity. For the human body was not entirely exempt from the laws of nature, so as not to receive from exterior sources more or less advantage and help.... So we may say that, according to the climate, or the movement of the stars, some would have been born more robust in body than others…however, in those who were thus surpassed, there would have been no defect or fault either in soul or body." Excerpts from Aquinas's *Summa* are from the English translation by the Fathers of the English Dominican Province (New York: Ave Maria Press, 1981).

[10] In response to that view, see *Salvifici Doloris*, no. 15: "When one says that Christ by his mission strikes at evil at its very roots, we have in mind not only evil and definitive, eschatological suffering (so that man 'should not perish, but have eternal life'), but also—at least indirectly *toil and suffering* in their *temporal and historical dimension*. For evil remains bound to sin and death. And even if we must use great caution in judging man's suffering as a consequence of concrete sins (this is shown precisely by the example of the just man Job [i.e., *Salvifici Doloris*, nos. 9-13]), nevertheless suffering cannot be divorced from the sin of the beginnings, from what Saint John calls 'the sin of the world,' *from the sinful background* of the personal actions and social processes in human history. Though it is not licit to apply here the narrow criterion of direct dependence (as Job's three friends did), it is equally true that one cannot reject the criterion that, at the basis of human suffering, there is a complex involvement with sin." Emphasis in original. See *Catechism*, nos. 1500-2: "In illness, man experiences his powerlessness, his limitations, and his finitude.... It is the experience of Israel that illness is mysteriously linked to sin and evil, and that faithfulness to God according to his law restores life."

in the image of God—*beings who are by nature, among other things, variously and unequally vulnerable to impairment, illness, injury, and decay.*[11] Second, any moral theological or Christian ethical account of human impairment, illness, and injury in the life of the Church is incomplete if it does not, and cannot, account for how the outlook held forth coheres with the basic doctrines of the Christian faith—*including, among other things, Christian doctrine on our specific intellectual dignity, the essential goodness and relative afflictions of corporeality, and the corporeal consequences of the Fall.*[12]

At the heart of this twofold contention is hope for an enterprise of self-recovery, within the discipline of moral theology.[13] The way contemporary moral theologians conceive and navigate the topic of "disability" in systematic, moral, and ethical discourse indicates the scope of that enterprise. The particular recovery I have in mind is one that is responsive to the diagnosis and prescription articulated for the discipline of moral theology by Fr. Servais Pinckaers, O.P., in his *Sources of Christian Ethics.* Specifically, Pinckaers is critical of any moral theology that fails to engage the ordinary human experience of privation or poverty ("suffering," in the broad theological sense, which includes our bare passive potency to externalities, the corporeal pains of affliction, and the affective pains of sorrow).[14] Pinckaers writes,

---

[11] For context, note the analogy between the incomplete theology that concerns me here (i.e., one that addresses the human good, but avoids or muddles Catholic doctrine on the goodness of our innate corporeal vulnerability) and Pope John Paul II's *argument against* certain problematic moral methodologies in *Veritatis Splendor,* nos. 46, 47. Further, note the analogy between my proposed correction for the incomplete theology that concerns me (i.e., the position that presumes an idealized caricature of the human being as naturally invulnerable and independent) and the correction offered by Pope John Paul II to problematic moral methodologies in *Veritatis Splendor,* nos. 48, 49.

[12] For context, note the analogy between the incomplete theology that concerns me here (i.e., one that addresses impairment/disability, but avoids or muddles Christian doctrine on the revealed history of the human condition) and Pope John Paul's *argument against* problematic moral methodologies in *Veritatis Splendor,* no. 46a. Further, note the analogy between my proposed correction for the incomplete theology that concerns me (the position that places a reductively material emphasis upon the reality of impairment and disability) and the correction offered by Pope John Paul II to problematic moral methodologies in *Veritatis Splendor,* no. 50.

[13] See Miguel J. Romero, "Profound Cognitive Impairment, Moral Virtue, and Our Life in Christ: Can My Brother Live a Happy and Holy Life?" *Church Life* 3, no. 4 (2015): 80-94.

[14] An important distinction is called for here. Given the kind of creatures we are, ultimately, every temporal joy and sorrow, every sensual gratification and painful affliction, is 'suffered' insofar as these are experiences we *undergo*. For that reason, it is theologically imprecise to categorically conflate or identify *corporeal impairment, illness, and injury* with the experience of *physical/spiritual pain or "suffering."* In the ordinary way, it is not difficult to imagine forms of impairment, illness, and injury that one could *undergo* and that do not coincide with an experience

Think of a person who has never known suffering [in the broad sense]. Is this person real? ... How is it that [Christian] ethicists have not grasped the importance of suffering and have built up moral systems that bypass it? The explanation is simple enough: once the idea of obligation becomes dominant and determines the scope of morality, the consideration of suffering becomes marginal, since it is not a matter of obligation. On the other hand, if the idea of happiness is the initial consideration in moral theology, the place of suffering will be obvious .... Suffering will then be an element of moral theology from the very start.... This is [the exact problem that] I have been describing: *a moral theology that excludes the question of suffering, and happiness as well, relegating them to a related science as if they were merely material for specialists, while in reality they are fundamental human experiences.* Actually, this banishment of the consideration of suffering from ethics is an outgrowth of a rationalistic conception of the human person.[15]

The essay is divided into five sections. First, instead of a theological typology of human "disability," I sketch a typology of three ways contemporary Christian theologians both avoid and engage the topic of "disability." The purpose of this *ad hoc* sketch is to highlight an underlying problem in the way contemporary theologians tend to think about the innate vulnerabilities and coordinate dependencies of the human body. Second, I discuss the Christian challenge to the concept of "disability" and the particular challenge the concept of "disability" presents to moral theological reflection on impairment, illness, and injury. The setting for the difference Catholic teaching on impairment, illness, and injury could make for moral theology is mapped in relation to a set of theologically suggestive threads drawn from Alasdair MacIntyre's book *Dependent Rational Animals* – in particular, MacIntyre's description of the way insular moral formation and disordered affective inclination can dispose

---

of physical or spiritual pain. Despite the common negative connotation among English speakers, the technical Christian theological use of the term *suffering* is not always in reference to something that is categorically 'bad.' Rather, *to suffer* is a condition of our creatureliness, our substantial passive potency to be subject to or affected by things and circumstances that we do not control—which includes both joys and sorrows, sensual gratification and painful affliction. So, in Christian theological terms, while there may be a correlation between *impairment* and *spiritual/physical pain*, there is nothing about impairment that necessitates *spiritual/physical pain*. Suffering in the negative sense, thus, would refer specifically to *spiritual pains of sorrow* and *corporeal pains of affliction*, insofar as these are *evils suffered* (*malum poenae*): the human experience of a spiritual or corporeal good that is missing or lacking.

[15] Servais Pinckaers, *Sources of Christian Ethics* (Washington, DC: The Catholic University of America Press, 1995), 24–27 [Emphasis added]. See Pinckaers's extended discussion of poverty in *The Pursuit of Happiness—God's Way: Living the Beatitudes* (Eugene, OR: Wipf and Stock Publishers, 2011), 39–54.

moralists to persist with incomplete or distorted accounts of the human being. Third, I offer a close reading of Aquinas's remarks in ST I q. 91, a. 3, on the "fittingness" of the vulnerable disposition and coordinate dependencies of the human body. There, Aquinas provides a Christian theological framework for understanding the connection between moral formation, aesthetic perception, and the Christian account of human dignity. Given the contemporary challenge, Aquinas's formulation of the goodness and beauty of our fragile flesh recommends three lines of remedial work: doctrine, encounter, and aesthetic perception. Fourth, I retrace certain doctrinal fundamentals of the Christian view and consider a key contemporary theological muddle concerning the way Christians think about the vulnerability of the human body. Fifth, I conclude with a brief discussion of why our personal and ongoing reception of the Christian understanding of the human being involves a discipline of moral conversion, by way of encounter, toward the transformation of one's affective inclination.[16] That constructive proposal is oriented by the moral witness of St. Francis of Assisi. I do not pretend that these remarks amount to much more than a collection of reminders and programmatic recommendations.[17] The most I can hope is that readers will be encouraged toward critical self-reflection on the way their own interpretive and speculative work on the human good and human happiness engages the goodness and beauty of our fragile flesh.

PART ONE: THEOLOGICAL AVOIDANCE AND ENGAGEMENT WITH "DISABILITY"

My first purpose in this section is to sketch the contours of three common ways contemporary theologians tend to avoid and/or engage the topic of "disability."[18] From the aspects of its construction and

---

[16] Although I intend that the aesthetic theory outlined here should, at the very least, be theologically defensible as a preliminary gesture, theological aesthetics is not my central concern. I lean heavily on the scholarship of Christopher Scott Sevier, *Aquinas On Beauty* (London: Lexington Books, 2015); Alex Garcia-Rivera, *A Wounded Innocence* (Collegeville: The Liturgical Press, 2003); Richard Viladesau, *The Beauty of the Cross* (Oxford: Oxford University Press, 2006); Kevin O'Reilly, *Aesthetic Perception* (Portland: Four Courts Press, 2007); and Natalie Carnes, *Beauty: A Theological Engagement with Gregory of Nyssa* (Eugene: Cascade Books, 2014).

[17] For examples of the anthropological outlook I am holding forth for recovery in Catholic moral theology—one that presumes our innate creaturely vulnerability and coordinate dependencies—see Pia Matthews, *Pope John Paul II and the Apparently 'Non-acting' Person* (Herefordshire, UK: Gracewing, 2013), 61-96; Jeffrey Tranzillo, *John Paul II on the Vulnerable* (Washington, DC: CUA Press, 2012), 309-358; Paul J. Wadell, *Happiness and the Christian Moral Life: An Introduction to Christian Ethics* (Lanham: Rowman & Littlefield, 2008), 69-91. See also Bishop Peter Comensoli, *In God's Image: Recognizing the Profoundly Impaired as Persons*, ed. Nigel Zimmerman (Eugene, OR: Cascade Books, 2017).

[18] The typology I've developed here draws from and improvises upon the approach and speculative framework(s) conceived by Licia Carlson in *The Faces of Intellectual*

deconstruction, however, this typology may offer more disappointment than delight—this is because the typology only maps the symptom, and not the underlying cause. The symptom, as I see it, is the various ways we theologically conceive and navigate the topic of "disability." The underlying cause, I'll go on to argue, is the predicate judgments (or presumptions) of the theologian on the constellation of distinctively Christian anthropological principles named at the outset: our specifically incarnate intellectual dignity, the fittingness of our vulnerability, and the enduring goodness of corporeality in light of the Fall. The various ways that this typology does not bear up to close scrutiny, I hope, will allow us to better appreciate the challenge of Christianity to the concept of "disability."[19] And, further, should help us understand the extent to which the concept of "disability," nevertheless, retains and presses an important challenge to the way contemporary moral theologians go about their work.

Three Types of Theological Discourse on Disability
It seems reasonable to presume that virtually every contemporary theology instructor has in some way, at some time, either been pressed to engage or attempted to engage the topic of "disability." Not even a living caricature of the quintessentially indifferent, abstraction-inebriated fuddy-duddy could wholly avoid the occasional student question about disability. For most of us, in our response to that student, we likely settle into one of the three, typical modes of theological discourse on disability: 1) principled avoidance, 2) practical specialization, or 3) instrumental use.

1) Principled Avoidance
In some quarters of Catholic theology (although there is nothing exclusively Catholic about it), on the understanding that no particular corporeal impairment, illness, or injury is essential to the human being, the normative or natural reference point for systematic and moral theological speculation is taken to be a person with an able-body

---

Disability: Philosophical Reflections (Bloomington: Indiana University Press, 2010), 105-208; and in "Philosophers of Intellectual Disability: A Taxonomy," *Metaphilosophy* 40, no. 3-4 (2009): 552-566.

[19] Thus, this *ad hoc* typology of the ways contemporary theologians engage and/or avoid disability is intended as scaffold for the later argument and not as summary of established, methodological approaches to disability. Its purpose is to help us recognize an underlying, contemporary problem in the way we tend to think about the human body. Although I am confident some readers will recognize the referent for many of my descriptions, I've opted for nonspecificity to underscore the provisional nature of these distinctions. I'd also add that there is no 'good-guy' or 'bad-guy' envisioned in these distinct modes of engagement. It shouldn't be difficult to envision both virtuous and vicious, faithful and unfaithful theological proposals arising from each type.

(a body abstracted from any particularizing disability). Everyone would agree, for example, that the lack of wings is *definitive* of the kind of body proper to the human being; however, the argument goes, no one claims that the lack of arms is *definitive* of the kind of body proper to the human being.

In the case of moral theology, for example, this would mean that the accidental lack of any particular natural faculty or organ would not be an appropriate theme to incorporate into fundamental moral theological discourse, except for the occasional illustration of principles, or to demonstrate the implications or application of a particular concept. So conceived, theological consideration of the human good and human happiness could not responsibly take a concept like "disability" as an anthropological principle in moral discourse—just as other human particularities like maleness or femaleness or race, likewise, cannot responsibly be taken as definitive of humanity, *as such*. Of course, as with the other human particularities just mentioned, there is nothing illicit about a specialized theological consideration of particular disabilities. Thus, for the *principled avoider*, the practical Christian response to disability is a perfectly intelligible and even commendable topic for focused study, so long as that special inquiry is not confused with the fundamental dogma, doctrine, and themes of traditional Christian theological discourse.

Principled avoidance, in other words, could sound like this: *I may have a personal experience of disability and an overflowing compassionate regard for persons who have a disability, but "disability" is not one of my research concerns and it is outside my competency as a scholar. It is better to leave the discussion of disability to specialists, professionals, and pastoral ministers.* This does not mean that these *principled avoiders* of disability harbor some deep seated bigotry or that their avoidance is a totalizing value judgment against theological discourse on disability. It simply means that "disability" is not a theological topic that interests them. In the ordinary way, their principled avoidance could even be taken as an expression of collegial trust that theologians who do indeed have a special interest and expertise in "disability" will make good use of solid theological resources when particular dilemmas or questions arise. Christian theology, of course, is a team sport.

2) Practical Specialization

Coordinate with the tendency toward *principled avoidance* is the tendency toward *practical specialization*. On this approach, the task of the practical theologian who has a special interest and cultivated expertise in "disability" is to apply the doctrinal and spiritual resources of the Christian tradition to practical Christian reflection on an anomalous, outlier aspect of the human condition. In so doing, the practical theologian provides both spiritual inspiration and/or theologically informed support whenever intra-personal, liturgical, socio-political, or ethical dilemmas arise. Although the disability specialist generally avoids discussing disability in these terms, their theological concern with disability or mental illness is animated by the intent to provide a practical Christian response *when something has gone wrong with someone's body*. Notions like human nature, evil, and the wounds of original sin certainly matter for the disability specialist, but not in a way that would change what could count as a Christian response to the reality and experience of disability—for that reason, there is a general tendency to avoid the cultural baggage and negative associations of those theological topics. For both the *avoider* and the *specialist*, Christian discourse on the theological significance and moral implications of disability tends to be regarded as a practice-oriented, accessory extension of standard Christian theology.

Practical specialization, in other words, could sound like this: *I may have an enduring concern for the theological principles relevant to disability, but my attentiveness to theology is ordered towards the practical difference it can make in the lives of Christians who have a disability and for the good of their families. It is better to leave abstract theological discussions about dogma and doctrine to trustworthy experts.* This does not necessarily mean that *practical specialists* in disability are incapable of nuanced theological speculation or that they are viciously dodging intellectual engagement. Rather, it simply indicates a decisive preference to see that the fruit of their theological labors will directly nourish the faith and support the wellbeing of particular Christians. In the ordinary way, their specialization and attentiveness to practical challenges can be understood as an expression of collegial trust that expert theologians will write and teach faithful theology.

3) Instrumental Use

The third type of theological discourse on disability is the most diverse. Nevertheless, there is a common characteristic that unites the various iterations of this approach from the past forty years. Specifically, what distinguishes this third mode of engagement is that "disability" as a concept, "the disabled" as a class, and narratives about particular persons who have a disability are invoked in view of something else. Insofar as theological discourse on "disability" is not *directly* addressed to a practical need or for the practical benefit of particular persons, the engagement and invocation of "disability" could be defined as an *instrumental use*—for example, engagements that aim to illustrate some other concept, justify a critique, defend a view, or underwrite some kind of disciplinary agenda or outlook. In other words, if the primary goal is to convince other theologians or academics of some claim or proposal, it is an *instrumental use* of the concept "disability." This is not necessarily a bad thing. Rather, it is simply a mode of engagement and use of the concept "disability" that is distinct from the practical preoccupations and aims that orient *practical specialist* theological engagement with disability. So conceived, with great consistency, the concept of "disability" is used instrumentally in Christian theological discourse to either *define a new boundary* or *problematize an old boundary*.

Although the following list is not exhaustive and is intentionally nonspecific, I intend it to be a fair reflection of the various ways contemporary theologians instrumentally use the concept "disability," "the disabled" as a class, or narratives about disability. In the areas of dogmatic and systematic theology, for example, it is not difficult to find instrumental uses of "disability" developed in view of some claim or proposal on:

(1) Christian community, where "disability" either defines or problematizes the boundary between non-disabled "us" and disabled "them";
(2) A particular Christian doctrine, where "disability" either defines or problematizes the boundary between faithful articulation and unfaithful articulation of the doctrine;
(3) A particular cultural practice, where "disability" either defines or problematizes the boundary between good practices and evil practices, from a Christian perspective;
(4) Christian liturgy, where "disability" either defines or problematizes the boundary between a licit and illicit performance;
(5) Individual Christian identity, where "disability" either defines or problematizes the boundary between 'self' and 'other';
(6) The human species, where "disability" either defines or problematizes the boundary between human and not-human, from a Christian perspective;
(7) Theological method, where "disability" either defines or problematizes the difference between stronger and weaker methodological practices;
(8) Anthropological norms, where "disability" either defines or problematizes the boundary between 'normal' human beings and 'abnormal' human beings, from a Christian perspective.

In the areas of moral theology and Christian ethics, we find instrumental uses of "disability" in service of claims or proposals on:

(1) Moral agency, where "disability" either defines or problematizes the boundary between human acts and acts of a human being, from a Christian perspective;

(2) Moral subjectivity, where "disability" either defines or problematizes the boundary between moral regard and moral disregard, from a Christian perspective;
(3) Moral acts, where "disability" either defines or problematizes the boundary between culpability and non-culpability, from a Christian perspective;
(4) Some social or political or ecclesial practice, where "disability" either defines or problematizes the boundary between inclusion and exclusion, enfranchisement and disenfranchisement, from a Christian perspective;
(5) The human good, where "disability" either defines or problematizes the boundary between a flourishing life and a life of languishing, from a Christian perspective;
(6) Justice, where "disability" either defines or problematizes the boundary between individual rights and collective responsibility, from a Christian perspective;
(7) Health, where "disability" either defines or problematizes the difference between strong and infirm, well and diseased, from a Christian perspective.

There is also a body of scholarly work treating the sources of Christian theology, where the concept of "disability" is used instrumentally to advance various claims or proposals about:

(1) Scripture, where "disability" helps define or problematize the difference between faithful and unfaithful interpretation;
(2) Christian tradition, where "disability" helps to either define or to problematize the difference between an accurate and inaccurate account of some historical figure, event, belief, or practice;
(3) The development of doctrine, where "disability" helps to either define or to problematize the difference between the "voiced" historical subject and the "voiceless" subaltern, from a Christian perspective.

Amid the above examples of *instrumental use*, some of the most interesting recent theological work has used the concept of "disability" and narratives from persons who have a disability to challenge commonly held, anthropological norms that (arguably) are insufficiently-Christian and theologically problematic. In particular, there has been a concerted effort to disrupt the theory-practice dialectic of *principled avoidance* and *practical specialization* on the topic of disability, targeting the doctrinal and speculative theological work (and evasions) of *principled avoiders* by drawing upon the practical knowledge and theological insight of *practical specialists*. As a governing sub-genre of contemporary *instrumental use*, these engagements tend to assert the normativity of human "disability" in view of Christian theological anthropology.

While there will be disagreement on the persuasiveness of the various arguments that use "disability" to think about the human being, charitably read, the most basic intent is an unambiguously Christian concern to hold fast to the faith of the Church and to reject dehumanizing modern anthropologies that are inconsistent with the Gospel. The strongest versions generally run like this: on the understanding that no human life is ever wholly free from impairment, illness, injury, and decay, the normative or natural reference point for Christian theological anthropology needs to be a person with a disabled-body (a body defined by its place along the spectrum of disability)—paradigmatically, the wounded and glorified body of Christ at the Resurrection.

From that Christological foundation, the argument goes, every Christian would agree that the experience of some form of impairment or illness is part of every human life. Likewise, virtually no Christian will claim that there has ever been a human being who lived a life without personally experiencing some kind of disabling impairment, illness, or injury.[20] So conceived, the universal reality of human disability implies that the notion of "disability" should be included among the foundational and central categories of Christian theological anthropology. For that reason, theological consideration of the human good and human happiness cannot responsibly take an idealized caricature of physical, cognitive, and mental health as an anthropological norm—just as Christian theological discourse cannot responsibly assume the anthropological norms of similarly defective accounts of the human being, like Angelism or Animalism (i.e., monistic materialism). Thus, on its own best terms, what this disability-normed, anthropological outlook promotes is a theological challenge to patently un-Christian, best-case anthropologies.

One could argue that most academic or scholarly work that falls under the heading "theology and disability" or "theology of disability" would fit into the generic framework of the *instrumental use type*. While most practical ecclesial guidelines, pastoral writings, personal theological memoirs, spiritual reflections on disability, and theological meditations on the experience of disability would fit into the framework of the *practical specialization type*. The *principled avoidance type* covers theological engagements with disability that appear as digressive illustrations, quick tests or proofs of methodology, and opening narrative hooks—and, also, any attempt at Christian theological anthropology that somehow (!) fails to mention that human beings are created with bodies that naturally differ in

---

[20] See note 29 below on the bodies of Adam, Eve, the Lord Jesus Christ, and the Immaculate Mother of God, Blessed Virgin Mary.

functionality, capability, get sick, sometimes break, age, etc. That last failure, specific to the *principled avoidance type*, is a common tendency in contemporary Catholic moral theology: for most of us, concrete examples of this are within an arm's reach—residing, as it were, in the canon for specialists in moral theology and the primer texts we assign our students.

PART TWO: A CHRISTIAN CHALLENGE TO THE CONCEPT OF "DISABILITY"

When we step back and take a global look at the typology mapped above, it seems to offer a common sense overview of the way the topic of "disability" is engaged and avoided across contemporary Christian theology. It is certainly true that some theologians intentionally avoid the topic of disability, not necessarily because they think the topic is unimportant but simply because disability is not among their special interests. It is also true that there are other theologians who have specially devoted their considerable practical wisdom, ecclesial knowledge, and spiritual insight toward addressing particular practical challenges that face persons who have a disability and toward inspiring the faith of Christians whose lives are somehow impacted by disability. Finally, it is true that in recent decades a loosely affiliated network of theologians has emerged who recognize how the reality and experience of "disability" can be used instrumentally to expose important conceptual problems and disciplinary blind spots in systematic theology, moral theology, and theorizing around the practical Christian response to the needs of particular persons.

Among the three modes of engagement outlined above, however, there is a constellation of common presumptions regarding the concept "disability."[21] These presumptions do not present equally in each case, but one could reasonably claim that most contemporary theologians who intentionally engage or intentionally avoid "disability" have, in some way, appropriated at least one of the following presumptions. *First*, there is a presumption that the ability-disability distinction is a self-evident and unproblematic natural division within humanity. *Second*, there is a presumption that the concept of "disability" can function as an internally coherent, conceptually stable, ahistorical category for Christian theological discourse (i.e., that it can stand as a specialized field of inquiry). *Third*, there is a presumption that the Christian theological tradition holds human impairment, illness, and injury (i.e., "disabilities") to be unequivocally bad, objectively ugly, and definitively tragic corporeal states.

What is interesting about these three presumptions concerning "disability" is that none of them comes even close, from the Christian

---

[21] Cf. Licia Carlson's 'map of the philosophical terrain' in *The Faces of Intellectual Disability*, 9-13.

perspective, to being historically demonstrable or theologically defensible in relation to Christian anthropology and the various ways that human beings experience corporeal impairment, illness, and injury (as I will discuss below and in Section 5).[22] In other words, the problem is a theologically unfounded contemporary confidence in the nature, meaning, and valuation of the concept "disability," by both those who intentionally engage disability theologically and theologians who intentionally avoid the topic of disability. If this is correct, my typology of the three modes of theological engagement (and avoidance) with disability only captures part of the picture. Specifically, just to the extent that the organizing concept "disability" lacks a consistent concrete reference and conceptual stability, it cannot serve as much more than a provisional, *ad hoc*, organizing heuristic for distinguishing between different modes of Christian theological engagement.[23]

One implication of the above is the need to find some other way to account for the unity and disunity of theological projects that intentionally use and intentionally do not use the concept "disability." Later, in Section 3, I show how Aquinas provides a way for us to recognize the chief doctrinal and theological matters relevant to the fragility of our bodies: Christian doctrine on our specific intellectual dignity, the fittingness of our vulnerability, and the enduring goodness of corporeality. For Christian theologians, there is reason to believe that contemporary disagreement on the theological significance and moral implications of "disability" is best defined and explored on the

---

[22] This critique of the typology sketched could be described as a "critical theological approach to disability" insofar as this evaluation of the concept "disability" in philosophical and theological discourse parallels what Lennard J. Davis (see Davis's *Enforcing Normalcy: Disability, Deafness, and the Body* [New York: Verso Press, 1995], 23-49) and Licia Carlson call "the critical theory approach to disability." I prefer to call it the traditional Christian account of the human being. In other words, when it comes to the concept "disability," I think the Christian tradition offers Christians better ways of talking about the fact that our bodies are sometimes impaired, get sick, present with a diversity of competencies and dependencies, and eventually die.

[23] If one was so inclined, this is the point where he or she should cry foul. Specifically, at the beginning I proposed to construct a typology based on modes of theological engagement with the concept "disability," so there is no surprise that disability is the common term of comparison. Moreover, it is hardly significant to discover that ambiguities embedded in the way we use the word "disability" would be inflected in our theological engagement or avoidance of disability. Nevertheless, what concerns me here is not the strength of the typology but the theological presumptions obscured when theologians opt to intentionally engage or intentionally avoid *the topic of disability*. Along with the contemporary presumption and/or invocation of a weak concept like "disability," the key theological and anthropological principles most relevant to the way Christians think and argue about impairment, illness, and injury are arranged in such a way that certain theological questions cannot be asked and certain theological implications cannot be parsed out.

ground of these three doctrinal themes—and not along the horizon of an ambiguous and conceptually unstable concept like "disability." This is not to say that the concept of "disability" is useless. Rather, it is only to suggest that "disability" might not be the best place to begin for Christian theologians concerned to think well about our innate vulnerability to impairment, illness, and injury. Before we discuss the theological utility of the concept "disability," however, I want to take a theological look at the above three presumptions about "disability." I discuss the first two presumptions here, and the third presumption in Section 5.

The Ability-Disability Distinction

The ability-disability distinction is descriptively accurate when focused on specific corporeal faculties, antecedently stipulated as determinative or valuable, at a particular time and in a particular context. From the perspective of Christian theology, what cannot be directly captured in the ability-disability distinction includes the following: each person's fundamental, ongoing creaturely dependence upon God for his or her existence; each person's natural, inalienable aptitude for apprehension and contemplation of intelligible truth; and, because we are incarnate intellectual creatures, the spectrum of spiritual-corporeal competencies and dependencies each person exercises in relation to her or his neighbor, over the course of a lifetime. Understood in this way, for Christians, "ability-disability" divides humanity in the same way "asleep-awake," "child-parent," or "mourner-comforter" divide humanity. These are meaningful distinctions, but their meaning is neither self-evident nor are they ever innocent of the explicitly or implicitly stipulated values that give conceptual form to the distinction.

To be clear, this does not mean that the ability-disability distinction has no use as a framework for Christian theologians. Rather, it means that any distinction between the disabled "us" and nondisabled "them" (or the nondisabled "us" and the disabled "them") is always qualified, circumscribed, and *ad hoc*. Specifically, the distinction is useful with reference to the particular experience of particular persons or groups but dramatically less useful as something definitive of humanity. For example, the concept is useful when describing a particular moment of a specific social or political dynamic, but that utility quickly dissolves when a socio-political reality is framed by the lifetime of the various individuals involved, with their various vulnerabilities and dependencies. In other words, when our theological thinking begins with a presumption that ability-disability, the "able-bodied" and the "disabled-bodied," is a natural division of humanity, a clear and stable distinction within the human species, we implicitly assume metaphysical categories and anthropological principles that make it difficult to articulate the unity of humanity. Moreover, we cede the dogmatic and doctrinal ground to formulate distinctively Christian theological critiques, moral arguments, and practical guidelines relevant to our innate vulnerability to impairment, illness, and injury.

Theological Use of the Concept "Disability"

Across the various modes of engagement, there is a theologically unfounded confidence that the concept "disability" stands as an internally coherent, conceptually stable, ahistorical category for Christian theological discourse. It is worth explaining why that confidence lacks warrant. On the level of grammar, the invocation of "disability" carries with it, either explicitly or implicitly, not only the semantic content of its contrast (i.e., whatever happens to constitute "ability" at a particular time and place) but also presumptions about the "disabled" subject. That is to say, *a disabled what?* A disabled human being, of course, but what is the aspect or horizon of consideration for the human being? What specifies the referential subject as distinct from other kinds of being? And what is the purpose of the distinction? In this way, basic judgments about what it means to be a human being are embedded in the way the concept "disability" is deployed in theoretical and theological discourse.

The standard "disability models," for example, each assume a particular aspect of consideration, referent, and outcome sought.[24] As most are aware, the "medical model of disability" works on the horizon of *function-dysfunction*, the referent is delimited to the faculties and operations of the human body, and the generic goal is to see dysfunctional bodies transition to a state of functionality. The standard amongst disability theorists, until recently, was to contrast the *impairment* defined by the "medical model of disability" with the *disability* defined by the "social model of disability." The social model of disability works on a horizon of *inclusion-exclusion* where the referent is the socio-political status of a person who has an impairment in a particular community, and the generic goal is to see persons who are impaired transition from a state of exclusion to a state of inclusion. Because the social model framework is widely and consistently used in contemporary Christian instrumental discourse on disability (as provisionally defined above), it affords us an apt illustration of the theologically unfounded confidence that many theologians seem to have in the concept "disability."

---

[24] See Deborah Creamer's theological introduction to the disability models and Christian theology in *Disability and Christian Theology* (Oxford: Oxford University Press, 2009), 3-33. Among other things, one of the most important contributions of Creamer's introduction is her identification of both the various strengths, weakness, and theological utility of the main disability models. By my reading, Creamer effectively shows the muddles that Christian theologians invite when they begin with the concept "disability" (however it is defined), instead of a Christian theological account of the human being.

To begin with, the social model of disability is not an ideology or philosophy, so much as it is an extremely useful and demonstratively effective conceptual shorthand that defines in advance what we mean when we say "disability." Like the other "disability models"— the medical model, cultural model, economic model, moral model, etc.— the social model of disability reflects a particular way of talking about disability and approaches the subject of disability (the human being) from a particular aspect. This framework amounts to rules or norms of discourse that include anthropological presuppositions that are rarely made explicit (metaphysical, political, moral, etc.); rules or norms that determine what kind of questions can be asked (e.g., socio-political inclusion doesn't help us think about friendship, works of mercy, or the cosmic meaning of our vulnerability) and that regulate what does and does not count as an answer (e.g., a discourse on theodicy cannot answer questions about access).

Theoretical and theological discourse following the social model of disability usually defines "disability" as the *state of exclusion* from community life, experienced by persons who have an impairment or abnormality of some anatomical or psychological function.[25] The state of exclusion is caused when a cultural preference for certain kinds of body function (an arbitrary ethos regarding what counts as unimpaired function) coalesces in the establishment of physical, social, or practical *barriers to inclusion*—those barriers limit access to the community life and common goods and directly affect the ability of socially "disabled" persons to participate in the community life.

Four theologically relevant presuppositions characterize the social model of disability.[26] *First*, the community being described is usually conceptualized as fundamentally divided along a material polarity of inclusion and exclusion, able-bodied persons vs. disable-bodied persons. That is to say, division and conflict is presumed, and, in most versions, individual "rights" are the central common claim— where competitive assertion, recognition, and concession regarding individual rights and community responsibilities frame social intercourse. *Second*, the dynamic between inclusion and exclusion is usually mapped (or imagined) as a spectrum relationship between a center (persons who *enjoy the dignity* of full participation) and diminishing degrees of inclusion, progressing outward toward an excluded periphery (persons who *suffer the indignity* of limited participation). *Third*, the terms or criteria for inclusion and exclusion

---

[25] See, for example, *Disability, Difference, Discrimination: Perspectives on Justice in Bioethics and Public Policy*, ed. Anita Silvers, David Wasserman, Mary Mahowald (Lanham: Rowman & Littlefield, 1998).
[26] See the engagements under the heading of "Justice" by Martha Nussbaum, Michael Bérubé, Cynthia Stark, and Sophia Isako Wong in *Cognitive Disability and its Challenge to Moral Philosophy*, ed. Eva Feder Kittay and Licia Carlson (Oxford: Wiley-Blackwell, 2010), 75-145.

are taken to be contingent cultural values, which are enforced through arbitrary physical, social, or practical barriers. These arbitrary barriers create arbitrary disability-specific needs that impinge upon the individual right of a particular "disabled" person to community inclusion, access, accommodation, and participation. *Fourth*, the implied goal or good outcome of the social model of disability is to aid in the identification and removal of physical, social, and practical barriers to inclusion. The main vehicle for this process is to gain concessions from those at the center of the community, in recognition of the rights belonging to those on the periphery of the communal life. The expectation is that by asserting and protecting rights, securing access, and enforcing accommodation in the common community life, the dignity of the disabled person will be established and affirmed.

A clarification is important here. *The theological problem with the social model of disability is not its use as an analytic tool and resource for description.* Certainly, as a theoretical framework for describing the socio-political experience of persons who have a physiological, psychological, or cognitive impairment, the social model of disability is a useful and effective framework for argument within a community that has no binding loyalties or shared conception of the human good. For example, there is no disagreement that the social model of disability (and its attendant aspect of consideration, referent, and purpose) has been politically expedient and conceptually useful for crafting U. S. legislation on the rights of Americans with disabilities (e.g., to protect rights, to secure fair access, to enforce civil accommodations). However, and this is the important point, *this tool is useful for Christian theology only so long as it is understood that theoretical models can only afford us an incomplete understanding of any given social situation.* Among the things that the social model of disability lacks, from a Christian theological perspective, are an integral account of what it means to be a human being, an authentic account of the common good (for Christians, the common good does not end at inclusion and access), and an account of the individual human good proffered by the excluded to the included (for Christians, the bigoted exclusion of one's neighbor from the common good constitutes a grave self-separation from the goodness of God).

The theological problem, thus, is not that Christians sometimes use the social model of disability to theorize or conceive the entailments of certain socio-political realities. Rather, a theological problem arises when Christian theologians *uncritically presume or attribute comprehensiveness* to the social model's way of framing and guiding theoretical discourse on disability. By one description, when the concept of "disability" is framed and directed according to the terms of the social model of disability, Christian theological discourse appropriates a relationally two-dimensional and reductively materialistic description of the spiritual-corporeal reality and experience of human impairment, illness, and injury. Moreover, when Christian theologians deploy a formulation of "disability" defined along the horizon of inclusion and exclusion, it becomes extraordinarily difficult to discuss the human experience of a particular impairment in relation to our specifically incarnate intellectual dignity, the fittingness of our vulnerability, and the enduring goodness of corporeality in light of the Fall. A temporary inclusion may have been won, but the conditions for friendship and the common good have not been established, according to the Christian outlook.[27]

When Christian theologians uncritically incorporate the terms, categories, and relative insights of the concept "disability" into our theological reflection on human impairment, illness, injury, we likewise incorporate a constellation of metaphysical and anthropological presuppositions. The consequence of inattentiveness to these implications is a thinning out of traditionally and conceptually thick biblical and theological concepts into two-dimensional socio-political metaphors: e.g., "exclusion," "inclusion," "rights," "alienation," "access," "barriers," "accommodation," "participation." There is nothing wrong with these concepts, but, absent the horizon and outlook of Christian discourse on the revelation of God's love for the world, revealed in and through Christ, Christians believe that the concepts can provide only a partial description of the problem and can only propose incomplete means for remediation.[28]

Recovering Creatureliness and Vulnerability for Moral Theology

I began with the claim that contemporary theological engagement with and avoidance of the topic of "disability" can help us recognize a deeper set of differences in the way we go about the work of moral theology. Toward that end, the first task was to map, in a commonsense way, how contemporary theologians tend to navigate the concept "disability." The second task was to outline why ambiguity on the nature and meaning of "disability" in Anglophone use limits both the analytic stability and theological utility of the concept. Among the various entailments that follow, it is clear that distinct anthropological outlooks and deliberative frameworks are embedded within every uncritical or haphazard theological use of the concept "disability," even if that use is only to say *I don't have a special interest or theological stake in "disability."* Consider, for

---

[27] For an alternative approach to the problem I have just described, see Hans S. Reinders, *Receiving the Gift of Friendship* (Grand Rapids: Eerdmans, 2008), 4-8.

[28] For an extended discussion of a similar theological dilemma relevant to the use of Marxist analytic categories in Christian theological discourse on the common good, see Miguel J. Romero, "Liberation, Development, and Human Advancement: Catholic Social Doctrine in *Caritas in Veritate*," *Nova et Vetera*, English Edition, 8, no. 4 (2010): 923–957.

example, the various anthropological outlooks and deliberative frameworks embedded within these familiar Christian theological uses: "God does not intend disability," "the disabled are God's gift to the world," "God is disabled," "*even* the profoundly disabled can be saved," "your disability will be healed at the resurrection."

The upshot here is that a deliberate decision to either avoid or engage an uncritical conception of "disability" certainly implicates and often underwrites a wide set of theological judgments, both implicit and explicit, on foundational doctrinal matters. Those implications are usually easy to tease out and are often integral to the rationale in the case of *practical specialist type* and *instrumental use type* of engagements with disability. However, in the case of the *principled avoidance type*, as described above, the implications and rationale are more subtle. Specifically, presuming the goodwill and moral integrity of theologians who intentionally avoid the topic of "disability," how might we account for both their clear-eyed decision and the implications of their avoidance?

On the disciplinary level, we could surmise at least two ways that uncritical theological use of the concept "disability," among some *practical specialist type* and *instrumental use type* engagement with disability, might have had a problematic impact upon the wider horizon of contemporary theological discourse. First, we could guess that uncritical use of the concept "disability" has made it possible for *principled avoiders* to imagine that our innate vulnerability to impairment, illness, and injury is a special, accessory, sub-discipline of theology. That is to say, alongside the invention of the genre "disability theology" or "theologies of disability" came the rationale to classify theological discourse on our innate vulnerability to impairment, illness, and injury as specialist—and, further, the practical, textual means to isolate extended theological discourse on impairment, illness, and injury from systematic and fundamental moral theology. Second, it is also possible that uncritical use of specialized jargon and theoretical frameworks associated with "disability" has made it difficult for theologians who intentionally avoid "disability" to recognize how their theological outlook is impoverished, absent serious engagement with the innate vulnerabilities and coordinate dependencies of the human body.

While these causes are certainly possible, it could also be said that the above two accounts of the tendency to *principled avoidance* bracket out his or her status as a vulnerable and limited being. That is to say, certainly wisdom and practical necessity commend the ordinary tendency toward academic specialization—*we can't all be experts in everything*. Indeed, if something important is truly lost when theologians avoid engagement with our innate vulnerability to impairment, illness, and injury (under the heading "disability"), what

The Goodness and Beauty of Our Fragile Flesh 227

keeps us from recognizing these implications and sensing the loss in our teaching and research?

I want to suggest that the difference between those who intentionally engage "disability" and those of us who intentionally avoid "disability" can be sourced to habits and practices of a more personal nature. Those habits and practices concern the way individual theologians learn to navigate the implications of our own creatureliness and vulnerability. Specifically, all of us, at some point in our lives, personally experience the innate vulnerability and coordinate dependencies of our bodies: universally as infants and at our death, for most of us during times of severe illness or injury, and for some of us as a profound, wholly debilitating, life-long impairment or illness.[29] Whatever the case may be, in each of our individual lives, over the course of a lifetime, we all directly experience the radical vulnerability and profound dependency of our own particular body. What makes the Christian understanding of these common experiences *Christian* is the evangelical narrative of God's love for the world, in and through Christ. The Gospel is how Christians locate and evaluate whatever meaning and significance there is to be gleaned from the ordinary experience of our various impairments, illnesses, and injuries. That is all well and good, but why claim that engagement with these aspects of our individual lives is important for the coherence and integrity of Catholic moral theology?

Presuming that there is a solid basis to Pinckaers's concern and critique, and in service of a rapprochement across the divisions mapped by my typology, in the remainder of this section I'd like to

---

[29] Here are the only possible exceptions, according to the Catholic tradition: Adam, Eve, Blessed Virgin Mary, and our Lord Jesus Christ. Adam and Eve cannot be exceptions because of the Fall. The Lord, of course, suffered the Passion of His cross. That only leaves Blessed Virgin Mary as possibly exempt from a personal experience with the innate vulnerability and coordinate dependencies of the human body. However, according to the teachings of the Catholic Church, even the Immaculate Mother of God, who was assumed body and soul into heavenly glory, "throughout the course of her earthly pilgrimage, led a life troubled by cares, hardships, and sorrows, and…what the holy old man Simeon had foretold actually came to pass, that is, that a terribly sharp sword pierced her heart as she stood under the cross of her divine Son, our Redeemer" (*Munificentissimus Deus*, no. 14). As Catholics affirm with the Church Fathers that "the Blessed Virgin was, through grace, entirely free from every stain of sin, and from all corruption of body, soul and mind" and that the Immaculate Mother of God was not wounded by the "common injuries" of original sin (*Ineffabilis Deus*), Catholics also understand that the exalted status of Mary Immaculate did not make her physically invulnerable to the ordinary corporeal defects and infirmities co-assumed by Jesus Christ in the Incarnation (*Munificentissimus Deus*, no. 14; *Salvifici Doloris*, no. 25; ST III qq. 14-15): free from the common spiritual corruptions and injuries of original sin, the body of Mary Immaculate "who conceived Christ, brought him forth, nursed him with her milk, held him in her arms, and clasped him to her breast" was, indeed, a vulnerable and dependent human body (*Munificentissimus Deus*, no. 38).

consider the perspective offered by Alasdair MacIntyre. Specifically, there is a useful parallel between the disciplinary tendencies of Catholic moral theology in the early 21st century and MacIntyre's assessment of late 20th century moral philosophy, as sketched in *Dependent Rational Animals: Why Human Beings Need the Virtues*.[30]

Diagnosing the Blind-Spots and Tendencies of Moralists

In *Dependent Rational Animals*, MacIntyre provides a way for us to think about how moral theologians both engage and avoid the topic of "disability," offering both a means of diagnosis and a prescription that is worth considering. Three threads of MacIntyre's argument are uniquely relevant to the way Catholic theologians navigate our specific dignity, the fittingness of our vulnerability, and the enduring goodness of corporeality: *habits of mind, the company we keep, and affective inclination*.

MacIntyre begins with the common sense recognition that human beings are vulnerable to a broad spectrum of impairments, illnesses, and infirmities—and that for many of us these conditions can be very serious and debilitating. Given the personal importance and universal implications of human vulnerability and dependency, MacIntyre contends that "no account of the human condition whose authors hoped to achieve credibility could avoid giving [the facts concerning our vulnerabilities and dependencies] central place."[31] Yet, he notes, in the history of Western moral philosophy, the basic vulnerability and coordinate dependencies of the human being are most often only acknowledged in the form of incomplete and passing references. This persistent lack of self-awareness among moral philosophers and the tendency to imagine humanity in terms of "us" and "them" has consequences in the work of moral analysis:

> [W]hen the ill, the injured and the otherwise disabled are presented in the pages of moral philosophy books, it is almost always exclusively as possible subjects of benevolence by moral agents who are themselves presented as though they were continuously rational, healthy, and untroubled. So we are invited, when we do think of disability, to think of "the disabled" as "them," as other than "us," as a separate class, not as ourselves as we have been, sometimes are now, and may well be in the future.[32]

---

[30] Alasdair MacIntyre, *Dependent Rational Animals*, (Chicago: Open Court, 1999).
[31] MacIntyre, *Dependent Rational Animals*, 1.
[32] MacIntyre, *Dependent Rational Animals*, 2. Speaking of his argument in *After Virtue* (Notre Dame: University of Notre Dame Press, 1981) and his effort to avoid the worst parts of Aristotle's 'metaphysical biology,' MacIntyre admits that he went too far and the need to correct his former outlook: "I was in error in supposing an ethics independent of biology to be possible...no account of the goods, rules, and virtues that are definitive of our moral life can be adequate that does not explain...how that form of life is possible for beings who are biologically constituted as we are"

MacIntyre's description of late-twentieth century moral philosophy is important for Catholic moral theologians for two reasons. First, there are suggestive parallels between MacIntyre's characterization of western moral philosophy and the most prominent streams of Catholic systematic and moral theology in the past seventy-five years (parallels that will not be discussed here). Second, and more relevant, are the questions that MacIntyre poses for moral philosophy: *What difference would it make for moral philosophy if the facts of human vulnerability, affliction, and dependency were treated as central to the human condition?* And, *how should moral philosophers approach the work of answering that first question?*[33]

My present interest is how particular moral theologians who are inclined to avoid the topic of "disability" might approach answering a version of MacIntyre's second question in the case of their own work. Specifically, how should a Catholic moral theologian approach a self-assessment of the way disability-relevant anthropological principles are inflected in his or her writing and teaching? A paraphrase of MacIntyre's disciplinary prescription might be useful here.[34] One possible starting point for the moral theologian would be to acknowledge that an unthematized, negative regard for the fact of our corporeal vulnerability and coordinate dependencies is something we must have learned—separate, for the moment, from questions about the origin of impairment, illness, and injury. Further, we should acknowledge the possibility that avoidance of these anthropological principles in our moral theologizing could have a serious impact in other parts of our teaching and research.

These habits of mind concerning the vulnerability and dependency of our bodies belong to the general outlook that we acquired through our academic training, scholarly pursuits, and the wider culture. Beginning with an acknowledgment of this sort should alert us, from the outset, that our habits of mind may create unnecessary problems. We may have an unwarranted confidence in bits of theological shorthand, or that we may be subject to a species of bias that could

---

(*Dependent Rational Animals*, x). Writing in the 1990s, MacIntyre acknowledges his own debt to philosophical arguments leveled against his position from feminist discussions and disability-focused scholarship—but, in so doing, he laments that the remedy from these "striking" and "important" areas of work had yet to be fully appreciated in mainstream moral philosophy (*Dependent Rational Animals*, 3-4). Since the publication of *Dependent Rational Animals*, of course, this lacuna in Anglophone moral philosophy has been addressed in important ways; nevertheless, there remains a species of that multi-form disciplinary blindness. See Carlson and Kittay, "Introduction: Rethinking Philosophical Presumptions in Light of Cognitive Disability," *Cognitive Disability and its Challenge to Moral Philosophy*, 1-25.

[33] MacIntyre, *Dependent Rational Animals*, 4.
[34] MacIntyre, *Dependent Rational Animals*, 4-9.

prevent us from sensing a lacuna in our theological outlook. Consider, for example, how an attitude of denial toward simply raising a methodological question about our corporeal vulnerability in relation to the terms of fundamental moral theology could imply either inadequate catechesis or moral depravity.[35] Specifically, the Christian creedal confession of belief in the "bodily resurrection of the dead" highlights the class of mental gymnastics one would need to perform to escape the theological and moral significance of having a body that will die and, per our hope, be raised in glory. As for moral depravity, it is somewhat ridiculous for a being that has a belly button, regularly defecates, and who lives only one blood clot away from death to imagine himself to be a naturally invulnerable and independent being. A calculated refusal or blithe forgetfulness concerning the full bodily dimensions of our creaturely existence betrays a severely defective self-understanding, at the levels of orthodoxy and common sense. *So, as we aspire toward the intellectual integrity and goodwill held forth in Christ's call to discipleship, we might ask: from where, then, do our tendencies toward avoidance arise?*

MacIntyre's overarching concern in *Dependent Rational Animals* is to describe the distinctive virtues that human beings need, as vulnerable and dependent beings, if we are to flourish as rational animals. He makes the case that these distinctive virtues are the same virtues we need if we are to rationally respond to the vulnerabilities and dependencies we encounter in ourselves and other persons.[36] As MacIntyre sees it, Aristotle-supplemented-and-corrected-by-Aquinas is the best way forward "because no philosopher has taken human animality more seriously." Over the course of the work, MacIntyre highlights three particular obstacles to the change in perspective that he is concerned to hold forth.[37] The first obstacle has to do with intellectual formation and acquired errors of interpretation, as described above. The second obstacle concerns the blindness that arises from political or social exclusions—specifically, a lack of relevant personal experience and encounter with the ordinary facts of human vulnerability and dependency.[38] Stemming from that lack of experience is a more general inability to recognize how the outcome of our philosophical (and theological) deliberations is in part the product of those whom we choose to include in our deliberations and, importantly, those whom we choose to exclude. For when persons with the relevant experience are the ones excluded, philosophical and

---

[35] MacIntyre, *Dependent Rational Animals*, 96; See Paul J. Griffiths, "How Reasoning Goes Wrong: A Quasi-Augustinian Account of Error and Its Implications," *Reason and the Reasons of Faith*, ed. Paul J. Griffiths and Reinhard Huetter (New York: T&T Clark: 2005), 145-159.
[36] MacIntyre, *Dependent Rational Animals*, 5.
[37] MacIntyre, *Dependent Rational Animals*, 5-8.
[38] MacIntyre, *Dependent Rational Animals*, 14, 18, 85, 91.

theological mistakes are inevitable. The third obstacle named by MacIntyre, particular to moral deliberation on the facts of vulnerability and dependency, is the affective inclination that arises from poorly chosen political and social associations.[39] MacIntyre argues that moralists can back themselves into ways of seeing that affect and can possibly distort their ability to recognize and truthfully describe what is the case.

On the disciplinary horizon of Catholic moral theology, our acquired interpretive habits, the associations we keep, and the affective outlook generated by those associations are all relevant to a consideration of the way contemporary theologians tend to conceive and navigate the theological questions relevant to disability. It is in this way, it seems to me, that a moral theologian can be rendered unable to recognize the general disciplinary loss that follows from one's avoidance of disability-relevant themes in his or her teaching and research.

In the next section, I transition from questions of moral methodology (whether philosophical or theological) to Christian theological anthropology, in particular, Aquinas's remarks in ST I q. 91, a. 3, on the "fittingness" of the vulnerable disposition and coordinate dependencies of the human body. Aquinas provides a Christian theological framework for understanding the connection between moral formation, aesthetic perception, and the Christian account of human dignity. Appropriating and extending MacIntyre's proposal and the disciplinary challenge of Pinckaers, I argue with the help of Aquinas that the constitutive vulnerabilities and particular dependencies of the human body are an essential part of any coherently Christian description of the inviolable dignity, vocational aptitude, and graced beatification of the human being.

PART THREE: AQUINAS ON THE FITTINGNESS OF OUR VULNERABLE AND DEPENDENT BODIES

My goal in this section is to explore what we might be able to learn from Aquinas's way of thinking about the vulnerability and dependency of our bodies and, further, Aquinas's theological reckoning of the significance and implications of our ordinary vulnerability to bodily impairment, illness, and injury. In ST I q. 91, a. 3, Aquinas makes an argument for the integrity and fittingness of our corporeal vulnerability. With respect to my overarching concern, the relevance of Aquinas's argument in question 91 is the constellation of themes he brings together in the formulation of his response. Specifically, Aquinas provides a Christian theological framework for understanding the connection between moral formation, aesthetic perception, and the Christian account of our creaturely dignity. Given

---

[39] MacIntyre, *Dependent Rational Animals*, 135-138.

the tendencies of contemporary Catholic moral theologians in our engagement (and avoidance) of the topic of "disability," and in response to the challenges issued by Pinckaers and MacIntyre on the distortions contemporary moralists are wont to presume about the human being, Aquinas's formulation of the goodness and beauty of our fragile flesh recommends three lines of remedial work: doctrine, encounter, and affect. Individual work along these three lines is necessary if we are to reconcile our contemporary moral theological engagement (and avoidance) of "disability" with the standard Christian account of the human being.

The Goodness and Beauty of a "Defective" Iron Saw (ST I q. 91, a. 3)

Aquinas's treatment of the fittingness of our corporeal vulnerabilities and dependencies appears at the beginning of the second half of his *Treatise on the Human Being* (qq. 75-102). In the first half of the *Treatise* (qq. 75-89), Aquinas concerns himself with a description of our composite nature (material and immaterial aspects), focusing on the unity and cooperation of the subsistent formal cause (incorruptible intellectual soul) and the material cause (corruptible body) of the human being. It is important to note the clear difference between Aquinas's discussion of the *what* and the *how* of the human being in the first half of the *Treatise* (qq.75-89) and his discussion of the *whence* and *whither* of the human being in the second half of the *Treatise* (qq. 90-102). While the first half of the treatise is focused on providing an *abstract description of human nature*, the second half of the treatise is focused on providing *the distinctively Christian narrative* of the origin (efficient cause) and end (final cause) of the human being.

The structure of Aquinas's *Treatise* makes plain his judgment that description of our essential nature (mortal rational animal) is only one part of the Christian understanding of what it means to be a human being (see *Sententia libri Metaphysicae* VII.5, 1378–9). For Aquinas, what makes an account of the human being Christian is not only Scripture-led deduction on the attributes that distinguish and specify *human nature* but the Gospel's radical illumination of the *dignity* and *destiny* of the human being. So conceived, the context of Aquinas's treatment of the fittingness of our corporeal vulnerabilities in question 91 is, first, God's immediate creative intent in the formation of human beings as such (qq. 90-92), i.e., God's relationship to the kind of beings that we are, and, second, God's ongoing creative intent or purpose for human beings in the hierarchy of creation (q. 93), i.e., God's relationship to the kind of beings we have the aptitude and call to become. These four questions (qq. 90-93) are a central pillar of the theological anthropology outlined in Aquinas's *Summa* and are arguably the climax of Aquinas's doctrine of creation in the *Summa* (qq. 44-119).

I have taken the time to outline both the general and immediate context of ST I q. 91 in order to highlight the pivotal nature of what Aquinas argues in article 3, on "Whether the body of man was given an apt disposition?" This article is not an accessory digression from the main thrust of Aquinas's theological anthropology. Rather, the particular question of this article is situated at the absolute heart of Aquinas's theological account of the human being. In that way, the organizing problem or doubt of article 3 drops with a bone-shaking thud—cold in its simplicity and nauseating in its implications: "It would seem that the body of man was not given an apt disposition."

For those who are able to ask this question, one need only stand naked before a mirror or pause after bathing to feel its force: we examine our lumpy, scarred, misshaped, and inglorious bodies, and we know the frail, weak, leaky, and deformed truth of our corporeality. In concert with the self-knowledge that only some have the courage to confront, Aquinas's three objections press some of the most basic, distinguishing concerns of any coherently Christian theological anthropology: Did God make a mistake in giving us bodies that are vulnerable? Do all the defects, impairments, illnesses, and disorders of my body diminish my dignity or signal my disqualification from God's providential intent for the human being?

These questions shine a light on many of the most precious conceits and hidden shames we bear in regard to our own, particular body—because when we look in the mirror or pause naked after bathing, considering our bodies as they are, it is unnervingly easy to consider with Aquinas the possibility that God may have made a mistake. First, the human being is supposed to be the most honored of God's creatures, but the human body—my body—is inferior when compared to the speed, strength, and sensitivity of the bodies that belong to others, even the bodies of non-human animals (a. 3, arg. 1). Second, perfect things are supposed to lack nothing, and *yet* the human body—my body—is disturbingly vulnerable and weak when compared to the bodies of others, even the bodies of many non-human animals (a. 3, arg. 2). Third, the human body—my body—is delicate, exposed, and impractical for survival, like fragile vegetation, having nothing of the sturdy, hearty, and practical utility of the bodies of others, including the bodies of many non-human animals (a. 3, arg. 3).

Earlier in the *Treatise*, responding to a related question, Aquinas notes a common tactic for evading the existential force of these types of questions. Specifically, the evasive supposition that the vulnerability of the human body to corruption, as we know it, is caused by an unnatural perversion of the soul's formal relationship to the body, consequent of original sin (ST I q. 76, a. 5, ad. 1; see q. 98, a. 2, co). This is the distorted idea that the "real, spiritual me" is somehow separate from the accidents inherent to my substantial form, the idea that the "real, spiritual me" is actually invulnerable to accidental corporeal defects. Aquinas firmly rejects that argument as insufficient, insofar as it erases the gift of Divine grace from the preternatural benefits of original innocence. Different from that earlier engagement, in question 91, article 3, Aquinas presumes (1) the distinctive spiritual-corporeal unity of human nature and our specific dignity in the hierarchy of creation, (2) the supernatural source of any preternatural corporeal perfections there were before the Fall, and (3) the incarnate, creaturely vulnerability of the human being to material corruption. Aquinas takes these three doctrines as anthropological principles in his response. Understood in this way, the driving force of question 91, article 3 is not an extension of "What is human nature?" Rather, the driving force is "What are we to think about human nature in light of the Gospel?" Specifically, is the corruptible aspect of human nature good and fitting, appropriate to the creaturely dignity and graced destiny of the human being?

Aquinas formulates his response around the somewhat generic affirmation from Ecclesiastes 7 that "God made man right" (*Deus fecit hominem rectum*). Elsewhere in the *Treatise*, Aquinas uses the same passage to deduce the kind of knowledge possible before the Fall (q. 94, a. 1, co.), to affirm that the human being was created in a state of grace (q. 95, a. 1, co.) and that infants in the state of innocence would have been physically weak and uncoordinated in the ordinary way (q. 99, a. 1, co.). In question 91, article 3, the emphasis of the reference to Ecclesiastes is not about the condition of the human being or the human body before the Fall, but *on God's creative agency* in the ongoing act of creation. This is important—the Christian response to whether or not our innate vulnerability to impairment, illness, and injury is consistent with God's intent and purpose for the human being *begins with the Creator, not the creature or accidental qualities of the creature*. Thus, Aquinas begins his response by reframing the question about the goodness and fittingness of the human body with an appeal to the artistry of Creator God:

> All natural things were produced by the Divine art, and so may be called God's works of art. Now every artist intends to give to his work the best disposition; not absolutely the best, but the best as regards the proposed end; and even if this entails some defect [*defectum*], the artist does not fret [*artifex non curat*]. (a. 3, co.)

Three things are noteworthy about how Aquinas frames his approach. First, the question about the fittingness of the human body's disposition is framed principally as a question about God's agency and not about human agency or aptitude.[40] Second, efficient causality and final causality are introduced as terms for evaluating the goodness of the artifact. Third, the definitive reference for evaluating the aptness of an artifact's disposition and the significance of any defect is the estimation of fittingness held by the artist (and not someone other than the artist).

According to Aquinas, in view of the creaturely dignity and proper end of the human being, the best and most fitting body for the human being is a body that is vulnerable to impairment, illness and injury (i.e., *defectum*, "limitation" or "impairment").[41] To illustrate this outlook, Aquinas gives the example of an artisan (*artefex*) making a saw for the purpose of cutting.

> [W]hen a man makes himself a saw for the purpose of cutting, he makes it of iron, which is suitable for the object in view; and he does not prefer to make it of glass, though this be a more beautiful material, because this very beauty [of glass] would be an obstacle to the end he has in view [for the saw]. (*ST* I q. 91, a. 3, co.)

From the aspect of material integrity and material proportionality, glass is a more beautiful material than iron; however, the artisan deems that the material splendor of glass would be an obstacle to the perfection of a tool ordained to cut. Umberto Eco comments on this passage from Aquinas, saying that if an artisan were to "construct a saw out of glass, because of some ill-conceived desire for beauty, it would be quite useless…imperfect, and thus ugly."[42]

Some useful exclusions and affirmations come to light when we consider this illustration by way of the four causes (formal cause, material cause, efficient cause, and final cause), around which Aquinas's *Treatise on the Human Being* seems to be organized. More precisely, we receive an indication of what kind of questions are

---

[40] For an account of how Aquinas uses the concept of fittingness (*convenientia*) in his theology, see Frederick Christian Bauerschmidt, *Thomas Aquinas: Faith, Reason, and Following Christ* (Oxford: Oxford University Press, 2013), 161-3.

[41] Aquinas discusses the necessity of our corporeal corruptibility in *ST* II-II q. 164, a. 1, co., where he writes "The form of man is his rational soul, which is, of itself, immortal: wherefore death is not natural to man on the part of his form. The matter of man is a body such as is composed of contraries, of which corruptibility is a necessary consequence, and in this respect death is natural to man. Now this condition attached to the nature of the human body results from a natural necessity, since it was necessary for the human body to be the organ of touch, and consequently a mean between objects of touch: and this was impossible, were it not composed of contraries." For an example of the distinct ways Aquinas uses the term 'defectum' in relation to the human body, see *ST* III q.14, where Aquinas discusses the defects of body co-assumed by Christ in the Incarnation.

[42] Umberto Eco, *The Aesthetics of Thomas Aquinas*, trans. Hugh Bredin (Cambridge: Harvard University Press, 1988), 181.

relevant to Christian theological anthropology, and we are directed toward a particular "way of seeing" that reflects the heart of the Christian theological outlook. Notice, for example, that for Aquinas the "fittingness" of the iron saw is not indexed to "sawness" as such (the formal cause of the saw) nor to the innate perfections and coordinate defects of iron (the material cause of the saw). Rather, the fittingness of the iron saw is indexed to the actualized intent of the artisan in crafting the saw and the final purpose of cutting intended by the artisan for the saw (efficient and final causes).[43] The *goodness* of the iron saw, as such, and the *fittingness* of the iron saw, in the good order purposed by the artisan, both depend on the actions and intentions of the artisan. Thus, for Aquinas, our consideration of the goodness and beauty of the iron saw does not begin with something intrinsic to the iron saw, accidental qualities of the iron saw, or a comparison of the iron saw to instances of sawness that are materially more or less splendid.

It is important to be clear, nevertheless, that this artisan-dependent goodness and fittingness does not magically transform the iron saw's actual material defects into splendid material perfections, comparable to the material splendor of glass. The defects of the iron remain material defects that are not sought in themselves (i.e., they are privations or an absence of some qualified good that is proper to sawness, but that does not specify sawness, as such). In *one, narrow sense*, then, it would be a qualified or relative good if the iron, of which the iron saw is composed, did not have the kind of defects that follow from the material attributes of iron. However, Aquinas seems to reason, the only way to eliminate the possibility of divots, warping, deformation, breaks, and iron's deep susceptibility to wear over time is to eliminate the most crucial element to the realization of the iron saw's ultimate purpose: the material contingency, malleability, and receptiveness of iron to the artisan's intent is exactly what makes it possible for the iron saw to realize its ultimate end *as saw*.[44]

The ultimate end or purpose of the saw is not to be a glittering, useless museum piece or an unaffected, idealized caricature of

---

[43] See C.S. Sevier on the objective components of beauty in the theology of Aquinas, *Aquinas on Beauty*, 103-147; See also Natalie Carnes in *Beauty: A Theological Engagement with Gregory of Nyssa* (Eugene: Cascade Books, 2014), 252: "Neither proportion, unity, and clarity, nor woundedness fully determine beauty. The radiant, scarred Christ names the beauty in which both woundedness and clarity participate.... Creation and fall are not displaced by but taken up into Christ's glory, where we find the final context for fittingness and gratuity."

[44] Elsewhere (ST I q. 76, a. 5, ad. 1), in service of a different but related point, Aquinas writes, "The artisan, for instance, for the form of the saw chooses iron adapted for cutting through hard material; but that the teeth of the saw may become blunt and rusted, follows by force of the matter itself."

"sawness." Rather, the perfection of "sawness" in cutting can only be realized alongside the possibility that the saw may be damaged, subject to material defects. However, even if the saw is damaged or bears some defect, those unsought material conditions cannot undermine, *from the perspective of the artisan,* the integral goodness of the iron saw or, *from the perspective of the artisan,* displace the fittingness of the iron saw for the good work intended by the artisan. If there are material defects in the iron of the iron saw, they only matter (so to speak) in the case of an aesthetic appraisal that prescinds from the actualized creative intent of the artisan and the final purpose for which the artisan crafts the iron saw.

In other words, the defects are only significant if one takes a perspective other than the *specific* integral good intended by the artist and the *particular* fittingness ordained by the artist. So conceived, following Aquinas's rationale, the *narrowly unappealing* defects of iron and the *narrowly appealing* perfections of the glass are both relativized. The horizon of the iron saw's integral perfection is conditioned by the dignity (*dignitas;* conferred or attributed goodness) given by the artisan. Likewise, the horizon of the iron saw's proportion (harmony) is conditioned by the end (*telos;* actualized and perfected nature) ordained by the artisan.

There is no question that the defects of the iron are still relative defects, and, likewise, the glass material of the glass saw does, indeed, communicate a certain integrity and proportionality that is splendid. However, a glass saw cannot fulfill the purpose that the artist intends for saws, as such. This, according to Umberto Eco, would make a splendid glass saw something imperfect and useless, *from the perspective of a carpenter who prefers imperfect saws that cut.* The defects of the iron saw remain defects, but they are attributes that have a proper place in the good order and final perfection established by the artisan. The glittering splendor of the glass saw has no place in the good order of the carpenter's workroom, nor is the glittering splendor of glass necessary for the proper perfection ordained by the artisan for the saws he crafts.

Anthropological Implications and the Challenge to See

Given the pivotal and prominent placement of ST I q. 91, a. 3, co. in Aquinas's *Treatise on the Human Being*, what are the anthropological implications of the iron saw analogy? Did God make a mistake in giving us bodies that are vulnerable? Do all the defects, impairments, illnesses, and disorders of my body diminish my dignity or disqualify me from God's providential intent for the human being? Is the corruptible aspect of human nature good and fitting, given the dignity of the human being? Thankfully, the anthropological implications of Aquinas's saw analogy do not require speculative leaps or interpretive stretches. Aquinas immediately makes the implications explicit:

> God gave to each natural being the best disposition; not absolutely so, but in the view of its proper end .... Now the proximate end of the human body is the rational soul and its operations; since matter is for the sake of the form, and instruments are for the action of the agent. I say, therefore, that God fashioned the human body in that disposition which was best, befitting [*optima dispositione secundum convenientiam*] to such a form and to such operations. If defect exists in the disposition of the human body, it is well to observe that such defect arises as a necessary result of the matter, from the conditions required in the body, in order to make it suitably proportioned to the soul and its operations. (ST I q. 91, a. 3, co.)

Thomas is concerned to reconcile the natural vulnerability of the human body to defect with the Christian presumption that the human being, composite creature, is given an apt disposition of body.[45] The reason this argument needs to be made surely has something to do with a tendency to regard the defects of our bodies (and the bodies of others) as repulsive and ugly, unnatural and unfitting conditions in view of the proper dignity and purpose of the human being. In other words, the argument needs to be made because many of us have a tendency to regard our vulnerability to impairment, illness, and injury, and our individual impairments, illnesses, and injuries as unnatural and ugly aspects of the human condition.

This common, affective disposition to be repulsed by the defects of our own bodies and the corporeal defects of other person's bodies owes primarily to the indirect, progressive, and sensory means by which human beings come to know creaturely goodness and truth and move towards knowledge of ultimate Goodness and Truth (ST I q. 39, a. 8, co.).[46] We know first through our senses, but what our senses tell us about the beauty of a thing is not all there is to know of the thing. This is true when it comes to our affective regard for our own bodies and the bodies of other persons. In his commentary on Psalm 25:4-5, Aquinas remarks on this distinction: "Every human being loves beauty: carnal people love carnal beauty, spiritual people love spiritual beauty [*Unde omnis homo amat pulchrum: carnales amant pulchrum*

---

[45] I am indebted to Scott Sevier for his reading and comments on an early draft of this interpretive argument.

[46] Aquinas writes, "Our intellect, which is led to the knowledge of God from creatures, must consider God according to the mode derived from creatures. In considering any creature four points present themselves to us in due order. Firstly, the thing itself taken absolutely is considered as a being.... For beauty includes three conditions, 'integrity' or 'perfection,' since those things which are impaired are by the very fact ugly; due 'proportion' or 'harmony'; and lastly, 'brightness' or 'clarity,' whence things are called beautiful which have a bright color."

carnale, spirituales amant pulchrum spirituale]" (*Super Psalmo*, 25, no. 5). It is important to understand that the designation of "carnal beauty" here is not a moral evaluation of the seer or negative evaluation of the thing perceived. Eco comments on Aquinas's interpretation:

> The purely physical beauty of an animal or a natural object is [what Aquinas means] by "carnal." As for spiritual beauty, we know that for Aquinas this referred to what was beautiful deep within itself [in a radical sense], and was therefore more honorable and sought after by "spiritual" people.[47]

According to Aquinas, human beings have an intuitive tendency to assess the integral goodness and proportionate fittingness of things in a way that is narrow and superficial (ST I-II, q. 57, a. 3, co.).[48] In the ordinary way, our wellbeing and survival as a species depends on the ability to recognize when something is out of place, diseased, or a potential threat. However, according to Aquinas, every human being also has the capacity to recognize a thing in reference to ultimate Goodness and Truth. The affective inclination to avoid superficially unattractive things is only vicious when the semblance of goodness and truth is deliberately chosen, over and against one's spiritual awareness or revelation-tutored understanding of what is ultimately Good and True. Thus, when it comes to the defects of the human body, Aquinas challenges Christians to attend to and appropriate the practical insight and intent of the architect of Creation, the Master Artisan. Aquinas's view here resonates with that of Augustine. Augustine writes, in Book Twelve of *City of God*,

> Of this order [the appointed order of things transitory], the beauty does not strike us, because by our mortal frailty we are so involved in a part of it, that we cannot perceive the whole, in which these fragments that offend us are harmonized with the most accurate fitness and beauty.

---

[47] Eco, *The Aesthetics of Thomas Aquinas*, 263, n. 75.
[48] Aquinas writes, "Art is nothing else but 'the right reason about certain works to be made.' And yet the good of these things depends, not on man's appetitive faculty being affected in this or that way, but on the goodness of the work done. For a craftsman, as such, is commendable, not for the will with which he does a work, but for the quality of the work. Art, therefore, properly speaking, is an operative habit. And yet it has something in common with the speculative habits: since the quality of the object considered by the latter is a matter of concern to them also, but not how the human appetite may be affected towards that object. For as long as the geometrician demonstrates the truth, it matters not how his appetitive faculty may be affected, whether he be joyful or angry: even as neither does this matter in a craftsman, as we have observed. And so art has the nature of a virtue in the same way as the speculative habits, in so far, to wit, as neither art nor speculative habit makes a good work as regards the use of the habit, which is the property of a virtue that perfects the appetite, but only as regards the aptness to work well."

And therefore, where we are not so well able to perceive the wisdom of the Creator, we are very properly enjoined to believe it, lest in the vanity of human rashness we presume to find any fault with the work of so great an Artificer. (*City of God*, Bk 12.4)[49]

For Aquinas, following Augustine, there is a basic understanding that the prelapsarian impassability and incorruptibility of the body was a supernatural gift (ST I q. 76, a. 5, ad. 1).[50] Aquinas argues that defects of body (analogous to the defects of iron) do not undermine the natural integrity and creaturely dignity of the human being. The integral perfection of a particular human being is not indexed solely to her or his status as intellectual creature. Rather, her or his integral perfection is indexed to the actualized intent of the Creator for this particular intellectual creature. Aquinas calls this the *first perfection* of the human being (ST I q. 93, a. 4, co.).[51] Likewise, the proportionality or

---

[49] Augustine continues, "At the same time, if we attentively consider even these faults of earthly things, which are *neither voluntary nor penal*, they seem to illustrate the excellence of the natures themselves, which are all originated and created by God; for it is that which pleases us in this nature which we are displeased to see removed by the fault—unless even the natures themselves displease men, as often happens when they become hurtful to them, and then men estimate them not by their nature, but by their utility.... Therefore it is not with respect to our convenience or discomfort, but with respect to their own nature, that the creatures are glorifying to their Artificer" [emphasis mine]. Notice that the faults or defects that Augustine references here are "neither voluntary nor penal." Augustine and Aquinas are of one mind (Aquinas, clearly, learned it from Augustine) that the vulnerability and dependency of the human body is essential to human nature, and distinct from the postlapsarian defects we experience consequent of original sin. Those postlapsarian defects, for Augustine, are usually, though not exclusively, conceived and theorized through the analogy of offense and penalty, as is evident from the immediate context of *City of God* Bk 12.4.

[50] See also: ST I q. 97, a. 1, co. & ad. 3, where Aquinas writes, "For man's body was indissoluble not by reason of any intrinsic vigor of immortality, but by reason of a supernatural force given by God to the soul, whereby it was enabled to preserve the body from all corruption so long as it remained itself subject to God.... This power of preserving the body was not natural to the soul, but was the gift of grace." ST I-II q. 81, a. 2, co., where Aquinas writes, "In this way original justice ... was a gift of grace, conferred by God on all human nature in our first parent. This gift the first man lost by his first sin. Wherefore as that original justice together with the nature was to have been transmitted to his posterity, so also was its disorder." ST III q. 14, a. 3, ad. 2, where Aquinas writes, "The cause of death and other corporeal defects of human nature is twofold: the first is remote, and results from the material principles of the human body, inasmuch as it is made up of contraries. But this cause was held in check by original justice. Hence the proximate cause of death and other defects is sin, whereby original justice is withdrawn." ST III q. 14, a. 4, ad. 1, where Aquinas writes, "All particular defects of men are caused by the corruptibility and passability of the body, some particular causes being added; and hence, since Christ healed the passability and corruptibility of our body by assuming it, He consequently healed all other defects."

[51] For those who consider St. Thomas to be a trustworthy guide, we ought to be wary of the tendency to amplify the conceptual shorthand "rational nature" in a way that

fittingness of a particular human being is not indexed solely to the transient splendors and/or corruptions of other bodies; rather, the fittingness is indexed to the final end purposed by the Creator, exemplified in the resurrection glory of Christ's scarred body. For Aquinas, the Creator's ultimate intent for the human being is a perfection in contemplation that cannot be frustrated, short of death, by corporeal or material defect.[52] Aquinas calls this the final perfection of the human being.

Now, a question could be raised about *why* God made us in this way, and it could be argued that God might have avoided the various pains that seem to define our corporeality at key moments in each person's life. To that, however, Aquinas responds

> If, however, it be said that God could avoid this, we answer that in the formation of natural things we do not consider what God might do; but what is suitable [*conveniat*] to the nature of things....God, however, provided in this case by applying a remedy against death in the gift of grace. (ST I q. 76, a. 5, ad. 1)

So conceived, for Aquinas, when it comes to the Christian account of the human being, there is no more determinative argument, theory, or framework than the bedrock of our faith in the providential goodness of the Creator. It would also seem that for Aquinas there is no more determinative argument, theory, or framework for the determination of the "fittingness" of our innate vulnerability than our faith in the providential goodness of the Creator. Classical aesthetic theories of beauty usually associate defect (*defectus*) with a privation of beauty, i.e., ugliness. Yet, in ST I q. 91, a. 3, co., Aquinas makes an argument for the "fittingness" of the human body, as it is, which includes its innate vulnerability to defect and the various defects that we encounter in ordinary life.

The analogy runs like this. From the perspective of the saw-making artisan, iron is the best material for making a saw that is purposed to cut, even though iron is vulnerable to defect and lacks the splendor of glass. A splendid and defect-free glass saw is in a narrow sense beautiful, but such a tool is ultimately unable to function as a saw, for the glass saw lacks the integrity and proportionality proper to the intent of the craftsman. In that way, the splendor of the glass is an obstacle to the *telos* of the saw. A glass saw has a proximate beauty that we can appreciate in a narrow sense, but that beauty should not be mistaken as comparable to the integral goodness of the iron saw or the

---

obscures the constellation of theological and anthropological principles that the shorthand is tuned to represent in the thought of Aquinas (See ST I q. 76, a. 1, co.).
[52] See Miguel J. Romero, "Aquinas on Happiness and 'Those Who Lack the Use of Reason,'" *The Thomist* 80, no. 1 (2016): 49-96.

final perfection proper to the saw. Analogously, from the perspective of the Creator of humanity, corruptible flesh is the best material for making an intellectual being that is purposed to learn through sensation, even though flesh is vulnerable to defect and lacks the superficially attractive splendor of corporeal invulnerability. A seemingly invulnerable and defect-free body could be considered beautiful in a narrow sense, but such a body would ultimately be unable to function in a way that is perfective of the human being. An invulnerable body would lack the integrity and proportionality proper to the intent of the Creator, and that invulnerability would be an obstacle to the ultimate or final *telos* of the human being.[53]

The (sometimes defective) iron saw has a beauty that the imaginary glass saw does not have. Likewise the (sometimes defective) human body has a beauty that the imaginary invulnerable and defect-free human body does not have. Aquinas argues that the Christian understanding of our inalienable creaturely dignity and aptitude for perfection includes the innate vulnerability of the human body to "defect." Moreover, Aquinas alerts us to how our diverse and unequal experience of corporeal "defect" manifests the integral goodness and fitting beauty of the human being.

With an eye toward the final two sections of this essay: Aquinas provides conceptual principles for a Christian theological approach to reflection on the way the various impairments, illnesses, and injuries we experience in our vulnerable bodies, our variously "disabled" bodies, are revealed by Christ as fitting and beautiful. Taking the wider view of Aquinas's anthropology and the inchoate aesthetic theory he seems to presuppose, Aquinas is saying that our various physical defects do not undermine the beauty of the human being (i.e., *integrity* indexed to essential human dignity and *proportionality* indexed to our perfection in love).[54]

Aquinas accepts that, yes, impaired, ill, and injured bodies lack something and, in a superficial sense, lack carnal beauty. However, the carnal beauty that our variously defective and impaired bodies lack is of limited significance. A theological outlook that places unwarranted emphasis on carnal agility, ability, or comeliness is an obstacle to the Christian theological consideration of our ultimate spiritual-corporeal beauty. Just as glass saws cannot cut, invulnerable bodies cannot learn and grow. In that way, for the human body, according to the Christian view outlined by Aquinas, both our innate vulnerability to defect and an instance of corporeal defect express something of the essential beauty of the human being in the good order

---

[53] Aquinas on this point does not conflict with his speculation on the subtlety, agility, and splendor of our resurrection bodies.

[54] See O'Reilly, *Aesthetic Perception,* 60-77, 99-117. See also Sevier, "Aquinas on the Relation of Goodness to Beauty," *De Medio Aevo* 2, no. 2 (2013): 103-126.

of God's creation. Aquinas's argument does not amount to a vapid "ugly on the outside, beautiful on the inside" proverb. Rather, he argues that what some people perceive as ugly is, in fact, evidence of what is ultimately beautiful about the human being.[55]

Aquinas acknowledges that we have a tendency to see some people as beautiful and others as ugly, but, in ST I q. 91, a. 3, co., he lays out a theological framework for describing and recognizing a spiritual beauty that one must learn to apprehend, just as the apprentice would need to learn to apprehend and discern from a master craftsman. We can think, for example, of St. Francis of Assisi, whose affective inclination was transformed through a process of encounter and transformation. Personal encounter and engagement with his own vulnerability liberated St. Francis to recognize the creaturely goodness and beauty of his neighbor (who also happened to have leprosy) without ignoring that the disease was a corruption of corporeal faculties, that the spiritual and physical pain caused by the illness was real, and that the disease is not something to be sought.

PART FOUR: THE BADNESS, UGLINESS, AND TRAGEDY OF "DISABILITY"?

At the beginning of Section II, I highlighted three presumptions about the concept "disability" that seem to inform the various ways theologians engage and avoid the topic. Although Christians raise the question in a particular way, there is nothing exclusively Christian about challenging the self-evidence of "ability-disability" as a natural division of humanity. Likewise, there is nothing exclusively Christian about challenging the internal coherence and conceptual stability of the concept "disability." The third presumption I noted was the common view that the Christian theological tradition holds human impairment, illness, and injury to be unequivocally bad, objectively ugly, and definitively tragic corporeal states.

In this Section (IV) and the final Section (V), my purpose is to discuss in outline some parts of the distinctively Christian understanding of our impairment, illness, and injury, as regulated by Christian belief in the origin, history, status, and destiny of the human being, amid the ongoing act of creation. My particular interest is to explain why Christians reject any doctrinal outlook that underwrites a categorically negative regard for the vulnerability of our bodies and our various and unequal experience of the same.

One contemporary theological muddle is the common view that our *actual vulnerability* to corporeal "defect" and "infirmity" is an original-sin-caused privation of a good that is natural to the human

---

[55] See my remarks on affective moral disorder in "The Call to Mercy: *Veritatis Splendor* and the Preferential Option for the Poor," *Nova et Vetera*, 11, no. 4 (2013): 1205–27. See also O'Reilly, *Aesthetic Perception,* 73-75, 78-98.

being; whereby, the privation of a particular person's relative corporeal good by impairment, illness, or injury would (1) be a corruption of her or his integral dignity and (2) would be an impediment to the realization of that person's specific good, in the good order of God's creation. Specifically, I am concerned here with a distorted view of our innate creaturely perfection, which leads to a distorted view of the theological significance and moral implications of impairment, illness, and injury. What worries me, in other words, is the tendency of some contemporary theologians to presume an idealized, anthropological caricature in the development of their moral reflection on the human good—presupposing a creature that is neither vulnerable nor dependent—and who do so in place of a properly Christian theological account of human nature, human dignity, and human destiny.

I begin with a concise, Aquinas-conversant sketch of the doctrines and anthropological principles outlined in the previous three sections: Christians believe that the immortal and incorruptible essence of the human being (the intellectual soul) is perfected in and through its union with a corruptible body.[56] Of the various ways Christians have imagined the impassibility, agility, and subtlety of the human body before the Fall, those preternatural qualities have always been understood as derivative corporeal goods or perfections—relative perfections originated in and sustained by a spiritual intimacy between creature and Creator.[57] Before the Fall, the glory of those spiritual intimacies and friendship, between God and the Image of God, "overflowed" to the human body and "elevated" the body to a condition above its nature.

Coordinate with the Christian understanding of that elevated state is the Christian understanding of the *event* of original sin and the *consequences* of original sin, that is, the Fall from grace. First and foremost, the spiritual wound of original sin was a primordial rupture or break in the intimate friendship shared between God and humanity. So conceived, notwithstanding the various "offense-penalty" metaphors we find and make proper use of throughout the tradition, the corporeal consequences of original sin, humanity's Fall from

---

[56] For an expanded discussion of this anthropological outlook, see Miguel J. Romero, "Aquinas on the *corporis infirmitas*: Broken Flesh and the Grammar of Grace," *Disability in the Christian Tradition: A Reader,* ed. Brian Brock and John Swinton (Grand Rapids: Eerdmans, 2012), 101-151.

[57] The tradition has also been careful to distinguish between the preternatural impassibility, agility, and subtlety of the human body *before the Fall* and the anticipated condition of our glorified bodies *at the resurrection.* For an extended discussion of how our innate corporeal vulnerability relates to the impassibility, agility, and subtlety of the resurrected body, see Paul Gondreau's essay in this issue, "Disability, the Healing of Infirmity, and the Theological Virtue of Hope: A Thomistic Approach," 70-111.

grace, were not the result of a violent retaliatory injury or a de-creative (privative) metaphysical insult inflicted by God upon the specific dignity of humanity. Rather, the various implications of original sin that we experience in our bodies are the result of humanity's self-separation from God, and the concomitant loss or withdrawal of the secondary benefits that followed from the primary good of humanity's intimacy with the Creator.

What, then, are these impairments, illnesses, and injuries? Created from the beginning to partake in the glory of the triune Lord of Creation, humanity "Fell" from a state of grace that allowed us to exceed our nature.[58] We are found universally alienated from the only grace that can preserve us (soul and body) in a preternaturally perfect state of corporeal integrity and harmony. Among the consequences of this primordial spiritual wound are the various impairments, illnesses, and injuries that coincide with our natural creaturely vulnerability.

Certainly, the postlapsarian disclosures of our innate vulnerability are privations of a relative corporeal good. However, because our corporeal vulnerability is an essential aspect of our creaturely nature, and not a perversion of our nature, those "defects" and "infirmities" do not diminish our incarnate, creaturely dignity, nor do they displace the fittingness of our composite nature in the good order of God's creation. Rather, in the light of the Gospel, and as illustrated by Aquinas on the apt disposition of the human body in ST I q. 91, a. 3, co., the various and unequal "defects" and "infirmities" of the human body manifest the integral goodness of corporeality and the fitting beauty of our fragile flesh. This does not amount to a presumptuous explanation of *why* a particular person might or might not experience impairment, illness, or injury in her or his life.[59] Nor does this imply a categorical association of corporeal defect and/or infirmity with the experience of spiritual/physical pain ("suffering" in the common sense of the word), as noted above in Aquinas's discussion of the innate vulnerabilities and coordinate dependencies of the human being *before* the Fall (*ST* I q. 96, a. 3, co.).

The Good News is that God does not abandon us to death and the dissolution of our being, as Christ came to reconcile humanity in the love of our Creator and to restore the supernatural benefits that were lost. Aquinas helps us understand the significance of our vulnerable nature in the cosmic history of Fall, Reconciliation, and Restoration. In particular, he provides us a way to see why no corporeal evil can

---

[58] For detailed account of Aquinas on these themes, see Rudi Te Velde, "Evil, Sin, and Death" in *The Theology of Thomas Aquinas*, ed. Rik Van Nieuwenhove and Joseph Wawrykow (Notre Dame: University of Notre Dame Press, 2005), 143-166.

[59] See Eleonore Stump, "Providence and The Problem of Evil," *The Oxford Handbook of Aquinas,* ed. Brian Davies and Eleonore Stump (Oxford: Oxford University Press, 2012), 401-417.

decisively undermine the inviolable dignity and vocational aptitude of a human being to receive and respond to the love of God, and why Christians look forward in faith to the bodily resurrection of the dead and the final consummation of our hope.

"The Wound" and "The Consequences" of Original Sin

In some quarters of contemporary Catholic theology, there is a bit of theological shorthand we tend to use that conflates the spiritual wound of original sin with the corporeal consequences of original sin. That theological shorthand is then, commonly, refracted through the various offense-penalty metaphors describing the human condition that we find throughout Scripture and in the Christian theological tradition. The problem, of course, is not the Pauline rubric of death as consequence of sin (Romans 5:12-21; I Corinthians 15:1-58). Rather, the problem develops when Christians amplify the offense-penalty metaphor beyond Paul's own circumscribed use and without due consideration for the absolute goodness of God's ongoing, direct, and universally expansive work in the gift of creation. When developed, the shorthand tends to transpose any defect or privation of a relative corporeal good (i.e., impairment, illness, infirmity, etc.) from an accidental quality of human being, toward an essential perversion of human being.

The overlooked distinction in short form is this: there is a tendency to collapse the innate vulnerability and coordinate dependencies of the human body into the postlapsarian evils we variously experience in our bodies consequent of original sin, as if the human being is *naturally invulnerable* and *naturally self-sufficient* and is now found in a sin-wrecked state of *unnatural vulnerability* and *unnatural dependency*. So conceived, a natural quality or characteristic (i.e., our innate vulnerability), coordinate with the first perfection of the human being, is awkwardly injected into theological discourse and engagement with the human experience of corporeal defect and infirmity, and the spiritual-moral significance of the same (concerning the second perfection of the human being). That problematic premise provides a basis for theologians to wrongly suppose that a vulnerable human body lacks a specific good proper to the human being, by the mere fact of being vulnerable (i.e., the *allegedly* natural good of being invulnerable to any impairment, illness, or injury that could hinder the relative perfection of the corporeal aspect of our nature).

According to that distorted view of human dignity, human nature, and the corporeal consequences of original sin, the human body's susceptibility to the material contingencies of our mortal state is taken to be a defect or privation of human nature, as such. Thus, when ordinary circumstances reduce this allegedly "unnatural" passive potency for corporeal defect to an actual corporeal defect, the corporeal aspect of our nature is said to have suffered a degradation of its proper perfection, proportionate to the degree of the defect. What this distortion of the Christian view implies is that a privation of any corporeal good amounts to a correlative privation of the goodness of corporeality. That conclusion is inconsistent with the traditional Christian account of our specifically incarnate intellectual dignity, the fittingness of our vulnerability, and the enduring goodness of corporeality in light of the Fall.

By way of that mistaken view, healthy, strong, and mature bodies are regarded as more-perfect actualizations of the integral dignity of the human being; infirm, weak, immature and/or aged bodies are regarded as less-perfect actualizations of the integral dignity of the human being. Likewise, the supposition follows from that mistaken view that persons whose bodies are free from corporeal defect are better able to realize the specific good of the human being in the good order of God's creation, and, correlatively, persons whose bodies have some defect are less able to realize the specific good of the human being in the good order of God's creation.

Impairment, Healing, and the Non-Competitive Transcendence of God

There are various ways that the mistaken view just outlined has been resisted in the Christian theological tradition. My own view, noted at the outset, is that the best response is to recover the significance of our status as creatures and the Good News about what God intends for the human being. When our innate vulnerability is considered in and through the Incarnation of God in Jesus Christ, the absolute transcendence of God beyond creation and the profound immanence of God in the ongoing act of creation challenge the theologian to re-evaluate the significance of "ability" and "disability" from the perspective of our creaturely origin and final perfection.[60]

Among the various implications of this "noncompetitive" understanding of God's transcendence, the vulnerabilities and dependencies of the human body can be understood in the light of the love-sustained, noninvasive immanence of God's liberative and nonviolent reconciliation of creation. So conceived, the Gospel accounts of Christ's healing ministry could be read as challenging categorically negative evaluations of impairment, illness, and injury. Specifically, because our postlapsarian experience of our corporeal vulnerability indicates only the loss of a supernatural benefit and not the loss of our specific creaturely dignity, it would be improper to frame the secondary consequences of original sin (our actual

---

[60] See Pope Saint John Paul II's remarks entitled "On the Dignity and Rights of the Mentally Disabled Person," no. 2, where he writes "The starting point for every reflection on disability is rooted in the fundamental convictions of Christian anthropology." See also Kathryn Tanner, *God and Creation in Christian Theology* (Minneapolis: Fortress Press, 2005), 81-119.

impairments, illnesses, and injuries) as direct punishments from God: for example, by supposing that our vulnerable condition is the result of God withdrawing God's love from humanity, God diminishing our dignity through privative insult, or God displacing the human being in the order of creation.

For that reason, in light of God's noninvasive immanence and activity in the world, the Gospel accounts of Christ's healing activity can be recognized not as a restoration of the "human nature" of particular persons, but as the supernatural endowment of relative corporeal goods that human beings might enjoy, but do not necessarily enjoy. Moreover, the liberation and freedom communicated in the Gospel accounts of Christ's healing activity—e.g., sight for the blind, hearing for the deaf, strength for the infirm, health for the ill, agility for those who are impeded—the proximate result of these particular liberations, for these particular people, can be appreciated for the ultimate purpose they serve in these individual lives.

Understood in that way, Christ's healing of various impairments, illnesses, and injuries in Scripture could not be taken as evidence for a Divine rejection of the material aspect and coordinate attributes of our composite nature, as if our innate vulnerabilities and coordinate dependencies were somehow in conflict with the act of healing. Rather, in the healing of persons who were somehow impaired, ill, or injured (and even dead), Christ offered particular people a particular liberation from the limitation, burden, and (perhaps) the suffering of their particular corporeal defect or infirmity. Three points are important here. First, the healing ministry of Christ did not change the nature of the beneficiary, placing the person in a state of corporeal invulnerability. Second, the healings did not wholly erase the condition from the beneficiary's life (it remained in her or his past). Third, the healings did not elevate the person to a preternatural physical state. In the healing ministry of Jesus, the goodness and beauty of the human body is shown not through an erasure of human vulnerability and dependency but by situating the human body (along with its innate passive potency to corporeal defect) within the unfolding drama of creation, fall, redemption, and resurrection.[61]

---

[61] We can identify additional analogous examples: The direct revelation of Christ's teaching ministry is a not divine judgment against the way human beings acquire knowledge—rather, Jesus offered particular people a particular liberation from the limitation, burden, and lack of their particular ignorance. Christ's multiplication of the loaves or increasing of the fisherman's catch is not a divine judgment against the dignified drudgery of a hard day's work—rather, Jesus offered particular hungry people a particular liberation from the limitation, burden, and lack associated with the struggles of survival, on that particular day. Christ's welcome of sinners was not a divine rebuke of communities who reject the shameful behavior of thieves, liars, oath breakers, corrupt politicians, and violent criminals—rather, Jesus offered particular

PART FIVE: ENCOUNTER AND LEARNING TO SEE

> Oliver could not move his own hands, could not wink, whisper, stand. He did not have the power to hold a spoon, to write a letter, to embrace.... Oliver's own heart laughed, and that was quite enough for him, but my vision had to be focused to see this laughter.... Oliver was physically and mentally retarded, but he was not spiritually retarded. –Christopher DeVinck, *The Power of the Powerless,* 38-40.

In his book *The Power of the Powerless*, Christopher DeVinck challenges his readers with the proposal that the ability to recognize the truth about persons like his brother Oliver is a skill that must be learned. In this final section, I briefly consider why some Christians and not others are able to recognize the incarnate goodness and fitting beauty of our vulnerable and dependent bodies. Receiving the fullness of the Christian account of our innate vulnerability is not merely a matter of collecting theological reminders and arranging anthropological principles from the Christian archive. It also involves the formation and habituation of our aesthetic sensibilities. As noted above, the moral witness of St. Francis can help us understand what kind of formation is necessary. I want to suggest that the formal coherence and precision of any particular Catholic moral theologian's interpretive and speculative work on the human good and human happiness can be refined through a discipline of moral conversion, by way of encounter, toward the transformation of one's affective inclination.

Beauty and Theological Anthropology

Christians recognize both the ugliness of the cross and the beauty of Christ's Passion. We understand that the beauty and goodness of *misericordia* presupposes the evil of affliction. We mourn the primordial, cosmic wound of original sin, as we sing at Easter Vigil *O felix culpa quae talem et tantum meruit habere redemptorem.* Is crucifixion beautiful? Can affliction be lovely? Can the impairment, illness, and injuries we bear in our bodies in any way be rendered sweet and delightful? Questions of this sort direct us toward the main themes of Christian theological aesthetics: What is beauty and the beautiful? What, for Christians, does beauty have to do with the goodness of creation, human dignity, the reality of evil, sin, suffering, grace, and conversion? To hold forth that our fragile flesh is good and beautiful—just as when we affirm the beauty of Christ's Passion—is

---

sinners a particular liberation from the limitation, burden, and suffering caused by their particular sins.

to lay claim to a distinctively Christian vision of beauty and to the kind of formation that allows one to recognize such beauty.[62]

This skill of aesthetic perception is well illustrated in the affective transformation and moral conversion experienced by Saint Francis of Assisi.

> One day, while he was praying enthusiastically to the Lord, Francis received this response: "Francis, everything you loved carnally and desired to have, you must despise and hate, if you wish to know my will. Because once you begin doing this, what before seemed delightful and sweet will be unbearable and bitter; and what before made you shudder will offer you great sweetness and enormous delight." He was overjoyed at this and was comforted by the Lord. One day he was riding his horse near Assisi, when he met a leper. And, even though he usually shuddered at lepers, he made himself dismount, and gave him a coin, kissing his hand as he did so. After he accepted a kiss of peace from him, Francis remounted and continued on his way. He then began to consider himself less and less, until, by God's grace, he came to complete victory over himself. After a few days, he moved to a hospice of lepers, taking with him a large sum of money. Calling them all together, as he kissed the hand of each, he gave them alms. When he left there, what before had been bitter, that is, to see and touch lepers, was turned into sweetness.... With the help of God's grace, he became such a servant and friend of the lepers, that, as he testified in his Testament, he stayed among them and served them with humility.[63]

For St. Francis, "what before had been bitter, that is, to see and touch lepers, was turned into sweetness." We might ask ourselves, *What, exactly, did St. Francis see?* Did Francis undergo a bizarre distortion of his sensory experience of the world, such that truly revolting sights and revolting smells were deceptively veiled with a delightful and sweet façade? Or, rather, could it be that Francis simply learned to recognize a goodness and beauty that is easy to ignore and avoid?

I want to suggest that the beauty Francis came to apprehend is the innate dignity and fitting purpose of the human being in the good order of God's creation. That integral creaturely goodness and proportionate harmony is not in conflict with the various ways the human body is vulnerable to defect and infirmity. Rather, it is through the innate vulnerabilities and coordinate dependencies of the human body that the specific goodness and beauty of the human body is manifest. Understood in this way, the conversion of St. Francis's affective inclination can be understood as one of the ordinary transformations

---

[62] This way of framing the question is drawn from Richard Viladesau, *The Beauty of the Cross* (Oxford: Oxford University Press, 2006), 9-12.

[63] *Legend of the Three Companions* (L3C 11: FAED II, 74), www.custodia.org/default.asp?id=1445.

capacitated and proffered by Christ to the Church. I have in mind a kind of affective transformation that, as with Francis, is available for every Christian to accept or to reject in response to our own vulnerability and the vulnerability of our neighbor. There stands an invitation, one that prompts a personal response: to either touch or withdraw from the beauty eternally revealed in Christ's Passion, celebrated in the Eucharist, and offered to doubting theologians in the splendor of Christ's glorified wounds: *"Thomas...put your finger here...."* (John 20:27).

What difference would it make if moral theologians learned to recognize the goodness and beauty of our fragile flesh from the perspective of the Creator? And how might a refusal to learn to see and love in the way modeled by St. Francis of Assisi affect the work of moral theology? It may be, if Victor Preller is correct, that the consequences of refusal could be quite profound and long-lasting. "Distorted love," he writes, "can affect our reasoning. It can even affect what we find intelligible and what we do not."[64]

Whether one provisionally identifies with the able-bodied or the disable-bodied, the strong or the weak, this is normative: There are many Christians, like St. Francis, who do not perceive an "unnatural," "sin-caused," aesthetically "ugly" state of the body when they encounter a person who has an impaired, ill, or injured body. Rather, while acknowledging the limitations and whatever pain there may be, these Christians have learned to recognize goodness and beauty in and through the vulnerability and impairment of the human body. Are these Christians confused, grasping at stupid delusions and romantic sentiment to cope with the awful and ugly wounds of the human condition? Or, perhaps, is there something here that Christian theologians are well-advised to remember?

We must also admit that some Christian theologians think "disability" is ugly. Like death and sin, the vulnerable and impaired human body is taken to be an irreducible and unredeemable corruption of our proper creaturely goodness. Here is one formulation of that view: since beauty is a matter of a thing's integrity (or perfection) and proportion (or harmony), and since "disability" refers precisely to those bodies that manifestly lack some manner of perfection and harmony, it follows that the bodies of disabled persons are objectively ugly. Theologians of the view just sketched could certainly affirm the inviolability of human dignity, champion the justice that is due to every person, and promote the lavish generosity that Christian mercy commends toward vulnerable and dependent persons, and these theologians could do so while maintaining that the postlapsarian

---

[64] Victor Preller, "Water into Wine," *Grammar and Grace: Reformulations of Aquinas and Wittgenstein,* ed. Jeffrey Stout and Robert MacSwain (London: SCM Press, 2004), 266.

defects and infirmities of the human body are ugly negations of the goodness and beauty of the human body. So conceived, the profundity of any particular corporeal defect is taken as directly correlative to that body's ugliness. Well and functional bodies are regarded as perfect (actualized good) and beautiful. Unwell and impaired bodies are regarded as defective (diminished good) and ugly. The greater the wellness and more agile the function, the greater the goodness and beauty. The greater the infirmity and impairment, the greater the evil and ugliness. Given the argument of the previous sections, we can see that the problem with the above view is an improperly truncated scope or context for consideration of the integrity and proportionality of the human body, where the goodness and beauty of the human body is indexed to the narrow horizon of the corporeal consequences of original sin and the presently incomplete realization of any particular human life. It is a tragedy that there are theologians who see the world in this way.

Against that view, there are other Christians who, likewise, recognize when a human body obviously lacks some kind of physical integrity or relative corporeal harmony—*and yet* do not experience revulsion and disgust when they encounter an impaired, ill, or injured body. Rather, they have learned to recognize a particular goodness and beauty in the vulnerability and dependencies of their own body. They recognize the beautiful in and through the body that belongs to a severely impaired brother, a profoundly dependent spouse, or the bent limbs of their newborn son. Like St. Francis, for whom the sight of leprosy was transformed from an offensive bitterness into sweetness and delight, the affective inclination of these Christians has been formed (or transformed, as the case may be) to recognize the beauty of our fragile, fractured, and failing flesh. Like the apostle Thomas, who, invited to touch the eternal wounds of Incarnate Love, they have responded to a challenge toward encounter and embarked on a process toward a truthful recognition of the place of our vulnerable and dependent bodies in the good order of God's creation.

The difference between these two ways of seeing can be understood as a matter of affective inclination and the conversion of one's aesthetic sensibilities: Some people have been habituated into a state of affective moral disorder such that they cannot perceive the beauty of a vulnerable and dependent human body. And there are other people whose affective inclination has been formed and shaped to apprehend the fittingness of our creaturely vulnerability and dependency. In the light of Christ, what is fitting is revealed for its proper and dignified place in the order of creation. In that way, the integral dignity of our creaturely status and the proportional fittingness of individual differences are communicated by our body, such that the goodness of what is communicated can be appreciated as truly beautiful by those whose affective dispositions and aesthetic sensibilities have been habituated to find pleasure in what is truly and objectively good. Wouldn't it be wonderful if moral theologians learned to see in this way?[65] ∎

---

[65] I am grateful to John Cavadini for prompting the central thesis of this essay. My friend Virgilio Elizondo, *requiescat in pace*, helped me appreciate the significance of cultural formation for my claim. Paul Griffiths and Stanley Hauerwas offered comments and suggestions on the first draft of this argument in 2010. Portions of my argument were worked out through formal and informal conversation with Reinhard Huetter, Alasdair MacIntyre, Luis Vera, Paul Gondreau, Brain Brock, Louis Albarran, Michael Hebbeler, Matthew Insley, and Scott Sevier. Sr. Kathleen Schipani and Jan Benton pressed me to reconsider and revise the practical entailments of my argument. Portions of this essay were presented at the Living Fully Symposium (Rome, 2016), where I received generous feedback from Pia Matthews, Hans Reinders, Cristina Gangemi, Bill Gaventa, Martin Benton, and Ann Masters. This paper was possible because of direct support I received from The Institute for Church Life at the University of Notre Dame; Salve Regina University; and the National Catholic Partnership on Disability. I am particularly indebted to Vicente Romero for his kindness and support.

Contributors

Jana Marguerite Bennett is associate professor of religious studies at the University of Dayton. Her most recent book is *Singleness and the Church: A New Theology of Single Life* (Oxford University Press, 2017). She is also a managing editor of the *Journal of Disability and Religion* and co-editor of the blog catholicmoraltheology.com.

Lorraine Cuddeback is a Teaching Scholar at the University of Notre Dame, where she received her PhD in 2017. Her research interests include theologies of disability, liberation theologies, feminist ethics, and the Catholic social tradition. She also contributes to Daily Theology (dailytheology.org) and Political Theology Today (politicaltheology.com/blog), and is an active member of the Society of Christian Ethics and the Catholic Theological Society of America.

Julia Fleming is currently professor and Chair of the Department of Theology at Creighton University. She received her doctorate from The Catholic University of America and served on the editorial board of *Theological Studies*. Her publications on the history of moral theology include *Defending Probabilism: The Moral Theology of Juan Caramuel* (Georgetown University Press). Her current research projects concern restitution and the evolution of punitive justice in the Roman Catholic tradition.

Matthew J. Gaudet teaches theology and philosophy at the University of San Francisco. His research lies at the intersection of Moral Theology and Political/Social Theory, with a particular interest in the topics of disability ethics, ethics of war and peace, and university ethics. His previous writings have appeared in the *Journal for the Society of Christian Ethics*, the *Journal for Peace and Justice Studies*, *America*, and the *National Catholic Reporter*.

Paul Gondreau is professor of theology at Providence College, Rhode Island, where he has been teaching since 1997. He earned his doctorate in sacred theology at the University of Fribourg, Switzerland. He has published numerous essays in the area of Thomistic Christology and Thomistic moral thought, with a special emphasis on sexual morality. He has a published manuscript on Christ's human passions in the theology of Thomas Aquinas. He is associate editor of the theological journal *Nova et Vetera* and has served as a consultant to the USCCB committee on marriage and family. And he is the proud father of a boy with severe cerebral palsy.

Jason Reimer Greig is a PhD candidate in theology and ethics at the VU Free University of Amsterdam. Before pursuing graduate theological studies, he lived for eleven years in two L'Arche communities in Canada.

Mary Jo Iozzio studied classical history at The Pennsylvania State University (BA), biblical studies at Providence College (MA), the history of religions (MA) and moral theology (PhD) at Fordham University; she is professor of moral theology at Boston College. Grounded in historical consciousness and dedicated to past and present contexts, she lectures, teaches, and writes on Catholic social thought, using virtue and liberation ethics at the intersection of disability, gender, and racial justice. In addition to *Self Determination and the Moral Act: A Study of the Contributions of Odon Lottin, OSB* (1995), her publications include: co-edited books and manuals on HIV/AIDS, Pax Christi USA work on racial justice, bioethics, Christian sexual ethics, and disability; she is former co-editor of the *Journal of the Society of Christian Ethics* and series editor of *Content and Context in Theological Ethics* (Palgrave Macmillan); and she has many publications in US and European journals. She is active in the American Academy of Religion, Catholic Theological Society of America, Catholic Theological Ethics in the World Church, and Society of Christian Ethics. She lives in Boston with her two beagle dogs, Maynard and Melrose.

Mary M. Doyle Roche is associate professor of religious studies at the College of the Holy Cross in Worcester, MA. She is the author of *Children, Consumerism, and the Common Good* (Lexington, 2009) and *Schools of Solidarity: Families and Catholic Social Teaching* (Liturgical, 2015). She is a co-editor of *Calling For Justice Throughout the World: Catholic Women Theologians of the HIV/AIDS Pandemic* (Continuum, 2009) with Mary Jo Iozzio and Elsie Miranda.

Miguel J. Romero is assistant professor of religious and theological studies at Salve Regina University. Romero's research interests include moral theology, Catholic social teaching, disability, and the theology of Thomas Aquinas. Romero received his doctoral and postdoctoral training at Duke University and University of Notre Dame. He currently serves on the board of directors for the National Catholic Partnership on Disability. Romero's published work includes "Aquinas on the *corporis infirmitas*: Broken Flesh and the Grammar of Grace," in *Disability in the Christian Tradition* (Eerdmans, 2012); "The Call To Mercy: *Veritatis Splendor* and the Preferential Option for the Poor," in *Nova et Vetera;* and "Aquinas on Happiness and Those Who Lack the Use of Reason," in *The Thomist*.

Articles available to view
or download at:

www.msmary.edu/jmt

The

Journal of Moral Theology

is proudly sponsored by the

Fr. James M. Forker Professorship
of Catholic Social Teaching

and the

College of Liberal Arts

at

Mount St. Mary's University

www.ingramcontent.com/pod-product-compliance
Lightning Source LLC
Chambersburg PA
CBHW050438240426
43661CB00055B/2423